SELECTED MESSAGES

Book 3

SELECTED MESSAGES

From the Writings of
Ellen G. White

Book   Three

Significant and ever-timely counsels gathered from periodical articles, manuscript statements, and certain valuable pamphlets and tracts long out of print.

REVIEW AND HERALD® PUBLISHING ASSOCIATION
HAGERSTOWN, MD 21740

ISBN 0-8280-0055-7

(PRINTED IN U.S.A.)

Contents

A Word to the Reader   PAGE 9

SECTION I—THE CHURCH
      Introduction   14
    1. What Is the Church   15
    2. Unity in the Church   20
    3. Independent Action   23

SECTION II—PRINCIPLES OF INSPIRATION
      Introduction   28
    4. The Primacy of the Word   29
    5. Experiences in Receiving the Visions . .   34
    6. Glimpses of How the Light Came to
        Ellen White   40
    7. Presenting the Divinely Revealed Mes-
        sage   48
    8. The Question of Influence   62
    9. Defining Sister White's Judgment and
        the Word of the Lord   68
   10. On Being an Inspired Messenger   71
   11. The Reception of the Messages   78

SECTION III—THE PREPARATION OF THE ELLEN G. WHITE
      BOOKS
      Introduction   88
   12. Literary Assistants in Work of Ellen G.
        White   89
   13. The *Testimonies for the Church*   94

14. Initial Steps in Writing and Publishing
    the Great Controversy Story   99
15. A Running Account of Ellen G. White's
    Experience in Writing on the Life of
    Christ in 1876   103
16. Expanding the Great Controversy Pre-
    sentation 109
17. The Experience of E. G. White in Pre-
    paring *The Desire of Ages* 115
18. Comments While at Work on the Con-
    flict Series Books 121

SECTION IV—THE INCARNATION
    Introduction   126
19. The Incarnation 127

SECTION V—PRINCIPLES OF SALVATION
    Introduction   144
20. Principles as Set Forth by Ellen White
    in Her Early Ministry   145
21. Ellen White Reports on the Minneapolis
    Conference   156
22. Emphasis on Salvation Theme—1890-
    1908   190

SECTION VI—EDUCATION—THE CHURCH SCHOOL,
    AND UNIVERSITIES OF THE WORLD
    Introduction   206
23. Appeal for a Church School   209
24. Counsel Regarding Age of School
    Entrance   214
25. General Guiding Principles   227
26. Attending Colleges and Universities
    of the Land   231

SECTION VII—STANDARDS
    Introduction   236
27. The Grace of Courtesy   237
28. Dress and Adornment   241

29. The Sabbath 256
30. The Propriety of Varying Postures
    in Prayer 266

SECTION VIII—THE HEALTH REFORM
    Introduction 272
31. Visions That Early Called for Reforms . 273
32. The 1863 Health Reform Vision 276
33. Proper Use of the Testimonies
    on Health Reform 283
34. Spiritual and Physical Hazards of In-
    dulged Appetite 289
35. Teaching Health Reform in the Family 293
36. Sister White and Prayer for the Sick . . 295

SECTION IX—COUNSELS ON MANY MATTERS
    Introduction 298
37. Seventh-day Adventists and Lawsuits . . 299
38. Science and Revelation 306
39. Questions About the Saved 313
40. The Question of the Date Line 317
41. Memorials, Are They Proper? 320
42. Renting our Churches to Other
    Denominations 322
43. Feelings of Despondency 324
44. Specific Light on Gardening 328
45. Balanced Counsel on Picture-making and
    Idolatry 330
46. Music and the Music Director 332
47. Work in the Spirit of Prayer 336
48. The Bible Prophets Wrote for Our
    Time 338
49. Can All Have the Gift of Prophecy? . . 340
50. Disparaging the Pioneers 342
51. Attacks on Ellen White and Her Work 348
52. Sinlessness and Salvation 353
53. Study the Testimonies 358

SECTION X—MEETING FANATICISM
    Introduction 362

    54. The Mackin Case 363

SECTION XI—LAST-DAY EVENTS
        Introduction 380
    55. Lessons From Meeting the Sunday Law
        Crisis of the Late 1880's and Early
        1890's 383
    56. As We Near the End 403
    57. The Last Great Struggle 413
APPENDIX
    A. *The Great Controversy*—1911 Edition . . . 433
    B. W. C. White Statement Made to W. W.
        Eastman 445
    C. W. C. White Letters to L. E. Froom . . 451
Scripture Index 467
General Index 468

A Word to the Reader

~~~~~~

The publication in 1958 of *Selected Messages,* books 1 and 2, provided the opportunity to bring to the church counsels that had become particularly significant since Ellen White issued volume 9 of the *Testimonies* in the year 1909. The content of books 1 and 2 included materials appearing in the *Review and Herald, The Youth's Instructor,* and *Signs of the Times* articles, in out-of-print pamphlets, and in E. G. White manuscripts and letters. These were reproduced in whole or in part, depending on the relevance of their contribution to a particular field of counsel. Subjects such as inspiration, the nature of Christ, and righteousness by faith were supplemented by a number of miscellaneous and general counsels that, through the passage of time, had become particularly pertinent, such as fanaticism, subversive movements, and the use of medicinal agencies. These volumes have come to be major source books supplementing the *Testimonies* and books of specialized counsels.

During the past two decades the Ellen G. White *Review and Herald* and *Signs of the Times* articles have been reprinted in facsimile form, thus providing a wealth of valuable materials that hitherto were not generally available. In these two decades routine research in the Ellen G. White manuscript and letter files has brought to the front some unusually helpful materials. Some of these have been published as articles in the *Adventist Review,* while others have become a part of study documents assembled for committees investigating certain doctrines or questions involving church policy.

Research conducted by graduate students has called attention to a number of choice statements, from E. G. White manuscript sources, that seemed to make a contribution over and above that which was already in print. A careful scrutiny of material concerning last-day events has also contributed to a better understanding, of certain aspects of that topic, that Seventh-day Adventists will treasure. An intensified concern in recent years on the question of inspiration, and interest in the manner in which the E. G. White books were prepared, has led to the assembling of pertinent statements, of which some are new and some are familiar.

It is these combined sources of inspired counsels that have provided the materials for *Selected Messages,* book 3. The making of such books is in harmony with Ellen White's expectation that through the years subsequent to her death, her literary resources, published and unpublished, would yield materials that would serve the needs of the growing church. Until 1938 these materials were housed in the manuscript vault connected with the Elmshaven office, close to her California home. Since that time they have been kept in the White Estate vault at the General Conference headquarters in Washington, D.C. It was Ellen White's expectation that her manuscripts and letters of counsel would provide a widening range of service to the church. Of this she wrote in 1905:

"I am endeavoring by the help of God to write letters that will be a help, not merely to those to whom they are addressed, but to many others who need them."—Letter 79, 1905.

The manuscript for this volume has been compiled under the authorization and by the direction of the Board of Trustees of the Ellen G. White Estate, in the offices of the White Estate in Washington, D.C., by the regularly employed staff.

The reader will notice that there is a difference in format from section to section, and at times within sections. In each instance the format thought best to present the material has been followed. This procedure is similar to that followed in the two earlier volumes of this series. The source of each item is given at the close of the selection. In most instances this includes the date of writing or of first publication.

The staff members who have prepared this compilation have endeavored, wherever possible, to include materials from the documents quoted to provide the reader with adequate context. There are some statements for which more of a setting would seem desirable, yet the original context contains nothing more that is relevant or that would be useful if added. This is a feature of Ellen White's writings well known to the White Trustees and staff. Truth, however, is truth, and in many instances it must stand alone without supporting context.

In a score or more of instances, items selected carried in the original text the name of the individual concerned. In a few cases where no confidence would be betrayed, the name has been left in the text. In most cases, initials have been employed in place of names, beginning with the letter A in the first instance and running consecutively through most of the alphabet. No relation exists between the initial used and the name of the individual concerned.

That this volume, presenting as it does important information and counsels in many lines, may be a source of particular usefulness, blessing, and encouragement to the church is the sincere wish of the

BOARD OF TRUSTEES OF THE
ELLEN G. WHITE ESTATE, INC.

SECTION I

The Church

INTRODUCTION

The Seventh-day Adventist Church was ever close to the heart of Ellen G. White. A thousand times and more through her long life, Heaven had drawn near to her with messages of encouragement, of instruction, of information, and of reproof and correction. These many visions were given to guide and guard the members of God's Sabbathkeeping remnant, both individually and collectively.

"The Lord loves His church," she declared when it was under attack *(Selected Messages,* book 2, p. 68). Tenderly she wrote, "The church of Christ, enfeebled and defective as it may be, is the only object on earth on which He bestows His supreme regard."—*Testimonies to Ministers,* p. 15.

Ellen White loved the church deeply. Her whole life was dedicated to its welfare and ultimate triumph.

How appropriate, then, that this volume of *Selected Messages* should open with a definition of what the church is, drawn from a letter of counsel to an administrator working outside North America. This is followed by admonitions calling for unity as a means of strength, and warning against independent action, which could only weaken the church's efforts to reach and rescue a confused world.—WHITE TRUSTEES.

1.

What Is the Church?

Christ's influence is to be felt in our world through His believing children. He who is converted is to exert the same kind of an influence which through God's instrumentality was made effectual in his conversion. All our work in this world is to be done in harmony and love and unity. We are to keep the example of Christ ever before us, walking in His footsteps.

Union is strength, and the Lord desires that this truth should be ever revealed in all the members of the body of Christ. All are to be united in love, in meekness, in lowliness of mind. Organized into a society of believers for the purpose of combining and diffusing their influence, they are to work as Christ worked. They are ever to show courtesy and respect for one another. Every talent has its place and is to be kept under the control of the Holy Spirit.

A Christian Society Formed for Its Members.— The church is a Christian society formed for the members composing it, that each member may enjoy the assistance of all the graces and talents of the other members, and the working of God upon them, according to their several gifts and abilities. The church is united in the holy bonds of fellowship in order that each member may be benefited by the influence of the other. All are to bind themselves to the covenant of love and harmony. The Christian principles and graces of the whole society of believers are to gather strength and force in harmonious action. Each believer is to be benefited and improved by the refining and transforming influence of the varied capabilities of the other members, that the things lacking in one may be more abundantly displayed in another. All the members are to draw together, that the church may become a spectacle to the world, to angels, and to men.

The covenant of agreement in church membership is that each member would walk in the footsteps of Christ, that all will take His yoke upon them, and learn of Him who is meek and lowly in heart. Doing this, "Ye shall," saith the dear Saviour, "find rest unto your souls. For my yoke is easy, and my burden is light" (Matthew 11:29, 30).

Those who wear Christ's yoke will draw together. They will cultivate sympathy and forbearance, and in holy emulation will strive to show to others the tender sympathy and love of which they feel such great need themselves. He who is weak and inexperienced, although he is weak, may be strengthened by the more hopeful and by those of mature experience. Although the least of all, he is a stone that must shine in the building. He is a vital member of the organized body, united to Christ, the living head, and through Christ identified with all the excellencies of Christ's character so that the Saviour is not ashamed to call him brother.

Usefulness Increased by Church Ties.—Why are believers formed into a church? Because by this means Christ would increase their usefulness in the world and strengthen their personal influence for good. In the church there is to be maintained a discipline which guards the rights of all and increases the sense of mutual dependence. God never designed that one man's mind and judgment should be a controlling power. He never designed that one man should rule and plan and devise without the careful and prayerful consideration of the whole body, in order that all may move in a sound, thorough, harmonious manner.

Believers are to shine as lights in the world. A city set on an hill cannot be hid. A church, separate and distinct from the world, is in the estimation of heaven the greatest object in all the earth. The members are pledged to be separate from the world, consecrating their service to one Master, Jesus Christ. They are to reveal that they have chosen Christ as their leader. . . . The church is to be as God designed it should be, a representative of God's family in another world.—Letter 26, 1900.

God Has an Organized Body

Beware of those who arise with a great burden to denounce the church. The chosen ones who are standing and breasting the storm of opposition from the world, and are uplifting the downtrodden commandments of God to exalt them as holy and honorable, are indeed the light of the world. . . .

I tell you, my brethren, the Lord has an organized body through whom He will work. There may be more than a score of Judases among them, there may be a rash Peter who will under circumstances of trial deny his Lord. There may be persons represented by John whom Jesus loved, but he may have a zeal that would destroy men's lives by calling down fire from heaven upon them to revenge an insult to Christ and the truth. But the great Teacher seeks to give lessons of instruction to correct these existing evils. He is doing the same today with His church. He is pointing out their dangers. He is presenting before them the Laodicean message.

He shows them that all selfishness, all pride, all self-exaltation, all unbelief and prejudice, which lead to resistance of the truth and turn away from the true light, are dangerous, and unless [these sins are] repented of, those who cherish these things will be left in darkness, as was the Jewish nation. Let every soul now seek to answer the prayer of Christ. Let every soul echo that prayer in mind, in petitions, in exhortations, that they all may be one, even as Christ is one with the Father, and work to this end.

In the place of turning the weapons of warfare within our own ranks, let them be turned against the enemies of God and of the truth. Echo the prayer of Christ with your whole heart: "Holy Father, keep through Thine own name those whom Thou hast given Me, that they may be one, as we are." (John 17:11) . . .

What Christ's Prayer Envisioned.—The prayer of Christ is not only for those who are now His disciples, but for all those who shall believe on Christ through the words of His disciples, even to the end of the world. Jesus was just about to yield up His life to bring life and immortality to light. Christ, amid His sufferings, and being daily rejected of men, looks down the lines two thousand years to His church which would be in existence in the last days, before the close of this earth's history.

The Lord has had a church from that day, through all the changing scenes of time to the present period, 1893. The Bible sets before us a model church. They are to be in unity with each other, and with God. When believers are united to Christ, the living vine, the result is that they are one with Christ, full of sympathy and tenderness and love.

Those Who Pronounce Judgment on the Church.—When anyone is drawing apart from the organized body of God's commandmentkeeping people, when he begins to weigh the church in his human scales and begins to pronounce judgment against them, then you may know that God is not leading him. He is on the wrong track.

Constantly, men and women are arising who become restless and uneasy, who want to set up some new contrivance, to do some wonderful thing. Satan watches his opportunity to give them something to do in his line. God has given to every man his work.

To Restore, Not Tear Down.—There are opportunities and privileges in the church to help those who are ready to die, and to inspire the church with zeal, but not to tear the church to pieces. There are plenty of opportunities in the church to walk in Christ's lines. If the heart is full of zeal to press on to a deeper sanctification and holiness, then work in that line in all humbleness and devotedness. The church needs freshness and the inspiration of men who breathe in the very atmosphere of heaven, to vitalize the church, notwithstanding the tares are among the wheat. . . .

I would caution all believers to learn to maintain a godly jealousy over yourselves, lest Satan shall steal your heart away from God and you slip unconsciously into work in Satan's lines, without perceiving that you have changed leaders, and be found in the treacherous power of a tyrant.

We are as a church to be wide awake, and to work for the erring among us as laborers together with God. We are furnished with spiritual weapons, mighty to the pulling down of the fortress of the enemy. We are not to hurl the thunderbolts against the church of Christ militant, for Satan is doing all he possibly can in this line, and you who claim to be the remnant of the people of God had better not be found helping him, denouncing, accusing, and condemning. Seek to restore, not to tear down, discourage, and destroy.—Manuscript 21, 1893. (Published in *The Review and Herald,* Nov. 8, 1956.)

2.

Unity in the Church

Present a United Front

The testimony of every believer in the truth must be as one. All your little differences, which arouse the combative spirit among brethren, are devices of Satan to divert minds from the great and fearful issue before us. The true peace will come among God's people when through united zeal and earnest prayer the false peace that exists to a large degree is disturbed. Now there is earnest work to do. Now is the time to manifest your soldierly qualities; let the Lord's people present a united front to the foes of God and truth and righteousness. . . .

When the Holy Spirit was poured out upon the early church, "the multitude of them that believed were of one heart and of one soul" (Acts 4:32). The Spirit of Christ made them one. This is the fruit of abiding in Christ. . . .

We have need of divine illumination. Every individual is striving to become a center of influence, and until God works for His people, they will not see that subordination to God is the only safety for any soul. His transforming grace upon human hearts will lead to unity that has not yet been realized, for all who are assimilated to Christ will be in harmony with one another. The Holy

Spirit will create unity.—Letter 25b, 1892.

Unity Our Creed

The prayer of Christ to His Father, contained in the seventeenth chapter of John, is to be our church creed. It shows us that our difference and disunion are dishonoring to God. Read the whole chapter, verse by verse.—Manuscript 12, 1899.

Not to Draw Apart

No advice or sanction is given in the Word of God to those who believe the third angel's message to lead them to suppose that they can draw apart. This you may settle with yourselves forever. It is the devising of unsanctified minds that would encourage a state of disunion. The sophistry of men may appear right in their own eyes, but it is not truth and righteousness. "For he is our peace, who hath made both one, and hath broken down the middle wall of partition between us; . . . that he might reconcile both unto God in one body by the cross" (Eph. 2:14-16).

Christ is the uniting link in the golden chain which binds believers together in God. There must be no separating in this great testing time. The people of God are, "fellow-citizens with the saints, and of the household of God; and are built upon the foundation of the apostles and prophets, Jesus Christ himself being the chief corner stone; in whom all the building fitly framed together groweth unto an holy temple in the Lord" (verses 19-21). The children of God constitute one united whole in Christ, who presents His cross as the center of attraction. All who believe are one in Him.

Human feelings will lead men to take the work into their own hands, and the building thus becomes disproportionate. The Lord therefore employs a variety of gifts to make the building symmetrical. Not one feature of the truth is to be hidden or made of little account. God cannot be glorified unless the building, "fitly framed together groweth unto an holy temple in the Lord." A great subject is here comprehended, and those who understand the truth for this time must take heed how they hear and how they build and educate others to practice.—Manuscript 109, 1899.

What Heaven Ratifies

"Verily I say unto you, Whatsoever ye shall bind on earth shall be bound in heaven: and whatsoever ye shall loose on earth shall be loosed in heaven" (Matt. 18:18). When every specification which Christ has given has been carried out in the true, Christian spirit, then, and then only, Heaven ratifies the decision of the church, because its members have the mind of Christ, and do as He would do were He upon the earth.—Letter 1c, 1890.

3.

Independent Action

Departing From the Faith

God is teaching, leading, and guiding His people, that they may teach, lead, and guide others. There will be, among the remnant of these last days, as there were with ancient Israel, those who wish to move independently, who are not willing to submit to the teachings of the Spirit of God, and who will not listen to advice or counsel. Let such ever bear in mind that God has a church upon the earth, to which He has delegated power. Men will want to follow their own independent judgment, despising counsel and reproof; but just as surely as they do this they will depart from the faith, and disaster and ruin of souls will follow. Those who rally now to support and build up the truth of God are ranging themselves on one side, standing united in heart, mind, and voice in defense of the truth.—Letter 104, 1894.

Strength From Concerted Action

The Lord would have all who act a part in His work bear testimony in their lives to the holy character of the truth. The end is near, and now is the time when Satan will make special efforts to distract the interest and separate it from the all-important subjects that should arrest every mind to concentrated action.

An army could do nothing successfully if its different parts did not work in concert. Should each soldier act without reference to the others, the army would soon become disorganized. Instead of gathering strength from concentrated action, it would be wasted in desultory, meaningless efforts. Christ prayed that His disciples might be one with Him, as He was one with the Father.
. . .

Whatever good qualities a man may have, he cannot be a good soldier if he acts independently. Good may occasionally be done but often the result is of little value, and often the end shows more mischief done than good. Those who act independently make a show of doing something, attract attention, and flash out brightly, and then are gone. All must pull in one direction in order to render efficient service to the cause.
. . .

God requires concerted action of His soldiers, and in order to have this in the church, self-restraint is essential; self-restraint must be exercised.—Letter 11a, 1886.

Counsel Together—Compare Plans

In every effort in every place where the truth is introduced there is need of different minds, different gifts, different plans and methods of labor being united. All should make it a point to counsel together, to pray together. Christ says that, "If two of you shall agree on earth as touching any thing that they shall ask, it shall be done for them of my Father which is in heaven" (Matt. 18:19). No one worker has all the wisdom that is needed. There should be a comparing of plans, a counseling together. No one man should think himself sufficient to manage an interest in any place without helpers.

One man may have tact in one direction, but may be a decided failure upon some essential points. This makes his work imperfect. He needs the tact of another man's mind and gift to blend with his efforts. All should be perfectly harmonious in the work. If they can work with only those who see just as they do and follow just their plans, then they will make a failure. The work will be defective because none of these laborers have learned the lessons in the school of Christ that makes them able to present every man perfect in Christ Jesus. All should be constantly improving. They should lay hold of every opportunity and make the most of every privilege, until they become better fitted for their great and solemn work.

But God has set in the church different gifts. These are all precious in their place, and all are to act a part in the perfecting of the saints.

This is God's order, and men must labor according to His rules and arrangements if they would meet with success. God will accept only those efforts that are made willingly and with humble hearts, without the trait of personal feelings or selfishness.—Letter 66, 1886.

Practice in the Early Days

When the cause was younger, my husband used to counsel with men who had sound judgment. The work was much smaller then than it is now, but he did not feel able to manage it alone. He chose counselors from among those bearing responsibility in all parts of the work. And after counseling together, these men would go back to their work feeling a still greater responsibility to carry the work forward in right lines, to uplift, to purify, to solidify, so that the cause of God might move forward in strength.—Manuscript 43, 1901.

Independence a Delusion of Satan

It is a delusion of the enemy for anyone to feel that he can disconnect from agencies which God has appointed and work on an independent line of his own, in his own supposed wisdom, and yet be successful. Although he may flatter himself that he is doing God's work, he will not prosper in the end. We are one body, and every member is to be united to the body, each person working in his respective capacity.—*Letter 104, 1894.*

It is not a good sign when men will not unite with their brethren, but prefer to act alone, when they will not take in their brethren because they do not just exactly meet their mind. If men will wear the yoke of Christ, they cannot pull apart. They will wear Christ's yoke, they will draw with Christ.—*Manuscript 56, 1898.*

As we near the final crisis, instead of feeling that there is less need of order and harmony of action, we should be more systematic than heretofore. All our work should be conducted according to well-defined plans.

I am receiving light from the Lord that there should be wise generalship at this time more than at any former period of our history.—*Letter 27a, 1892.*

Thorough Organization Essential

Oh, how Satan would rejoice if he could succeed in his efforts to get in among this people, and disorganize the work at a time when thorough organization is essential, and will be the greatest power to keep out spurious uprisings and to refute claims not endorsed by the Word of God! We want to hold the lines evenly, that there shall be no breaking down of the system of organization and order that has been built up by wise, careful labor. License must not be given to disorderly elements that desire to control the work at this time.

Some have advanced the thought that as we near the close of time, every child of God will act independently of any religious organization. But I have been instructed by the Lord that in this work there is no such thing as every man's being independent. The stars of heaven are all under law, each influencing the other to do the will of God, yielding their common obedience to the law that controls their action. And in order that the Lord's work may advance, healthfully and solidly, His people must draw together (May 30, 1909).—*Testimonies,* vol. 9, pp. 257, 258.

SECTION II

Principles of Inspiration

INTRODUCTION

Our confidence in that which comes to us as messages inspired by God is based on our faith in God and His Word, as well as upon the convicting work of the Holy Spirit on our hearts. It is also based upon the observation of fulfilled and fulfilling prophecy and the fruitage of these messages in our own lives and in the lives of others. The influence of the counsels on the development and work of the church provides additional evidence of their supernatural origin.

A knowledge of some of the facets of inspiration and revelation helps to sustain such confidence. These may be found in expressions—often incidental—employed by the inspired writers themselves. These words maintaining our confidence appear in the Bible, as well as in the writings of Ellen G. White. The author's Introduction to *The Great Controversy* has contributed much to our understanding of her inspiration.

From time to time the White Estate has brought out Ellen White statements from her published as well as from her unpublished writings relating to the question of revelation and inspiration. These often-used statements, together with material heretofore unpublished, are now brought together in this section entitled "Principles of Inspiration."

As in the case of the Bible writers, Ellen White makes only incidental reference to her visions. She explains only briefly how the light came to her, and how the messages were delivered. These incidental references, appearing in different sources, and often consisting of only a few lines, are now for the first time brought together in this volume.—WHITE TRUSTEES.

4.

The Primacy of the Word

Relation of E. G. White Writings to the Bible Recognized in First Book.—I recommend to you, dear reader, the Word of God as the rule of your faith and practice. By that Word we are to be judged. God has, in that Word, promised to give visions in the "last days"; not for a new rule of faith, but for the comfort of His people, and to correct those who err from Bible truth. Thus God dealt with Peter when He was about to send him to preach to the Gentiles.—*A Sketch of the Christian Experience and Views of Ellen G. White*, p. 64 (1851). (Reprinted in *Early Writings*, p. 78.)

Not to Take the Place of the Word.—The Lord desires you to study your Bibles. He has not given any additional light to take the place of His Word. This light is to bring confused minds to His Word, which, if eaten and digested, is as the lifeblood of the soul. Then good works will be seen as light shining in darkness.— Letter 130, 1901.

Get Proofs From the Bible.—In public labor do not make prominent, and quote that which Sister White has written, as authority to sustain your positions. To do this will not increase faith in the testimonies. Bring your evidences, clear and plain, from the Word of God. A

"Thus saith the Lord" is the strongest testimony you can possibly present to the people. Let none be educated to look to Sister White, but to the mighty God, who gives instruction to Sister White.—Letter 11, 1894.

Bible Principles First, Then the Testimonies.—It is my first duty to present Bible principles. Then, unless there is a decided, conscientious reform made by those whose cases have been presented before me, I must appeal to them personally.—Letter 69, 1896.

E. G. White Work Not Unlike That of Bible Prophets.—In ancient times God spoke to men by the mouth of prophets and apostles. In these days He speaks to them by the testimonies of His Spirit. There was never a time when God instructed His people more earnestly than He instructs them now concerning His will and the course that He would have them pursue.—*Testimonies,* vol. 5, p. 661.

Scripture and Spirit of Prophecy Have Same Author.—The Holy Ghost is the author of the Scriptures and of the Spirit of Prophecy. These are not to be twisted and turned to mean what man may want them to mean, to carry out man's ideas and sentiments, to carry forward man's schemes at all hazards.—Letter 92, 1900.

Relationship of E. G. White Writings to Bible—The Lesser Light.—Little heed is given to the Bible, and the Lord has given a lesser light to lead men and women to the greater light.—*The Review and Herald,* Jan. 20, 1903. (Quoted in *Colporteur Ministry,* p. 125.)

Tested by the Bible.—The Spirit was not given—nor can it ever be bestowed—to supersede the Bible; for the Scriptures explicitly state that the Word of God is the standard by which all teaching and experience must be tested. . . . Isaiah declares, "To the law and to the testimony: if they speak not according to this word, it is because there is no light in them" (Isa. 8:20).—*The Great Controversy,* Introduction, p. vii.

Not for the Purpose of Giving New Light.—Brother J would confuse the mind by seeking to make it appear that the light God has given through the *Testimonies* is an addition to the Word of God, but in this he presents the matter in a false light. God has seen fit in this manner to bring the minds of His people to His Word, to give them a clearer understanding of it.

The Word of God is sufficient to enlighten the most beclouded mind, and may be understood by those who have any desire to understand it. But notwithstanding all this, some who profess to make the Word of God their study are found living in direct opposition to its plainest teachings. Then, to leave men and women without excuse, God gives plain and pointed testimonies, bringing them back to the Word that they have neglected to follow.

The Word of God abounds in general principles for the formation of correct habits of living, and the testimonies, general and personal, have been calculated to call their attention more especially to these principles.—*Testimonies*, vol. 5, pp. 663, 664.

Testimonies to Bring Plain Lessons From the Word.—In the Scriptures God has set forth practical lessons to govern the life and conduct of all; but though He has given minute particulars in regard to our character, conversation, and conduct, yet in a large measure, His lessons are disregarded and ignored. Besides the instruction in His Word, the Lord has given special testimonies to His people, not as a new revelation, but that He may set before us the plain lessons of His Word, that errors may be corrected, that the right way may be pointed out, that every soul may be without excuse.— Letter 63, 1893. (See *Testimonies*, vol. 5, p. 665.)

Ellen White Enabled to Clearly Define Truth and Error.—At that time [after the 1844 disappointment] one error after another pressed in upon us; ministers and doctors brought in new doctrines. We would search the Scriptures with much prayer, and the Holy Spirit would bring the truth to our minds. Sometimes whole nights would be devoted to searching the Scriptures and earnestly asking God for guidance. Companies of devoted men and women assembled for this purpose. The power of God would come upon me, and I was enabled clearly to define what is truth and what is error.

As the points of our faith were thus established, our feet were placed upon a solid foundation. We accepted the truth point by point, under the demonstration of the Holy Spirit. I would be taken off in vision, and explanations would be given me. I was given illustrations of heavenly things, and of the sanctuary, so that we were placed where light was shining on us in clear, distinct rays.—*Gospel Workers,* p. 302.

To Correct Error and Specify Truth.—I have much written in the diary* I have kept in all my journeys that should come before the people if essential, even if I did not write another line. I want that which is deemed worthy to appear, for the Lord has given me much light that I want the people to have; for there is instruction that the Lord has given me for His people. It is light that they should have, line upon line, precept upon precept, here a little and there a little. This is now to come before the people, because it has been given to correct specious errors and to specify what is truth. The Lord has revealed many things pointing out the truth, thus saying, "This is the way, walk ye in it."—Letter 117, 1910.

Testimonies Never Contradict the Bible.—The Bible must be your counselor. Study it and the testimonies God has given; for they never contradict His Word.—Letter 106, 1907.

If the *Testimonies* speak not according to the word of God, reject them. Christ and Belial cannot be

---

* While Mrs. White kept from time to time a daily diary of her experience, yet this is not what she referred to primarily in using the term "diary." Her writing was often done in ruled blank books, more than a score of which are now in the White Estate vault, and many of the manuscripts that appear in the file are found to have been written first in these books. Some manuscripts on file bear the general heading "Diary," used in this particular sense. It will be remembered that this term is used by her in the *Testimonies* in referring to her writings in manuscript form. (See *Testimonies,* vol. 8, p. 206, where she says, "In my diary I find the following written one year ago," and it is plain from what follows that she is referring to testimony matter.)

united.—*Testimonies*, vol. 5, p. 691.

On Quoting Sister White.—How can the Lord bless those who manifest a spirit of "I don't care," a spirit which leads them to walk contrary to the light which the Lord has given them? But I do not ask you to take my words. Lay Sister White to one side. Do not quote my words again as long as you live until you can obey the Bible.* When you make the Bible your food, your meat, and your drink, when you make its principles the elements of your character, you will know better how to receive counsel from God. I exalt the precious Word before you today. Do not repeat what I have said, saying, "Sister White said this," and "Sister White said that." Find out what the Lord God of Israel says, and then do what He commands.—Manuscript 43, 1901. (From an address to church leaders the night before the opening of the General Conference session of 1901.)

---

* Ellen White was meeting the leaders of the church as a group for the first time in ten years. Situations in both the General Conference and in our Battle Creek-based institutions had in many cases reached a low ebb. Testimonies calling for a return to Bible principles had been received, theoretically, but no real improvement had taken place.

Most delegates coming to the General Conference session, which would open the next morning, sensed that there must be changes. Ellen White would in the opening meeting rebuke institutional leaders and call for a reorganization of the General Conference. It was her burden that the changes that needed to be made would be based on Bible principles and not just on the word of Ellen White. In this address she declared:

"God has told me that my testimony must be borne to this conference, and that I must not try to make men believe it. My work is to leave the truth with the people, and those who appreciate the light from Heaven will accept the truth."—Manuscript 43, 1901.

Counsel would come through her as the messenger of the Lord and this counsel should be heeded, but work in depth must be done, work based on the principles set forth in God's Word.—COMPILERS.

5.

Experiences in Receiving the Visions

First Vision. —While I was praying at the family altar, the Holy Ghost fell upon me. —*Early Writings*, p. 14.

Five of us, all women, were kneeling quietly at the family altar. While we were praying, the power of God came upon me as I had never felt it before. I seemed to be surrounded with light, and to be rising higher and higher from the earth. At this time I had a view of the experience of the Advent believers, the coming of Christ, and the reward to be given to the faithful. —*Testimonies*, vol. 5, pp. 654, 655.

The Experience Recounted. —When the gleams of the glory of God came to me first, they thought that I was dead, and there they watched and cried and prayed so long, but to me it was heaven, it was life, and then the world was spread out before me and I saw darkness like the pall of death.

What did it mean? I could see no light. Then I saw a little glimmer of light and then another, and these lights increased and grew brighter, and multiplied and grew stronger and stronger till they were the light of the world. These were the believers in Jesus Christ. . . .

I never thought that I should come to the world

again. When my breath came again to my body, I could not hear anything. Everything was dark. The light and glory that my eyes had rested upon had eclipsed the light and thus it was for many hours. Then gradually I began to recognize the light, and I asked where I was.

"You are right here in my house," said the owner of the house.

"What, here? I here? Do you not know about it?" Then it all came back to me. Is this to be my home? Have I come here again? Oh, the weight and the burden which came upon my soul.—Manuscript 16, 1894.

Entirely Lost to Earthly Things.—When the Lord sees fit to give a vision, I am taken into the presence of Jesus and angels, and am entirely lost to earthly things.* I can see no farther than the angel directs me. My attention is often directed to scenes transpiring upon earth.

At times I am carried far ahead into the future and shown what is to take place. Then again I am shown things as they have occurred in the past.—*Spiritual Gifts,* vol. 2, p. 292 (1860).

At Times Visions Received While Conscious.— Friday, March 20, I arose early, about half past three o'clock in the morning. While writing upon the fifteenth chapter of John suddenly a wonderful peace came upon me. The whole room seemed to be filled with the atmosphere of heaven. A holy, sacred presence seemed to be in my room. I laid down my pen and was in a waiting attitude to see what the Spirit would say unto me. I saw no person. I heard no audible voice, but a heavenly watcher seemed close beside me; I felt that I was in the presence of Jesus.

The sweet peace and light which seemed to be in my room it is impossible for me to explain or describe. A

---

* This accounts for the fact that Ellen White rarely speaks of the physical phenomenon that accompanied many of the visions. She herself had to depend on the testimony of eyewitnesses for a knowledge of these manifestations as she did in 1906 when she referred to evidences of her call and work. See the item closing this chapter.

sacred, holy atmosphere surrounded me, and there were presented to my mind and understanding matters of intense interest and importance. A line of action was laid out before me as if the unseen presence was speaking with me. The matter I had been writing upon seemed to be lost to my mind and another matter distinctly opened before me. A great awe seemed to be upon me as matters were imprinted upon my mind.—Manuscript 12c, 1896.

Another Vision While Writing.—I arose early Thursday morning, about two o'clock, and was writing busily upon the True Vine, when I felt a presence in my room, as I have many times before, and I lost all recollection of what I was about. I seemed to be in the presence of Jesus. He was communicating to me that in which I was to be instructed. Everything was so plain that I could not misunderstand.

I was to help one whom I thought I should never be called upon to be troubled with again. I could not understand what it meant, but at once decided not to try to reason about this, but follow the directions. Not an audible word was spoken to my ear, but to my mind. I said, "Lord, I will do as Thou has commanded."—Letter 36, 1896.

Wonderful Representation While Writing and Speaking.—Not only when I am standing before large congregations is special help bestowed upon me; but when I am using my pen, wonderful representations are given me of past, present, and future.—Letter 86, 1906.

Ellen White Could Not Control the Visions.—It is utterly false that I have ever intimated I could have a vision when I pleased. There is not a shade of truth in this. I have never said I could throw myself into visions when I pleased, for this is simply impossible. I have felt for years that if I could have my choice and please God as well, I would rather die than have a vision, for every vision places me under great responsibility to bear testimonies of reproof and of warning, which has ever been against my feelings, causing me affliction of soul that is inexpressible. Never have I coveted my position, and yet I dare not resist the Spirit of God and seek an easier position.

The Spirit of God has come upon me at different times, in different places, and under various circumstances.* My husband has had no control of these manifestations of the Spirit of God. Many times he has been far away when I have had visions.—Letter 2, 1874.

Dared Not Doubt.—In the confusion I was sometimes tempted to doubt my own experience. While at family prayers one morning, the power of God began to rest upon me, and the thought rushed into my mind that it was mesmerism, and I resisted it. Immediately I was struck dumb. . . . After that I dared not doubt or for a moment resist the power of God, however others might think of me.—*Early Writings*, pp. 22, 23.

Ellen White Recounts Evidences of Her Call and Work.—There is in our world a spirit of belief and also a spirit of unbelief. In the latter days some shall depart from the faith, giving heed to seducing spirits and doctrines of devils. We expect that those who refuse to harmonize with Christ will develop into a warring element; but we should not think that this will do us harm. We must remember that they that are for us are more than they that can be against us. This is my hope and strength and power. I believe in God. I know in whom I believe. I believe the messages that God has given to His remnant church. From childhood I have had many, many experiences that have strengthened my faith in the work that God has given me to do.

Enabled to Write.—Early in my public labors I was bidden by the Lord, "Write, write the things that are revealed to you." At the time this message came to me, I

---

* Elder J. N. Loughborough reports that the last vision accompanied by physical phenomena was on the campground at Portland, Oregon, in 1884. He was present and he made mention of this in a talk he gave on January 20, 1893, on "The Study of the Testimonies," at the General Conference session, held in Battle Creek. See *General Conference Bulletin*, 1893, pp. 19, 20.—Compilers.

could not hold my hand steady. My physical condition made it impossible for me to write. But again came the word, "Write the things that are revealed to you." I obeyed; and as the result it was not long before I could write page after page with comparative ease. Who told me what to write? Who steadied my right hand, and made it possible for me to use a pen? It was the Lord.

When we come into right relation with Him, and give ourselves wholly to Him, we shall see the miracle-working power of God in word and deed.

The Visions Confirmed Conclusions From Bible Study.—In the early days of the message, when our numbers were few, we studied diligently to understand the meaning of many Scriptures. At times it seemed as if no explanation could be given. My mind seemed to be locked to an understanding of the Word; but when our brethren who had assembled for study came to a point where they could go no farther, and had recourse to earnest prayer, the Spirit of God would rest upon me, and I would be taken off in vision, and be instructed in regard to the relation of Scripture to Scripture. These experiences were repeated over and over and over again. Thus many truths of the third angel's message were established, point by point.

Think you that my faith in this message will ever waver? Think you that I can remain silent, when I see an effort being made to sweep away the foundation pillars of our faith? I am as thoroughly established in these truths as it is possible for a person to be. I can never forget the experience I have passed through. God has confirmed my belief by many evidences of His power.

The light that I have received, I have written out, and much of it is now shining forth from the printed page. There is, throughout my printed works, a harmony with my present teaching.

While in Vision She Did Not Breathe.—Some of the instruction found in these pages was given under circumstances so remarkable as to evidence the wonder-working power of God in behalf of His truth. Sometimes while I was in vision, my friends would approach me, and exclaim, "Why, she does not breathe!" Placing a mirror before my lips, they found that no moisture gathered on the glass. It was while there was no sign of any breathing that I kept talking of the things that were being presented before me. These messages were thus given to substantiate the faith of all, that in these last days we might have confidence in the Spirit of Prophecy.

Voice Miraculously Preserved.—I thank God that He has preserved my voice, which in my early youth physicians and friends declared would be silent within three months. The God of heaven saw that I needed to pass through a trying experience in order to be prepared for the work He had for me to do.

For the past half century my faith in the ultimate triumph of the third angel's message and everything connected with it, has been substantiated by the wonderful experiences through which I have passed. This is why I am anxious to have my books published and circulated in many languages. I know that the light contained in these books is the light of heaven.

Study the Instruction.—I ask you to study the instruction that is written in these books. To John, the aged apostle, came the message, "Write the things which thou hast seen, and the things which are, and the things which shall be hereafter." The Lord has bidden me write that which has been revealed to me. This I have done, and it is now in printed form. . . .

Amid the error that is overspreading the whole earth, let us strive to stand firm on the platform of eternal truth. Let us put on the whole armor of God; for we are told that in this time Satan himself will work miracles before the people; and as we see these things, we must be prepared to withstand their deceptive influence. Whatever is presented by the enemy as truth, ought not to influence us; for we should be under the instruction of the great Author of all truth.—*The Review and Herald*, June 14, 1906.

6.

Glimpses of How the Light Came to Ellen White

In the First Vision—Seemingly Present, Participating in Events.—While I was praying at the family altar, the Holy Ghost fell upon me, and I seemed to be rising higher and higher, far above the dark world. I turned to look for the Advent people in the world, but could not find them, when a voice said to me, "Look again, and look a little higher." At this I raised my eyes, and saw a straight and narrow path, cast up high above the world. On this path the Adventist people were traveling to the city, which was at the farther end of the path.—*Early Writings*, p. 14.

Broad Panoramic Views.—Through the illumination of the Holy Spirit, the scenes of the long-continued conflict between good and evil have been opened to the writer of these pages. From time to time I have been permitted to behold the working, in different ages, of the great controversy between Christ, the Prince of Life, the Author of our salvation, and Satan, the prince of evil, the author of sin, the first transgressor of God's holy law.—*The Great Controversy*, Introduction, pp. x, xi.

An Angel Explains the Significance.—While at Loma Linda, California, April 16, 1906, there passed before me a most wonderful representation. During a vision of the night, I stood on an eminence, from which I could see houses shaken like a reed in the wind. Buildings, great and small, were falling to the ground. Pleasure resorts, theaters, hotels, and the homes of the wealthy were shaken and shattered. Many lives were blotted out of existence, and the air was filled with the shrieks of the injured and the terrified. . . . The awfulness of the scenes that passed before me I cannot find words to describe. It seemed that the forbearance of God was exhausted, and that the judgment day had come.

Terrible as was the representation that passed before me, that which impressed itself most vividly upon my mind was the instruction given in connection with it. The angel that stood by my side declared that God's supreme rulership and the sacredness of His law must be revealed to those who persistently refuse to render obedience to the King of kings. Those who choose to remain disloyal must be visited in mercy with judgments, in order that, if possible, they may be aroused to a realization of the sinfulness of their course.—*Testimonies*, vol. 9, pp. 92, 93.

A Vivid View Relating to a Family.—The angel of God said, "Follow me." I seemed to be in a room in a rude building, and there were several young men playing cards. They seemed to be very intent upon the amusement in which they were engaged and were so engrossed that they did not seem to notice that anyone had entered the room. There were young girls present observing the players, and words were spoken not of the most refined order. There was a spirit and influence that were sensibly felt in that room that was not of a character calculated to purify and uplift the mind and ennoble the character. . . .

I inquired, "Who are these and what does this scene represent?"

The word was spoken, "Wait." . . .

I had another representation. There was the imbibing of the liquid poison, and the words and actions under its influence were anything but favorable for serious thoughts, clear perception in business lines, pure morals, and the uplifting of the participants. . . .

I asked again, "Who are these?"

The answer came, "A portion of the family where you are visiting. The adversary of souls, the great enemy of God and man, the head of principalities and powers, and the ruler of the darkness of this world is presiding here tonight. Satan and his angels are leading on with his temptations these poor souls to their own ruin.—Letter 1, 1893.

As If the Whole Thing Were Transacting.—Now I have light, mostly in the night season, just as if the whole thing were transacting, and I viewing it, and as [if] I am listening to the conversation. I am moved to get up and meet it.—Manuscript 105, 1907.

Symbolic Representations.—You were represented to me as a general, mounted on a horse, and carrying a banner. One came and took out of your hand the banner bearing the words, "The commandments of God and the faith of Jesus," and it was trampled in the dust. I saw you surrounded by men who were linking you up with the world.—Letter 239, 1903.

Some of the work that has been done [for outcasts] is represented as being like men rolling large stones up a hill with great effort. When nearly at the top of the hill, the stones rolled again to the bottom. The men only succeeded in taking a few to the top. In the work done for the degraded—what effort it has taken to reach them, what expense, and then to lead them to stand against appetite and base passions!—Letter 232, 1899.

Enabled to Comprehend Symbolic Visions.—My mind and perceptions are still clear. That which the Lord presents to me in figure, He enables me to understand.—Letter 28, 1907.

Warned of Peril Threatening a Physician.—In a vision last night I saw you writing. One looked over your shoulder and said, "You, my friend, are in danger." . . .

Let me tell you of a scene that I witnessed while in Oakland. Angels clothed with beautiful garments, like angels of light, were escorting Dr. A from place to place, and inspiring him to speak words of pompous boasting that were offensive to God.

Soon after the Oakland conference, in the night season the Lord portrayed before me a scene, in which Satan, clothed in a most attractive disguise, was earnestly pressing close to the side of Dr. A. I saw and heard much. Night after night I was bowed down in agony of soul as I saw this personage talking with our brother.—Letter 220, 1903.

Revealed in a Flash of Light.—The question is asked, How does Sister White know in regard to the matters of which she speaks so decidedly, as if she had authority to say these things? I speak thus because they flash upon my mind when in perplexity like lightning out of a dark cloud in the fury of a storm. Some scenes presented before me years ago have not been retained in my memory, but when the instruction then given is needed, sometimes even when I am standing before the people, the remembrance comes sharp and clear, like a flash of lightning,* bringing to mind distinctly that particular instruction. At such times I cannot refrain from saying the things that flash into my mind, not because I have had a new vision, but because that which was presented to me, perhaps years in the past, has been recalled to my mind forcibly.—Manuscript 33, 1911.

Scenes in a Sanitarium Lobby.—In my dreams I was at ———, and I was told by my Guide to mark everything I heard and to observe everything I saw. I was in a retired place, where I could not be seen, but could see all that went on in the room. Persons were settling

---

* Commenting on the manner light often came to Ellen White, W. C. White, her son, in a statement she fully endorsed, declared: "The things which she has written out, are descriptions of flashlight pictures and other representations given her regarding the actions of men, and the influence of these actions upon the work of God for the salvation of men, with views of past, present, and future history in its relation to this work" (WCW Oct. 30, 1911, before GC Council; see Appendix A).—COMPILERS.

accounts with you, and I heard them remonstrating with you in regard to the large sum charged for board and room and treatment. I heard you with firm, decided voice refuse to lower the charge. I was astonished to see that the charge was so high.

You seemed to be the controlling power. I saw that the impression made by your course on the minds of those who were settling their bills was unfavorable to the institution. I heard some of your brethren pleading with you, telling you that your course was unwise and unjust, but you were as firm as a rock in your adherence to your course. You claimed that in what you were doing, you were working for the good of the institution. But I saw persons go from ———— anything but satisfied.—Letter 30, 1887.

Scenes of Familiarity and Adultery.—While in Europe the things that transpired in ———— were opened before me. A voice said, "Follow me, and I will show you the sins that are practiced by those who stand in responsible positions." I went through the rooms, and I saw you, a watchman upon the walls of Zion, were very intimate with another man's wife, betraying sacred trusts, crucifying your Lord afresh. Did you consider that there was a Watcher, the Holy One, who was witnessing your evil work, seeing your actions and hearing your words, and these are also registered in the books of heaven?

She was sitting on your lap; you were kissing her, and she was kissing you. Other scenes of fondness, sensual looks and deportment, were presented before me, which sent a thrill of horror through my soul. Your arm encircled her waist, and the fondness expressed was having a bewitching influence. Then a curtain was lifted, and I was shown you in bed with ————. My Guide said, "Iniquity, adultery."—Letter 16, 1888.

The Message Represented as Fruit Being Given Out.—Your work has been represented to me in figures. You were passing round to a company a vessel filled with most beautiful fruit. But as you offered them this fruit, you spoke words so harsh, and your attitude was so forbidding, that no one would accept it. Then Another came to the same company, and offered them the same fruit. And so courteous and pleasant were His words and manner as He spoke of the desirability of the fruit, that the vessel was emptied.—Letter 164, 1902.

One of Authority Counsels Regarding Locating a Sanitarium.—In the night season I was in a council meeting where the brethren were discussing the matter of the sanitarium in Los Angeles. One of the brethren presented the advantages of establishing the sanitarium in the city of Los Angeles. Then One of Authority arose and presented the matter with clearness and force.—Letter 40, 1902.

Contrasting Scenes; Illustrating Missionary Fervor.—I seemed to be in a large gathering. One of authority was addressing the company, before whom was spread out a map of the world. He said that the map pictured God's vineyard, which must be cultivated. As light from heaven shone upon anyone, that one was to reflect the light to others. Lights were to be kindled in many places, and from these lights still other lights were to be kindled. . . .

I saw jets of light shining from cities and villages, and from the high places and the low places of the earth. God's word was obeyed, and as a result there were memorials for Him in every city and village. His truth was proclaimed throughout the world.

Then this map was removed and another put in its place. On it light was shining from a few places only. The rest of the world was in darkness, with only a glimmer of light here and there. Our Instructor said: "This darkness is the result of men's following their own course. They have cherished hereditary and cultivated tendencies to evil. They have made questioning and faultfinding and accusing the chief business of their lives. Their hearts are not right with God. They have hidden their light under a bushel."—*Testimonies*, vol. 9, pp. 28, 29.

The Study of the Word and Special Knowledge.—With the light communicated through the study of His Word, with the special knowledge given of individual cases among His people under all circumstances and in every phase of experience, can I now be in the same ignorance, the same mental uncertainty and spiritual blindness, as at the beginning of this experience? Will my brethren say that Sister White has been so dull a scholar that her judgment in this direction is no better than before she entered Christ's school, to be trained and disciplined for a special work? Am I no more intelligent in regard to the duties and perils of God's people than are those before whom these things have never been presented?—*Testimonies*, vol. 5, p. 686.

Holy Spirit Impressed Ellen White's Mind and Heart.—God has given me a marked, solemn experience in connection with His work; and you may be assured that so long as my life is spared, I shall not cease to lift a warning voice as I am impressed by the Spirit of God, whether men will hear or whether they will forbear. I have no special wisdom in myself; I am only an instrument in the Lord's hands to do the work He has set for me to do. The instructions that I have given by pen or voice have been an expression of the light that God has given me. I have tried to place before you the principles that the Spirit of God has for years been impressing upon my mind and writing on my heart.

And now, brethren, I entreat you not to interpose between me and the people, and turn away the light which God would have come to them. Do not by your criticisms take out all the force, all the point and power, from the *Testimonies*. Do not feel that you can dissect them to suit your own ideas, claiming that God has given you ability to discern what is light from heaven and what is the expression of mere human wisdom. If the *Testimonies* speak not according to the Word of God, reject them.—*Testimonies*, vol. 5, p. 691.

Illustrated in the Location of a Food Factory.—In the visions of the night, these principles were presented to me in connection with the proposal for the establishment of a bakery* at Loma Linda. I was shown a large building where many foods were made. There were also some smaller buildings near the bakery. As I stood by, I heard loud voices in dispute over the work that was being done. There was a lack of harmony among the workers, and confusion had come in.

Then I saw Brother Burden approach. His countenance bore a look of anxiety and distress as he endeavored to reason with the workmen, and bring them into harmony. The scene was repeated, and Brother Burden was often drawn away from his legitimate work as manager of the sanitarium, to settle variances. . . .

I then saw patients standing on the beautiful sanitarium grounds. They had heard the disputes between the workmen. The patients did not see me, but I could see them and hear them, and their remarks were brought to my ears. They were expressing words of regret that a food factory should be established on these beautiful grounds, in such close proximity to an institution for the care of the sick. Some were disgusted. . . .

Then One appeared on the scene, and said: "All this has been caused to pass before you as an object lesson, that you might see the result of carrying out certain plans. . . .

Then, lo, the whole scene changed. The bakery building was not where we had planned it, but at a distance from the sanitarium buildings, on the road toward the railway. It was a humble building, and a small work was carried on there. The commercial idea was lost sight of, and, in its stead, a strong spiritual influence pervaded the place.—Letter 140, 1906.

---

* Note: Plans called for its location about one hundred yards from the main sanitarium building.

7.

Presenting the Divinely Revealed Message

Instruction to Ellen White.—As the Spirit of God has opened to my mind the great truths of His Word, and the scenes of the past and the future, I have been bidden to make known to others that which has thus been revealed.—*The Great Controversy*, p. xi.

From the beginning of my work . . . I have been called upon to bear a plain, pointed testimony, to reprove wrongs, and to spare not.—*Testimonies*, vol. 5, p. 678.

Bearing Testimony—Aided by the Spirit of God.—After I come out of vision I do not at once remember all that I have seen, and the matter is not so clear before me until I write, then the scene rises before me as was presented in vision, and I can write with freedom. Sometimes the things which I have seen are hid from me after I come out of vision, and I cannot call them to mind until I am brought before a company where the vision applies, then the things which I have seen come to my mind with force.

I am just as dependent upon the Spirit of the Lord in relating or writing the vision as in having the vision. It is impossible for me to call up things which have been shown me unless the Lord brings them before me at the time that He is pleased to have me relate or write them.—*Spiritual Gifts*, vol. 2, pp. 292, 293.

Must Be Impressed by the Holy Spirit.—I cannot at my own impulse take up a work and launch out into it. I have to be impressed by the Spirit of God. I cannot write unless the Holy Spirit helps me. Sometimes I cannot write at all. Then again I am aroused at eleven, twelve, and one o'clock; and I can write as fast as my hand can move over the paper.—Letter 11, 1903.

When Pen Taken in Hand.—As soon as I take my pen in hand I am not in darkness as to what to write. It is as plain and clear as a voice speaking to me, "I will instruct thee and teach thee in the way which thou shalt go." "In all thy ways acknowledge him, and he shall direct [make plain] thy paths."—Manuscript 89, 1900.

I am very busy with my writing. Early and late, I am writing out the matters that the Lord opens before me. The burden of my work is to prepare a people to stand in the day of the Lord.—Letter 371, 1907. (Published in *Writing and Sending Out of the Testimonies to the Church*, p. 15.)

The Integrity of Her Message.—I speak that which I have seen, and which I know to be true.—Letter 4, 1896.

In the line of my work I speak the things the Lord gives me. And in my words to you I would . . . [not] dare to say that the Lord did not move me to make the remarks which I made in that talk all the way through.—Letter 18d, 1890.

I write all that the Lord gives me to write.—Letter 52, 1906.

Testimony Expressed in Her Own Words.—Although I am as dependent upon the Spirit of the Lord in writing my views as I am in receiving them, yet the words I employ in describing what I have seen are my own, unless they be those spoken to me by an angel, which I always enclose in marks of quotation.*—*Review*

---

* General Conference session action on inspiration: "We believe the light given by God to His servants is by the enlightenment of the mind, thus

and Herald, Oct. 8, 1867.)

I Must Write These Things Over and Over.—I have faithfully written out the warnings that God has given me. They have been printed in books, yet I cannot forbear. I must write these same things over and over. I ask not to be relieved. As long as the Lord spares my life, I must continue to bear these earnest messages.—Manuscript 21, 1910.

Ellen G. White's Understanding of Her Writings.—

a. The Testimonies: Those who carefully read the testimonies as they have appeared from the early days, need not be perplexed as to their origin. The many books, written by the help of the Spirit of God, bear a living witness to the character of the testimonies.—Letter 225, 1906. (Published in *Selected Messages,* book 1, p. 49.)

b. The Conflict of the Ages Books: Sister White is not the originator of these books. They contain the instruction that during her lifework God has been giving her. They contain the precious, comforting light that God has graciously given His servant to be given to the world.—*Colporteur Ministry,* p. 125.

c. The Articles: I do not write one article in the paper expressing merely my own ideas. They are what God has opened before me in vision—the precious rays of light shining from the throne.—*Testimonies,* vol. 5, p. 67.

d. The Letters (testimonies): Weak and trembling, I arose at three o'clock in the morning to write to you. God was speaking through clay. You may say that this communication was only a letter. Yes, it was a letter, but prompted by the Spirit of God, to bring before your minds things that had been shown me. In these letters which I write, in the testimonies I bear, I am presenting to you that which the Lord has presented to me.—*Testimonies,* vol. 5, p. 67.

imparting the thoughts, and not (except in rare cases) the very words in which the ideas should be expressed."—General Conference proceedings, *Review and Herald,* Nov. 27, 1883.

e. The Interviews: He [Elder G. A. Irwin] has with him a little notebook in which he has noted down perplexing questions which he brings before me, and if I have any light upon these points, I write it out for the benefit of our people, not only in America but in this country [Australia].—Letter 96, 1899.

f. When There Was No Light: I have no light on the subject [as to just who would constitute the 144,000]. . . . Please tell my brethren that I have nothing presented before me regarding the circumstances concerning which they write, and I can set before them only that which has been presented to me.—Quoted in a letter by C. C. Crisler to E. E. Andross, Dec. 8, 1914. (In White Estate Document File, Number 164.)

I am not at liberty to write to our brethren concerning your future work. . . . I have received no instruction regarding the place where you should locate. . . . If the Lord gives me definite instruction concerning you, I will give it you; but I cannot take upon myself responsibilities that the Lord does not give me to bear.—Letter 96, 1909.

God-given Representations Reproduced as Vividly as Possible.—I want every jot and tittle of my strength to reproduce the representations the Lord has given me, and to make them as vivid as possible while I can do so.—Letter 325, 1905.

Holy Spirit Gives Appropriate Words.—The goodness of the Lord to me is very great. I praise His name that my mind is clear on Bible subjects. The Spirit of God works upon my mind and gives me appropriate words with which to express the truth. I am also greatly strengthened when I stand before large congregations.—Letter 90, 1907.

The Spirit's Help in Choice of Appropriate Words.—I am trying to catch the very words and expressions that were made in reference to this matter, and as my pen hesitates a moment, the appropriate words come to my mind.—Letter 123, 1904.

When writing these precious books, if I hesitated,

the very word I wanted to express the idea was given me.—Letter 265, 1907.

Choosing Words Carefully.—I am exceedingly anxious to use words that will not give anyone a chance to sustain erroneous sentiments. I must use words that will not be misconstrued and made to mean the opposite of that which they were designed to mean.—Manuscript 126, 1905.

Not One Heretical Sentence.—I am now looking over my diaries* and copies of letters written for several years back. . . . I have the most precious matter to reproduce and place before the people in testimony form. While I am able to do this work, the people must have things to revive past history, that they may see that there is one straight chain of truth, without one heretical sentence, in that which I have written. This, I am instructed, is to be a living letter to all in regard to my faith.—Letter 329a, 1905.

First a General Presentation, Then Specific Application.—I was carried from one sickroom to another where Dr. B was the physician. In some cases I was made sad to see a great inefficiency. He did not have sufficient knowledge to understand what the case demanded and what was essential to be done to baffle disease.

The one of authority that has often instructed me, said, "Young man, you are not a close student. You skim the surface. You must make close study, make use of your opportunities, learn more; and what lessons you learn, learn thoroughly. You go too lightly loaded. It is a solemn thing to have human life in your hands, where any mistake you may make, any neglect of deep insight on your part, may cut short the existence of those who might live. This danger would be lessened, if the physician had more thorough intelligence how to treat the sick."

I never have written this to you, but I have presented all, in a general manner, without applying it to your

---

* See Footnote, p. 32.

case. I feel now that you should know these things, that the light which has been given to the workers at the sanitarium, in some things meant you. I tell you in the spirit of love for your soul, and with an interest in your success as a medical practitioner, you must drink deeper at the fountain of knowledge, before you are prepared to be first or alone in an institution for the sick.—Letter 7, 1887.

Case Not Varnished Over.—In the last vision given me your case was presented before me. . . . From what has been shown me you are a transgressor of the seventh commandment. How then can your mind be in harmony with the precious Word of God, truths which cut you at every turn? If you had been betrayed into this folly unwittingly it would be more excusable, but you have not. You have been warned. You have been reproved and counseled. . . .

My soul is stirred within me. . . . I will not varnish over your case. You are in a fearful state and you need to be entirely transformed.—Letter 52, 1876.

Not Always a Special Vision.—I write this for I dare not withhold it. You are far from doing the will of God, far from Jesus, far from heaven. It is no marvel to me that God has not blessed your labors. You may say, "God has not given Sister White a vision in my case, why, then, does she write as she does?"

I have seen the cases of others who like you are neglecting their duties. I have seen many things in your case in your past experience. And when I enter a family and see a course pursued that God has reproved and condemned, I am in grief and distress, whether the special sins have been shown me or the sins of another who has neglected similar duties. I know whereof I speak. I feel deeply over the matter. I say, then, for Christ's sake make haste to come on the right ground, and harness up for the battle.—Letter 52, 1886.

Testimony Counsel Based on Many Visions.— God has given me a testimony of reproof for parents who treat their children as you do your little one.—Letter 1, 1877.

This matter has been brought before my mind in other cases where individuals have claimed to have messages for the Seventh-day Aventist Church, of a similar character, and the word has been given me, "Believe them not."—Letter 16, 1893. (Quoted in *Selected Messages,* book 2, pp. 63, 64.)

Bearing Testimony Unexpectedly.—Sabbath morning early, I went into meeting and the Lord gave me a testimony directly to them, all unexpected to me. I poured it out upon them, showing them that the Lord sent His ministers with a message and the message they brought was the very means God had ordained to reach them, but they felt at liberty to pick it in pieces and make of none effect the Word of God. . . . I can tell you there was great astonishment and marveling that I dared to speak to them thus.—Letter 19, 1884.

Bearing Reproofs an Unpleasant Task for Ellen White.—Were I to go to the [General] Conference [session], I should be compelled to take positions that would cut some to the quick. It greatly hurts me to do this, and it is a long time before I recover from the strain that such an experience brings on me.—Letter 17, 1903.

Work Made Sure by Both Oral and Written Messages.—The messages that God has given me have been communicated to His people both by word of mouth and in printed form. Thus my work has been made doubly sure.

I am instructed that the Lord, by His infinite power, has preserved the right hand of His messenger for more than half a century, in order that the truth may be written out as He bids me write it for publication in periodicals and books.—Letter 136, 1906.

Whether Past or Future She Could Not Say.—I have been urged by the Spirit of the Lord to fully warn our people in regard to the undue familiarity of married men with women, and women with men. This lovesick sentimentalism existed in the [city] mission at —— before you were connected with it. I was shown you with others manifesting the same; whether this was in the past or the future I cannot say, for often things are presented to me long before the circumstances take place.—Letter 17, 1891.

Shown as If Work Was Done.—I have been thinking of how, after we began sanitarium work in Battle Creek, sanitarium buildings all ready for occupation were shown to me in vision. The Lord instructed me as to the way in which the work in these buildings should be conducted in order for it to exert a saving influence on the patients.

All this seemed very real to me, but when I awoke I found that the work was yet to be done, that there were no buildings erected.

Another time I was shown a large building going up on the site on which the Battle Creek Sanitarium was afterward erected. The brethren were in great perplexity as to who should take charge of the work. I wept sorely. One of authority stood up among us, and said, "Not yet. You are not ready to invest means in that building, or to plan for its future management."

At this time the foundation of the sanitarium had been laid. But we needed to learn the lesson of waiting.—Letter 135, 1903.

Paul Shown in Advance Dangers That Would Arise.—Paul was an inspired apostle, yet the Lord did not reveal to him at all times just the condition of His people. Those who were interested in the prosperity of the church, and saw evils creeping in, presented the matter before him, and from the light which he had previously received he was prepared to judge of the true character of these developments. Because the Lord had not given him a new revelation for that special time, those who were really seeking light did not cast his message aside as only a common letter. No, indeed. The Lord had shown him the difficulties and dangers which would arise in the churches, that when they should develop he might know just how to treat them.—*Testimonies*, vol. 5, p. 65.

Ellen White Could Now Speak.—This morning I

attended a meeting where a select few were called together to consider some questions that were presented to them by a letter soliciting consideration and advice on these subjects. Of some of these subjects I could speak, because at sundry times and in divers places many things have been presented to me. . . . As my brethren read the selections from letters, I knew what to say to them; for this matter has been presented to me again and again in regard to the southern field. I have not felt at liberty to write out the matter until now. . . . The light that the Lord has given me at different times has been that the southern field, where the greatest share of the population of the colored race is, cannot be worked after the same methods as other fields.—Letter 73, 1895. (Published in *The Southern Work,* p. 72.)

When the Time Is Fully Come.—I must not write more now, although there is much more that I shall write when I know that the time has fully come.—Letter 124, 1902.

Deferred for a Year.—The Lord did help and bless me in a signal manner during the conference in Melbourne. I labored, before I entered it, very hard, giving personal testimonies which I had written out one year before, but could not feel clear to send them. I thought of the words of Christ, "I have yet many things to say unto you, but ye cannot bear them now" (John 16:12). When I enclosed the communication all ready to mail, it seemed that a voice spoke to me saying, "Not yet, not yet, they will not receive your testimony."—Letter 39, 1893.

Visions Not Always First Understood.—On one occasion when we were talking together about your experience in your work, you asked me, "Have you told me all?" I could not say more at that time. Often representations are given me which at first I do not understand, but after a time they are made plain by a repeated presentation of those things that I did not at first comprehend, and in ways that make their meaning clear and unmistakable.—Letter 329, 1904.

What I Wrote Seemed New.—In the night I am aroused from my sleep, and I write in my diary many things that appear as new to me when read, as to any who hear them. If I did not see the matter in my own handwriting I should not think my pen had traced it.—Letter 118, 1898.

Former Writings Timely.—I have a large amount of precious matter, written at Cooranbong [Australia], and dated December 20, 1896, which is just what is needed at this time. I will have it copied today, and if it is possible get it off in the evening mail. I had lost all trace of these manuscripts, but this morning a pile of copies attracted my attention, which on looking over, I found to my surprise to be just what I wanted.—Letter 262, 1907.

Minds Must Be Prepared Spiritually.—I have tried to not shun to give to our people the whole counsel of God, but have sometimes deferred matters with the injunction, "They cannot bear them now." Even truth cannot be presented in its fullness before minds that are in no preparation spiritually to receive it. I have many things to say, but persons to whom the messages apply cannot in their present unconsecrated state bear them.—Letter 55, 1894.

Why Paul Could Not Tell All.—The great apostle had many visions. The Lord showed him many things that it is not lawful for a man to utter. Why could he not tell the believers what he had seen? Because they would have made a misapplication of the great truths presented. They would not have been able to comprehend these truths. And yet all that was shown to Paul molded the messages that God gave him to bear to the churches.—Letter 161, 1903.

No Claim for Special Light for Biographical Writings.—In preparing the following pages [*Spiritual Gifts*, vol. 2, which is an autobiographical account], I have labored under great disadvantages, as I have had to depend in many instances on memory, having kept no journal till within a few years. In several instances I have sent the manuscripts to friends who were present when the circumstances related occurred, for their examination before they were put in print. I have taken great care, and have spent much time, in endeavoring to state the simple facts as correctly as possible.

I have, however, been much assisted in arriving at dates by the many letters which I wrote.—Preface to *Spiritual Gifts*, vol. 2.

A special request is made that if any find incorrect statements in this book they will immediately inform me. The edition will be completed about the first of October; therefore send before that time.—*Ibid.*, Appendix in first 400 copies.

Distinction Between Common and Religious Subjects.—There are times when common things must be stated, common thoughts must occupy the mind, common letters must be written and information given that has passed from one to another of the workers. Such words, such information, are not given under the special inspiration of the Spirit of God. Questions are asked at times that are not upon religious subjects at all, and these questions must be answered. We converse about houses and lands, trades to be made, and locations for our institutions, their advantages and disadvantages.— Manuscript 107, 1909. (Published in *Selected Messages*, book 1, p. 39.)

The Point Illustrated.—I have not been given the message, Send for Brother C to come to Australia. No; therefore I do not say, I know that this is the place for you. But it is my privilege to express my wishes, even though I say, I speak not by commandment.

But I do not want you to come because of any persuasion of mine. I want you to seek the Lord most earnestly, and then follow where He shall lead you. I want you to come when God says, Come, not one moment before.

Nevertheless, it is my privilege to present the wants of the work of God in Australia. Australia is not my country only as it is the Lord's province. The country is

God's; the people are His. A work is to be done here, and if you are not the one to do it, I shall feel perfectly resigned to hear that you have gone to some other locality.—Letter 129, 1897. (From a letter concerning the need for a sanitarium in Australia and the possibility of this man coming to Australia to launch such an enterprise.)

Information Gained From Those Who Should Know.—The information given concerning the number of rooms in the Paradise Valley Sanitarium was given, not as a revelation from the Lord, but simply as a human opinion. There has never been revealed to me the exact number of rooms in any of our sanitariums; and the knowledge I have obtained of such things I have gained by inquiring of those who were supposed to know. In my words, when speaking upon these common subjects, there is nothing to lead minds to believe that I receive my knowledge in a vision from the Lord and am stating it as such.—Manuscript 107, 1909. (Quoted in *Selected Messages,* book 1, p. 38.)

Two Kinds of Letters.—Dear Children [Edson and Emma]: I have had many matters to write out, and I have been hard at work. My heart is fixed, trusting in the Lord. We are in no case to be doubtful, but hopeful.

This morning I found your letter under my door. I was glad to hear from you. Yesterday I wrote you a letter on common, everyday topics. [See next quotation.] This letter will be sent today. I have written a long letter on the subject spoken of in your letter, and have given it out to be copied. This will be sent to you soon. . . .

From the instruction that the Lord has given me from time to time, I know that there should be workers who make medical evangelistic tours among the towns and villages. Those who do this work will gather a rich harvest of souls, both from the higher and the lower classes.—Letter 202, 1903.

The Letter Dealing With Common Matters.—Dear Children Edson and Emma.—It has been a long time since I have written to you. I should be very much

pleased to visit you in your own home. Willie writes me
that he is much pleased with your situation. I have not
heard from you for a long time. I should be so glad to
get a letter from you, even if it is only a few lines. And
remember that if at any time you wish to pay us a visit,
to counsel about your work and about the books that we
are trying to get out, I shall be more than glad to see
you.

It seems a long time since Willie left us. He went
away the last of June, and it is now the tenth of
September. He will not be home for a week yet.
. . .—Letter 201, 1903.

Sister White's Judgment.—You have evidenced
your opinion of your own judgment—that it was more
reliable than Sister White's. Did you consider that Sister
White has been dealing with just such cases during her
life of service for the Master, that cases similar to your
own and many varieties of cases have passed before her
that should make her know what is right and what is
wrong in these things? Is a judgment that has been
under the training of God for more than fifty years of no
preference to those who have not had this discipline and
education? Please consider these things.—Letter 115,
1895.

**Dared Not Speak When There Was No Special
Light.**—I find myself frequently placed where I dare
give neither assent nor dissent to propositions that are
submitted to me; for there is danger that any words I
may speak shall be reported as something that the Lord
has given me. It is not always safe for me to express my
own judgment; for sometimes when someone wishes to
carry out his own purpose, he will regard any favorable
word I may speak as special light from the Lord. I shall
be cautious in all my movements.—Letter 162, 1907, p.
2.

NOTE: Except for that which is in the nature of everyday matters or
biographical, that which Mrs. White set before the people was based upon the
visions given to her, whether or not she used the term "I saw." She, in her
day, and we today, draw the line, not between books and letters, et cetera, but

between the sacred and the common. No one need be confused.

Mrs. White, in books intended for the reading of the general public, designedly left out all expressions such as "I saw" and "I was shown," lest the readers, being unfamiliar with her experience, should have their minds diverted from the message itself. One looks in vain through the five volumes of the Conflict Series for one such expression, yet in her introduction to *The Great Controversy*, the first of the series that appeared in 1888, and elsewhere, she makes it known that she witnessed events take place and was "bidden to make known to others that which has been revealed" (p. xi). See also *Steps to Christ, Thoughts From the Mount of Blessing, Christ's Object Lessons, Education*, and *The Ministry of Healing*. "Sister White is not the originator of these books," she wrote.

8.

The Question of Influence

Who Has Told Sister White?—Those who have disregarded the messages of warning have lost their bearings. Some, in their self-confidence, have dared to turn from that which they knew to be truth, with the words, "Who has told Sister White?" These words show the measure of their faith and confidence in the work that the Lord has given me to do. They have before them the result of the work that the Lord has laid upon me, and if this does not convince them, no arguments, no future revelations, would affect them. The result will be that God will speak again in judgment as He has spoken heretofore.—*Review and Herald,* May 19, 1903, p. 8.

Did Anyone Tell Her These Things?—Some are ready to inquire: "Who told Sister White these things?" They have even put the question to me: "Did anyone tell you these things?" I could answer them: "Yes; yes, the angel of God has spoken to me." But what they mean is: "Have the brethren and sisters been exposing their faults?" For the future, I shall not belittle the testimonies that God has given me, to make explanations to try to satisfy such narrow minds, but shall treat all such questions as an insult to the Spirit of God. God has seen fit to thrust me into positions in which He has not placed any other one in our ranks. He has laid upon me burdens of reproof that He has not given to any other one.—*Testimonies*, vol. 3, pp. 314, 315.

Someone Has Told Sister White.—Even now unbelief is expressed by the words, "Who has written these things to Sister White?" But I know of no one who knows them as they are, and no one who could write that which he does not suppose has an existence. Someone has told me—He who does not falsify, misjudge, or exaggerate any case.—*Special Instruction Relating to the Review and Herald Office and the Work in Battle Creek*, p. 16.

Untrustworthy if Influenced.—You think individuals have prejudiced my mind. If I am in this state, I am not fitted to be entrusted with the work of God.—Letter 16, 1893.

Mrs. White Did Not Read Certain Letters or Articles.—You may blame me for not reading your package of writings. I did not read them, neither did I read the letters that Dr. Kellogg sent. I had a message of stern rebuke for the publishing house, and I knew that if I read the communications sent to me, later on, when the testimony came out, you and Dr. Kellogg would be tempted to say, "I gave her that inspiration."—Letter 301, 1905.

I have not been in the habit of reading any doctrinal articles in the paper [the *Review and Herald*], that my mind should not have any understanding of anyone's ideas and views, and that not a mold of any man's theories should have any connection with that which I write.—Letter 37, 1887.

A Question Raised in Early Ministry.—What if you had said ever so much, would that affect the visions that God gives me? If so, then the visions are nothing. . . . What you or anyone else has said is nothing at all. God has taken the matter in hand. . . . What you have said, Sister D, influenced me not at all. My opinion has nothing to do with what God has shown me in vision.—Letter 6, 1851.

Reproof Not From Hearsay.—I received your letter and will endeavor to answer it. You say that you received the testimonies, but the portion in regard to deception you do not receive. Nevertheless, my brother, it is true, and hearsay has nothing to do with this case of reproof.—Letter 28, 1888.

An Attempt to Guide Mrs. White.—Brother E suggests that it would please the people if I speak less about duty and more in regard to the love of Jesus. But I wish to speak as the Spirit of the Lord shall impress me. The Lord knows best what this people needs. I spoke in the forenoon [Sabbath, October 17] from Isaiah 58. I did not round the corners at all.—Manuscript 26, 1885.

Manipulated by One Mighty in Counsel.—There are those who say, "Someone manipulates her writings." I acknowledge the charge. It is One who is mighty in counsel, One who presents before me the condition of things.—Letter 52, 1906.

Why Inquiries Were at Times Made.—I am told by one who made a confession to me that doubts and unbelief had been cherished by them against the testimonies because of the words spoken to them by Sister F. One thing mentioned was that the testimonies to individuals had been told me by others and I gave them, purporting to be a message from God. Does my sister know that in this she is making me a hypocrite and a liar? . . .

One case was mentioned by Sister F, that she had told me all about the case of Brother G's family, and the next thing she heard I was relating the very things she had told me as what the Lord had shown me.

Let me explain. I am often shown families and individuals and when I have an opportunity with those who are acquainted with them, I make inquiry how that family is standing for the purpose of ascertaining if ministers or people have any knowledge of the existing evils.

This was the fact in the case concerning Brother G's family. I wished to see if the testimony was substantiated by facts. But that information given did not originate the testimony, although shortsighted, tempted souls may thus interpret it.—Letter 17, 1887.

Who Told Paul and Sister White?—When a testimony from the Lord is borne to the erring there is often a question asked: Who told Sister White? This must have been the case in the days of Paul, for someone must have [had] the interest of the church at heart to present before the apostle, God's appointed minister, the dangers of the members of the church which threatened its prosperity. There is a time to speak and a time to keep silence. Of course, something must be done, and the Lord's appointed minister must not fail in his work to correct these evils. Now these evils were existing, and Paul had a work to do to counteract them. . . .

We know that Paul had presented before him the state of the churches. God has given him light and knowledge in regard to the order that should be maintained in the churches, the evils that would arise, and which would have to be corrected and firmly dealt with corresponding to their aggravated character. The Lord had revealed to Paul the purity, the devotion and piety that should be maintained in the church, and things arising contrary to this he knew must be reproved according to the light given him of God.

Why Inquiries Are Made.—When matters are brought before my mind in regard to a church, sometimes there flashes, as it were, a light from heaven revealing particulars that God had presented before me of that case, and when the burden is bearing upon my mind in reference to special churches, families or individuals, I frequently inquire the condition of things in the church, and the matter is all written out before I come to that church.

But I want facts to substantiate the testimonies, and I am burdened to know in what manner I should bring out the light God has given me. If the errors have been manifestly affecting the church, the examples of a character to mislead the church, weaken it in faith and strengthen unbelief, then the work to be done must not be confined to families privately or to individuals alone, but must come before the whole church to stay the evil and flash light into the minds of those who have been deceived by deceptive works and misinterpretations.

Again, when before the people, there flashes upon me light that God has given me in the past in reference to the faces which were before me, and I have been impelled by the Spirit of the Lord to speak. This is the way I have been used, viewing many cases, and before I bring these cases out, I wish to know whether the case is known by others; whether their influence is calculated to injure the church generally. Questions are sometimes asked and sometimes it determines the manner of treating these cases, whether before many or few, or before the persons themselves.

If the case is such that it can be dealt with privately, and others need not know, I greatly desire to do all possible to correct and not give publicity to the matter.—Letter 17, 1887.

I Stand Alone, Severely Alone.—I have a statement to make. When the Lord presents before me any matter and instruction and I have a message to bear concerning the said matter, then I shall, to the best of my God-given ability, make known the matter, presenting the mind and will of God just as clearly as my human capabilities, guided and controlled by the Holy Spirit, shall bring all the matter before me to present to others. In regard to the serious matters given me I have not given anyone—man or woman—any right to have the least control over my work the Lord has given me to do.

Since twenty-one years ago, when I was deprived of my husband by death, I have not had the slightest idea of ever marrying again. Why? Not because God forbade it. No. But to stand alone was the best for me, that no one should suffer with me in carrying forward my work entrusted to me of God. And no one should have a right to influence me in any way in reference to my responsibility and my work in bearing my testimony of encouragement and reproof.

My husband never stood in my way to do this, although I had help and encouragement from him and oft his pity. His sympathy and prayers and tears I have missed so much, so very much. No one can understand this as myself. But my work has to be done. No human power should give the least supposition that I would be influenced in the work God has given me to do in bearing my testimony to those for whom He has given me reproof or encouragement.

I have been alone in this matter, severely alone with all the difficulties and all the trials connected with the work. God alone could help me. The last work that is to be done by me in this world will soon be finished. I must express myself plainly, in a manner, if possible, not to be misunderstood.

I have not one person in the world who shall put any message in my mind or lay one duty upon me. I am now to say to you, Brother F, when the Lord gives me a burden for you or for anyone, you shall have it in the way and manner the Lord gives it to me.—Manuscript 227, 1902.

9.

Defining Sister White's Judgment and the Word of the Lord

Sister White's Opinion?

The Position of Part Human, Part Divine.— Many times in my experience I have been called upon to meet the attitude of a certain class, who acknowledged that the testimonies were from God, but took the position that this matter and that matter were Sister White's opinion and judgment. This suits those who do not love reproof and correction, and who, if their ideas are crossed, have occasion to explain the difference between the human and the divine.

If the preconceived opinions or particular ideas of some are crossed in being reproved by testimonies, they have a burden at once to make plain their position to discriminate between the testimonies, defining what is Sister White's human judgment, and what is the word of the Lord. Everything that sustains their cherished ideas is divine, and the testimonies to correct their errors are human—Sister White's opinions. They make of none effect the counsel of God by their tradition.—Manuscript 16, 1889.

Virtually Rejecting the Testimonies.—You have talked over matters as you viewed them, that the communications from Sister White are not all from the Lord, but a portion is her own mind, her own judgment, which is no better than anybody else's judgment and ideas. This is one of Satan's hooks to hang your doubts upon to deceive your soul and the souls of others who will dare to draw the line in this matter and say, this portion which pleases me is from God, but that portion which points out and condemns my course of conduct is from Sister White alone, and bears not the holy signet. You have in this way virtually rejected the whole of the messages, which God in His tender, pitying love has sent to you to save you from moral ruin. . . .

There is One back of me which is the Lord, who has prompted the message which you now reject and disregard and dishonor. By tempting God you have unnerved yourselves, and confusion and blindness of mind has been the result.—Letter 16, 1888.

This Is Not My Opinion.—After I wrote you the long letter which has been belittled by Elder H as merely an expression of my own opinion, while at the Southern California Camp Meeting, the Lord partially removed the restriction, and I write what I do. I dare not say more now, lest I go beyond what the Spirit of the Lord has permitted me.

When Professor I came, I put to him a few pointed questions, more to learn how he regarded the condition of things, than to obtain information. I felt that the crisis had come. Had Elder H, and those united with him, been standing in the light, they would have recognized the voice of warning and reproof; but he calls it a human work, and casts it aside. The work he is doing he will wish undone ere long. He is weaving a net around himself that he cannot easily break. This is not my opinion.

What voice will you acknowledge as the voice of God? What power has the Lord in reserve to correct your errors, and show you your course as it is? What power to work in the church? You have, by your own course, closed every avenue whereby the Lord would reach you.

Will He raise one from the dead to speak to you? . . .

In the testimonies sent to Battle Creek, I have given you the light God has given to me. In no case have I given my own judgment or opinion. I have enough to write of what has been shown me, without falling back on my own opinions. You are doing as the children of Israel did again and again. Instead of repenting before God, you reject His words, and attribute all the warnings and reproof to the messenger whom the Lord sends.—*Testimony for the Battle Creek Church*, pp. 50-58 (1882).

Permit me to express my mind, and yet not my mind, but the word of the Lord.—*Letter 89, 1899.* (Quoted in *Counsels to Writers and Editors*, p. 112.)

Satan Will Help Those Who Feel They Must Discriminate.—I have my work to do, to meet the misconceptions of those who suppose themselves able to say what is testimony from God and what is human production. If those who have done this work continue in this course, satanic agencies will choose for them. . . .

Those who have helped souls to feel at liberty to specify what is of God in the Testimonies and what are the uninspired words of Sister White, will find that they were helping the devil in his work of deception. Please read Testimony No. 33, page 211 [*Testimonies*, vol. 5, p. 682], "How to Receive Reproof."—*Letter 28, 1906.*

How Can God Reach Them?—What reserve power has the Lord with which to reach those who have cast aside His warnings and reproofs, and have accredited the testimonies of the Spirit of God to no higher source than human wisdom? In the judgment, what can you who have done this, offer to God as an excuse for turning from the evidences He has given you that God was in the work?—*Testimonies to Ministers*, p. 466.

10.

On Being an Inspired Messenger

Experiences as God's Messenger Recounted. —
For half a century I have been the Lord's messenger, and
as long as my life shall last I shall continue to bear the
messages that God gives me for His people. I take no
glory to myself. In my youth the Lord made me His
messenger, to communicate to His people testimonies of
encouragement, warning, and reproof. For sixty years I
have been in communication with heavenly messengers,
and I have been constantly learning in reference to divine
things, and in reference to the way in which God is
constantly working to bring souls from the error of their
ways to the light in God's light.

Many souls have been helped because they have
believed that the messages given me were sent in mercy
to the erring. When I have seen those who needed a
different phase of Christian experience, I have told them
so, for their present and eternal good. And so long as the
Lord spares my life, I will do my work faithfully,
whether or not men and women shall hear and receive
and obey. My work is clearly given me to do, and I shall
receive grace in being obedient.

I love God. I love Jesus Christ, the Son of God, and
I feel an intense interest in every soul who claims to be a
child of God. I am determined to be a faithful steward so

long as the Lord shall spare my life. I will not fail nor be discouraged.

But for months my soul has been passing through intense agony on account of those who have received the sophistries of Satan and are communicating the same to others,* making every conceivable interpretation in various ways to destroy confidence in the gospel message for this last generation, and in the special work which God has given me to do. I know that the Lord has given me this work, and I have no excuse to make for what I have done.

In my experience I am constantly receiving evidence of the sustaining miracle-working power of God upon my body and my soul, which I have dedicated to the Lord. I am not my own; I have been bought with a price and I have such assurance of the Lord's working in my behalf that I must acknowledge His abundant grace. . . .

Why should I complain? So many times has the Lord raised me up from sickness, so wonderfully has He sustained me, that I can never doubt. I have so many unmistakable evidences of His special blessings, that I could not possibly doubt. He gives me freedom to speak His truth before large numbers of people. Not only when I am standing before large congregations is special help bestowed upon me, but when I am using my pen, wonderful representations are given me of past, present, and future.—Letter 86, 1906.

Given Tongue and Utterance.—Of all the precious assurances God has given me regarding my work, none has been more precious to me than this, that He would give me tongue and utterance wherever I should go. In places where there was the greatest opposition, every tongue was silenced. I have spoken the plain message to our own people and to the multitude, and my words have been accepted as coming from the Lord.—Letter 84, 1909.

---

* Reference to pantheistic teachings.

Ellen G. White Message Consistent Through the Years.—The meeting on Sunday afternoon was attended by many of the citizens of Battle Creek. They paid the best of attention. At this meeting I had opportunity to state decidedly that my views have not changed. The blessing of the Lord rested upon many of those who heard the words spoken. I said: "You may be anxious to know what Mrs. White believes. You have heard her speak many times. . . . She has the same service to do for the Master that she had when she addressed the people of Battle Creek years ago. She receives lessons from the same Instructor. The directions given her are, 'Write the messages that I give you, that the people may have them.' These messages have been written as God has given them to me."—Letter 39, 1905.

E. G. White's Confidence in the Divine Source of Her Revelations.—What a battle I am obliged to fight! My brethren seem to judge me as taking positions that are not necessary. They do not see that God in His own wisdom has made revelations to me which cannot successfully be contradicted or disputed. Nothing can rub out that which has been presented to me and imprinted on the tablets of my soul. All the oppositions or gainsaying to make my testimony of none effect only compels from me, by the urgency of the Spirit of God, a more decided repetition, and to stand on the light revealed with all the force of the strength God has given me.—Manuscript 25, 1890.

Meet the Danger Positively.—Satan will continue to bring in his erroneous theories and to claim that his sentiments are true. Seducing spirits are at work. I am to meet the danger positively, denying the right of anyone to use my writings to serve the devil's purpose to allure and deceive the people of God.* God has spared my life that I may present the testimonies given me, to vindicate

---

* Advocates of pantheistic teachings used E. G. White writings to bolster their erroneous views.

that which God vindicates, and to denounce every vestige of Satan's sophistry. One thing will follow another in spiritual sophistry, to deceive if possible the very elect.—Manuscript 126, 1905.

Unmoved by Opposition.—The greatest tirade may be made against me, but it will not change in the least my mission or my work. We have had this to meet again and again. The Lord gave me the message when I was only 17 years old. . . . The message the Lord has given me to bear has been in a straight line from light to light, upward and onward from truth to advanced truth.—Manuscript 29, 1897.

No Claim to the Title "Prophetess."—During the discourse [at Battle Creek, October 2, 1904], I said that I did not claim to be a prophetess. Some were surprised at this statement, and as much is being said in regard to it, I will make an explanation. Others have called me a prophetess, but I have never assumed that title. I have not felt that it was my duty thus to designate myself. Those who boldly assume that they are prophets in this our day are often a reproach to the cause of Christ.

My work includes much more than this name signifies. I regard myself as a messenger, entrusted by the Lord with messages for His people.—Letter 55, 1905. (In *Selected Messages*, book 1, pp. 35, 36.)

The Work of a Prophet and More.—I am now instructed that I am not to be hindered in my work by those who engage in suppositions regarding its nature, whose minds are struggling with so many intricate problems connected with the supposed work of a prophet. My commission embraces the work of a prophet, but it does not end there. It embraces much more than the minds of those who have been sowing the seeds of unbelief can comprehend.—Letter 244, 1906. (Addressed to elders of the Battle Creek church; See *Selected Messages*, book 1, pp. 34-36.)

No Self-vindication.—My heart feels very sad that Brethren J and K have taken the position which they have. . . . You may inquire, "What effect does this have upon you?" Sorrow only, sorrow of soul, but peace and perfect rest and trust in Jesus. To vindicate myself, my position, or my mission, I would not utter ten words. I would not seek to give evidence of my work. "By their fruits ye shall know them" (Matt. 7:20).—Letter 14, 1897.

Leaving Consequences With God.—I am sometimes greatly burdened in the night season. I rise from my bed, and walk the room, praying to the Lord to help me bear the burden, and say nothing to *make* the people believe that the message He has given me is truth. When I can lay this burden on the Lord, I am free indeed. I enjoy a peace that I cannot express. I feel lifted up, as if borne by the everlasting arms, and peace and joy fill my soul.

I am again and again reminded that I am not to try to clear away the confusion and contradiction of faith and feeling and unbelief that is expressed. I am not to be depressed, but am to speak the words of the Lord with authority, and then leave with Him all the consequences.

I am instructed by the Great Physician to speak the word that the Lord gives me, whether men will hear or whether they will forebear. I am told that I have nothing to do with the consequences, that God, even the Lord Jehovah, will keep me in perfect peace if I will rest in His love and do the work He has given me.—Letter 146, 1902.

Will Not Confess the Sins Known Only to Those Involved.—Your brethren, or many of them, do not know that which you yourself and the Lord know. . . . I have determined that I will not confess the sins of those who profess to believe the truth, but leave these things for them to confess.—Letter 113, 1893.

E. G. White Benefited by the Message Given.—I long to speak to large congregations, knowing that the message is not of myself but that which the Lord impresses upon my mind to utter. I am never left alone when I stand before the people with a message. When before the people there seems to be presented before me the most precious things of the gospel and I participate in the gospel message and feed upon the Word as much as any of the hearers. The sermons do me good, for I have new representations every time I open my lips to speak to the people.

I can never doubt my mission, for I am a participant in the privileges and am nourished and vivified, knowing that I am called unto the grace of Christ. Every time I set forth the truth to the people, and call their attention to eternal life which Christ has made possible for us to obtain, I am as much benefited as they with most gracious discoveries of the grace and love and the power of God in behalf of His people, in justification and reconciliation with God.—Manuscript 174, 1903.

The Privilege of Being God's Messenger.—I am very thankful that the Lord has given me the privilege of being His messenger to communicate precious truth to others.—Letter 80, 1911.

After Ellen White's Death

E. G. White's Writings to Continue to Witness.—I am to trace this testimony on paper, that should I fall asleep in Jesus, the witness to the truth might still be borne.—Letter 116, 1905.

To Speak to the End.—Abundant light has been given to our people in these last days. Whether or not my life is spared, my writings will constantly speak, and their work will go forward as long as time shall last. My writings are kept on file in the office, and even though I should not live, these words that have been given to me by the Lord will still have life and will speak to the people.—Letter 371, 1907. (Published in *Selected Messages*, book 1, p. 55.)

Messages to Be of Greater Force After Prophet's Death.—Physically, I have always been as a broken vessel; and yet in my old age the Lord continues to move upon me by His Holy Spirit to write the most important books that have ever come before the churches and the world. The Lord is evidencing what He can do through weak vessels. The life that He spares I will use to His glory. And, when He may see fit to let me rest, His messages shall be of even more vital force than when the frail instrumentality through whom they were delivered, was living.—Manuscript 122, 1903.

11.

The Reception of the Messages

Messages of Encouragement, Warning, and Reproof.—For half a century I have been the Lord's messenger, and as long as my life shall last I shall continue to bear the messages that God gives me for His people. I take no glory to myself; in my youth the Lord made me His messenger, to communicate to His people testimonies of encouragement, warning, and reproof. For sixty years I have been in communication with heavenly messengers, and I have been constantly learning in reference to divine things, and in reference to the way in which God is constantly working to bring souls from the error of their ways to the light in God's light.—Letter 86, 1906.

Some Receive, Some Reject.—I have a work to do for those who will be helped, even if the light given does not harmonize with their ideas. They will recognize the light from God, because they have the fruits of the work which the Lord has been pleased to do through His humble instrument in the last forty-five years. They acknowledge this work to be of God, and are therefore willing to be corrected in their ideas and to change their course of action.

But those who will maintain and retain their own

ideas, and because they are corrected, conclude that Sister White is influenced to take a certain course of action which is not in harmony with their ideas . . . could not be benefited. I would not consider such friends to be of any value in a hard place, especially in a crisis. Now you have my mind. I do not want to do the work of God in a bungling manner. I want to know what duty is and move in harmony with the Spirit of God.—Letter 3, 1889.

Ellen White's Letter a Message From God.—You ask if the Lord gave me that letter to give to you. I say He did. The Holy God of Israel will not serve with your sins. That message was given of God. If you have had, since that message was given, a new sense of what constitutes sin, if you have become truly converted, a child of God in place of being a transgressor of His law, then there is no one who will be more pleased than myself.—Letter 95, 1893.

Truthfulness of Testimonies Publicly Acknowledged.—I spoke to the people [in Bloomfield, California] in the forenoon in regard to the necessity of having the defects in their characters removed, that they may stand before the Son of God blameless when He shall appear. There was deep feeling in the meeting. I addressed several personally, pointing out the wrongs I had been shown in their cases. They all responded and many with weeping confessed their sins and the truthfulness of the testimony.—Letter 7, 1873.

Interpreted in Light of Preconceived Positions.—There are many who interpret that which I write in the light of their own preconceived opinions. You know what this means. A division in understanding and diverse opinions is the sure result.

How to write in a way to be understood by those to whom I address important matter, is a problem I cannot solve. But I will endeavor to write much less. Owing to the influence of mind upon mind, those who misunderstand can lead others to misunderstand, by the interpretation they place upon the subjects from my pen. One understands them as he thinks they should be, in accordance with his ideas. Another puts his construction upon the written matter, and confusion is the sure result.—Letter 96, 1899.

Partial Acceptance.—For many months, excepting for a few nights, I have not been able to sleep past one o'clock. I find myself sitting in conversation with you, and others, pleading with you as a mother would plead with her son. . . .

You are doubtless surprised, as I expected you would be, that I write to you in so plain and decided a manner. But this I must do, for I am made a steward of the grace of Christ, and I must do this errand for the Lord. You may feel well satisfied with yourself. You may deny the representation given me of your case. Some are doing this today. . . .

This is the reason that men and women do not always see their errors and mistakes, even when these are pointed out to them. They claim to believe the testimonies that come to them, until the message comes that they must change their plans and methods, that their character-building must be altogether different, else the storm and tempest will sweep it from its foundation. Then the enemy tempts them to justify themselves.

After reading this message, you will doubtless be tempted to say, "This is not so. I am not as I am represented here. Someone has filled Sister White's mind with a mass of trash about me." But I tell you in the name of the Lord that the words of this writing are from God. If you choose thus to dispose of the matter, you show the measure of your faith in the work that the Lord has given His servant to do.—Letter 13, 1902.

The Portions Condemning Favorite Indulgences.—There are some professed believers who accept certain portions of the testimonies as the message of God, while they reject those portions which condemn their favorite indulgences. Such persons are working contrary to their own welfare and the welfare of the church. It is essential that we walk in the light while we have the light.—Manuscript 71, 1908.

Trifling With the Messages.—Frequently I do not anticipate saying the things I do say when I am speaking before the people. God may give me words of reproof, of warning, or encouragement as He sees fit, for the benefit of souls. I shall speak these words, and they may cut across the track of my brethren, whom I sincerely love and respect in the truth.

I expect to have these words distorted, misapprehended by unbelievers, and it is no surprise to me. But to have my brethren, who are acquainted with my mission and my work, trifle with the message that God gives me to bear, grieves His Spirit.

It is discouraging to me to have them pick out portions in the testimonies that please them which they construe to justify their own course of action and give the impression that that portion they accept as the voice of God, and then when other testimonies come that bring rebuke upon their course, when words are spoken that do not coincide with their opinions and judgment, they dishonor God's work by saying, "Oh, this we do not accept—it is only Sister White's opinion, and it is no better than my opinion or that of anyone else."—Letter 3, 1889.

Watching for Words on Which Human Interpretation Is Placed.—I am sensible of the fact that I am mortal, and that I must guard my physical, mental, and moral powers. The constant changing from place to place necessitated by travel, and the taking hold of public labor wherever I have gone, have been too much for me, in addition to the writings that I have been preparing day and night as the Lord has worked my mind by His Holy Spirit.

And when I am meeting with evidences that these communications will be treated by some in accordance with the human judgment of those who shall receive them, when I realize that some are watching keenly for some words which have been traced by my pen and upon which they can place their human interpretations in order to sustain their positions and to justify a wrong course of action—when I think of these things, it is not very encouraging to continue writing.

Some of these who are certainly reproved, strive to make every word vindicate their own statements. The twistings and connivings and misrepresentations and misapplications of the Word are marvelous! Persons are linked together in this work. What one does not think of, another mind supplies.—Letter 172, 1906.

Wresting the Scriptures and the Testimonies.—The lessons of Christ were often misunderstood, not because He did not make them plain, but because the minds of the Jews, like the minds of many who claim to believe in this day, were filled with prejudice. Because Christ did not take sides with the Scribes and Pharisees, they hated Him, opposed Him, sought to counteract His efforts, and to make His words of no effect.

Why will not men see and live the truth? Many study the Scriptures for the purpose of proving their own ideas to be correct. They change the meaning of God's Word to suit their own opinions. And thus they do also with the testimonies that He sends. They quote half a sentence, leaving out the other half, which, if quoted, would show their reasoning to be false. God has a controversy with those who wrest the Scriptures, making them conform to their preconceived ideas.—Manuscript 22, 1890.

Words Wrested and Misunderstood.—It seems impossible for me to be understood by those who have had the light but have not walked in it. What I might say in private conversations would be so repeated as to make it mean exactly opposite to what it would have meant had the hearers been sanctified in mind and spirit. I am afraid to speak even to my friends; for afterwards I hear, Sister White said this, or, Sister White said that.

My words are so wrested and misinterpreted that I am coming to the conclusion that the Lord desires me to keep out of large assemblies and refuse private interviews. What I say is reported in such a perverted light that it is new and strange to me. It is mixed with words spoken by men to sustain their own theories.—Letter 139, 1900.

From the First a Voice in Our Midst.—We call upon you to take your stand on the Lord's side, and act your part as a loyal subject of the kingdom. Acknowledge the gift that has been placed in the church for the guidance of God's people in the closing days of earth's history. From the beginning the church of God has had the gift of prophecy in her midst as a living voice to counsel, admonish, and instruct.

We have now come to the last days of the work of the third angel's message, when Satan will work with increasing power because he knows that his time is short. At the same time there will come to us through the gifts of the Holy Spirit, diversities of operations in the outpouring of the Spirit. This is the time of the latter rain.—Letter 230, 1908.

The Protective Barrier Torn Away.—The enemy has made his masterly efforts to unsettle the faith of our own people in the Testimonies, and when these errors come in they claim to prove all the positions by the Bible, but they misinterpret the Scriptures. They make bold assertions, as did Elder Canright, and misapply the prophecies and the Scriptures to prove falsehood. And, after men have done their work in weakening the confidence of our churches in the Testimonies, they have torn away the barrier, that unbelief in the truth shall become widespread, and there is no voice to be lifted up to stay the force of error.

This is just as Satan designed it should be, and those who have been preparing the way for the people to pay no heed to the warnings and reproofs of the Testimonies of the Spirit of God will see that a tide of errors of all kinds will spring into life. They will claim Scripture as their evidence, and deceptions of Satan in every form will prevail.—Letter 109, 1890.

Secure From Satan's Seductive Delusions.—Men

may get up scheme after scheme, and the enemy will seek to seduce souls from the truth, but all who believe that the Lord has spoken through Sister White, and has given her a message, will be safe from the many delusions that will come in these last days.—Letter 50, 1906.

It Is Not I Whom You Betray, but the Lord.—I have tried to do my duty to you and to the Lord Jesus, whom I serve and whose cause I love. The testimonies I have borne you have in truth been presented to me by the Lord. I am sorry that you have rejected the light given. . . .

Are you betraying your Lord because in His great mercy He has shown you just where you are standing spiritually? He knows every purpose of the heart. Nothing is hid from Him. It is not I whom you are betraying. It is not I against whom you are so embittered. It is the Lord, who has given me a message to bear to you.—Letter 66, 1897.

Giving Up Faith in the Testimonies.—One thing is certain: Those Seventh-day Adventists who take their stand under Satan's banner will first give up their faith in the warnings and reproofs contained in the Testimonies of God's Spirit.

The call to great consecration and holier service is being made, and will continue to be made.—Letter 156, 1903.

Two Typical Examples

1. **Personal Testimony Gratefully Received.**—We returned December 12 [1892]. On the evening of the next day, Brother Faulkhead called to see me.* The burden of his case was upon my mind. I told him that I had a message for him and his wife, which I had several times prepared to send them, but I had felt forbidden by the Spirit of the Lord to do so. I asked him to appoint a

---

* See *Selected Messages*, book 2, pp. 125-140, for the message given to N. D. Faulkhead.

time when I could see them.

He answered, "I am glad that you did not send me a written communication; I would rather have the message from your lips; had it come in another way I do not think it would have done me any good." He then asked, "Why not give me the message now?" I said, "Can you remain to hear it?" He replied that he would do so.

I was very weary, for I had attended the closing exercises of the school that day; but I now arose from the bed where I was lying and read to him for three hours. His heart was softened, tears were in his eyes, and when I ceased reading, he said, "I accept every word; all of it belongs to me."

Much of the matter I had read related to the [Australian] Echo Office and its management from the beginning. The Lord also revealed to me Brother Faulkhead's connection with the Free Masons, and I plainly stated that unless he severed every tie that bound him to these associations he would lose his soul.

He said, "I accept the light the Lord has sent me through you. I will act upon it. I am a member of five lodges, and three other lodges are under my control. I transact all of their business. Now I shall attend no more of their meetings, and shall close my business relations with them as fast as possible."

I repeated to him the words spoken by my guide in reference to these associations. Giving a certain movement that was made by my guide, I said, "I cannot relate all that was given to me." Brother Faulkhead told Elder Daniells and others that I gave the particular sign known only by the highest order of Masons, which he had just entered. He said that I did not know the sign, and that I was not aware that I was giving the sign to him. This was special evidence to him that the Lord was working through me to save his soul.—Letter 46, 1892.

2. **A Brother and the Visitor on the Camp-ground.**—I took some of our brethren aside in our tent [at the Milton, Washington, camp meeting] and read the matter I had written three years ago in regard to their

course. They had pledged to the General Conference and taken it all back again. I read to them straight, clear, and pointed testimonies, but here was the trouble—they had felt no obligations to believe the Testimonies. Brother L had been one of the Marion Party* when he lived in LaPort, Iowa, and what to do with these folks was a mystery. There was no minister or his message which they respected above their own judgment. How to bring anything to bear upon them was the question. We could only pray, and work for them as though they did believe every word of testimony, and yet be so cautious, as though they were unbelievers. . . .

Early Sabbath morning [June 7, 1884] I went into meeting and the Lord gave me a testimony directly to them, all unexpected to me. I poured it out upon them, showing them that the Lord sent His ministers with a message and the message they brought was the very means God had ordained to reach them, but they felt at liberty to pick it in pieces and make of none effect the Word of God. . . .

Sabbath, June 14. We had meetings long to be remembered. Sabbath forenoon Brother [J. N.] Lough-borough talked. I talked in the afternoon. The Lord helped me. I then called them forward. Thirty-five responded. They were mostly young men and women, and old men and women. We had a most precious meeting. Some who had left the truth came back with repentance and confession. Many were starting for the first time. The Lord was there Himself. This seemed to break down the prejudice and melting testimonies were borne. We had a recess, and then began again, and the good work went on. . . .

Friday afternoon I read important matter written three years ago. This was acknowledged to be of God. The testimonies were accepted heartily and confessions made of great value to the wrongdoer.—Letter 19, 1884.

---

* An offshoot movement that sprang up in Marion, Iowa, in the mid-1860's.

SECTION III

The Preparation of the Ellen G. White Books

INTRODUCTION

Much of Ellen White's life was spent preparing books that carried the messages God gave her for His people and in some instances to the general public. The White Estate files contain relatively few of her statements concerning the details of this work. However, others working with her wrote more fully. Her relatively few statements, however, do take us into the very heart of her work. We present here some of these statements relative to the preparation and publication of the *Testimonies for the Church* and certain of her books that present the conflict of the ages story, particularly *The Great Controversy* and *The Desire of Ages*.

Since the initial writings on various components of the conflict of the ages story were enlarged two or three times, it is not possible to present a precise chronological sequence of Ellen White's work depicting the events of the agelong controversy. It should also be noted that Ellen White considered all parts of this narrative as part of the great controversy story, whether Old Testament, New Testament, or post-Biblical history.

Statements explaining the work of her literary assistants are included, constituting the opening chapter of this section. Another chapter traces her work in writing on the life of Christ, in which she was assisted by her niece in 1876 and by Marian Davis in the 1890's.

Ellen White's son William was closely associated with her in the production of her books after 1881, the year James White died. On several occasions he wrote from his intimate knowledge of his mother's work in book preparation. Several enlightening statements from his pen, as well as from the pen of Marian Davis, appear as appendix items.—WHITE TRUSTEES.

12.

Literary Assistants in Work of

Ellen G. White

James White and Others Assisted.—While my husband lived, he acted as a helper and counselor in the sending out of the messages that were given to me. We traveled extensively. Sometimes light would be given to me in the night season, sometimes in the daytime before large congregations. The instruction I received in vision was faithfully written out by me, as I had time and strength for the work. Afterward we examined the matter together, my husband correcting grammatical errors and eliminating needless repetition. Then it was carefully copied for the persons addressed, or for the printer.

As the work grew, others assisted me in the preparation of matter for publication. After my husband's death, faithful helpers joined me, who labored untiringly in the work of copying the testimonies and preparing articles for publication.

But the reports that are circulated, that any of my helpers are permitted to add matter or change the meaning of the messages I write out, are not true.—Letter 225, 1906, published in 1913 in *Writing and Sending Out of the Testimonies for the Church*, p. 4. (*Selected Messages*, book 1, p. 50.)

E. G. White Feeling of Inadequacy in 1873.—

This morning I take into candid consideration my writings. My husband is too feeble to help me prepare them for the printer, therefore I shall do no more with them at present. I am not a scholar. I cannot prepare my own writings for the press. Until I can do this I shall write no more. It is not my duty to tax others with my manuscript.—Manuscript 3, 1873. (Diary Jan. 10, 1873.)

Determined to Develop Her Literary Skills.—We rested well last night. This Sabbath morning opens cloudy. My mind is coming to strange conclusions. I am thinking I must lay aside my writing I have taken so much pleasure in, and see if I cannot become a scholar. I am not a grammarian. I will try, if the Lord will help me, at forty-five years old to become a scholar in the science. God will help me. I believe He will.—Manuscript 3, 1873. (Diary Jan. 11, 1873.)

Sense of Inadequacy in 1894.—Now I must leave this subject so imperfectly presented that I fear you will misinterpret that which I feel so anxious to make plain. Oh, that God would quicken the understanding, for I am but a poor writer, and cannot with pen or voice express the great and deep mysteries of God. Oh, pray for yourselves, pray for me.—Letter 67, 1894.

Refuting Reports of Changes in the Writings.—My copyists you have seen. They do not change my language. It stands as I write it. . . .

My work has been in the field since 1845. Ever since then I have labored with pen and voice. Increased light has come to me as I have imparted the light given me. I have very much more light on the Old and New Testament Scriptures, which I shall present to our people.—Letter 61a, 1900.

Final Reading of All Writings Published and Unpublished.—I am still as active as ever. I am not in the least decrepit. I am able to do much work, writing and speaking as I did years ago.

I read over all that is copied, to see that everything is as it should be. I read all the book manuscript before it is sent to the printer. So you can see that my time must be fully occupied. Besides writing, I am called upon to speak to the different churches and to attend important meetings. I could not do this work unless the Lord helped me.—Letter 133, 1902.

The Work of Marian Davis

Miss Davis a Faithful Assistant.—Marian had been with me about twenty-five years. She was my chief worker in arranging the matter for my books. She ever appreciated the writings as sacred matter placed in her hands, and would often relate to me what comfort and blessing she received in performing this work, that it was her health and her life to do this work. She ever handled the matters placed in her hands as sacred. I shall miss her so much. Who will fill her place?—Manuscript 146, 1904.

Marian Is My Bookmaker.—Marian's work is of a different order altogether. She is my bookmaker. Fanny [Bolton]* never was my bookmaker. How are my books made? Marian does not put in her claim for recognition.

She does her work in this way: She takes my articles which are published in the papers, and pastes them in blank books. She also has a copy of all the letters I write. In preparing a chapter for a book, Marian remembers that I have written something on that special point, which may make the matter more forcible. She begins to search for this, and if when she finds it, she sees that it will make the chapter more clear, she adds it.

The books are not Marian's productions, but my own, gathered from all my writings. Marian has a large field from which to draw, and her ability to arrange the matter is of great value to me. It saves my poring over a mass of matter, which I have no time to do.

So you understand that Marian is a most valuable help to me in bringing out my books. Fanny had none of

---

* Fanny Bolton, a newspaper writer, after becoming a Seventh-day Adventist, was drawn into Ellen White's literary work and soon after accompanied her to Australia.

this work to do. Marian has read chapters to her, and Fanny has sometimes made suggestions as to the arrangement of the matter.

This is the difference between the workers. As I have stated, Fanny has been strictly forbidden to change my words for her words. As spoken by the heavenly agencies, the words are severe in their simplicity; and I try to put the thoughts into such simple language that a child can understand every word uttered. The words of someone else would not rightly represent me.

I have written thus fully in order that you may understand the matter. Fanny may claim that she has made my books, but she has not done so. This has been Marian's field, and her work is far in advance of any work Fanny has done for me.—Letter 61a, 1900.

Marian's Caution While Working on *Patriarchs and Prophets* in 1889.—Willie [W. C. White]* is in meeting early and late, devising, planning for the doing of better and more efficient work in the cause of God. We see him only at the table.

Marian will go to him for some little matters that it seems she could settle for herself. She is nervous and hurried and he so worn he has to just shut his teeth together and hold his nerves as best he can. I have had a talk with her and told her she must settle many things herself that she has been bringing Willie.

Her mind is on every point and the connections, and his mind has been plowing through a variety of difficult subjects until his brain reels and then his mind is in no way prepared to take up these little minutiae. She must just carry some of these things that belong to her part of the work, and not bring them before him nor worry his mind with them. Sometimes I think she will kill us both, all unnecessarily, with her little things she can just as well settle herself as to bring them before us. Every

---

* William C. White, son of Ellen White, at the time serving as acting president of the General Conference.

little change of a word she wants us to see.—Letter 64a, 1889.

Her Faithful Services Greatly Prized.—I feel very thankful for the help of Sister Marian Davis in getting out my books. She gathers materials from my diaries, from my letters, and from the articles published in the papers. I greatly prize her faithful service. She has been with me for twenty-five years, and has constantly been gaining increasing ability for the work of classifying and grouping my writings.—Letter 9, 1903.

We Worked Together, Just Worked Together.—Marian, my helper, faithful and true as the compass to the pole in her work, is dying.* . . .

I am leaving tomorrow for Battle Creek. Yet my soul is drawn to the dying girl who has served me for the last twenty-five years. We have stood side by side in the work, and in perfect harmony in that work. And when she would be gathering up the precious jots and tittles that had come in papers and books and present it to me, "Now," she would say, "there is something wanted [needed]. I cannot supply it." I would look it over, and in one moment I could trace the line right out.

We worked together, just worked together in perfect harmony all the time. She is dying. And it is devotion to the work. She takes the intensity of it as though it were a reality, and we both have entered into it with an intensity to have every paragraph that shall stand in its right place, and show its right work.—Manuscript 95, 1904.

---

* This was written Sept. 24, 1904. Marian Davis died Oct. 25, 1904, and was buried at St. Helena, California.—COMPILERS.

13.

The Testimonies for the

Church

1855 Vision Published in First Testimony. *—
November 20, 1855, while in prayer, the Spirit of the
Lord came suddenly and powerfully upon me, and I was
taken off in vision. I saw that the Spirit of the Lord has
been dying away from the church.—*Testimonies*, vol. 1,
p. 113.

Sent Out by the Author Without Charge.—I
have sent out (postpaid) to brethren in different States
about 150 copies of "Testimony for the Church." It can
be had by addressing me at Battle Creek, Michigan. I
shall be happy to hear from those who may receive it.
Those who would encourage the circulation of such

---

* The publication of the November 20, 1855, vision and the May 27,
1856, vision in 16-page pamphlets titled "Testimony for the Church," was
initiated by eyewitnesses in the Battle Creek church, as noted in each
pamphlet: "We the undersigned, being eyewitnesses when the above vision
was given, deem it highly necessary that it should be published, for the
benefit of the church, on account of the important truths and warnings which
it contains. Signed: Jos. Bates, J. H. Waggoner, G. W. Amadon, M. E.
Cornell, J. Hart, Uriah Smith."—*Testimony for the Church* [No. 1, 1855], p.
8.

"To the Saints Scattered Abroad.—The foregoing testimony was given in
the presence of about one hundred brethren and sisters assembled in the house
of prayer, on whose minds it apparently made a deep impression. It has since
been read before the church at Battle Creek, who gave their unanimous vote in
favor of its publication for the benefit of the saints scattered abroad. Signed:
Cyrenius Smith, J. P. Kellogg."—*Testimony for the Church* [No. 2, 1856 ed.].

matter can do so by assisting in its publication.—*Review and Herald*, Dec. 18, 1855.

Condensation of First Ten Testimony Pamphlets Republished in 1864.—During the last nine years, from 1855 to 1864, I have written ten small pamphlets, entitled, Testimony for the Church, which have been published and circulated among Seventh-day Adventists. The first edition of most of these pamphlets being exhausted, and there being an increasing demand for them, it has been thought best to re-print them, as given in the following pages, omitting local and personal matters, and giving those portions only which are of practical and general interest and importance. Most of Testimony No. 4 may be found in the second volume of Spiritual Gifts, hence, it is omitted in this volume.†—*Spiritual Gifts*, vol. 4a, p. 2.

Personal Testimonies Published.—Since the warning and instruction given in testimony for individual cases applied with equal force to many others who had not been specially pointed out in this manner, it seemed to be my duty to publish the personal testimonies for the benefit of the church. . . .

I know of no better way to present my views of general dangers and errors, and the duty of all who love God and keep His commandments than by giving these testimonies. Perhaps there is no more direct and forcible way of presenting what the Lord has shown me.

In a vision given me June 12, 1868, I was shown that which fully justified my course in publishing personal testimonies: "When the Lord singles out individual cases, and specifies their wrongs, others, who have not been shown in vision, frequently take it for granted that they are right, or nearly so. If one is reproved for a special wrong, brethren and sisters should carefully examine themselves to see wherein they have failed, and wherein they have been guilty of the same sin."—*Tes-*

---

† By popular demand the first ten were reprinted, in 1874, in full in book form, together with a reprinting of numbers 11-20.—COMPILERS.

timonies, vol. 5, pp. 658, 659.

Editing the Published Testimonies in 1884.— Dear Brother Smith: I have today mailed you a letter, but information has been received from Battle Creek that the work upon *Testimonies* is not accepted.*

I wish to state some matters, which you can do what you please with. These statements you have heard me make before—that I was shown years ago that we should not delay publishing the important light given me because I could not prepare the matter perfectly. My husband was at times very sick, unable to give me the help that I should have had and that he could have given me had he been in health. On this account I delayed putting before the people that which has been given me in vision.

But I was shown that I should present before the

---

* Reference is to the work being done in response to the General Conference session action of November 16, 1883, which reads:

"32. *Whereas,* Some of the bound volumes of the *Testimonies to the Church,* are out of print, so that full sets cannot be obtained at the office; and,

"*Whereas,* There is a constant and urgent call for the reprinting of these volumes; therefore,

"*Resolved,* That we recommend their republication in such a form as to make four volumes of seven or eight hundred pages each.

"33. *Whereas,* Many of these testimonies were written under the most unfavorable circumstances, the writer being too heavily pressed with anxiety and labor to devote critical thought to the grammatical perfection of the writings, and they were printed in such haste as to allow these imperfections to pass uncorrected; and,

"*Whereas,* We believe the light given by God to His servants is by the enlightenment of the mind, thus imparting the thoughts, and not (except in rare cases) the very words in which the ideas should be expressed; therefore,

"*Resolved,* That in the republication of these volumes, such verbal changes be made as to remove the above-named imperfections, as far as possible, without in any measure changing the thought; and further,

"34. *Resolved,* That this body appoint a committee of five to take charge of the republication of these volumes according to the above preambles and resolutions."—*Review and Herald,* Nov. 27, 1883.

"The committee of five to take charge of the republication of the testimonies provided for in the thirty-fourth resolution was announced as follows, the Chair having been empowered to select four persons besides himself for this purpose: W. C. White, Uriah Smith, J. H. Waggoner, S. N. Haskell, George I. Butler."—*Ibid.*

The work was submitted to Ellen White and was approved by her. The letter to Elder Smith intimates that she was more ready to accept the improvements than some in Battle Creek. The product was our present *Testimonies,* vols. 1-4, published in 1885.—COMPILERS.

people in the best manner possible the light received; then as I received greater light, and as I used the talent God had given me, I should have increased ability to use in writing and in speaking. I was to improve everything, as far as possible bringing it to perfection, that it might be accepted by intelligent minds.

As far as possible every defect should be removed from all our publications. As the truth should unfold and become widespread, every care should be exercised to perfect the works published.

I saw in regard to Brother Andrews' *History of the Sabbath*, that he delayed the work too long. Other erroneous works were taking the field and blocking the way, so that minds would be prejudiced by the opposing elements. I saw that thus much would be lost. After the first edition was exhausted, then he could make improvements; but he was seeking too hard to arrive at perfection. This delay was not as God would have it.

Ellen G. White Desired Language Correctly Used

Now, Brother Smith, I have been making a careful, critical examination of the work that has been done on the *Testimonies*, and I see a few things that I think should be corrected in the matter brought before you and others at the General Conference [November, 1883]. But as I examine the matter more carefully I see less and less that is objectionable. Where the language used is not the best, I want it made correct and grammatical, as I believe it should be in every case where it can be without destroying the sense. This work is delayed, which does not please me. . . .

My mind has been exercised upon the question of the *Testimonies* that have been revised. We have looked them over more critically. I cannot see the matter as my brethren see it. I think the changes will improve the book. If our enemies handle it, let them do so. . . .

I think that anything that shall go forth will be criticized, twisted, turned, and boggled, but we are to go forward with a clear conscience, doing what we can and leaving the result with God. We must not be long in delaying the work.

Now, my brethren, what do you propose to do? I do not want this work dragging along any longer. I want something done, and done now.—Letter 11, 1884. (Written from Healdsburg, California, Feb. 19, 1884.)

The Work of E. G. White Selecting Matter for the *Testimonies*.—I must select the most important matters for the *Testimony* (vol. 6) and then look over everything prepared for it, and be my own critic; for I would not be willing to have some things which are all truth to be published; because I fear that some would take advantage of them to hurt others.

After the matter for the *Testimony* is prepared, every article must be read by me. I have to read them myself; for the sound of the voice in reading or singing is almost unendurable to me.

I try to bring out general principles, and if I see a sentence which I fear would give someone excuse to injure someone else, I feel at perfect liberty to keep back the sentence, even though it is all perfectly true.—Letter 32, 1901.

Letters to Help Others

Anticipated Use of Letters.—I am endeavoring by the help of God to write letters that will be a help not merely to those to whom they are addressed, but to many others who need them.—Letter 79, 1905.

14.

Initial Steps in Writing and Publishing The Great Controversy Story

The 1858 Great Controversy Vision

The Vision March 14, 1858.—In this vision at Lovett's Grove,* most of the matter of the great controversy which I had seen ten years before, was repeated, and I was shown that I must write it out. That I should have to contend with the powers of darkness, for Satan would make strong efforts to hinder me, but angels of God would not leave me in the conflict, that in God must I put my trust.—*Spiritual Gifts*, vol. 2, p. 270. (See *Life Sketches*, p. 162.)

Satan's Attack.—Monday we commenced our journey homeward. . . . While riding in the cars we arranged our plans for writing and publishing the book called the *Great Controversy*, immediately on our return home. I was then as well as usual. On the arrival of the train at Jackson, we went to Bro. Palmer's. We had been in the house but a short time, when, as I was conversing with Sr. P., my tongue refused to utter what I wished to say, and seemed large and numb. A strange, cold

---

* Elder and Mrs. White, who resided in Battle Creek, Michigan, were holding meetings with the believers at Lovett's Grove, Ohio. The vision here referred to was given to Ellen White while attending a funeral service conducted by her husband on Sunday afternoon, March 14, 1858.—COMPILERS.

sensation struck my heart, passed over my head, and down my right side. For a while I was insensible; but was aroused by the voice of earnest prayer. I tried to use my left arm and limb, but they were perfectly useless. For a short time I did not expect to live.—*Ibid.*, p. 271.

Writing the Controversy Story.—For several weeks I could not feel the pressure of the hand, nor the coldest water poured upon my head. In rising to walk, I often staggered, and sometimes fell to the floor. In this condition I commenced to write the *Great Controversy*. I could write at first but one page a day, then rest three; but as I progressed, my strength increased. The numbness in my head did not seem to becloud my mind, and before I closed that work [*Spiritual Gifts*, vol. 1*], the effect of the shock had entirely left me.—*Ibid.*, p. 272.

Shown Satan's Hindering Tactics.—At the time of the conference at Battle Creek, June, 1858, . . . I was taken off in vision. In that vision I was shown that in the sudden attack at Jackson, Satan designed to take my life to hinder the work I was about to write; but angels of God were sent to my rescue, to raise me above the effects of Satan's attack. I saw, among other things, that I should be blessed with better health than before the attack at Jackson.—*Ibid.*

Spiritual Gifts, *Volumes III and IV*

Writing Old Testament History 1863-1864.—
After we returned from the East [December 21, 1863], I

---

* Notice of the publication of the book, *Spiritual Gifts—The Great Controversy Between Christ and His Angels and Satan and His Angels*, with a listing of its chapters, was given by James White in the *Review and Herald* of September 9, 1858, in two last page notes:

"Spiritual Gifts

"This is a work of 224 pages written by Mrs. White, with an introductory article on the perpetuity of Spiritual Gifts, by Bro. R. F. Cottrell. Price 50 cents.

"*Spiritual Gifts*, or the *Great Controversy*, has now been sent to all who have ordered. If any do not receive it in due time, let notice be given."

The book was eagerly secured and ran through two or more printings.—COMPILERS.

commenced to write [*Spiritual Gifts*] Volume III, expecting to have a book of a size to bind in with the testimonies which help compose [*Spiritual Gifts*] Volume IV. As I wrote, the matter opened before me and I saw it was impossible to get all I had to write [on Old Testament history] in as few pages as I at first designed. The matter opened and Volume III was full [304 pages].

Then I commenced on Volume IV, but before I had my work finished, while preparing the health matter for the printers, I was called to go to Monterey. We went, and could not finish the work there as soon as we expected. I was obliged to return to finish the matter for the printers. . . .

I had written almost constantly for above one year. I generally commenced writing at seven in the morning and continued until seven at night, and then left writing to read proof sheets.*—Manuscript 7, 1867.

Author's Preface Recognized Vision Source.—In presenting this, my third little volume to the public, I am comforted with the conviction that the Lord has made me His humble instrument in shedding some rays of precious light upon the past. Sacred history, relating to holy men of old, is brief. . . .

Since the great facts of faith, connected with the history of holy men of old, have been opened to me in vision; also, the important fact that God has nowhere lightly regarded the sin of the apostate, I have been more than ever convinced that ignorance as to these facts, and the wily advantage taken of this ignorance by some who know better, are the grand bulwarks of infidelity. If what I have written upon these points shall help any mind, let God be praised.

When I commenced writing, I hoped to bring all into this volume, but am obliged to close the history of

---

* Book publishing at this time was done somewhat in piecemeal. While the writing was in progress, the type was hand set and actual printing might commence before the last of the manuscript was completed. Thus writing and reading proof sheets could run at the same time.—COMPILERS.

the Hebrews, take up the cases of Saul, David, Solomon, and others, and treat upon the subject of health, in another volume.*—*Spiritual Gifts*, vol. 3, pp. 5, 6 (E.G.W. Preface).

------

* *Spiritual Gifts*, volume 4, was published in 1864. Enlargements of this initial presentation appeared in *The Spirit of Prophecy*, vol. 1 (1870), and *Patriarchs and Prophets* (1890).—COMPILERS.

15.

*A Running Account of Ellen G. White's Experience in Writing on the Life of Christ in 1876**

March 25, 1876.—Mary Clough† and I will do all we can to forward the work of my writings. I cannot see any light shining to Michigan for me.‡ This year I feel that my work is writing. I must be secluded, stay right here, and I must not let inclination or persuasion of others shake my resolution to keep closely to my work until it is done. God will help me if I trust in Him.—Letter 63, 1876. (To James White, March 25, 1876.)

April 4.—We have been having company about every day for some days back, but I try to stick to my writing and do as much each day as I dare. I cannot write but one half of a day each day. . . .

---

* Published as *The Spirit of Prophecy*, vol. 2, dealing with the life of Christ from His birth to the triumphal entry into Jerusalem.

† Ellen G. White's niece, daughter of her sister Caroline. An earnest Christian girl, but not herself a Seventh-day Adventist, Mary served for a time as Mrs. White's literary assistant, and during the travels of Elder and Mrs. White, as a publicity agent, writing articles for local newspapers particularly about Mrs. White's sermons and temperance lectures.—COMPILERS.

‡ On March 22, James White left Oakland, where they had just built a home, for a special session of the General Conference at Battle Creek, Michigan. He and his wife were separated for sixty-six days, until they met again on May 27 at the Kansas camp meeting. During this period she wrote her husband almost every day and occasionally to others.—COMPILERS.

Mary [is] in the office, I upstairs writing. . . .

I have had much freedom in prayer and sweet communion with God in my waking hours at night and early in the morning. I am gaining some strength, but find that any taxation affects me seriously, so that it takes time to recover from it. My trust [is] in God. I have confidence that He will help me in my efforts to get out the truth and light He has given me to [give to] His people.—Letter 3, 1876.

April 7.—The precious subjects open to my mind well. I trust in God and He helps me to write. I am some twenty-four pages ahead of Mary. She does well with my copy. It will take a clear sense of duty to call me from this work to camp meetings. I mean to finish my writings on one book, at any rate, before I go anywhere. . . . The East will not see me for one year unless I feel that God calls me to go. He has given me my work. I will do it, if I can be left free.—Letter 4, 1876.

April 8.—I have liberty in writing and I plead with God daily for counsel and that I may be imbued with His Spirit. I then believe that I shall have help and strength and grace to do the will of God. . . .

I never had such an opportunity to write in my life, and I mean to make the most of it. . . .

How will it do to read my manuscript to Elders [J. H.] Waggoner and [J. N.] Loughborough? If there is any wording of doctrinal points not so clear as might be, he might discern it (W.* I mean).—Letter 4a, 1876.

April 8.—My husband writes that an appeal is to be sent to me from the [General] Conference [session], but I shall not be moved from that which I believe to be my duty at this time. I have a special work at this time to write out the things which the Lord has shown me. . . .

I have a work to do which has been a great burden to my soul. How great, no one but the Lord knows.

Again, I want time to have my mind calm and

---

* Elder J. H. Waggoner when he became a Seventh-day Adventist was a newspaper editor and publisher.—COMPILERS.

composed. I want to have time to meditate and pray while engaged in this work. I do not want to be wearied myself or be closely connected with our people who will divert my mind. This is a great work, and I feel like crying to God every day for His Spirit to help me to do this work all right.—Letter 59, 1876. (To Lucinda Hall, April 8, 1876.)

April 14.—It seems to me my writings are important, and I [am] so feeble, so unable to do the work with justice. I have pleaded with God to be imbued with His Holy Spirit, to be connected with heaven, that this work may be done right. I can never do this work without the special blessing of God.—Letter 7, 1876, p. 2.

April 16.—I have written quite a number of pages today. Mary is hard after me. She gets so enthusiastic over some subjects, she brings in the manuscript after she has copied it, to read it to me. She showed me today quite a heavy pile of manuscripts she had prepared.* . . .

I am feeling very free and peaceful. I feel the precious love of Christ in my heart. It humbles me in my own sight, while Jesus is exalted before me. Oh, how I do long for that social and mysterious connection with Jesus that elevates us above the temporal things of life. It is my anxiety to be right with God, to have His Spirit continually witnessing with me that I am indeed a child of God.—Letter 8, 1876.

April 18.—We went to the city [San Francisco] Sunday night. I spoke to quite a large congregation of outsiders with acceptance, taking up the subject of the loaves and fishes with which Jesus, by His miraculous power, fed about ten thousand people . . . that were continually collecting, after the Saviour had blessed the small portion of food; Christ walking on the sea, and the Jews requiring a sign that He was the Son of God. The neighbor next to the church near the public garden was

---

* All work was at this time in handwritten sheets. Typewriters did not come into Ellen White's work until 1883, two years after her husband's death.—COMPILERS.

there. Cragg, I believe his name is. They all listened
with wide-open eyes and some open mouths. . . .

I would feel pleased to meet my brethren and sisters
in camp meeting. It is just such work as I enjoy. Much
better than the confinement of writing. But this will
break up my work and defeat the plans of getting out my
books, for I cannot do both—travel and write. Now
seems to be my golden opportunity. Mary is with me,
the best copyist I can ever have. Another such chance
may never be mine.—Letter 9, 1876.

April 21.—I have just completed quite a lengthy
article on several miracles; makes fifty pages. We have
prepared about 150 pages since you left. We feel the
best of satisfaction in what we have prepared.—Letter
12, 1876.

April 24.—Mary has just been reading to me two
articles—one on the loaves and fishes, Christ walking on
the water, and stating to His hearers He was the Bread of
life, which caused some of His disciples to turn from
Him. This takes fifty pages and comprises many subjects. I do think it the most precious matter I have ever
written. Mary is just as enthusiastic over it. She thinks it
is of the highest value. I am perfectly satisfied with it.

The other article was upon Christ going through the
cornfield, plucking the ears of corn, and healing the
withered hand—twelve pages. If I can, with Mary's
help, get out these subjects of such intense interest, I
could say, "Lord, now lettest Thou Thy servant depart in
peace." These writings are all I can see now. . . .

My heart and mind are in this work, and the Lord
will sustain me in doing this work. I believe the Lord
will give me health. I have asked Him, and He will
answer my prayer.

I love the Lord. I love His cause. I love His people. I
feel great peace and calmness of mind. There seems to be
nothing to confuse and distract my mind, and with so
much hard thinking, my mind could not be perplexed
with anything without being overtaxed.—Letter 13,
1876.

April 25.—I cannot merely portion my writing to one half the day, as some of the time my head troubles me, and then I have to rest, lie down, stop thinking, and take my time for writing when I can do so comfortably. I cannot rush business. This work must be done carefully, slowly, and accurately. The subjects we have prepared are well gotten up. They please me.—Letter 14, 1876.

April 27.—I have written fifteen pages today. Mary Clough is hard after me. She has copied fifteen pages today—a good, large day's work. . . . Never have I had such an opportunity in my life before. I will improve it. We have written about 200 pages since you left, all copied, ready for printers. . . .

I feel that I am less than nothing, but Jesus is my all—my righteousness, and my wisdom, and my strength.—Letter 16a, 1876.

May 5.—I have been writing more than usual, which was too much for me. I cannot and must not write more than half a day, but I continue to step over the bounds and pay for it. My mind is on my subjects day and night. I have strong confidence in prayer. The Lord hears me and I believe in His salvation. In His strength I trust. In His strength I shall complete my writings. I cling firmly to His hand with unwavering confidence. . . .

I have important subjects coming in next paper [*Signs of the Times*] on Jeremiah. My mind was urged to this by the Spirit of God. The view I had sixteen years ago was forcefully impressed on my mind. I saw that important matter was to be seen applicable to the people of God. This was in reference to testimony God had given me to bear in reproving wrong.—Letter 21, 1876.

May 11.—If I get my writings [*Spirit of Prophecy,* vol. 2] all in manuscript, my part of the work is done and I shall be relieved.—Letter 24, 1876.

October 19.—We have decided to have the printers [at the Review and Herald office in Battle Creek] go on my book and not transport these books across the plains again. Part of the book is here already printed. We shall not have them stereotyped,* because we shall not wait to have matters of my book so very, very exact, but get out this first edition and get it in market. Then we can take time to get out a more perfect edition on Pacific Coast and have [it] stereotyped. Then your father's and my life will be written and printed in the Pacific Printing Office. But we have all used our best judgment and think we had better remain here [Battle Creek] till December and complete this edition. Letter 45, 1876.

October 26.—We are in the very worst drive and hurry getting off my volume two, *Spirit of Prophecy.* Three new forms are already printed. If we remain here [Battle Creek] four weeks longer, we shall have the book completed and removed from my mind a great burden of care.†—Letter 46, 1876. (To W. C. White and wife, Oct. 26, 1876.)

---

* Pages would not be made into printing plates, but left in standing type, allowing changes to be made if desired.—COMPILERS.

† The Book Advertised.—The second volume of the *Spirit of Prophecy,* by Mrs. E. G. White, will be ready in a few days. This work is a thrilling description of the first advent, life, teachings, and miracles of Christ, and will be regarded by the friends of Mrs. W. as a book of almost priceless value. It can be furnished only by mail until New Year's, and after that at one-fourth discount for cash with all orders. Price, postage paid, $1. J.W.—*Review and Herald,* Nov. 9, 1876.

Commended by Uriah Smith, the Editor of the *Review and Herald.*—We are prepared to speak of this volume, now just issued, as the most remarkable volume that has ever issued from this Office. It covers that portion of the great controversy between Christ and Satan, which is included in the life and mission, teachings and miracles, of Christ here upon the earth. Many have endeavored to write the life of Christ; but their work, as compared with this, seems to be only like the outer garments to the body. Here we have, so to speak, an interior view of the wonderful work of God during this time. And if the reader has a heart that can be impressed, feelings that can be stirred, an imagination that can respond to the most vivid portraiture of the most thrilling scenes, and a spirit to drink in lessons of purity, faith, and love from Christ's divine example, he will find in this volume that which will call into liveliest play all these faculties. But the best of all is the lasting impression it must make for good upon all who read. It should have an unlimited circulation. Post-paid, by mail, as per previous notices, $1. U.S.—*Review and Herald,* Nov. 30, 1876.

16.

Expanding the Great Controversy Presentation

Preparing Manuscript for Spirit of Prophecy, Volume 4, * the Forerunner of The Great Controversy

Intensity of Feeling While Writing (February 19, 1884).—I write from fifteen to twenty pages each day. It is now eleven o'clock and I have written fourteen pages of manuscript for Volume Four and seven pages of letters to different ones besides this. I feel continually grateful to God for His merciful kindness. . . .

As I write upon my book I feel intensely moved. I want to get it out as soon as possible, for our people need it so much. I shall complete it next month if the Lord gives me health as He has done. I have been unable to sleep nights, thinking of the important things to take place. Three hours' sleep, and sometimes five, is the most I get. My mind is stirred so deeply I cannot rest. Write, write, write, I feel that I must, and not delay.

Great things are before us, and we want to call the people from their indifference, to get ready for that day. Things that are eternal crowd upon my vision day and

---

* While in Ellen White's mind all materials comprising the agelong conflict were a part of the great controversy story, this chapter focuses on the post-Biblical part of the narration as found in *Spirit of Prophecy*, vol. 4, published in 1884, and *The Great Controversy*, which appeared in 1888. The enlarged writing on the life of Christ for *The Desire of Ages* follows in the next chapter.—COMPILERS.

night. The things that are temporal fade from my sight. We are not now to cast away our confidence, but to have firm assurance, firmer than ever before. Hitherto hath the Lord helped us, and He will help us to the end. We will look to the monumental pillars, reminders of what the Lord hath done for us, to comfort and to save us from the hand of the destroyer.—Letter 11a, 1884.

History Opened Up in Scenic Visions From Time to Time.—Through the illumination of the Holy Spirit, the scenes of the long-continued conflict between good and evil have been opened to the writer of these pages. From time to time I have been permitted to behold the working, in different ages, of the great controversy between Christ, the Prince of life, the Author of our salvation, and Satan, the prince of evil, the author of sin, the first transgressor of God's holy law.—*The Great Controversy,* Introduction, p. x.

Visions of the Past and Future While Writing.—When I am using my pen, wonderful representations are given me of past, present, and future.—Letter 86, 1906.

Reformation History Presented in Vision.—The banner of the ruler of the synagogue of Satan was lifted high, and error apparently marched in triumph, and the reformers, through the grace given them of God, waged a successful warfare against the hosts of darkness. Events in the history of the reformers have been presented before me. I know that the Lord Jesus and His angels have with intense interest watched the battle against the power of Satan, who combined his hosts with evil men, for the purpose of extinguishing the divine light, the fire of God's kingdom. They suffered for Christ's sake scorn, derision, and the hatred of men who knew not God. They were maligned and persecuted even unto death, because they would not renounce their faith.—Letter 48, 1894.

Shown Ellen White Years Before Visiting Europe in 1885-1887.—Years ago, the work of the first message in these countries [Sweden and other northern countries] was presented before me, and I was shown circumstances similar to those related above [Swedish child-preaching].—Ellen G. White, in *Historical Sketches of the Foreign Missions of Seventh-day Adventists* (Basel, 1886), p. 108.

Chapter on Time of Trouble.—We have just read the matter in regard to the time of trouble. Brother Smith thinks that chapter by no means should be left out of Volume 4. He says there is not a sentence in it that is not essentially needed. This seemed to make a very deep impression upon his mind and I thought I would write to you in reference to this matter. I have read it and it has just a thrilling power with it. I see nothing that will exclude it from the book for general sale among unbelievers.*—Letter 59, 1884.

The 1888 Edition of The Great Controversy

Work Begins on the Enlargement of *The Great Controversy.*—Basel, Switzerland, June 11, 1886. I think you will want to hear some particulars in regard to our family. We now number ten. W.C.W. [White] and Mary and Ella are well. Sarah McEnterfer is well, and just as busy as she can be taking letters by dictation and writing them out on the calligraph [typewriter]. Marian's [Davis] health is about as it usually is. She is at work on volume 4, "Great Controversy."—Manuscript 20, 1886.

Bidden to Portray Scenes of the Past and the Future.—As the Spirit of God has opened to my mind the great truths of the past and the future, I have been bidden to make known to others that which has thus been revealed—to trace the history of the controversy in past ages, and especially so to present it as to shed a light

---

* The book was published by the Pacific Press in late September, 1884, and gained favorable notice: *"The Great Controversy, Vol. IV:* This volume, so long looked for, is now out. And we are confident that it will more than meet the expectations of those who have anxiously waited for it. We judge from our own reading of it; we found the contents of deeper interest than our imagination could have reached."—*Signs of the Times*, Oct. 2, 1884.—COMPILERS.

on the fast-approaching struggle of the future. In pursuance of this purpose, I have endeavored to select and group together events in the history of the church in such a manner as to trace the unfolding of the great testing truths that at different periods have been given to the world, that have excited the wrath of Satan, and the enmity of a world-loving church, and that have been maintained by the witness of those who "loved not their lives unto the death."—*The Great Controversy*, Introduction, p. xi.

Scenes Presented Anew While Writing.—While writing the manuscript of "Great Controversy," I was often conscious of the presence of the angels of God. And many times the scenes about which I was writing were presented to me anew in visions of the night, so that they were fresh and vivid in my mind.—Letter 56, 1911.

Vivid Scenes of Christ's Second Advent.—The sky opened and shut, and was in commotion. The mountains shook like a reed in the wind, and cast out ragged rocks all around. The sea boiled like a pot, and cast out stones upon the ground. And as God spoke the day and hour of Jesus' coming, and delivered the everlasting covenant to His people, He spoke one sentence and then paused while the words were rolling through the earth. . . .

I have not the slightest knowledge as to the time spoken by the voice of God. I heard the hour proclaimed, but had no remembrance of that hour after I came out of vision. Scenes of such thrilling, solemn interest passed before me as no language is adequate to describe. It was all a living reality to me, for close upon this scene appeared the great white cloud, upon which was seated the Son of man.—Letter 38, 1888. (Published in *Selected Messages*, book 1, pp. 75, 76.)

Reading the Page Proofs—Last Work on the Book.—I have just read the manuscript of the three last chapters. I cannot see but that it is all right and of the most intense and thrilling interest. I am glad you have sent these pages and I want the book—the very first one from the press—sent to me. . . .

Last Sabbath was an impressive, solemn time. I spoke upon some of the very scenes described in these last chapters and there was deep feeling in the meeting.—Letter 57, 1884.

Steps Taken to Make It the Best Possible.—In the preparation of this book, competent workers were employed and much money was invested in order that the volume might come before the world in the best style possible. . . .

The Lord impressed me to write this book, in order that without delay it might be circulated in every part of the world, because the warnings it contains are necessary for preparing a people to stand in the day of the Lord.—Manuscript 24, 1891.

Experience of Ellen White While Writing *The Great Controversy.*—I was moved by the Spirit of the Lord to write that book, and while working upon it, I felt a great burden upon my soul. I knew that time was short, that the scenes which are soon to crowd upon us would at the last come very suddenly and swiftly, as represented in the words of Scripture: "The day of the Lord so cometh as a thief in the night" (1 Thess. 5:2).

The Lord has set before me matters which are of urgent importance for the present time, and which reach into the future. The words have been spoken in a charge to me, "Write in a book the things which thou hast seen and heard, and let it go to all people; for the time is at hand when past history will be repeated." I have been aroused at one, two, or three o'clock in the morning, with some point forcibly impressed upon my mind, as if spoken by the voice of God. I was shown that many of our own people were asleep in their sins, and although they claimed to be Christians, they would perish unless they were converted.

The solemn impressions made upon my mind as the truth was laid out in clear lines before me, I tried to bring before others, that each might feel the necessity of having a religious experience for himself, of having a knowledge of the Saviour for himself, of seeking repentance, faith, love, hope, and holiness for himself.

I was assured that there was no time to lose. The appeals and warnings must be given; our churches must be aroused, must be instructed, that they may give the warning to all whom they can possibly reach, declaring that the sword is coming, that the Lord's anger upon a profligate world will not long be deferred. I was shown that many would listen to the warning. Their minds would be prepared to discern the very things that it pointed out to them.

I was shown that much of my time had been occupied in speaking to the people, when it was more essential that I should devote myself to writing out the important matters for Volume IV,* that the warning must go where the living messenger could not go, and that it would call the attention of many to the important events to occur in the closing scenes of this world's history.

As the condition of the church and the world was opened before me, and I beheld the fearful scenes that lie just before us, I was alarmed at the outlook; and night after night, while all in the house were sleeping, I wrote out the things given me of God. I was shown the heresies which are to arise, the delusions that will prevail, the miracle-working power of Satan—the false Christs that will appear—that will deceive the greater part even of the religious world, and that would, if it were possible, draw away even the elect.

Is this work of the Lord? I know that it is, and our people also profess to believe it. The warning and instruction of this book are needed by all who profess to believe the present truth.—Letter 1, 1890.

---

* To Ellen White the 1888 edition of *The Great Controversy* was still Volume IV in the presentation of the great controversy story, and was often referred to by her as such.—COMPILERS.

17.

The Experience of E. G. White in Preparing The Desire of Ages

Notations From Letters and Diaries

July 15, 1892.—This week I have been enabled to commence writing on the life of Christ. Oh, how inefficient, how incapable I am of expressing the things which burn in my soul in reference to the mission of Christ! I have hardly dared to enter upon the work. There is so much to it all. And what shall I say, and what shall I leave unsaid? I lie awake nights pleading with the Lord for the Holy Spirit to come upon me, to abide upon me. . . .

I walk with trembling before God. I know not how to speak or trace with pen the large subject of the atoning sacrifice. I know not how to present subjects in the living power in which they stand before me. I tremble for fear lest I shall belittle the great plan of salvation by cheap words. I bow my soul in awe and reverence before God and say, "Who is sufficient for these things?"—Letter 40, 1892.

May 23, 1893.—It is cloudy and raining this morning. I have been writing upon the life of Christ since four o'clock. Oh, that the Holy Spirit may rest and abide upon me, that my pen may trace the words which will communicate to others the light which the Lord has been pleased in His great mercy and love to give to me.—Manuscript 80, 1893.

June 15, 1893.—I am anxious to get out the life of Christ. Marian [Davis] specifies chapters and subjects for me to write upon that I do not see really need to be written upon. I may see more light in them. These I shall not enter upon without the Lord's Spirit seems to lead me. The building [of] a tower, the war of kings, these things do not burden my mind, but the subjects of the life of Christ, His character representing the Father, the parables essential for us all to understand and practice the lessons contained in them, I shall dwell upon.—Letter 131, 1893.

July 2, 1893.—I write some every day on the life of Christ. One chapter sets my mind fresh upon other subjects so that I have several scratch books that I am writing upon. I hardly dare send manuscript by young Linden, fearing it may get lost, and I wish to give more time to some subjects.—Letter 132, 1893. (Written from New Zealand.)

July 7, 1893.—I have written you a little bit every mail we heard of that went to . . . [America], and when Brother Linden went, sent you a letter and manuscript . . . some on the life of Christ. . . . That on life of Christ can be used for articles for the paper.—Letter 133, 1893.

Late 1894.—It is decided in council I shall write on the life of Christ; but how any better than in the past? Questions and the true condition of things here and there are urged upon me. . . .

I have done scarcely anything on the life of Christ, and have been obliged to often bring Marian to my help, irrespective of the work on the life of Christ which she has to do under great difficulties, gathering from all my writings a little here and a little there, to arrange as best she can. But she is in good working order, if I could only feel free to give my whole attention to the work. She has her mind educated and trained for the work; and now I think, as I have thought a few hundred times, I shall be able after this mail [American] closes to take the life of

Christ and go ahead with it, if the Lord will.—Letter 55, 1894.

October 25, 1894.—Marian is working at the greatest disadvantage. I find but little time in which to write on the life of Christ. I am continually receiving letters that demand an answer, and I dare not neglect important matters that are brought to my notice. Then there are churches to visit, private testimonies to write, and many other things to be attended to that tax me and consume my time. Marian greedily grasps every letter I write to others in order to find sentences that she can use in the life of Christ. She has been collecting everything that has a bearing on Christ's lessons to His disciples, from all possible sources. After the camp meeting is ended, which is a very important meeting, I shall locate myself in some place where I can give myself to the work of writing on the life of Christ. . . .

There is much to be done in the churches, and I cannot act my part in keeping up the interest and do the other work that is necessary for me to do without becoming so weary that I cannot devote strength to writing on the life of Christ. I am much perplexed as to what is my duty. . . .

I have about decided to . . . devote all my time to writing for the books that ought to be prepared without further delay. I would like to write on the life of Christ, on Christian Temperance [*Ministry of Healing*], and prepare Testimony No. 34 [volume 6] for it is very much needed. I will have to stop writing so much for the papers, and let the *Review and Herald,* the *Signs of the Times,* and all other periodicals go without articles from my pen for this year.

All articles that appear under my signature are fresh, new writings from my pen. I am sorry that I have not more literary help. I need this kind of help very much. Fanny [Bolton] could help me a great deal on the book work if she had not so many articles to prepare for the papers, and so many letters and testimonies to edit to meet the demands of my correspondence and the needs of the people.

It is of no use to expect anything from Marian [Davis] until the life of Christ is completed. I wish I could procure another intelligent worker who could be trusted to prepare matter for the press. Such a worker would be of great value to me. But the question is, Where shall I find such an one? I am brain weary much of the time. I write many pages before breakfast. I rise in the morning at two, three, and four o'clock. . . .

You know that my whole theme both in the pulpit and in private, by voice and pen, is the life of Christ. Hitherto nearly all that I have written on this theme has been written during the hours when others are sleeping.—Letter 41, 1895.

June 6, 1896.—That which is holy and elevated in heavenly things, I scarcely dare represent. Often I lay down my pen and say, Impossible, impossible for finite minds to grasp eternal truths, and deep holy principles, and to express their living import. I stand ignorant and helpless. The rich current of thought takes possession of my whole being, and I lay down my pen, and say, O Lord, I am finite, I am weak, and simple and ignorant; Thy grand and holy revelations I can never find language to express.

My words seem inadequate. I despair of clothing the truth God has made known concerning His great redemption, which engrossed to itself His undivided attention in the only-begotten Son of the Infinite One. The truths that are to last through time and through eternity, the great plan of redemption, which cost so much for the salvation of the human race, presenting before them a life that measures with the life of God— these truths are too full, deep, and holy for human words or human pen to adequately express.—Manuscript 23, 1896.

July 29, 1897.—I awaken at half past two, and offer up my prayer to God in the name of Jesus. I am weak in physical strength; my head is not free from pain; my left eye troubles me. In writing upon the life of Christ I am deeply wrought upon. I forget to breathe as I should. I cannot endure the intensity of feeling that comes over me as I think of what Christ has suffered in our world.—Manuscript 70, 1897.

July 16, 1896.—The manuscript for the "Life of Christ" is just about to be sent to America.* This will be handled by the Pacific Press. I have employed workers to prepare this book, especially Sister Davis, and this has cost me three thousand dollars. Another three thousand will be needed to prepare it to be scattered broadcast through the world in two books. We hope that they will have a large sale. I have devoted little time to these books, for speaking, writing articles for the papers, and writing private testimonies to meet and repress the evils that are coming in keeps me busy.—Letter 114, 1896.

Meeting Criticisms of The Desire of Ages

June 20, 1900.—I received your letter, Edson.† In regard to *The Desire of Ages*, when you meet with those who have criticisms to make, as will always be the case, do not take any notice of the supposed mistakes, but praise the book, tell of its advantages. *The Desire of Ages* would have been the same size as the two former books [*Patriarchs and Prophets* and *The Great Controversy*], had it not been for the strong recommendation of Brother O who was then general canvassing agent. What you say about the appendix is the first objection we have heard regarding that feature. Many have spoken of the great help they have found in the appendix. If people are prejudiced against anything that makes prominent the

---

* Contrary to her expectation, it was not until early 1898 that the manuscript was ready to send to the Pacific Press. It was sent in piecemeal, for new revelations led to many additions to the manuscript thought to be complete.—COMPILERS.
† James Edson White wrote to his mother on May 11, 1900, presenting criticisms of the size, format, price, and illustrations of *The Desire of Ages*. He also objected to the appendix in the first edition, asking, "What is the use of pitching into other people's beliefs in the way it is done in this appendix?" He argued that such material made it difficult for literature evangelists to sell the book.

Sabbath, that very objection shows the necessity of it being there to convict minds.

Let us be guarded. Let us refuse to allow the criticisms of anyone to imprint objections on our minds. Let criticizers live by their trade of criticism. They cannot speak in favor of the very best of blessings without attaching a criticism to cast a shadow of reproach. Let us educate ourselves to praise that which is good when others criticize. Murmurers will always pick flaws, but let us not be saddened by the accusing element. Let us not consider it a virtue to make and suggest difficulties which one mind and another will bring in to harass and perplex.—Letter 87, 1900.

18.

Comments While at Work on the Conflict Series Books

_____

The Result of Visions Spanning Her Lifetime

I had been, during the forty-five years of experience, shown the lives, the character and history of the patriarchs, and prophets, who had come to the people with messages from God, and Satan would start some evil report, or get up some difference of opinion or turn the interest in some other channel, that the people should be deprived of the good the Lord had to bestow upon them.
. . .

I could but have a vivid picture in my mind from day to day of the way reformers were treated, how slight difference of opinion seemed to create a frenzy of feeling. Thus it was in the betrayal, trial, and crucifixion of Jesus. All this had passed before me point by point.—Letter 14, 1889.

Constructive Criticisms Appreciated (1885)

Tell her [Marian Davis] I have just one minute ago read the letters in which she has specified the improvements to be made in articles for Volume 1 [*Patriarchs and Prophets*]. I thank her. Tell her that she has a point about Zedekiah's having his eyes put out. That needs to be more carefully worded—also the rock, when the water flowed—something in reference to this. I think I can make the articles specified more full.—Letter 38, 1885.

Books Sought Giving Order of Events

Well, my dear Willie and Edson and Emma, let us draw very nigh to God. Let us live daily as we would wish we had lived when the judgment shall sit and the books shall be opened, and when everyone will be rewarded according to his works. . . . Tell Mary to find me some histories of the Bible that would give me the order of events.* I have nothing and can find nothing in the library here [Basel, Switzerland].—Letter 38, 1885, p. 8.

Holy Spirit Traced Truths on Ellen White's Heart

How many have read carefully *Patriarchs and Prophets, The Great Controversy,* and *The Desire of Ages?* I wish all to understand that my confidence in the light that God has given stands firm, because I know that the Holy Spirit's power magnified the truth, and made it honorable, saying: "This is the way; walk ye in it." In my books, the truth is stated, barricaded by a "Thus saith the Lord."

The Holy Spirit traced these truths upon my heart and mind as indelibly as the law was traced by the finger of God upon the tables of stone, which are now in the ark, to be brought forth in that great day when sentence will be pronounced against every evil, seducing science produced by the father of lies.—Letter 90, 1906. (*Colporteur Ministry,* p. 126.)

---

* In the preparation of *The Desire of Ages* such works were used in determining the order of events. On this point Marian Davis, writing to the manager of the Pacific Press, stated on November 23, 1896, "In the order of chapters we followed Andrews' Harmony as given in his Life of Christ. He is generally regarded as the very best authority, and is quoted by leading writers. We know of no better arrangement than his." Samuel J. Andrews, *The Life of Our Lord Upon the Earth,* first published in 1862. The 1891 edition was in Ellen White's library. His "Harmony of the Gospels" appears on pages xii to xxvii.—COMPILERS.

The 1911 Revision of The Great Controversy

The Author Explains What and Why
—Sanitarium, Cal., July 25, 1911

Dear Brother [F. M.] Wilcox:

A few days ago I received a copy of the new edition of the book *Great Controversy,* recently printed at Mountain View, and also a similar copy printed at Washington. The book pleases me. I have spent many hours looking through its pages, and I see that the publishing houses have done good work.

The book *Great Controversy* I appreciate above silver or gold, and I greatly desire that it shall come before the people. While writing the manuscript of *Great Controversy,* I was often conscious of the presence of the angels of God. And many times the scenes about which I was writing were presented to me anew in visions of the night, so that they were fresh and vivid in my mind.

Recently it was necessary for this book to be reset, because the electrotype plates were badly worn. It has cost me much to have this done, but I do not complain; for whatever the cost may be, I regard this new edition with great satisfaction.

Yesterday I read what W. C. White has recently written to canvassing agents and responsible men at our publishing houses regarding this latest edition of *Great Controversy,* and I think he has presented the matter correctly and well.*

When I learned that *Great Controversy* must be reset, I determined that we would have everything closely examined, to see if the truths it contained were stated in the very best manner, to convince those not of our faith that the Lord had guided and sustained me in the writing of its pages.

---

* See Appendix A for the Ellen G. White-approved W. C. White statements explaining the involvements of revising *The Great Controversy* in 1911. Appendices B and C present his answers to questions relative to the writing of the great controversy story and explaining how the light came to her, et cetera.—COMPILERS.

As a result of the thorough examination by our most experienced workers, some changing in the wording has been proposed. These changes I have carefully examined, and approved. I am thankful that my life has been spared, and that I have strength and clearness of mind for this and other literary work.

While preparing the book on the *Acts of the Apostles,* the Lord has kept my mind in perfect peace. This book will soon be ready for publication. When this book is ready for publication, if the Lord sees fit to let me rest, I shall say Amen, and Amen. If the Lord spares my life, I will continue to write, and to bear my testimony in the congregation of the people, as the Lord shall give me strength and guidance. . . .

(Signed) Ellen G. White
—Letter 56, 1911

The Incarnation

INTRODUCTION

The plan of salvation, of which the Incarnation is the very heart, is an exhaustless theme into which we may now look, and that will be the prime topic of study through the ceaseless ages of eternity. Again and again through the years Ellen White, in sermons preached, in letters written, in periodical articles and books, touched feelingly on this sublime topic of God and man becoming one. This is particularly so in *The Desire of Ages.*

A number of enlightening statements appear in *The Youth's Instructor.* Excerpts from many of these and from like materials from other sources have already appeared in *Selected Messages,* book 1, pages 242-289; the 1965 devotional book, *"That I May Know Him"*; and Ellen G. White releases in *The SDA Bible Commentary,* volume 5, page 1126-1131; and volume 7a, pages 443-456, the latter being a reprint of Appendix B of *Seventh-day Adventists Answer Questions on Doctrine.*

Yet, from time to time further choice items come to the front from sources not commonly available. Several of these have been drawn together here to make up this section, "The Incarnation."

As we review these beautiful, and at times seemingly unfathomable, truths, we are reminded of this Ellen G. White statement: "The incarnation of Christ has ever been, and will ever remain a mystery."—*Letter* 8, 1895 (published in *The SDA Bible Commentary,* vol. 5, p. 1129).

But these great truths, as we can grasp them by faith, are for us.—WHITE TRUSTEES.

19.

The Incarnation

***

The Completeness of Christ's Humanity

We cannot understand how Christ became a little, helpless babe. He could have come to earth in such beauty that He would have been unlike the sons of men. His face could have been bright with light, and His form could have been tall and beautiful. He could have come in such a way as to charm those who looked upon Him; but this was not the way that God planned He should come among the sons of men.

He was to be like those who belonged to the human family and to the Jewish race. His features were to be like those of other human beings, and He was not to have such beauty of person as to make people point Him out as different from others. He was to come as one of the human family, and to stand as a man before heaven and earth. He had come to take man's place, to pledge Himself in man's behalf, to pay the debt that sinners owed. He was to live a pure life on the earth, and show that Satan had told a falsehood when he claimed that the human family belonged to him forever, and that God could not take men out of his hands.

Men first beheld Christ as a babe, as a child. . . .

The more we think about Christ's becoming a babe here on earth, the more wonderful it appears. How can it be that the helpless babe in Bethlehem's manger is still the divine Son of God? Though we cannot understand it, we can believe that He who made the worlds, for our sakes became a helpless babe. Though higher than any of the angels, though as great as the Father on the throne of heaven, He became one with us. In Him God and man became one, and it is in this fact that we find the hope of our fallen race. Looking upon Christ in the flesh, we look upon God in humanity, and see in Him the brightness of divine glory, the express image of God the Father.— *The Youth's Instructor,* Nov. 21, 1895.

Christ Descended to the Level of Fallen Humanity

Christ has made an infinite sacrifice. He gave His own life for us. He took upon His divine soul the result of the transgression of God's law. Laying aside His royal crown, He condescended to step down, step by step, to the level of fallen humanity.— *The Review and Herald,* April 30, 1901.

From the Jordan, Jesus was led into the wilderness of temptation. "And when he had fasted forty days and forty nights, he was afterward an hungred. And when the tempter came to him, he said, If thou be the Son of God, command that these stones be made bread" (Matt. 4:2, 3).

Christ was suffering the keenest pangs of hunger, and this temptation was a severe one. But He must begin the work of redemption just where the ruin began. Adam had failed on the point of appetite, and Christ must conquer here. The power that rested upon Him came directly from the Father, and He must not exercise it in His own behalf. With that long fast there was woven into His experience a strength and power that God alone could give. He met and resisted the enemy in the strength of a "Thus saith the Lord." "Man shall not live by bread alone," He said, "but by every word that proceedeth out of the mouth of God" (verse 4).

This strength it is the privilege of all the tempted ones of earth to have. Christ's experience is for our benefit. His example in overcoming appetite points out the way for those to overcome who would be His followers.

Christ was suffering as the members of the human family suffer under temptation; but it was not the will of God that He should exercise His divine power in His own behalf. Had He not stood as our representative, Christ's innocence would have exempted Him from all this anguish, but it was because of His innocence that He felt so keenly the assaults of Satan. All the suffering which is the result of sin was poured into the bosom of the sinless Son of God. Satan was bruising the heel of Christ, but every pang endured by Christ, every grief, every disquietude, was fulfilling the great plan of man's redemption. Every blow inflicted by the enemy was rebounding on himself. Christ was bruising the serpent's head.—*The Youth's Instructor*, Dec. 21, 1899.

Was Christ Capable of Yielding to Temptation?

In your letter in regard to the temptations of Christ, you say: "If He was One with God He could not fall." . . . The point you inquire of me is, In our Lord's great scene of conflict in the wilderness, apparently under the power of Satan and his angels, was He capable, in His human nature, of yielding to these temptations?

I will try to answer this important question: As God He could not be tempted: but as a man He could be tempted, and that strongly, and could yield to the temptations. His human nature must pass through the same test and trial Adam and Eve passed through. His human nature was created; it did not even possess the angelic powers. It was human, identical with our own. He was passing over the ground where Adam fell. He was now where, if He endured the test and trial in behalf of the fallen race, He would redeem Adam's disgraceful failure and fall, in our own humanity.

Christ Had a Human Body and a Human Mind.—A human body and a human mind were His.

He was bone of our bone and flesh of our flesh. He was subjected to poverty from His first entrance into the world. He was subject to disappointment and trial in His own home, among His own brethren. He was not surrounded, as in the heavenly courts, with pure and lovely characters. He was compassed with difficulties. He came into our world to maintain a pure, sinless character, and to refute Satan's lie that it was not possible for human beings to keep the law of God. Christ came to live the law in His human character in just that way in which all may live the law in human nature if they will do as Christ was doing. He had inspired holy men of old to write for the benefit of man: "Let him take hold of my strength, that he may make peace with me; and he shall make peace with me" (Isaiah 27:5).

Abundant provision has been made that finite, fallen man may so connect with God that, through the same Source by which Christ overcame in His human nature, he may stand firmly against every temptation, as did Christ. He was subject to inconveniences that human nature is subjected to. He breathed the air of the same world we breathe. He stood and traveled in the same world we inhabit, which, we have positive evidence, was no more friendly to grace and righteousness than it is today.

His Attributes May Be Ours.—The higher attributes of His being it is our privilege to have, if we will, through the provisions He has made, appropriate these blessings and diligently cultivate the good in the place of the evil. We have reason, conscience, memory, will, affections—all the attributes a human being can possess. Through the provision made when God and the Son of God made a covenant to rescue man from the bondage of Satan, every facility was provided that human nature should come into union with His divine nature. In such a nature was our Lord tempted. He could have yielded to Satan's lying suggestions as did Adam, but we should adore and glorify the Lamb of God that He did not in a single point yield one jot or one tittle.

Two Natures Blended in Christ.—Through being partakers of the divine nature we may stand pure and holy and undefiled. The Godhead was not made human, and the human was not deified by the blending together of the two natures. Christ did not possess the same sinful, corrupt, fallen disloyalty we possess, for then He could not be a perfect offering.—Manuscript 94, 1893.

The Reality of Christ's Temptations.—When the follower of Christ meets with trial and perplexity, he is not to become discouraged. He is not to cast away his confidence if he does not realize all his expectations. When buffeted by the enemy, he should remember the Saviour's life of trial and discouragement. Heavenly beings ministered to Christ in His need, yet this did not make the Saviour's life one of freedom from conflict and temptation. He was in all points tempted like as we are, yet without sin. If His people will follow this example, they will be imbued with His Spirit, and heavenly angels will minister to them.

The temptations to which Christ was subjected were a terrible reality. As a free agent He was placed on probation, with liberty to yield to Satan's temptations and work at cross-purposes with God. If this were not so, if it had not been possible for Him to fall, He could not have been tempted in all points as the human family is tempted.

The temptations of Christ, and His sufferings under them, were proportionate to His exalted, sinless character. But in every time of distress, Christ turned to His Father. He "resisted unto blood" in that hour when the fear of moral failure was as the fear of death. As He bowed in Gethsemane, in His soul agony, drops of blood fell from His pores, and moistened the sods of the earth. He prayed with strong crying and tears, and He was heard in that He feared. God strengthened Him, as He will strengthen all who will humble themselves, and throw themselves, soul, body, and spirit, into the hands of a covenant-keeping God.

Upon the cross Christ knew, as no other can know, the awful power of Satan's temptations, and His heart was poured out in pity and forgiveness for the dying thief, who had been ensnared by the enemy.—*The Youth's Instructor*, Oct. 26, 1899.

Christ's heart was pierced by a far sharper pain than that caused by the nails driven into His hands and feet. He was bearing the sins of the whole world, enduring our punishment—the wrath of God against transgression. His trial involved the fierce temptation of thinking that He was forsaken by God. His soul was tortured by the pressure of great darkness, lest He should swerve from His uprightness during the terrible ordeal.

Unless there is a possibility of yielding, temptation is no temptation. Temptation is resisted when man is powerfully influenced to do a wrong action; and, knowing that he can do it, resists, by faith, with a firm hold upon divine power. This was the ordeal through which Christ passed.—*The Youth's Instructor*, July 20, 1899.

We May Overcome as Christ Overcame.—The love and justice of God, and also the immutability of His law, are made manifest by the Saviour's life, no less than by His death. He assumed human nature, with its infirmities, its liabilities, its temptations. . . . He was "in all points tempted like as we are" (Heb. 4:15). He exercised in His own behalf no power which man cannot exercise. As man He met temptation, and overcame in the strength given Him of God. He gives us an example of perfect obedience. He has provided that we may become partakers of the divine nature, and assures us that we may overcome as He overcame. His life testified that by the aid of the same divine power which Christ received, it is possible for man to obey God's law.—Manuscript 141, 1901.

God Sent a Sinless Being to This World

God did for us the very best thing that He could do when He sent from heaven a Sinless Being to manifest to this world of sin what those who are saved must be in character—pure, holy, and undefiled, having Christ formed within. He sent His ideal in His Son, and bade men build characters in harmony with this ideal.—Letter 58, 1906.

Man Created With Sinless Moral Nature

In the councils of heaven God said, "Let us make man in our image, after our likeness. . . . So God created man in his own image, in the image of God created he him" (Gen. 1:26, 27). The Lord created man's moral faculties and his physical powers. All was a sinless transcript of Himself. God endowed man with holy attributes, and placed him in a garden made expressly for him. Sin alone could ruin the beings created by the hand of the Almighty.—*The Youth's Instructor*, July 20, 1899.

Sicknesses of Others Carried Vicariously

Christ alone was able to bear the afflictions of all the human family. "In all their affliction he was afflicted." He never bore disease in His own flesh, but He carried the sickness of others. When suffering humanity pressed about Him, He who was in the health of perfect manhood was as one afflicted with them. . . .

In His life on earth, Christ developed a perfect character, He rendered perfect obedience to His Father's commandments. In coming to the world in human form, in becoming subject to the law, in revealing to men that He bore their sickness, their sorrow, their guilt, He did not become a sinner. Before the Pharisees He could say, "Which of you convinceth me of sin?" Not one stain of sin was found upon Him. He stood before the world the spotless Lamb of God.—*The Youth's Instructor*, Dec. 29, 1898.

Christ's Sinlessness Disturbed Satan

Christ, the Redeemer of the world, was not situated where the influences surrounding Him were the best calculated to preserve a life of purity and untainted morals, yet He was not contaminated. He was not free from temptation. Satan was earnest and persevering in his efforts to deceive and overcome the Son of God by his devices.

Christ was the only one who walked the earth upon whom there rested no taint of sin. He was pure, spotless, and undefiled. That there should be One without the defilement of sin upon the earth, greatly disturbed the author of sin, and he left no means untried to overcome Christ with his wily, deceptive power. But our Saviour relied upon His heavenly Father for wisdom and strength to resist and overcome the tempter. The Spirit of His heavenly Father animated and regulated His life. He was sinless. Virtue and purity characterized His life.—*The Youth's Instructor,* February, 1873.

Our Fallen Human Nature Connected With Christ's Divinity

Though He had no taint of sin upon His character, yet He condescended to connect our fallen human nature with His divinity. By thus taking humanity, He honored humanity. Having taken our fallen nature, He showed what it might become, by accepting the ample provision He has made for it, and by becoming partaker of the divine nature.—Letter 81, 1896.

Tempted as Children Today Are

One may think that Christ, because He was the Son of God, did not have temptations as children now have. The Scriptures say He was tempted in all points like as we are tempted.—*The Youth's Instructor,* April, 1873.

What the Incarnation Accomplishes

The Lord did not make man to be redeemed, but to bear His image. But through sin man lost the image of God. It is only by man's redemption that God can accomplish His design for him in making him a son of God.

"As many as received him, to them gave he power to

become the sons of God, even to them that believe on his name: which were born, not of blood, nor of the will of the flesh, nor of the will of man, but of God. And the Word was made flesh, and dwelt among us, (and we beheld his glory, the glory as of the only begotten of the Father,) full of grace and truth. . . . And of his fulness have all we received, and grace for grace" (John 1:12-16).

Because of the ransom paid for him, man, by his own choice, by obedience, may accomplish the design of God, and through the grace given of God bear the image that was first impressed upon him, and afterwards lost through the fall. . . .

Christ's Obedience Not Altogether Different From Ours.—The great teacher came into our world, not only to atone for sin but to be a teacher both by precept and example. He came to show man how to keep the law in humanity, so that man might have no excuse for following his own defective judgment. We see Christ's obedience. His life was without sin. His lifelong obedience is a reproach to disobedient humanity. The obedience of Christ is not to be put aside as altogether different from the obedience He requires of us individually. Christ has shown us that it is possible for all humanity to obey the laws of God. . . .

The work of Christ was not a divided heart service. Christ came not to do His own will but the will of Him that sent Him. Jesus says, "Step in the footprints of my Sonship in all obedience. I obey as in partnership with the great firm. You are to obey as in co-partnership with the Son of God. Often you will not see the path clearly; then ask of God, and He will give you wisdom and courage and faith to move forward, leaving all issues with Him." We want to comprehend so far as possible the truly human nature of our Lord. The divine and human were linked in Christ, and both were complete.

Our Saviour took up the true relationship of a human being as the Son of God. We are sons and daughters of God. In order to know how to behave ourselves circumspectly, we must follow where Christ leads the way. For thirty years He lived the life of a perfect man, meeting the highest standard of perfection. Then let man, however imperfect, hope in God, saying not, "If I were of a different disposition I would serve God," but bring himself to Him in true service. . . . That nature has been redeemed by Me. "As many as received him, to them gave he power to become the sons of God, even to them that believe on his name" (John 1:12)—you are not degraded, but raised, ennobled, refined by Me. You can find refuge in Me. You can obtain victory and be more than conquerors in My name.—Letter 69, 1897.

Satan Declared That Man Could Not Keep God's Law

The world's Redeemer passed over the ground where Adam fell because of his disobeying the expressed law of Jehovah; and the only begotten Son of God came to our world as a man, to reveal to the world that men could keep the law of God. Satan, the fallen angel, had declared that no man could keep the law of God after the disobedience of Adam. He claimed the whole race under his control.

The Son of God placed Himself in the sinner's stead, and passed over the ground where Adam fell, and endured the temptation in the wilderness, which was a hundredfold stronger than was or ever will be brought to bear upon the human race. Jesus resisted the temptations of Satan in the same manner that every tempted soul may resist, by referring him to the inspired record and saying, "It is written."

Humanity Can Keep God's Law by Divine Power.—Christ overcame the temptations of Satan as a man. Every man may overcome as Christ overcame. He humbled Himself for us. He was tempted in all points like as we are. He redeemed Adam's disgraceful failure and fall, and was conqueror, thus testifying to all the unfallen worlds and to fallen humanity that man could keep the commandments of God through the divine power granted to him of heaven. Jesus the Son of God humbled Himself for us, endured temptation for us, overcome in our behalf to show us how we may overcome. He has thus bound up His interests with humanity by the closest ties, and has given the positive assurance that we shall not be tempted above that we are able, for with the temptation He will make a way of escape.

The Holy Spirit Enables Us to Be Victorious. — The Holy Spirit was promised to be with those who were wrestling for victory, in demonstration of all mightiness, endowing the human agent with supernatural powers, and instructing the ignorant in the mysteries of the kingdom of God. That the Holy Spirit is to be the grand helper, is a wonderful promise. Of what avail would it have been to us that the only begotten Son of God had humbled Himself, endured the temptations of the wily foe, and wrestled with him during His entire life on earth, and died the Just for the unjust that humanity might not perish, if the Spirit had not been given as a constant, working, regenerating agent to make effectual in our cases what has been wrought out by the world's Redeemer?

The imparted Holy Spirit enabled His disciples, the apostles, to stand firmly against every species of idolatry and to exalt the Lord and Him alone. Who, but Jesus Christ by His Spirit and divine power, guided the pens of the sacred historians that to the world might be presented the precious record of the sayings and works of Jesus Christ?

The promised Holy Spirit, whom He would send after He ascended to His Father, is constantly at work to draw the attention to the great official sacrifice upon the cross of Calvary, and to unfold to the world the love of God to man, and to open to the convicted soul the precious things in the Scriptures, and to open to darkened minds the bright beams of the Sun of Righteousness, the truths that make their hearts burn within them with the awakened intelligence of the truths of eternity.

Who but the Holy Spirit presents before the mind

the moral standard of righteousness and convinces of sin, and produces godly sorrow which worketh repentance that needeth not to be repented of, and inspires the exercise of faith in Him who alone can save from all sin.

Who but the Holy Spirit can work with human minds to transform character by withdrawing the affections from those things which are temporal, perishable, and imbues the soul with earnest desire by presenting the immortal inheritance, the eternal substance which is imperishable, and recreates, refines, and sanctifies the human agents that they may become members of the royal family, children of the heavenly king. . . .

Christ Overcame Sin as a Man.—The fall of our first parents broke the golden chain of implicit obedience of the human will to the divine. Obedience has no longer been deemed an absolute necessity. The human agents follow their own imaginations, which the Lord said of the inhabitants of the old world were evil and that continually. The Lord Jesus declares, I have kept My Father's commandments. How? As a man. Lo, I come to do Thy will, O God. To the accusations of the Jews He stood forth in His pure, virtuous, holy character and challenged them, "Who of you convinceth me of sin?"

Our Example and Sacrifice for Sin.—The world's Redeemer came not only to be a sacrifice for sin but to be an example to man in all things, a holy, human character. He was a Teacher, such an educator as the world never saw or heard before. He spake as one having authority, and yet He invites the confidence of all. "Come unto me, all ye that labour and are heavy laden, and I will give you rest. Take my yoke upon you, and learn of me; for I am meek and lowly in heart: and ye shall find rest unto your souls. For my yoke is easy, and my burden is light" (Matt. 11:28-30).

The only begotten Son of the infinite God has, by His words [and], His practical example left us a plain pattern which we are to copy. By His words He has educated us to obey God, and by His own practice He has showed us how we can obey God.

Not only did Christ give explicit rules showing how we may become obedient children but He showed us in His own life and character just how to do those things which are right and acceptable with God, so there is no excuse why we should not do those things which are pleasing in His sight.

He Disproved Satan's Claim.—We are ever to be thankful that Jesus has proved to us by actual facts that man can keep the commandments of God, giving contradiction to Satan's falsehood that man cannot keep them. The Great Teacher came to our world to stand at the head of humanity, to thus elevate and sanctify humanity by His holy obedience to all of God's requirements showing it is possible to obey all the commandments of God. He has demonstrated that a lifelong obedience is possible. Thus He gives chosen, representative men to the world, as the Father gave the Son, to exemplify in their life the life of Jesus Christ.

He Stood the Test as a True Human Being.—We need not place the obedience of Christ by itself as something for which He was particularly adapted, by His particular divine nature, for He stood before God as man's representative and tempted as man's substitute and surety. If Christ had a special power which it is not the privilege of man to have, Satan would have made capital of this matter. The work of Christ was to take from the claims of Satan his control of man, and He could do this only in the way that He came—a man, tempted as a man, rendering the obedience of a man.

. . .

Bear in mind that Christ's overcoming and obedience is that of a true human being. In our conclusions, we make many mistakes because of our erroneous views of the human nature of our Lord. When we give to His human nature a power that it is not possible for man to have in his conflicts with Satan, we destroy the completeness of His humanity. His imputed grace and power He gives to all who receive Him by faith. The obedience of Christ to His Father was the same obedience that is required of man.

Man cannot overcome Satan's temptations without divine power to combine with His instrumentality. So with Jesus Christ, He could lay hold of divine power. He came not to our world to give the obedience of a lesser God to a greater, but as a man to obey God's Holy Law, and in this way He is our example.

Jesus Showed What Man Could Do.—The Lord Jesus came to our world, not to reveal what a God could do, but what a man could do, through faith in God's power to help in every emergency. Man is, through faith, to be a partaker in the divine nature, and to overcome every temptation wherewith he is beset. The Lord now demands that every son and daughter of Adam through faith in Jesus Christ, serve Him in [the] human nature which we now have.

The Lord Jesus has bridged the gulf that sin has made. He has connected earth with heaven, and finite man with the infinite God. Jesus, the world's Redeemer, could only keep the commandments of God in the same way that humanity can keep them. "Whereby are given unto us exceeding great and precious promises: that by these ye might be partakers of the divine nature, having escaped the corruption that is in the world through lust" (2 Peter 1:4). . . .

We must practice the example of Christ, bearing in mind His Sonship and His humanity. It was not God that was tempted in the wilderness, nor a God that was to endure the contradiction of sinners against Himself. It was the Majesty of heaven who became a man— humbled Himself to our human nature.

How We Are to Serve God.—We are not to serve God as if we were not human, but we are to serve Him in the nature we have, that has been redeemed by the Son of God; through the righteousness of Christ we shall stand before God pardoned, and as though we had never sinned. We will never gain strength in considering what we might do if we were angels. We are to turn in faith to Jesus Christ, and show our love to God through obedience to His commands. Jesus "was in all points tempted like as we are, yet without sin." Jesus says, "Follow me." "If any man will come after me, let him deny himself, and take up his cross, and follow me."—Manuscript 1, 1892.

Real Meaning of the Incarnation

Christ took upon Himself humanity, and laid down His life a sacrifice, that man, by becoming a partaker of the divine nature, might have eternal life. Not only was Christ the Sacrifice but He was also the Priest who offered the sacrifice. "The bread that I will give," said He, "is my flesh, which I will give for the life of the world" (John 6:51). He was innocent of all guilt. He gave Himself in exchange for the people who had sold themselves to Satan by transgression of God's law—His life for the life of the human family, who thereby became His purchased possession.

"Therefore doth my Father love me," said Christ, "because I lay down my life, that I might take it again. No man taketh it from me, but I lay it down of myself. I have power to lay it down, and I have power to take it again. This commandment have I received of my Father" (John 10:17, 18).

"The wages of sin is death" (Rom. 6:23). To Adam before his fall the Lord said, "In the day that thou eatest thereof thou shalt surely die" (Gen. 2:17). "If you transgress my law, death will surely be your punishment." By disobeying God's command, he forfeited his life.

Before his fall Adam was free from the results of the curse. When he was assailed by the tempter, none of the effects of sin were upon him. He was created perfect in thought and in action. But he yielded to sin, and fell from his high and holy estate.

In the Likeness of Sinful Flesh.—Christ, the second Adam, came in the likeness of sinful flesh. In man's behalf, He became subject to sorrow, to weariness, to hunger, and to thirst. He was subject to temptation, but He yielded not to sin. No taint of sin was upon Him. He declared, "I have kept my Father's commandments [in My earthly life]" (John 15:10). He had infinite power only because He was perfectly obedient to His Father's will. The second Adam stood the test of trial and temptation that He might become the Owner of all humanity.—Manuscript 99, 1903.

INTRODUCTION

The basic elements of salvation are presented in one form or another in almost every Ellen G. White book and in innumerable periodical articles. The Bible studies and discussions at the 1888 Minneapolis General Conference brought into focus the elements of salvation by faith in Christ alone, which was a truth that had been largely lost sight of by many, both ministers and laity. *Selected Messages,* book 1, in its 51-page section on "Christ Our Righteousness," sets forth this emphasis in the setting of Minneapolis. How Ellen White rejoiced as the great basic truth of justification by faith was brought prominently to the front at this conference, and as she entered with others into carrying the blessed message to the churches! This was a truth, however, that had entered into her sermons and writings down through the years, always presented in a balanced manner. This is attested to by the several presentations that make up the Ellen G. White book *Faith and Works,* containing discourses and articles from 1881 to 1902.

This section brings together in three chapters the vital truths relating to faith and works. The first chapter is devoted to typical statements made by Ellen White from 1850 to 1888 showing her clear-cut stand in a balanced presentation of justification by faith. The third chapter brings to view her consistent declarations, showing a unity of teaching all through her ministry. Only a few typical statements are included to remind us of her work in presenting this vital truth, which is the very heart of the gospel. Chapter two, historical in nature, presents her review of the experience at the Minneapolis General Conference and the work on her part, related to this experience, in the months that followed that conference. This chapter is introduced by a somewhat extended statement giving a background for her historical review.—WHITE TRUSTEES.

20.

Principles as Set Forth by Ellen White in Her Early Ministry

Look Away From Self to Jesus—1850.—Said the angel, "Have faith in God." I saw some tried too hard to believe. Faith is so simple, ye look above it. Satan tried to deceive some of the honest children and had got them looking to self to find worthiness there. I saw they must look away from self to the worthiness of Jesus and throw themselves just as dependent and unworthy as they are upon His mercy and draw by faith strength and nourishment from Him.—Letter 8, 1850.

Depend Solely on Merits of Jesus—1862.—Every member of the family should bear in mind that all have just as much as they can do to resist our wily foe, and with earnest prayers and unyielding faith each must rely upon the merits of the blood of Christ and claim His saving strength.

The powers of darkness gather about the soul and shut Jesus from our sight, and at times we can only wait in sorrow and amazement until the cloud passes over. These seasons are sometimes terrible. Hope seems to fail, and despair seizes upon us. In these dreadful hours we must learn to trust, to depend solely upon the merits of the atonement, and in all our helpless unworthiness cast ourselves upon the merits of the crucified and risen Saviour. We shall never perish while we do this—

never!—Testimonies, vol. 1, pp. 309, 310 (1862).

The Truth to Sanctify the Life—1869.—Brother and Sister P have a work to do to set their own house and hearts in order. . . . He [Brother P] has not seen and felt the necessity of the Spirit of God upon the heart to influence the life, the words, and acts. He has made his religious experience too much of a form.

The theory of the truth he has seen and acknowledged, but the special work of sanctification through the truth he has not become acquainted with. Self has appeared. If anything was spoken in meeting which did not meet his standard, he would rebuke, not in love and humility, but harshly with severe cutting words. This strong language is not proper for any Christian to use, especially one who has need of much greater experience himself, and who has very many wrongs to correct.—Manuscript 2, 1869.

The Fruit True Sanctification Produces—1874.—You have held views of sanctification and holiness which have not been of that genuine article which produces fruit of the right quality. Sanctification is not an outward work. It does not consist in praying and exhorting in meeting but it takes hold of the very life and molds the words and actions, transforming the character. . . .

There seem to be important positions that need to be filled by men who are truly sanctified, having the spirit of the Master. And there is a most positive necessity of overcoming self that their work and efforts should not be marred by the defects in their character.—Manuscript 6, 1874.

Character Perfected by Enoch and Elijah—1874.—Some few in every generation from Adam resisted his every artifice and stood forth as noble representatives of what it was in the power of man to do and to be—Christ working with human efforts, helping man in overcoming the power of Satan. Enoch and Elijah are the correct representatives of what the race might be through faith in Jesus Christ if they chose to be. Satan was greatly disturbed because these noble, holy men stood untainted amid the moral pollution surrounding them, perfected righteous characters, and were accounted worthy for translation to heaven. As they had stood forth in moral power in noble uprightness, overcoming Satan's temptations, he could not bring them under the dominion of death. He triumphed that he had power to overcome Moses with his temptations, and that he could mar his illustrious character and lead him to the sin of taking glory to himself before the people which belonged to God.—*The Review and Herald*, March 3, 1874.

Faith and Works in Salvation—1878.—All your good works cannot save you; but it is nevertheless impossible for you to be saved without good works. Every sacrifice made for Christ will be for your eternal gain.—*The Review and Herald*, March 21, 1878.

Trust in Christ Essential—1879.—Christ has been loved by you, although your faith has sometimes been feeble and your prospects confused. But Jesus is your Saviour. He does not save you because you are perfect, but because you need Him and in your imperfection have trusted in Him. Jesus loves you, my precious child. You may sing, "Under the shadow of Thy throne Still may we dwell secure; Sufficient is Thine arm alone, And our defense is sure."—Letter 46, 1879.

Works of Righteousness Weighed in the Judgment—1881.—Ministers sometimes tell the people that they have nothing to do but believe; that Jesus has done it all, and their own works are nothing. But the Word of God plainly states that in the Judgment the scales will be balanced accurately, and the decisions will be based on the evidence adduced.

One man becomes ruler of ten cities, another of five, another of two, each man receiving exactly in proportion to the improvement he has made on the talents entrusted to his keeping. Our efforts in works of righteousness, in our own behalf and for the salvation of souls, will have a decided influence on our recompense.—*The Review and*

Herald, Oct. 25, 1881.

Ellen White's Only Hope in Christ—1881.—In my recent bereavement, I have had a near view of eternity. I have, as it were, been brought before the great white throne, and have seen my life as it will there appear. I can find nothing of which to boast, no merit that I can plead.

"Unworthy, unworthy of the least of Thy favors, O my God," is my cry. My only hope is in a crucified and risen Saviour. I claim the merits of the blood of Christ. Jesus will save to the uttermost all who put their trust in Him.—*The Review and Herald,* Nov. 1, 1881.

Strive for Perfection of Character—1882.—We can never see our Lord in peace, unless our souls are spotless. We must bear the perfect image of Christ. Every thought must be brought into subjection to the will of Christ. As expressed by the great apostle, we must come "unto the measure of the stature of the fulness of Christ." We shall never attain to this condition without earnest effort. We must strive daily against outward evil and inward sin, if we would reach the perfection of Christian character.—*The Review and Herald,* May 30, 1882.

Basic Elements Presented at the 1883 General Conference

INTRODUCTORY NOTE: At the General Conference session held in 1883 at Battle Creek, Michigan, Ellen White addressed the ministers at thirteen consecutive morning meetings and spoke to the conference on the closing Sabbath. The *Review and Herald* the next year carried the entire series. In four of the addresses she set forth the principles of righteousness by faith, as presented in the selections which follow. A further basic address, "Christ Our Righteousness," keyed to these meetings, was first published in *Gospel Workers,* 1893 edition, page 411, and reprinted in *Selected Messages,* book 1, pp. 350-354, and *Faith and Works,* pp. 35-39.—COMPILERS.

Friday, November 9, 1883—Look to Jesus.—On this morning there was a spirit of earnest intercession for the Lord to reveal Himself among us in power. My heart was especially drawn out in prayer, and the Lord heard and blessed us. Testimonies were borne by many discouraged ones, who felt that their imperfections were so great that the Lord could not use them in His cause. This was the language of unbelief.

I tried to point these dear souls to Jesus, who is our refuge, a present help in every time of need. He does not give us up because of our sins. We may make mistakes and grieve His Spirit, but when we repent, and come to Him with contrite hearts, He will not turn us away. . . .

Sabbath, November 10, 1883—Come As You Are.—I have listened to testimonies like this: "I have not the light that I desire; I have not the assurance of the favor of God." Such testimonies express only unbelief and darkness.

Are you expecting that your merit will recommend you to the favor of God, and that you must be free from sin before you trust His power to save? If this is the struggle going on in your mind, I fear you will gain no strength, and will finally become discouraged. As the brazen serpent was lifted up in the wilderness, so was Christ lifted up to draw all men unto Him. All who looked upon that serpent, the means that God had provided, were healed; so in our sinfulness, in our great need, we must "look and live."

While we realize our helpless condition without Christ, we must not be discouraged; we must rely upon the merits of a crucified and risen Saviour. Poor sin-sick, discouraged soul, look and live. Jesus has pledged His word; He will save all who come unto Him. Then let us come confessing our sins, bringing forth fruits meet for repentance.

Jesus is our Saviour today. He is pleading for us in the most holy place of the heavenly sanctuary, and He will forgive our sins. It makes all the difference in the world with us spiritually whether we rely upon God without doubt, as upon a sure foundation, or whether we are seeking to find some righteousness in ourselves before we come to Him. Look away from self to the Lamb of God, that taketh away the sin of the world. It is a sin to doubt. The least unbelief, if cherished in the heart, involves the soul in guilt, and brings great darkness and discouragement. . . .

Some seem to feel that they must be on probation and must prove to the Lord that they are reformed before they can claim His blessing. But these dear souls may claim the blessing of God even now. They must have His grace, the spirit of Christ to help their infirmities, or they cannot form Christian characters. Jesus loves to have us come to Him just as we are—sinful, helpless, dependent. We claim to be children of the light, not of the night nor of darkness; what right have we to be unbelieving?—*The Review and Herald,* April 22, 1884.

Wednesday, November 14, 1883—True Religion Means Conformity to God's Will.—Some are ever looking to themselves instead of to Jesus; but, brethren, you want to be clothed in Christ's righteousness. If you are trusting in your own righteousness, you are weak indeed; for you are exposed to the darts of Satan, and after the privileges you are now enjoying, you will have severe conflicts to meet. You are too cold. The work is hindered by your want of that love which burned in the heart of Jesus. You have too little faith. You expect little, and as the result you receive little; and you are satisfied with very small success. You are liable to self-deception, and to rest satisfied with a form of godliness. This will never do.

You must have living faith in your hearts; the truth must be preached with power from above. You can reach the people only when Jesus works through your efforts. The Fountain is open; we may be refreshed, and in our turn refresh others. If your own souls were vitalized by the solemn, pointed truths you preach, cold-heartedness, listlessness, and indolence would disappear, and others would feel the influence of your zeal and earnestness.

True religion is nothing short of conformity to the will of God, and obedience to all things that He has commanded; and in return, it gives us spiritual life, imputes to us the righteousness of Christ, and promotes the healthful and happy exercise of the best faculties of the mind and heart. Infinite riches, the glory and blessedness of eternal life, are bestowed upon us on conditions so simple as to bring the priceless gift within the reach of the poorest and most sinful. We have only to obey and believe. And His commandments are not grievous; obedience to His requirements is essential to our happiness even in this life.—*The Review and Herald*, May 27, 1884.

Monday, November 19, 1883—Look to Him and Live.—How many are making laborious work of walking in the narrow way of holiness. To many the peace and rest of this blessed way seems no nearer today than it did years in the past. They look afar off for that which is nigh; they make intricate that which Jesus made very plain. He is "the way, the truth, and the life." The plan of salvation has been plainly revealed in the Word of God; but the wisdom of the world has been sought too much, and the wisdom of Christ's righteousness too little. And souls that might have rested in the love of Jesus, have been doubting, and troubled about many things.

The testimonies borne here are not expressive of great faith. It is not hard to believe that Jesus will pardon others, but it seems impossible for each to exercise living faith for himself. But, dear brethren, is it profitable to express doubts in regard to the willingness of Christ to accept you? I fear you are depending too much on feeling, making that a criterion. You are losing much by this course; you are not only weakening your own souls, but the souls of others who look to you.

You must trust Jesus for yourselves, appropriate the promises of God to yourselves, or how can you educate others to have humble, holy confidence in Him? You feel that you have neglected duties, that you have not prayed as you should.

You seem at a distance from Jesus, and think that He has withdrawn from you; but it is you who have separated from Him. He is waiting for you to return. He will accept the contrite heart. His lips have assured us that He is more willing to give the Holy Spirit to them that ask Him than parents are to give good gifts to their children.

We are wounded, polluted with sin; what shall we do to be healed from its leprosy? As far as it is in your power to do so, cleanse the soul-temple of every defilement, and then look to the "Lamb of God, which taketh away the sin of the world" (John 1:29).

If you are conscious of your wants, do not devote all your powers to representing them and mourning over them, but look and live. Jesus is our only Saviour; and notwithstanding millions who need to be healed will reject His offered mercy, not one who trusts in His merits will be left to perish.

Why do you refuse to come to Jesus and receive rest and peace? You may have the blessing this morning. Satan suggests that you are helpless, and cannot bless yourself. It is true; you are helpless. But lift up Jesus before him: "I have a Saviour. In Him I trust, and He will never suffer me to be confounded. In His name I triumph. He is my righteousness, and my crown of rejoicing." Let not one here feel that his case is hopeless, for it is not.

It may seem to you that you are sinful and undone; but it is just on this account that you need a Saviour. If you have sins to confess, lose no time. These moments are golden. "If we confess our sins, he is faithful and just to forgive us our sins, and to cleanse us from all unrighteousness" (1 John 1:9). Those who hunger and thirst after righteousness will be filled; for Jesus has promised it. Precious Saviour! His arms are open to receive us, and His great heart of love is waiting to bless us.—*The Review and Herald,* July 1, 1884.

False Sanctification—1885.—There was a man, a non-SDA minister by the name of Brown, perhaps you know him.* He claimed to be holy. "The idea of

---

* Ellen White, speaking to the members of the Santa Rosa, California, SDA church, on March 7, 1885, recounted an experience that took place on shipboard the year before, when she traveled from Portland, Oregon, to San Francisco, California.—Compilers.

repentance," said he, "is not in the Bible." "If," says he, "a man comes to me and says that he believes in Jesus, I take him right into the church, whether he is baptized or not; I have done so with a good many." "And," says he, "I have not committed a sin in six years."

"There are some on this boat," says he, "that believe that we [are] sanctified by [keeping] the law. There is a woman on this boat, by the name of White that teaches this."

I heard this, and I stepped up to him and said, "Elder Brown, you hold right on. I cannot permit that statement to go. Mrs. White has never said such a thing in any of her writings, nor has she ever spoken such a thing, for we do not believe that the law sanctifies anyone.

"We believe that we must keep that law or we will not be saved in the kingdom of heaven. The transgressor cannot be saved in the kingdom of glory. It is not the law that sanctifies anyone, nor saves us; that law stands and cries out, 'Repent that your sins may be blotted out.' And then the sinner goes to Jesus, and as the sinner promises that he will obey the requirements of the law, He blots out their guilty stains and sets them free, and gives them power with God."—Manuscript 5, 1885.

Freedom to Violate Commandments a Deception—1886.—You will hear the cry "Only believe." Satan believed and trembled. We must have a faith that works by love and purifies the heart. The idea prevails that Christ has done all for us, and that we can go on transgressing the commandments and will not be held accountable for it. This is the greatest deception that the enemy ever devised. We must take our position that we will not violate the commandments at any cost, and be in that spiritual condition that we can educate others in spiritual things.—Manuscript 44, 1886.

Moral Power Through Jesus—1886.—Christ knew that man could not overcome without His help. Therefore He consented to lay off His royal robes and clothe His divinity with humanity that we might be rich. He came to this earth, suffered, and knows just how to sympathize with us and to assist us in overcoming. He came to bring man moral power, and He would not have man to understand that he has nothing to do, for every one has a work to do for himself, and through the merits of Jesus we can overcome sin and the devil.—Manuscript 46, 1886.

Goody-goody Religion That Makes Light of Sin—1887.—"A new heart will I give you and a new spirit will I put within you." I believe with all my heart that the Spirit of God is being withdrawn from the world, and those who have had great light and opportunities and have not improved them, will be the first to be left. They have grieved away the Spirit of God. The present activity of Satan in working upon hearts, and upon churches and nations should startle every student of prophecy. The end is near. Let our churches arise. Let the converting power of God be experienced in the heart of the individual members, and then we shall see the deep moving of the Spirit of God. Mere forgiveness of sin is not the sole result of the death of Jesus. He made the infinite sacrifice not only that sin might be removed, but that human nature might be restored, rebeautified, reconstructed from its ruins, and made fit for the presence of God. . . .

Christ is the ladder which Jacob saw whose base rested on the earth and whose topmost round reached the highest heavens. This shows the appointed method of salvation. We are to climb round after round of this ladder. If any one of us shall finally be saved, it will be by clinging to Jesus as to the rounds of a ladder. Christ is made unto the believer wisdom and righteousness, sanctification, and redemption. . . .

There will be some terrible falls by those who think they stand firm because they have the truth; but they have it not as it is in Jesus. A moment's carelessness may plunge a soul into irretrievable ruin. One sin leads to the second, and the second prepares the way for a third and so on. We must as faithful messengers of God, plead with Him constantly to be kept by His power. If we swerve a single inch from duty we are in danger of following on in a course of sin that ends in perdition. There is hope for every one of us, but only in one way—by fastening ourselves to Christ, and exerting every energy to attain to the perfection of His character.

This goody-goody religion that makes light of sin and that is forever dwelling upon the love of God to the sinner, encourages the sinner to believe that God will save him while he continues in sin and he knows it to be sin. This is the way that many are doing who profess to believe present truth. The truth is kept apart from their life, and that is the reason it has no more power to convict and convert the soul. There must be a straining of every nerve and spirit and muscle to leave the world, its customs, its practices, and its fashions. . . .

If you put away sin and exercise living faith, the riches of heaven's blessings will be yours.—Letter 53, 1887.

Second Advent Ends Soul Preparation— 1888.—The robe of your character must be washed till it is spotless, in the fountain opened for all uncleanness. Your moral worth will be weighed in the balances of the sanctuary, and if you are found wanting, you will be at an eternal loss. All the coarseness, all the roughness, must be removed from your character before Jesus comes; for when He comes, the preparation for every soul is ended.

If you have not laid aside your envy, your jealousies, your hatred one against another, you cannot enter into the kingdom of God. You would only carry the same disposition with you; but there will be nothing of this character in the world to come. Nothing will exist there but love and joy and harmony. Some will have brighter crowns than others, but there will be no jealous thoughts in any heart among the redeemed. Each one will be perfectly satisfied, for all will be rewarded according to their work.—Signs of the Times, Feb. 10, 1888.

21.

Ellen G. White Reports on the Minneapolis Conference

A Statement Presenting the Historical Backgrounds

This chapter presents a statement by Ellen White prepared a few weeks after the close of the General Conference of 1888. She looks back upon the scene and describes what took place. The meetings at Minneapolis came into better perspective as the months elapsed, and Ellen White's statement is most enlightening and significant. A brief review of the historical setting is in place.

The Minneapolis General Conference was notable for the Bible studies and discussions on the law in Galatians and on the righteousness of Christ received by faith.

This session, attended by ninety-one delegates, was held October 17 to November 4 in Minneapolis, Minnesota, in our newly built church. As is customary, a number of Seventh-day Adventists who were not delegates were also present. The session was preceded by a seven-day ministerial institute, which met from October 10 through October 16. The Bible studies commenced in the institute in some cases continued into the General Conference session, occupying the Bible study hour.

Ellen White was present and participated in both the institute and the nineteen-day session. The session itself was quite routine, but constructive. Reports were received and meetings of various associations, such as

Sabbath School, Health and Temperance, and Tract and Missionary, were held. Fields of labor were assigned to the ministers, plans were laid for the advancement of the cause, officers were elected, and committees appointed.

An on-the-ground review of accomplishments and sentiments comes to us from the pen of W. C. White, who, two days before the close of the session, wrote to a fellow minister laboring in the Southern States:

"We are just at the close of another General Conference, and in a few days the delegates will be scattered to their respective fields, and another year's work begun.

"This has been a very interesting conference, and although not accompanied with all that peace and harmony that sometimes has been manifest, it is perhaps as profitable a meeting as was ever held, for many important principles were made prominent, and some conclusions arrived at, that will be of great value, as they may influence our future work. Many go forth from this meeting determined to study the Bible as never before, and this will result in clearer preaching.

"As you have no doubt noticed in the *Bulletin,* many advance steps have been taken as to our foreign missions, also some good moves for the advancement of the work in the South."—W. C. White letter to Smith Sharp, written from Minneapolis, Minnesota, Nov. 2, 1888.

It will be observed that together with his report of progress, Elder White made mention of the lack of "peace and harmony that sometimes has been manifest" in our General Conference sessions. In this he was referring to the theological discussions that made the 1888 meeting different from any other General Conference in Adventist history.

These discussions began in the week-long ministerial institute, when, according to the agenda, such topics as the ten kingdoms, the divinity of Christ, the healing of the deadly wound, and justification by faith were to be considered. The discussion of the ten kingdoms grew bitter and consumed a disproportionate amount of time. Some topics scheduled were crowded out. Near the close of the institute Elder E. J. Waggoner, associate editor of the *Signs of the Times,* began a series of studies, on the law in Galatians, that merged into his presentation of the Christian's faith and the righteousness of Christ. These continued through the first week of the General Conference session.

It was this series of studies, especially those that touched on the divisive subject of the law in Galatians, that sparked the controversy that followed. No transcription of the discussions was made, but the sketchy notes of one or two delegates, Ellen White's records, and the recollections of many who were present reveal the bitterness of the controversy and the baleful effects of the negative attitude of several prominent church leaders.

Even before the delegates assembled at Minneapolis there had been dispute on the key theological topics for several years. There was also building in the hearts of some an attitude of resistance to and nonacceptance of Ellen White's messages of warning and reproof. She early observed a strange and antagonistic attitude manifested toward her by some of the leading ministers.

As E. J. Waggoner led into an examination of the law in Galatians and salvation by faith, a debating spirit dominated some in the discussions. This greatly troubled Ellen White. Although she was not ready to agree with Elder Waggoner on all the fine points of his presentations on the law in Galatians, her heart was warmed by his clear enunciation of the principles of justification by faith and of righteousness obtained through faith in Christ. She spoke twenty times in Minneapolis, and especially in the early morning ministers' meetings she pleaded for open-minded Bible study. She herself did not speak on the topic of righteousness by faith.

The reactions to the emphasis on this vital truth were mixed. At the 1893 General Conference session, A. T. Jones, speaking of the reception of the truths set forth at Minneapolis, reported: "I know that some there accepted it; others rejected it entirely. You know the same thing.

Others tried to stand half way between, and get it that way."—*General Conference Bulletin*, 1893, p. 185.

The discussions were at times heated. Some, fearing that the new emphasis would weaken the church's strong position on God's law, particularly the Sabbath truth, strongly resisted the message on righteousness by faith. No conference actions were taken on this point or any other point brought forward in the Bible studies.

Ellen White reported in a letter written on the closing day of the session, a letter appearing in this section, "My courage and faith have been good," notwithstanding the almost "incomprehensible tug of war" they had been through, and she expressed the conviction, as she saw it at close range, that the "meeting will result in great good" (Letter 82, 1888). A few weeks later she wrote her statement looking back at the Minneapolis General Conference, a major portion of which is embodied in this section.

In the weeks and months following the session a hard core of opposition developed in Battle Creek, the church headquarters and the location of three of its major institutions. Ellen White frequently absented herself from Battle Creek, going into the field to carry the message to the churches. At times she worked with Elders Jones and Waggoner as all three engaged in presenting the precious truths of the gospel. She led out in an important and successful meeting of our ministers in January, 1889, in South Lancaster, where many were "greatly blessed." A report is included in this chapter.

The Ellen G. White files carry a powerful address on the basic principles of salvation by faith as given at the Ottawa, Kansas, camp meeting, May 11, 1889. This and her report on the response appear in the E. G. White book *Faith and Works*, pages 63-84.

There was victory in Chicago, and at Denver, Colorado, where at the camp meeting held in September, 1889, she spoke to the workers on the need for a true concept of righteousness by faith. The Denver address appears in this section.

While attending the General Conference session of 1889, held just a year after the Minneapolis meeting, she reported:

"We are having most excellent meetings. The spirit that was in the meeting at Minneapolis is not here. All moves off in harmony. There is a large attendance of delegates. Our five o'clock morning meeting is well attended, and the meetings good. All the testimonies to which I have listened have been of an elevating character. They say that the past year has been the best of their life; the light shining forth from the Word of God has been clear and distinct—justification by faith, Christ our righteousness. The experiences have been very interesting."—Manuscript 10, 1889 (published in *Selected Messages*, book 1, p. 361).

On February 3, 1890, as she addressed the ministers assembled in Battle Creek for a ministerial institute, she reviewed her experiences in the field during 1889. Her statement forms an appropriate part of this introduction:

"We have traveled all through to the different places of the meetings that I might stand side by side with the messengers of God that I knew were His messengers— that I knew had a message for His people. I gave my message with them right in harmony with the very message they were bearing. What did we see?

"We saw a power attending the message. In every instance we worked—and some know how hard we worked—I think it was a whole week, going early and late, at Chicago, in order that we might get these ideas in the minds of the brethren.

"The devil has been working for a year to obliterate these ideas—the whole of them. And it takes hard work to change their old opinions; they think they have got to trust in their own righteousness, and in their own works, and keep looking at themselves, and not appropriating the righteousness of Christ, and bringing it into their life, and into their character. And we worked there for one week. . . . One week had passed away before there was a break, and the power of God, like a tidal wave, rolled over that congregation. I tell you, it was to set men free; it was to point them to the Lamb of God which taketh away the sins of the world.

"And there at South Lancaster, the mighty movings of the Spirit of God were there. Some are here that were in that meeting. God revealed His glory, and every student in the College was brought to the door there in confession; and the movings of the Spirit of God were there.

"And thus [it was] from place to place. Everywhere we went we saw the movings of the Spirit of God.

"Do you think, like the ten lepers, I shall keep silent, that I shall not raise my voice to sing the righteousness of God and praise Him and glorify Him? I try to present it to you, that you may see the evidence that I saw: but it seems that the words go as into empty air; and how long is it to be thus? How long will the people at the heart of the work hold themselves against God? How long will men here sustain them in doing this work? Get out of the way, brethren. Take your hand off the ark of God, and let the Spirit of God come in and work in mighty power."—Manuscript 9, 1890.

Note the sentiment of the last paragraph just quoted. While the reception of the message of salvation by faith was resisted by some at the Minneapolis General Conference and accepted by others in the days that followed, resistance built up rapidly at the heart of the work. The reception among church members in the field, as reported by Ellen White, was quite different. The stubborn resistance participated in by "some" (see *Testimonies to Ministers*, p. 363) at the very headquarters of the church greatly retarded the work that the Lord intended should be accomplished.

Of this Ellen White wrote as the year 1890 came to a close: "The prejudices and opinions that prevailed at Minneapolis are not dead by any means; the seeds sown there in some hearts are ready to spring into life and bear a like harvest" (*Testimonies to Ministers*, p. 467).

In this same connection she wrote: "Some have failed

to distinguish between pure gold and mere glitter."—
Ibid. And she added, "The true religion, the only
religion of the Bible, that teaches forgiveness only
through the merits of a crucified and risen Saviour, that
advocates righteousness by the faith of the Son of God,
has been slighted, spoken against, ridiculed, and rejected."—*Ibid.*, p. 468.

In his book *Through Crisis to Victory*, Elder A. V.
Olson recounts the history and documents the gradual
change for better that ensued in the five or six years after
Minneapolis.

Nonetheless, there was a tragic setback in the advancement of the cause of God. Ellen White recognized
this and at times mentioned it, usually in incidental
statements. At no time, however, did she intimate or
declare that there was an official rejection by church
leaders of the precious message brought to the attention
of the General Conference in 1888. Rather, on December 19, 1892, just four years after that notable Conference, in a letter addressed to "Dear Brethren of the
General Conference," she triumphantly declared:

"In reviewing our past history, having traveled over
every step of advance to our present standing, I can say,
Praise God! As I see what God has wrought, I am filled
with astonishment and with confidence in Christ as
Leader. We have nothing to fear for the future, except as
we shall forget the way the Lord has led us, and His
teaching in our past history. We are now a strong
people, if we will put our trust in the Lord; for we are
handling the mighty truths of the word of God. We
have everything to be thankful for."—*General Conference
Bulletin,*1893, p. 24 (see *Life Sketches*, p. 196; *Testimonies
to Ministers*, p. 31).

Again, in 1907 she wrote: "The church is to increase
in activity and to enlarge her bounds. . . . While there
have been fierce contentions in the effort to maintain our
distinctive character, yet we have as Bible Christians ever
been on gaining ground."—*Letter 170, 1907 (Selected
Messages*, book 2, pp. 396, 397).

With this background we introduce the historical chapter of this section.—COMPILERS.

Precious Promises Versus Gloomy Pictures

It was by faith I ventured to cross the Rocky Mountains for the purpose of attending the General Conference held in Minneapolis. . . .

At Minneapolis we met a large delegation of ministers. I discerned at the very commencement of the meeting a spirit which burdened me. Discourses were preached that did not give the people the food which they so much needed. The dark and gloomy side of the picture was presented before them to hang in memory's hall. This would bring no light and spiritual freedom, but discouragement.

I felt deeply moved by the Spirit of the Lord Sabbath afternoon [Oct. 13, 1888] to call the minds of those present to the love God manifests to His people. The mind must not be permitted to dwell on the most objectionable features of our faith. In God's Word, which may be represented as a garden filled with roses and lilies and pinks, we may pluck by faith the precious promises of God, appropriate them to our own hearts, and be of good courage—yes, joyful in God—or we may keep our attention fastened on the briars and thistles and wound ourselves severely and bemoan our hard lot.

God is not pleased to have His people hanging dark and painful pictures in memory's hall. He would have every soul plucking the roses and the lilies and the pinks, hanging memory's hall with the precious promises of God blooming all over the garden of God. He would have us dwelling upon them, our senses sharp and clear, taking them in in their full richness, talking of the joy that is set before us. He would have us living in the world, yet not of it, our affections taking hold of eternal things. He would have us talking of the things which He has prepared for those that love Him. This will attract our minds, awaken our hopes and expectations, and strengthen our souls to endure the conflicts and trials of this life. As we dwell on these scenes the Lord will encourage our faith and confidence. He will draw aside the veil and give us glimpses of the saints' inheritance.

As I presented the goodness, the love, the tender compassion of our heavenly Father, I felt that the Spirit of the Lord was resting not only upon me but upon the people. Light and freedom and blessing came to the hearers and there was hearty response to the words spoken. The social meeting that followed evidenced that the Word had found lodgment in the hearts of the hearers. Many bore testimony that this day was the happiest of their lives, and it was indeed a precious season, for we knew the presence of the Lord Jesus was in the assembly and that to bless. I knew that the special revealing of the Spirit of God was for a purpose, to quell the doubts, to roll back the tide of unbelief which had been admitted into hearts and minds concerning Sister White and the work the Lord had given her to do.

Many Refreshed, but Not All.—This was a season of refreshing to many souls, but it did not abide upon some. Just as soon as they saw that Sister White did not agree with all their ideas and harmonize with the propositions and resolutions to be voted upon in that conference, the evidence they had received had as little weight with some as did the words spoken by Christ in the synagogue to the Nazarenes. Their hearts [the hearers at Nazareth] were touched by the Spirit of God. They heard as it were God speaking to them through His Son. They saw, they felt the divine influence of the Spirit of God and all witnessed to the gracious words that proceeded from His mouth. But Satan was at their side with his unbelief and they admitted the questioning and the doubts, and unbelief followed. The Spirit of God was quenched. In their madness they would have hurled Jesus from the precipice had not God protected Him that their rage did not harm Him. When Satan once has control of the mind he makes fools and demons of those who have been esteemed as excellent men. Prejudice, pride, and stubbornness are terrible elements to take possession of the human mind.

Ellen White Counsels With Some of the Leaders.—I had received a long epistle from Elder Butler,* which I read carefully. I was surprised at its contents. I did not know what to do with this letter, but as the same sentiments expressed in it seemed to be working and controlling my brother ministers I called a few of them together in an upper room and read this letter to them. They did not, any of them, seem to be surprised at its contents, several saying they knew this was the mind of Elder Butler, for they had heard him state the same things.

I then explained many things. I stated that which I knew was a right and righteous course to be pursued, brother toward brother, in the exercise of investigating the Scriptures. I knew the company before me were not viewing all things in a correct light, therefore I stated many things. All my statements set forth correct principles to be acted upon, but I feared that my words made no impression upon them. They understood things in their way, and the light which I told them had been given me was to them as idle tales.

Appeals at the Morning Meetings.—I felt very much pained at heart over the condition of things. I made most earnest appeals to my brethren and sisters when assembled in the morning meetings, and entreated that we should make this occasion a season of profit, searching the Scriptures together with humility of heart. I entreated that there should not be such freedom in talking in regard to things of which they knew but little.

All needed to learn lessons in the school of Christ. Jesus has invited, "Come unto me, all ye that labour and are heavy laden, and I will give you rest. Take my yoke upon you, and learn of me; for I am meek and lowly in heart: and ye shall find rest unto your souls. For my yoke

---

* The president of the General Conference was detained in Battle Creek because of illness.

is easy, and my burden is light" (Matt. 11:28-30). If we daily learn the lessons of humility and lowliness of heart, there will not be the feelings which existed at this meeting.

There are some differences of views on some subjects, but is this a reason for sharp, hard feelings? Shall envy and evil surmisings and imaginings, evil suspicion, hatred, and jealousies become enthroned in the heart? All these things are evil and only evil. Our help is in God alone. Let us spend much time in prayer and in searching the Scriptures with a right spirit—anxious to learn and willing to be corrected or undeceived on any point where we may be in error. If Jesus is in our midst and our hearts are melted into tenderness by His love we shall have one of the best conferences we have ever attended.

A Busy and Important Session.—There was much business to be done. The work had enlarged. New missions had been opened and new churches organized. All should be in harmony freely to consult together as brethren at work in the great harvest field, all working interestedly in the different branches of the work, and unselfishly considering how the Lord's work could be done to the best advantage. If ever there was a time when, as a conference, we needed the special grace and enlightenment of the Spirit of God, it was at this meeting. There was a power from beneath moving agencies to bring about a change in the constitution and laws of our nation, which will bind the consciences of all those who keep the Bible Sabbath, plainly specified in the fourth commandment as the seventh day.

The time has come when every man should be found doing his duty to the utmost of his ability to hold up and vindicate the law of God before our own people and the world, working to the limit of his capacity and entrusted talents. Many are blinded, deceived by men who claim to be ministers of the gospel, and they influence very many to consider they are doing a good work for God when it is the work of Satan.

Satan's Divisive Strategy.—Now, Satan had a council as to how he should keep pen and voice of Seventh-day Adventists silent. If he could only engage their attention and divert their powers in a direction to weaken and divide them his prospect would be fair.

Satan has done his work with some success. There has been variance of feelings, and division. There has been much jealousy and evil surmising. There have been many unsanctified speeches, hints, and remarks. The minds of the men who should be heart and soul at work, prepared to do mighty strokes for God at this very time are absorbed in matters of little consequence. Because the ideas of some are not exactly in accordance with their own on every point of doctrine involving minor ideas and theories which are not vital questions, the great question of the nation's religious liberty, now involving so much, is to many a matter of little consequence.

Satan has been having things his own way; but the Lord has raised up men and given them a solemn message to bear to His people, to wake up the mighty men to prepare for battle, for the day of God's preparation. This message Satan sought to make of none effect, and when every voice and every pen should have been intensely at work to stay the workings and powers of Satan there was a drawing apart; there were differences of opinion. This was not at all the way of the Lord.

The Law in Galatians One Point of Difference.—At this meeting the subject of the law in Galatians was brought before the ministers. This subject had been brought into the conference three years before.

. . .

We know that if all would come to the Scriptures with hearts subdued and controlled by the influence of the Spirit of God, there would be brought to the examination of the Scriptures a calm mind, free from prejudice and pride of opinion. The light from the Lord would shine upon His Word and the truth would be revealed. But there should be prayerful, painstaking effort and much patience, to answer the prayer of Christ that His disciples may be one as He is one with the Father. The earnest, sincere prayer will be heard and the Lord will answer. The Holy Spirit will quicken the mental faculties and there will be a seeing eye to eye. "The entrance of thy words giveth light; it giveth understanding unto the simple" (Ps. 119:130).

Justification and Christ's Righteousness Presented.—Elder E. J. Waggoner had the privilege granted him of speaking plainly and presenting his views upon justification by faith and the righteousness of Christ in relation to the law. This was no new light, but it was old light placed where it should be in the third angel's message. . . . What is the burden of that message? John sees a people. He says, "Here is the patience of the saints: here are they that keep the commandments of God, and the faith of Jesus" (Rev. 14:12). This people John beholds just before he sees the Son of man "having on his head a golden crown, and in his hand a sharp sickle" (verse 14).

The faith of Jesus has been overlooked and treated in an indifferent, careless manner. It has not occupied the prominent position in which it was revealed to John. Faith in Christ as the sinner's only hope has been largely left out, not only of the discourses given but of the religious experience of very many who claim to believe the third angel's message.

Truths Ellen White Had Presented Since 1844.—At this meeting I bore testimony that the most precious light had been shining forth from the Scriptures in the presentation of the great subject of the righteousness of Christ connected with the law, which should be constantly kept before the sinner as his only hope of salvation. This was not new light to me, for it had come to me from higher authority for the last forty-four years, and I had presented it to our people by pen and voice in the testimonies of His Spirit. But very few had responded except by assent to the testimonies borne upon this subject. There was altogether too little spoken and written upon this great question. The discourses of some might be correctly represented as like the offering of Cain—Christless.

The Mystery of Godliness.—The standard by which to measure character is the royal law. The law is the sin detector. By the law is the knowledge of sin. But the sinner is constantly being drawn to Jesus by the wonderful manifestation of His love in that He humiliated Himself to die a shameful death upon the cross. What a study is this! Angels have striven, earnestly longed, to look into the wonderful mystery. It is a study that can tax the highest human intelligence, that man, fallen, deceived by Satan, taking Satan's side of the question, can be conformed to the image of the Son of the infinite God. That man shall be like Him, that, because of the righteousness of Christ given to man, God will love man—fallen but redeemed—even as He loved His Son. Read it right out of the living oracles.

This is the mystery of godliness. This picture is of the highest value to be placed in every discourse, to be hung in memory's hall, to be uttered by human lips, to be traced by human beings who have tasted and known that the Lord is good, to be meditated upon, to be the groundwork of every discourse. There have been dry theories presented and precious souls are starving for the bread of life. This is not the preaching that is required or that the God of heaven will accept, for it is Christless. The divine picture of Christ must be kept before the people. He is that Angel standing in the sun of heaven. He reflects no shadows. Clothed in the attributes of deity, shrouded in the glories of deity, and in the likeness of the infinite God, He is to be lifted up before men. When this is kept before the people, creature merit sinks into insignificance. The more the eye looks upon Him, the more His life, His lessons, His perfection of character are studied, the more sinful and abhorrent will sin appear.

By beholding, man can but admire and become more attracted to Him, more charmed, and more desirous to be like Jesus until he assimilates to His image and has the mind of Christ. Like Enoch he walks with God. His mind is full of thoughts of Jesus. He is his best Friend. . . .

Study Jesus Our Pattern.—"Wherefore, holy brethren, partakers of the heavenly calling, consider the Apostle and High Priest of our profession, Christ Jesus" (Heb. 3:1). Study Christ. Study His character, feature by feature. He is our Pattern that we are required to copy in our lives and our characters, else we fail to represent Jesus, but present to the world a spurious copy. Do not imitate any man, for men are defective in habits, in speech, in manners, in character. I present before you the Man Christ Jesus. You must individually know Him as your Saviour before you can study Him as your pattern and your example.

Said Paul, "I am not ashamed of the gospel of Christ: for it is the power of God unto salvation to every one that believeth; to the Jew first, and also to the Greek. For therein is the righteousness of God revealed from faith to faith: as it is written, The just shall live by faith. . . . Because that which may be known of God is manifest in them; for God hath shewed it unto them" (Rom. 1:16-19).

Grateful That Minds Were Stirred by God's Spirit.—We felt deeply and solemnly grateful to God that minds were being stirred by the Spirit of God to see Christ in the living oracles and to represent Him to the world, but not in words merely. They see the Scripture requirements that all who claim to be followers of Christ are under obligation to walk in His footsteps, to be imbued with His Spirit, and thus to present to the world Jesus Christ, who came to our world to represent the Father.

In representing Christ we represent God to our world. "If any man have not the Spirit of Christ, he is none of his" (Rom. 8:9). Let us inquire, Are we reflecting in the church and before the world the character of Jesus Christ? A great deal deeper study is required of us in searching the Scriptures. Placing the righteousness of

Christ in the law distinctly reveals God in His true character and reveals the law as holy, just, and good, glorious indeed when seen in its true character.

If all our ministering brethren could have come to their Bibles together, with the spirit of Christ, respecting each other, and with true Christian courtesy, the Lord would have been their instructor. But the Lord has no chance to impress minds over which Satan has so great power. Everything that does not harmonize with their mind and their human judgment will appear in shadows and dark outlines. . . .

The Spirit of Many Burdened Ellen White.—My burden during the meeting was to present Jesus and His love before my brethren, for I saw marked evidences that many had not the spirit of Christ. My mind was kept in peace, stayed upon God, and I felt sad to see that a different spirit had come into the experience of our brother ministers, and that it was leavening the camp. There was, I knew, a remarkable blindness upon the minds of many, that they did not discern where the Spirit of God was and what constituted true Christian experience. And to consider that these were the ones who had the guardianship of the flock of God was painful. The destitution of true faith, the hands hung down, because not lifted up in sincere prayer!

Some felt no need of prayer. Their own judgment, they felt, was sufficient, and they had no sense that the enemy of all good was guiding their judgment. They were as soldiers going unarmed and unarmored to the battle. Can we marvel that the discourses were spiritless, that the living water of life refused to flow through obstructed channels, and that the light of heaven could not penetrate the dense fog of lukewarmness and sinfulness?

I was able to sleep but a few hours. I was writing all hours of the morning, frequently rising at two and at three A.M. and relieving my mind by writing upon the subjects that were presented before me. My heart was pained to see the spirit that controlled some of our ministering brethren, and this spirit seemed to be contagious. There was much talking done.

A Presentation of Truth She Could Endorse.— When I stated before my brethren that I had heard for the first time the views of Elder E. J. Waggoner, some did not believe me. I stated that I had heard precious truths uttered that I could respond to with all my heart, for had not these great and glorious truths, the righteousness of Christ and the entire sacrifice made in behalf of man, been imprinted indelibly on my mind by the Spirit of God? Has not this subject been presented in the testimonies again and again? When the Lord had given to my brethren the burden to proclaim this message I felt inexpressibly grateful to God, for I knew it was the message for this time.

The third angel's message is the proclamation of the commandments of God and the faith of Jesus Christ. The commandments of God have been proclaimed, but the faith of Jesus Christ has not been proclaimed by Seventh-day Adventists as of equal importance, the law and the gospel going hand in hand. I cannot find language to express this subject in its fullness.

"The faith of Jesus." It is talked of, but not understood. What constitutes the faith of Jesus, that belongs to the third angel's message? Jesus becoming our sin-bearer that He might become our sin-pardoning Saviour. He was treated as we deserve to be treated. He came to our world and took our sins that we might take His righteousness. And faith in the ability of Christ to save us amply and fully and entirely is the faith of Jesus.

The only safety for the Israelites was blood upon the doorposts. God said, "When I see the blood, I will pass over you" (Ex. 12:13). All other devices for safety would be without avail. Nothing but the blood on the doorposts would bar the way that the angel of death should not enter. There is salvation for the sinner in the blood of Jesus Christ alone, which cleanseth us from all sin. The man with a cultivated intellect may have vast stores of knowledge, he may engage in theological speculations, he may be great and honored of men and be considered the repository of knowledge, but unless he has a saving knowledge of Christ crucified for him, and by faith lays hold of the righteousness of Christ, he is lost. Christ "was wounded for our transgressions, he was bruised for our iniquities: the chastisement of our peace was upon him; and with his stripes we are healed" (Isa. 53:5). "Saved by the blood of Jesus Christ," will be our only hope for time and our song throughout eternity.

Battling Prejudice and False Accusations.— When I plainly stated my faith there were many who did not understand me and they reported that Sister White had changed; Sister White was influenced by her son W. C. White and by Elder A. T. Jones. Of course, such a statement coming from the lips of those who had known me for years, who had grown up with the third angel's message and had been honored by the confidence and faith of our people, must have influence.

I became the subject of remarks and criticism, but no one of our brethren came to me and made inquiries or sought any explanation from me. We tried most earnestly to have all our ministering brethren rooming in the house meet in an unoccupied room and unite our prayers together, but did not succeed in this but two or three times. They chose to go to their rooms and have their conversation and prayers by themselves. There did not seem to be any opportunity to break down the prejudice that was so firm and determined, no chance to remove the misunderstanding in regard to myself, my son, and E. J. Waggoner and A. T. Jones.

I tried to make another effort. I had that morning at an early hour written matter that should come before our brethren, for then my words would not be misstated. Quite a number of our leading responsible men were present, and I deeply regretted that a much larger number were not taken into this council, for some of those present, I knew, began to see things in a different light, and many more would have been benefited had they had the opportunity to hear what I had to say. But they did not know and were not benefited by my explanations and with the plain "Thus saith the Lord" which I gave them.

Questions were asked at that time. "Sister White, do you think that the Lord has any new and increased light for us as a people?" I answered, "Most assuredly. I do not only think so, but can speak understandingly. I know that there is precious truth to be unfolded to us if we are the people that are to stand in the day of God's preparation."

Ellen White Encourages Open-minded Study.— Then the question was asked whether I thought the matter had better drop where it was, after Brother Waggoner had stated his views of the law in Galatians. I said, "By no means. We want all on both sides of the question." But I stated that the spirit I had seen manifested at the meeting was unreasonable. I should insist that there be a right spirit, a Christlike spirit, manifested such as Elder E. J. Waggoner had shown all through the presentation of his views; and that this matter should not be handled in a debating style. The reason I should urge that this matter should be handled in a Christlike spirit was that there should be no thrust made against their brethren differing with them. As Elder E. J. Waggoner had conducted himself like a Christian gentleman they should do the same, giving the arguments on their side of the question in a straightforward manner. . . .

The Question of the Law in Galatians Not Vital.—The remark was made, "If our views of Galatians are not correct, then we have not the third angel's message, and our position goes by the board; there is nothing to our faith."

I said, "Brethren, here is the very thing I have been telling you. This statement is not true. It is an extravagant, exaggerated statement. If it is made in the discussion of this question I shall feel it my duty to set this matter before all that are assembled, and whether they hear or forbear tell them the statement is incorrect.

The question at issue is not a vital question and should not be treated as such. The wonderful importance and magnitude of this subject has been exaggerated, and for this reason—through misconception and perverted ideas—we see the spirit that prevails at this meeting, which is unchristlike, and which we should never see exhibited among brethren. There has been a spirit of Pharisaism coming in among us which I shall lift my voice against wherever it may be revealed." . . .

I could see a great want of wise discrimination and of good judgment. The evil of such things has often been presented before me. The difference of opinion was made apparent to both believers and unbelievers. These things made such an impression upon my mind that I felt that my brethren had met with a great change. This matter had been set before me while I was in Europe, in figures and symbols, but the explanation was given me afterwards so that I was not left in the dark in regard to the state of our churches and of our ministering brethren. . . .

I returned to my room questioning what was the best course for me to pursue. Many hours that night were spent in prayer in regard to the law in Galatians. This was a mere mote. Whichever way was in accordance with a "Thus saith the Lord," my soul would say, Amen, and Amen. But the spirit that was controlling our brethren was so unlike the spirit of Jesus, so contrary to the spirit that should be exercised toward each other, it filled my soul with anguish.

In the next morning's meeting for the ministers I had some plain things to say to my brethren, which I dared not withhold. The salt had lost its savor, the fine gold become dim. Spiritual darkness was upon the people and many evidenced that they were moved with a power from beneath, for the result was just such as would be the case when they were not under the illumination of the Spirit of God.

What pages of history were being made by the recording angel! The leaven had indeed done its sharp work, and nearly leavened the lump. I had a message of reproof and warning for my brethren, I knew. My soul was pressed with anguish. To say these things to my brethren causes me far greater anguish than they caused those to whom they were addressed. Through the grace of Christ I experienced a divine compelling power to stand before my ministering brethren, in the name of the Lord, hoping and praying that the Lord would open the blind eyes. I was strengthened to say the words which my secretary took in shorthand.—Manuscript 24, 1888.

Minneapolis a Proving Ground.—The Lord was testing and proving His people who had had great light, whether they would walk in it or turn from it under temptation, for but few know what manner of spirit they are of until circumstances shall be of a character to test the spirit which prompts to action. In many the natural heart is a controlling power, and yet they do not suppose that pride and prejudice are entertained as cherished guests, and work in the words and actions against light and truth. Our brethren who have occupied leading positions in the work and the cause of God should have been so closely connected with the Source of all light that they would not call light darkness and darkness light. . . .

Righteousness by Faith Does Not Downgrade the Law.—Holding up Christ as our only source of strength, presenting His matchless love in having the guilt of the sins of men charged to His account and His own righteousness imputed to man, in no case does away with the law or detracts from its dignity. Rather, it places it where the correct light shines upon and glorifies it. This is done only through the light reflected from the cross of Calvary. The law is complete and full in the great plan of salvation, only as it is presented in the light shining from the crucified and risen Saviour. This can only spiritually discerned. It kindles in the heart of the beholder ardent faith, hope, and joy that Christ is his righteousness. This joy is only for those who love and keep the words of Jesus, which are the words of God.

Were my brethren in the light the words that the Lord gave me for them would find a response in the hearts of those for whom I labored. As I saw that the hearts with which I longed to be in harmony were padlocked by prejudice and unbelief, I thought best for me to leave them. My purpose was to go from Minneapolis the first of the week. . . .

I wished to meditate, to pray, [that I might know] in what manner we could work to present the subject of sin and atonement in the Bible light before the people. They were greatly needing this kind of instruction that they might give the light to others and have the blessed privilege of being workers together with God in gathering in and bringing home the sheep of His fold. What power must we have from God that icy hearts, having only a legal religion, should see the better things provided for them—Christ and His righteousness! A life-giving message was needed to give life to the dry bones.—Manuscript 24, 1888.

Ellen White's Appraisal on the Closing Day

(Written to a member of her home family, November 4, 1888)

Our meeting [The Minneapolis General Conference session] is closed. I have on last Sabbath given my last discourse. There seemed for the first time to be considerable feeling in the congregation. I called them forward for prayers although the church was densely packed. Quite a number came forward. The Lord gave me the spirit of supplication and His blessing came upon me. I did not go out to meeting this morning. This has been a most laborious meeting for Willie, and I have had to watch at every point lest there should be moves made, resolutions passed, that would prove detrimental to the future work.

I have spoken nearly twenty times with great freedom and we believe that this meeting will result in great good. We know not the future, but we feel that Jesus stands at the helm and we shall not be shipwrecked. My courage and faith have been good and have not failed me, notwithstanding we have had the hardest and most incomprehensible tug of war we have ever had among our people. The matter cannot be explained by pen unless I should write many, many pages; so I had better not undertake the job.

Elder Olsen is to be president of the General Conference and Brother Dan Jones, of Kansas, is to help him. Elder Haskell will serve until Brother Olsen shall come from Europe.* I cannot tell what the future may reveal, but we shall remain for about four weeks in Battle Creek and get out a testimony that should come out just now without delay. Then we can see how matters move at the great center of the work. We are determined to do all we can in the fear of God to help our people in this emergency.

A sick man's mind has had a controlling power over the General Conference Committee and the ministers have been the shadow and echo of Elder Butler about as long as it is healthy and for the good of the cause. Envy, evil surmisings, jealousies have been working like leaven until the whole lump seemed to be leavened. . . .

Today, Sunday, I have not attended meeting, but have had to visit considerably. I am grateful to God for the strength and freedom and power of His spirit in bearing my testimony, although it has made the least impression upon many minds than at any period before in my history. Satan has seemed to have power to hinder my work in a wonderful degree, but I tremble to think what would have been in this meeting if we had not been here. God would have worked in some way to prevent this spirit brought to the meeting, having a controlling power. But we are not the least discouraged. We trust in the Lord God of Israel. The truth will triumph and we

---

* In the absence of George I. Butler, president of the General Conference, Elder Haskell chaired the General Conference session. Shortly after the close of the session, W. C. White was asked to serve as acting General Conference president, which he did for nearly six months.

mean to triumph with it.

We think of you all at home and would be pleased to be with you, but our wishes are not to be consulted. The Lord is our Leader, let Him direct our course and we will follow where He leads the way.—Letter 82, 1888.

Two Excerpts From Minneapolis Sermons*

Now what we want to present is, how you may advance in the divine life. We hear many excuses: I cannot live up to this or that.

What do you mean by this or that? Do you mean that it was an imperfect sacrifice that was made for the fallen race upon Calvary, that there is not sufficient grace and power granted us that we may work away from our own natural defects and tendencies, that it was not a whole Saviour that was given us?

Or do you mean to cast reproach upon God? Well, you say, It was Adam's sin. You say, I am not guilty of that, and I am not responsible for his guilt and fall. Here all these natural tendencies are in me, and I am not to blame if I act out these natural tendencies. Who is to blame? Is God?

Why did God let Satan have this power over human nature? These are accusations against the God of heaven, and He will give you an opportunity, if you want it, of finally bringing your accusations against Him. Then He will bring His accusations against you when you are brought into His court of judgment.—Manuscript 8, 1888, Sabbath, Oct. 20, 1888.†

If God could have changed His law to meet man in his fallen condition, Christ need not have come to this world. Because the law was immutable, unchangeable, God sent His only begotten Son to die for the fallen race. But did the Saviour take upon Himself the guilt of

---

* Ellen White spoke twenty times at Minneapolis, but did not there enter into presentations on righteousness by faith. Rather, she labored to lead men and women to open their minds to Bible-based truth.

† Her talks that were reported appear as a 60-page appendix (pp. 242-302) in the book *Through Crisis to Victory*.—Compilers.

human beings and impute to them His righteousness in
order that they might continue to violate the precepts of
Jehovah? No, no! Christ came because there was no
possibility of man's keeping the law in his own strength.
He came to bring him strength to obey the precepts of
the law. And the sinner, repenting of his transgression,
may come to God and say, "O Father, I plead forgiveness
through the merits of a crucified and risen Saviour." God
will accept all who come to Him in the name of
Jesus.—Manuscript 17, 1888, Sunday, Oct. 21, 1888.

Three Months After Minneapolis

When We Do Our Best.—Thank God it is not too
late for wrongs to be righted. Christ looks at the spirit,
and when He sees us carrying our burden with faith, His
perfect holiness atones for our shortcomings. When we
do our best, He becomes our righteousness. It takes
every ray of light that God sends to us to make us the
light of the world.—Letter 22, 1889. (Published in
Selected Messages, book 1, p. 368.)

The Reception in the Field of the Message of
Righteousness by Faith

Special meetings began at South Lancaster on Friday,
January 11 [1889]. We were glad to find the church well
filled with those who had come to receive benefit from
the meetings.* . . . Delegates were present from Maine,
Connecticut, Massachusetts, and other States. We realized that there was a work to be done in setting things
in order, which man's best efforts could not accomplish
without the aid of God. Our hearts were drawn out in
earnest supplication to God that He would work in our
behalf. . . .

We felt burdened for those who had been bearing

---

* This was among the first meetings in which Ellen White participated in
presenting the message of righteousness by faith in the field subsequent to the
Minneapolis Conference. Through 1889 she frequently led out in carrying the
message to the churches. Some of her sermons were reported, as was the one at
Ottawa, Kansas, on May 11. This typical sermon is published in *Faith and
Works*, pp. 63-79.

the message of truth to others, lest they should close their hearts to some of the precious rays of heaven's light that God has sent them. Jesus rejoiced when His followers received His messages of truth. . . .

On Sabbath afternoon, many hearts were touched, and many souls were fed on the bread that cometh down from heaven. After the discourse we enjoyed a precious social meeting. The Lord came very near, and convicted souls of their great need of His grace and love. We felt the necessity of presenting Christ as a Saviour who was not afar off, but nigh at hand. When the Spirit of God begins to work upon the hearts of men, the fruit is seen in confession of sin and restitution for wrongs. All through the meetings, as the people sought to draw nearer to God, they brought forth works meet for repentance by confessing one to another where they had wronged each other by word or act. . . .

There were many, even among the ministers, who saw the truth as it is in Jesus in a light in which they had never before reviewed it. They saw the Saviour as a sin-pardoning Saviour, and the truth as the sanctifier of the soul. "If we confess our sins, he is faithful and just to forgive us our sins, and to cleanse us from all unrighteousness." . . .

Many Hold Distorted Views.—There are many who seem to feel that they have a great work to do themselves before they can come to Christ for His salvation. They seem to think that Jesus will come in at the very last of their struggle, and give them help by putting the finishing touch to their lifework. It seems difficult for them to understand that Christ is a complete Saviour, and able to save to the uttermost all that come unto God by Him. They lose sight of the fact that Christ Himself is "the way, the truth, and the life." When we individually rest upon Christ, with full assurance of faith, trusting alone to the efficacy of His blood to cleanse from all sin, we shall have peace in believing that what God has promised He is able to perform. . . .

The Very Message Presented.—As our brethren

and sisters opened their hearts to the light, they obtained a better knowledge of what constitutes faith. The Lord was very precious; He was ready to strengthen His people. The meetings continued a week beyond their first appointment. The school was dismissed, and all made earnest work of seeking the Lord. Elder Jones came from Boston, and labored most earnestly for the people, speaking twice and sometimes three times a day. The flock of God were fed with soul-nourishing food. The very message the Lord has sent to the people of this time was presented in the discourses. Meetings were in progress from early morning till night, and the results were highly satisfactory.

Both students and teachers have shared largely in the blessing of God. The deep movings of the Spirit of God have been felt upon almost every heart. The general testimony was borne by those who attended the meeting that they had obtained an experience beyond anything they had known before. They testified their joy that Christ had forgiven their sins. Their hearts were filled with thanksgiving and praise to God. Sweet peace was in their souls. They loved everyone, and felt that they could rest in the love of God.

I have never seen a revival work go forward with such thoroughness, and yet remain so free from all undue excitement.

There were many who testified that as the searching truths had been presented, they had been convicted in the light of the law as transgressors. They had been trusting in their own righteousness. Now they saw it as filthy rags, in comparison with the righteousness of Christ, which is alone acceptable to God.

While they had not been open transgressors, they saw themselves depraved and degraded in heart. They had substituted other gods in the place of their heavenly Father. They had struggled to refrain from sin, but had trusted in their own strength. We should go to Jesus just as we are, confess our sins, and cast our helpless souls upon our compassionate Redeemer.—*The Review and Herald,* March 5, 1889.

Need for a Proper Concept of Righteousness by Faith

By invitation I made some remarks in the ministers' tent,* to the ministers. We talked some in regard to the best plans to be arranged to educate the people here upon this very ground in reference to home religion.

Many people seem to be ignorant of what constitutes faith. Many complain of darkness and discouragements. I asked, "Are your faces turned toward Jesus? Are you beholding Him, the Sun of Righteousness? You need plainly to define to the churches the matter of faith and entire dependence upon the righteousness of Christ. In your talks and prayers there has been so little dwelling upon Christ, His matchless love, His great sacrifice made in our behalf, that Satan has nearly eclipsed the views we should have and must have of Jesus Christ. We must trust less in human beings for spiritual help and more, far more, in approaching Jesus Christ as our Redeemer. We may dwell with a determined purpose on the heavenly attributes of Jesus Christ; we may talk of His love, we may tell and sing of His mercies, we may make Him our own personal Saviour. Then we are one with Christ. We love that which Christ loved, we hate sin, that which Christ hated. These things must be talked of, dwelt upon."

I address the ministers. Lead the people along step by step, dwelling upon Christ's efficiency until, by a living faith, they see Jesus as He is—see Him in His fullness, a sin-pardoning Saviour, One who can pardon all our transgressions. It is by beholding that we become changed into His likeness. This is present truth. We have talked the law. This is right. But we have only casually lifted up Christ as the sin-pardoning Saviour.

We are to keep before the mind the sin-pardoning

---

* Counsel to ministers at the Colorado camp meeting, September 13, 1889, on presenting righteousness by faith.

Saviour. But we are to present Him in His true position—coming to die to magnify the law of God and make it honorable, and yet to justify the sinner who shall depend wholly upon the merits of the blood of a crucified and risen Saviour. This is not made plain.

The soul-saving message, the third angel's message, is the message to be given to the world. The commandments of God and the faith of Jesus are both important, immensely important, and must be given with equal force and power. The first part of the message has been dwelt upon mostly, the last part casually. The faith of Jesus is not comprehended. We must talk it, we must live it, we must pray it, and educate the people to bring this part of the message into their home life. "Let this mind be in you, which was also in Christ Jesus" (Phil. 2:5).

Christ-filled Discourses Needed.—There have been entire discourses, dry and Christless, in which Jesus has scarcely been named. The speaker's heart is not subdued and melted by the love of Jesus. He dwells upon dry theories. No great impression is made. The speaker has not the divine unction, and how can he move the hearts of the people? We need to repent and be converted—yes, the preacher converted. The people must have Jesus lifted up before them, and they must be entreated to "Look and live."

Why are our lips so silent upon the subject of Christ's righteousness and His love for the world? Why do we not give to the people that which will revive and quicken them into a new life? The apostle Paul is filled with transport and adoration as he declares, "Without controversy great is the mystery of godliness: God was manifest in the flesh, justified in the Spirit, seen of angels, preached unto the Gentiles, believed on in the world, received up into glory" (1 Tim. 3:16).

"Let this mind be in you, which was also in Christ Jesus: who, being in the form of God, thought it not robbery to be equal with God: but made himself of no reputation, and took upon him the form of a servant, and was made in the likeness of men: and being found in fashion as a man, he humbled himself, and became obedient unto death, even the death of the cross. . . . That at the name of Jesus every knee should bow, of things in heaven, and things in earth, and things under the earth; and that every tongue should confess that Jesus Christ is Lord, to the glory of God the Father" (Phil. 2:5-11).

"In whom we have redemption through his blood, even the forgiveness of sins: who is the image of the invisible God, the firstborn of every creature: for by him were all things created, that are in heaven, and that are in earth, visible and invisible, whether they be thrones, or dominions, or principalities, or powers: all things were created by him, and for him: and he is before all things, and by him all things consist" (Col. 1:14-17).

This is the grand and heavenly theme that has in a large degree been left out of the discourses because Christ is not formed within the human mind. And Satan has had his way that it shall be thus, that Christ should not be the theme of contemplation and adoration. This name, so powerful, so essential, should be on every tongue.

"Whereof I am made a minister, according to the dispensation of God which is given to me for you, to fulfill the word of God; even the mystery which hath been hid from ages and from generations, but now is made manifest to his saints: to whom God would make known what is the riches of the glory of this mystery among the Gentiles; which is Christ in you, the hope of glory: whom we preach, warning every man, and teaching every man in all wisdom; that we may present every man perfect in Christ Jesus: whereunto I also labor, striving according to his working, which worketh in me mightily" (Col. 1:25-29).

Here is the work of the ministers of Christ. Because this work has not been done, because Christ and His character, His words, and His work have not been brought before the people, the religious state of the

churches testifies against their teachers. The churches are
ready to die because little of Christ is presented. They
have not spiritual life and spiritual discernment.

**Fear of the Message of Righteousness by
Faith.**—The teachers of the people have not themselves
become acquainted by living experience with the Source
of their dependence and their strength. And when the
Lord raises up men and sends them with the very
message for this time to give to the people—a message
which is not a new truth, but the very same that Paul
taught, that Christ Himself taught—it is to them a
strange doctrine. They begin to caution the people—
who are ready to die because they have not been
strengthened with the lifting up of Christ before
them—"Do not be too hasty. Better wait, and not take
up with this matter until you know more about it." And
the ministers preach the same dry theories, when the
people need fresh manna.

The character of Christ is an infinitely perfect character, and He must be lifted up, He must be brought
prominently into view, for He is the power, the might,
the sanctification and righteousness of all who believe in
Him. The men who have had a Pharisaical spirit, think
if they hold to the good old theories, and have no part in
the message sent of God to His people, they will be in a
good and safe position. So thought the Pharisees of old,
and their example should warn ministers off that self-
satisfied ground.

Present Inspiring Themes of the Gospel.—We
need a power to come upon us now and stir us up to
diligence and earnest faith. Then, baptized with the
Holy Spirit, we shall have Christ formed within, the
hope of glory. Then we will exhibit Christ as the divine
object of our faith and our love. We will talk of Christ,
we will pray to Christ and about Christ. We will praise
His holy name. We will present before the people His
miracles, His self-denial, His self-sacrifice, His sufferings, and His crucifixion, His resurrection and triumphant ascension. These are the inspiring themes of the

gospel, to awaken love and intense fervor in every heart. Here are the treasures of wisdom and knowledge, a fountain inexhaustible. The more you seek of this experience, the greater will be the value of your life.

The living water may be drawn from the fountain and yet there is no diminution of the supply. Ministers of the gospel would be powerful men if they set the Lord always before them and devoted their time to the study of His adorable character. If they did this, there would be no apostasies, there would be none separated from the conference because they have, by their licentious practices, disgraced the cause of God and put Jesus to an open shame. The powers of every minister of the gospel should be employed to educate the believing churches to receive Christ by faith as their personal Saviour, to take Him into their very lives and make Him their Pattern to learn of Jesus, believe in Jesus, and exalt Jesus. The minister should himself dwell on the character of Christ. He should ponder the truth, and meditate upon the mysteries of redemption, especially the mediatorial work of Christ for this time.

Dwell More on the Incarnation and Atonement.—If Christ is all and in all to every one of us, why are not His incarnation and His atoning sacrifice dwelt upon more in the churches? Why are not hearts and tongues employed in the Redeemer's praise? This will be the employment of the powers of the redeemed through the ceaseless ages of eternity.

We need to have a living connection with God ourselves in order to teach Jesus. Then we can give the living personal experience of what Christ is to us by experience and faith. We have received Christ and with divine earnestness we can tell that which is an abiding power with us. The people must be drawn to Christ. Prominence must be given to His saving efficacy.

The true learners, sitting at Christ's feet, discover the precious gems of truth uttered by our Saviour, and will discern their significance and appreciate their value. And more and more, as they become humble and teachable, will their understanding be opened to discover wondrous things out of His law, for Christ has presented them in clear, sharp lines.

The doctrine of grace and salvation through Jesus Christ is a mystery to a large share of those whose names are upon the church books. If Christ were upon the earth speaking to His people, He would reproach them for their slowness of comprehension. He would say to the slow and uncomprehending, "I have left in your possession truths which concern your salvation, of which you do not suspect the value."

Oh, that it might be said of ministers who are preaching to the people and to the churches, "Then opened he their understanding, that they might understand the scriptures"! (Luke 24:45). I tell you in the fear of God that up to this time, the Bible truths connected with the great plan of redemption are but feebly understood. The truth will be continually unfolding, expanding, and developing, for it is divine, like its Author.

How Jesus Taught the People.—Jesus did not give full comments or continued discourses upon doctrines, but He oft spoke in short sentences, as one sowing the heavenly grains of doctrines like pearls which need to be gathered up by a discerning laborer. The doctrines of faith and grace are brought to view everywhere He taught. Oh, why do not ministers give to the churches the very food which will give them spiritual health and vigor? The result will be a rich experience in practical obedience to the Word of God. Why do the ministers not strengthen the things that remain that are ready to die?

When about to leave His disciples, Christ was in search of the greatest comfort He could give them. He promised them the Holy Spirit—the Comforter—to combine with man's human effort. What promise is less experienced, less fulfilled to the church, than the promise of the Holy Spirit? When this blessing, which would bring all blessings in its train, is dropped out, the sure result is spiritual drought. This is the reproach that meets the sermonizer. The church must arise and no longer be content with the meager dew.

Our Need for the Holy Spirit.—Oh, why do our church members stop short of their privileges? They are not personally alive to the necessity of the influence of the Spirit of God. The church may, like Mary, say, "They have taken away my Lord, and I know not where they have laid him" (John 20:13).

Ministers preaching present truth will assent to the necessity of the influence of the Spirit of God in the conviction of sin and the conversion of souls, and this influence must attend the preaching of the Word, but they do not feel its importance sufficiently to have a deep and practical knowledge of the same. The scantiness of the grace and power of the divine influence of the truth upon their own hearts prevents them from discerning spiritual things and from presenting its positive necessity upon the church. So they go crippling along, dwarfed in religious growth, because they have in their ministry a legal religion. The power of the grace of God is not felt to be a living, effectual necessity, an abiding principle.

Oh, that all could see this and embrace the message given them of God! He has raised up His servants to present truth that, because it involves lifting the cross, has been lost sight of, and is buried beneath the rubbish of formality. It must be rescued and be reset in the framework of present truth. Its claims must be asserted, and its position given it in the third angel's message.

Let the many ministers of Christ sanctify a fast, call a solemn assembly, and seek God while He is to be found. Call upon Him while you are now lying at the foot of the cross of Calvary. Divest yourselves of all pride and as representative guardians of the churches, weep between the porch and the altar, and cry "Spare Thy people, Lord, and give not Thine heritage to reproach. Take from us what Thou wilt, but withhold not Thy Holy Spirit from us, Thy people." Pray, oh, pray for the outpouring of the Spirit of God!—Manuscript 27, 1889.

22.

Emphasis on Salvation
Theme—1890-1908

The Provision for Salvation.—Penances, mortifications of the flesh, constant confession of sin, without sincere repentance; fasts, festivals, and outward observances, unaccompanied by true devotion—all these are of no value whatever. The sacrifice of Christ is sufficient; He made a whole, efficacious offering to God; and human effort without the merit of Christ, is worthless. We not only dishonor God by taking this course but we destroy our present and future usefulness. A failure to appreciate the value of the offering of Christ, has a debasing influence; it blights our expectations, and makes us fall short of our privileges; it leads us to receive unsound and perilous theories concerning the salvation that has been purchased for us at infinite cost. The plan of salvation is not understood to be that through which divine power is brought to man in order that his human effort may be wholly successful.

To be pardoned in the way that Christ pardons, is not only to be forgiven, but to be renewed in the spirit of our mind. The Lord says, "A new heart will I give unto thee." The image of Christ is to be stamped upon the very mind, heart, and soul. The apostle says, "But we have the mind of Christ" (1 Cor. 2:16). Without the transforming process which can come alone through divine power, the original propensities to sin are left in the heart in all their strength, to forge new chains, to impose a slavery that can never be broken by human power. But men can never enter heaven with their old tastes, inclinations, idols, ideas, and theories. Heaven would be no place of joy to them; for everything would be in collision with their tastes, appetites, and inclinations, and painfully opposed to their natural and cultivated traits of character.

Happiness is the result of holiness and conformity to the will of God. Those who would be saints in heaven must first be saints upon the earth; for when we leave this earth, we shall take our character with us, and this will be simply taking with us some of the elements of heaven imparted to us through the righteousness of Christ.—*Review and Herald*, Aug. 19, 1890.

Justification and Sanctification Accomplished Through Faith—1890.—When through repentance and faith we accept Christ as our Saviour, the Lord pardons our sins, and remits the penalty prescribed for the transgression of the law. The sinner then stands before God as a just person; he is taken into favor with Heaven, and through the Spirit has fellowship with the Father and the Son.

Then there is yet another work to be accomplished, and this is of a progressive nature. The soul is to be sanctified through the truth. And this also is accomplished through faith. For it is only by the grace of Christ, which we receive through faith, that the character can be transformed.

It is important that we understand clearly the nature of faith. There are many who believe that Christ is the Saviour of the world, that the gospel is true and reveals the plan of salvation, yet they do not possess saving faith. They are intellectually convinced of the truth, but this is not enough; in order to be justified, the sinner must have that faith that appropriates the merits of Christ to his own soul. We read that the devils "believe, and tremble," but their belief does not bring them justification, neither will the belief of those who give a merely intellectual assent to the truths of the Bible bring them the benefits of salvation. This belief fails of reaching the vital point, for the truth does not engage the heart or transform the character.

In genuine, saving faith, there is trust in God, through the belief in the great atoning sacrifice made by the Son of God on Calvary. In Christ, the justified believer beholds his only hope and deliverer. Belief may exist without trust, but confidence born of trust cannot exist without faith. Every sinner brought to a knowledge of the saving power of Christ, will make manifest this trust in greater degree as he advances in experience.— *Signs of the Times,* Nov. 3, 1890.

Resisting Temptation—1891.—Many seem to think that it is impossible not to fall under temptation, that they have no power to overcome, and they sin against God with their lips, talking discouragement and doubt, instead of faith and courage. Christ was tempted in all points like as we are, yet without sin. He said, "The prince of this world cometh, and hath nothing in me." What does this mean? It means that the prince of evil could find no vantage ground in Christ for his temptation; and so it may be with us.—*The Review and Herald,* May 19, 1891.

Perfection Not Reached by One Bound—1891.—We are looking beyond time; we are looking to eternity. We are trying to live in such a way that Christ can say, "Well done, good and faithful servant." Let us live, every one of us, in that way. We may make mistakes; we may err; but God will not leave us in error. "If we sin we have an advocate with the Father, Jesus Christ the righteous." There is hope for us; we are prisoners of hope.

Let us grasp the rich promises of God. The garden of God is full of rich promises. Oh, let us gather them; let us take them home; let us show that we believe in God. Let us take Him at His word; let not one of us be found distrusting God or doubting Him.

Let us be growing Christians. We are not to stand still. We are to be in advance today of what we were yesterday; every day learning to be more trustful, more fully relying upon Jesus. Thus we are to grow up. You do not at one bound reach perfection; sanctification is the work of a lifetime. . . .

I remember in 1843 a man and his wife . . . who expected the Lord to come in 1844, and they were waiting and watching. And every day they would pray to God; before they would bid each other goodnight, they would say, "It may be the Lord will come when we are asleep, and we want to be ready." The husband would ask his wife if he had said a word during the day that she had thought was not in accordance with the truth and the faith which they professed, and then she would ask him the same question. Then they would bow before the Lord and ask Him if they had sinned in thought or word or action, and if so that He would forgive that transgression. Now we want just such simplicity as this.

You want to be like little children, hanging upon the merits of a crucified and risen Saviour, and then you will be fortified. How? The angels of God will be around you as a wall of fire. The righteousness of Christ, which you claim, goes before you, and the glory of God is your rearward. God sanctify the tongues; God sanctify the thoughts; God sanctify our minds, that we may dwell upon heavenly themes, and then that we may impart that knowledge and light to others. There is great advancement for us, and do not stop here. May God help you to make the most of your responsibilities.—Manuscript 9, 1891.

Justification Explained—1891.—Justification by faith is to many a mystery. A sinner is justified by God when he repents of his sins. He sees Jesus upon the cross of Calvary. Why all this suffering? The law of Jehovah has been broken. The law of God's government in heaven and earth has been transgressed, and the penalty of sin is pronounced to be death. But "God so loved the world, that he gave his only begotten Son, that whosoever believeth in him should not perish, but have everlasting life." Oh, what love, what matchless love! Christ, the Son of God, dying for guilty man!

The sinner views the spirituality of the law of God and its eternal obligations. He sees the love of God in providing a substitute and surety for guilty man, and that substitute is One equal with God. This display of grace in the gift of salvation to the world fills the sinner with amazement. This love of God to man breaks every barrier down. He comes to the cross, which has been placed midway between divinity and humanity, and repents of his sins of transgression, because Christ has been drawing him to Himself. He does not expect the law to cleanse him from sin, for there is no pardoning quality in the law to save the transgressors of the law. He looks to the atoning Sacrifice as his only hope, through repentance toward God—because the laws of His government have been broken—and faith toward our Lord Jesus Christ as the One who can save and cleanse the sinner from every transgression.

The mediatorial work of Christ commenced with the commencement of human guilt and suffering and misery, as soon as man became a transgressor. The law was not abolished to save man and bring him into union with God. But Christ assumed the office of his surety and deliverer in becoming *sin for man,* that man might become the righteousness of God in and through Him who was one with the Father. Sinners can be justified by God only when He pardons their sins, remits the punishment they deserve, and treats them as though they were really just and had not sinned, receiving them into divine favor and treating them as if they were righteous. They are justified alone through the imputed righteousness of Christ. The Father accepts the Son, and through the atoning sacrifice of His Son accepts the sinner.

A General Faith Is Not Enough.—A general faith is entertained by many, and their assent is given that Christianity is the only hope for perishing souls. But to believe this intellectually is not sufficient to the saving of the soul. . . .

There will be need not only of faith but of a trust in God. This is the true faith of Abraham, a faith which produced fruits. "Abraham believed God, and it was imputed unto him for righteousness" (James 2:23). When God told him to offer his son as a sacrifice it was the same voice that had spoken telling him to leave his country and go into a land which God would show him. Abraham was saved by faith in Christ as verily as the sinner is saved by faith in Christ today.

The faith that justifies always produces first true repentance, and then good works, which are the fruit of that faith. There is no saving faith that does not produce good fruit. God gave Christ to our world to become the sinner's substitute. The moment true faith in the merits of the costly atoning sacrifice is exercised, claiming Christ as a personal Saviour, that moment the sinner is justified before God, because he is pardoned.—Manuscript 46, 1891.

How to Overcome—1891.—John pointed the people to the Lamb of God who taketh away the sins of the world. He said, "Behold the Lamb of God, which taketh away the sin of the world." There is a great deal in that "taketh away." The question is, Shall we keep on sinning as though it were an impossibility for us to overcome? How are we to overcome? As Christ overcame, and that is the only way. He prayed to His heavenly Father. We can do the same. . . . When tempted to speak wrong and do wrong resist Satan and say, I will not surrender my will to your control. I will cooperate with divine power and through grace be conqueror.—Manuscript 83, 1891.

Christ Makes Up for Our Unavoidable Deficiencies—1891.—Jesus loves His children, even if they err. They belong to Jesus and we are to treat them as the purchase of the blood of Jesus Christ. Any unreasonable course pursued toward them is written in the books as against Jesus Christ. He keeps His eye upon them, and when they do their best, calling upon God for His help, be assured the service will be accepted, although imperfect.

Jesus is perfect. Christ's righteousness is imputed unto them, and He will say, "Take away the filthy garments from him and clothe him with change of raiment." Jesus makes up for our unavoidable deficiencies. Where Christians are faithful to each other, true and loyal to the Captain of the Lord's host, never betraying trusts into the enemy's hands, they will be transformed into Christ's character. Jesus will abide in their hearts by faith.—Letter 17a, 1891. (See also a similar statement made in 1885 in *Faith and Works*, p. 50.)

Flee to Christ as Soon as Sin Is Committed—1892.—Many do not pray. They feel under condemnation for sin, and they think they must not come to God until they have done something to merit His favor or until God has forgotten about their transgressions. They say, "I cannot hold up holy hands before God without wrath or doubting, and therefore I cannot come." So they remain away from Christ, and are committing sin all the time in so doing, for without Him you can do nothing but evil.

Just as soon as you commit sin, you should flee to the throne of grace, and tell Jesus all about it. You should be filled with sorrow for sin, because through sin you have weakened your own spirituality, grieved the heavenly angels, and wounded and bruised the loving heart of your Redeemer. When you have asked Jesus in contrition of soul for His forgiveness, believe that He has forgiven you. Do not doubt His divine mercy or refuse the comfort of His infinite love.—*Bible Echo*, Feb. 1, 1892. (Discourse at Melbourne, Australia, Dec. 19, 1891.)

What If We Sin After We Have Been Forgiven?—1892.—It is the Holy Spirit that imparts repentance to us. Jesus draws us to Himself through the agency of His divine Spirit; and through faith in His blood we are cleansed from sin: "for the blood of Jesus

Christ his Son, cleanseth us from all sin" (1 John 1:7). "If we confess our sins, he is faithful and just to forgive us our sins, and to cleanse us from all unrighteousness" (verse 9).

But suppose that we sin after we have been forgiven, after we have become the children of God, then need we despair?—No: for John writes: "My little children, these things I write unto you, that ye sin not. And if any man sin, we have an advocate with the Father, Jesus Christ the righteous" (chap. 2:1). Jesus is in the heavenly courts, pleading with the Father in our behalf. He presents our prayers, mingling with them the precious incense of His own merit, that our prayers may be acceptable to the Father. He puts the fragrance into our prayers, and the Father hears us because we ask for the very things which we need, and we become to others a savor of life unto life.

Jesus came to suffer in our behalf, that He might impart to us His righteousness. There is but one way of escape for us, and that is found only in becoming partakers of the divine nature.

But many say that Jesus was not like us, that He was not as we are in the world, that He was divine, and that we cannot overcome as He overcame. But Paul writes, "Verily he took not on him the nature of angels; but he took on him the seed of Abraham. Wherefore in all things it behooved him to be made like unto his brethren, that he might be a merciful and faithful high priest in things pertaining to God, to make reconciliation for the sins of the people. For in that he himself hath suffered being tempted, he is able to succour them that are tempted" (Heb. 2:16-18). "For we have not an high priest which cannot be touched with the feeling of our infirmities; but was in all points tempted like as we are, yet without sin. Let us therefore come boldly unto the throne of grace, that we may obtain mercy, and find grace to help in time of need" (chap. 4:15, 16). Jesus says, "To him that overcometh will I grant to sit with me in my throne, even as I also overcame, and am set down with my father in his throne" (Rev. 3:21).

Jesus encircled the race with His humanity, and united divinity with humanity; thus moral power is brought to man through the merits of Jesus. Those who profess His name through His grace are to sanctify themselves that they may exert a sanctifying influence on all with whom they associate.—*The Review and Herald,* March 1, 1892.

No Time to Fold Our Hands—1892.—As we come to feel our utter reliance upon Christ for salvation, are we to fold our hands, and say, "I have nothing to do; I am saved; Jesus has done it all"?—No, we are to put forth every energy that we may become partakers of the divine nature. We are to be continually watching, waiting, praying, and working.

But do all that we may, we cannot pay a ransom for our souls. We can do nothing to originate faith, for faith is the gift of God; neither can we perfect it, for Christ is the finisher of our faith. It is all of Christ. All the longing after a better life is from Christ, and is an evidence that He is drawing you to Himself, and that you are responding to His drawing power.—*Bible Echo,* May 15, 1892.

Christ's Nature Implanted in Us—1894.—Truth, precious truth, is sanctifying in its influence. The sanctification of the soul by the operation of the Holy Spirit is the implanting of Christ's nature in humanity. It is the grace of our Lord Jesus Christ revealed in character, and the grace of Christ brought into active exercise in good works. Thus the character is transformed more and more perfectly after the image of Christ in righteousness and true holiness. There are broad requirements in divine truth stretching out into one line after another of good works. The truths of the gospel are not unconnected; uniting they form one string of heavenly jewels, as in the personal work of Christ, and like threads of gold they run through the whole of Christian work and experience.

Christ is the complete system of truth. He says, "I

am the way, the truth, and the life." All true believers center in Christ, their character is irradiated by Christ; all meet in Christ, and circulate about Christ. Truth comes from Heaven to purify and cleanse the human agent from every moral defilement. It leads to benevolent action, to kind, tender, thoughtful love toward the needy, the distressed, the suffering. This is practical obedience to the words of Christ.—Manuscript 34, 1894.

Satan Claimed to Be Sanctified—1894.—Satan claimed to be sanctified, and exalted himself above God even in the courts of heaven. So great was his deceptive power that he corrupted a large number of angels, and enlisted their sympathy in his selfish interest. When he tempted Christ in the wilderness he claimed that he was sanctified, that he was a pure angel from the heavenly courts; but Jesus was not deceived by his pretensions and neither will those be deceived who live by every word that proceedeth out of the mouth of God.

God will not accept a willful, imperfect obedience. Those who claim to be sanctified, and yet turn away their ears from hearing the law prove themselves to be the children of disobedience, whose carnal hearts are not subject to the law of God, and neither indeed can be.—Manuscript 40, 1894.

Faith and Good Works—1895.—Our acceptance with God is sure only through His beloved Son, and good works are but the result of the working of His sin-pardoning love. They are no credit to us, and we have nothing accorded to us for our good works by which we may claim a part in the salvation of our souls. Salvation is God's free gift to the believer, given to him for Christ's sake alone. The troubled soul may find peace through faith in Christ, and his peace will be in proportion to his faith and trust. He cannot present his good works as a plea for the salvation of his soul.

But are good works of no real value? Is the sinner who commits sin every day with impunity, regarded of God with the same favor as the one who through faith in

Christ tries to work in his integrity? The Scripture answers, "We are his workmanship, created in Christ Jesus unto good works, which God hath before ordained that we should walk in them."

In His divine arrangement, through His unmerited favor, the Lord has ordained that good works shall be rewarded. We are accepted through Christ's merit alone; and the acts of mercy, the deeds of charity, which we perform, are the fruits of faith; and they become a blessing to us; for men are to be rewarded according to their works.

It is the fragrance of the merit of Christ that makes our good works acceptable to God, and it is grace that enables us to do the works for which He rewards us. Our works in and of themselves have no merit. When we have done all that it is possible for us to do, we are to count ourselves as unprofitable servants. We deserve no thanks from God. We have only done what it was our duty to do, and our works could not have been performed in the strength of our own sinful natures.

The Lord has bidden us to draw nigh to Him and He will draw nigh to us; and drawing nigh to Him, we receive the grace by which to do those works which will be rewarded at His hands.—*Review and Herald*, Jan. 29, 1895.

Surrounded With Heaven's Atmosphere— 1898.—"We love him, because he first loved us" (1 John 4:19). True conversion, true sanctification, will be the cause of the change in our views and our feelings toward one another and toward God. "We have known and believed the love that God hath to us. God is love; and he that dwelleth in love dwelleth in God, and God in him" (verse 16). We must increase in faith. We must know the sanctification of the Spirit. In earnest prayer we must seek God, that the divine Spirit may work in us. God then will be glorified by the example of the human agent. We shall be workers together with God.

Sanctification of soul, body, and spirit will surround us with the atmosphere of heaven. If God has chosen us from eternity, it is that we might be holy, our conscience purged from dead works to serve the living God. We must not in any way make self our god. God has given Himself to die for us, that He might purify us from all iniquity. The Lord will carry on this work of perfection for us if we will allow ourselves to be controlled by Him. He carries on this work for our good and His own name's glory.

The Importance of Simple, Implicit Faith.—We must bear a living testimony to the people, presenting before them the simplicity of faith. We must take God at His word, and believe that He will do just as He has said. If He chastises us, it is that we may be partakers of His divine nature. It runs through all His designs and plans to carry on a daily sanctification in us. Shall we not see our work? Shall we not present to others their duty, the privilege they have of growing in grace and in the knowledge of Jesus Christ?

"This is the will of God, even your sanctification" (1 Thess. 4:3). We have not pressed forward to the mark of the prize of our high calling. Self has found too much room. Oh, let the work be done under the special direction of the Holy Spirit. The Lord demands all the powers of the mind and being. It is His will that we should be conformed to Him in will, in temper, in spirit, in our meditations. The work of righteousness cannot be carried forward unless we exercise implicit faith.

Move every day under God's mighty working power. The fruit of righteousness is quietness and assurance forever. If we had exercised more faith in God and had trusted less to our own ideas and wisdom, God would have manifested His power in a marked manner on human hearts. By a union with Him, by living faith, we are privileged to enjoy the virtue and efficacy of His mediation. Hence we are crucified with Christ, dead with Christ, risen with Christ, to walk in newness of life with Him.—Letter 105, 1898.

True Sanctification Needed—1902.—Two nights

ago, I awoke at ten o'clock, heavily burdened in regard to the lack of the Holy Spirit's working among our people. I rose and walked the room, pleading with the Lord to come closer, very much closer, to His people, endowing them with such power that they may work His work so mightily that through them may be revealed the abundant grace of Christ. . . .

In the Sermon on the Mount, Christ has given a definition of true sanctification. He lived a life of holiness. He was an object lesson of what His followers are to be. We are to be crucified with Christ, buried with Him, and then quickened by His Spirit. Then we are filled with His life.

The Work of a Lifetime.—Our sanctification is God's object in all His dealing with us. He has chosen us from eternity that we may be holy. Christ gave Himself for our redemption, that through our faith in His power to save from sin, we might be made complete in Him. In giving us His Word, He has given us bread from heaven. He declares that if we eat His flesh and drink His blood, we shall receive eternal life.

Why do we not dwell more upon this? Why do we not strive to make it easily understood, when it means so much? Why do not Christians open their eyes to see the work God requires them to do. Sanctification is the progressive work of a lifetime. The Lord declares, "This is the will of God, even your sanctification" (1 Thess. 4:3). Is it your will that your desires and inclinations shall be brought into conformity to the divine will?

As Christians, we have pledged ourselves to realize and fulfill our responsibilities and to show to the world that we have a close connection with God. Thus, through the godly words and works of His disciples, Christ is to be represented.

God demands of us perfect obedience to His law— the expression of His character. "Do we then make void the law through faith? God forbid: yea, we establish the law" (Rom. 3:31). This law is the echo of God's voice, saying to us, Holier, yes, holier still. Desire the fullness of the grace of Christ; yea, long—hunger and thirst—after righteousness. The promise is, "Ye shall be filled." Let your heart be filled with an intense longing for this righteousness, the work of which God's Word declares is peace, and its effect quietness and assurance forever.

Partakers of the Divine Nature.—It is our privilege to be partakers of the divine nature, having escaped the corruption that is in the world through lust. God has plainly stated that He requires us to be perfect; and because He requires this, He has made provision that we may be partakers of the divine nature. Only thus can we gain success in our striving for eternal life. The power is given by Christ. "As many as received him, to them gave he power to become the sons of God" (John 1:12).

God requires of us conformity to His image. Holiness is the reflection from His people of the bright rays of His glory. But in order to reflect this glory, man must work with God. The heart and mind must be emptied of all that leads to wrong. The Word of God must be read and studied with an earnest desire to gain from it spiritual power. The bread of heaven must be eaten and digested, that it may become a part of the life. Thus we gain eternal life. Then is answered the prayer of the Saviour, "Sanctify them through thy truth: thy word is truth."—Letter 153, 1902.

Opinions and Practices to Be Conformed to God's Word.—There are many who claim that they have been sanctified to God, and yet when the great standard of righteousness is presented to them they become greatly excited and manifest a spirit which proves that they know nothing of what it means to be sanctified. They have not the mind of Christ; for those who are truly sanctified will reverence and obey the Word of God as fast as it is opened to them, and they will express a strong desire to know what is truth on every point of doctrine. An exultant feeling is no evidence of sanctification. The assertion, "I am saved, I am saved," does not prove that the soul is saved or sanctified.

Many who are greatly excited are told that they are sanctified, when they have no intelligent idea of what the term means, for they know not the Scriptures or the power of God. They flatter themselves that they are in conformity to the will of God because they feel happy; but when they are tested, when the Word of God is brought to bear upon their experience, they stop their ears from hearing the truth, saying, "I am sanctified," and that puts an end to the controversy. They will have nothing to do with searching the Scriptures to know what is truth, and prove that they are fearfully self-deceived. Sanctification means very much more than a flight of feeling.

Excitement is not sanctification. Entire conformity to the will of our Father which is in heaven is alone sanctification, and the will of God is expressed in His holy law. The keeping of all the commandments of God is sanctification. Proving yourselves obedient children to God's Word is sanctification. The Word of God is to be our guide, not the opinions or ideas of men.—*The Review and Herald*, March 25, 1902.

Sanctification, An Experience in Continued Growth—1908.—If we keep our minds stayed upon Christ, He will come unto us as the rain, as the former and latter rain upon the earth. As the Sun of Righteousness, He will arise with healing in His wings. We may grow as the lily, revive as the corn, and grow as the vine.

By constantly looking to and patterning after Christ as our personal Saviour, we shall grow up into Him in all things. Our faith will grow, our conscience will be sanctified. We will more and more become like Christ in all our works and words. Thank God, we shall believe His Word. "The fruit of the Spirit is love, joy, peace, longsuffering, gentleness, goodness, faith, meekness, temperance: against such there is no law."—Letter 106, 1908.

Education—The Church School, and Universities of the World

INTRODUCTION

_____

In 1902 the community surrounding the St. Helena Sanitarium, a community in which Ellen White resided from 1901 until her death, was served by the one-room Crystal Springs public school. It was taught by a dedicated Seventh-day Adventist teacher, Mr. Anthony.

At the turn of the century, Seventh-day Adventists in some parts of the United States, largely as the result of Ellen White's counsel, were just moving into the establishment of church schools for the children of grade-school age. At 6:00 A.M. on Monday, July 14, 1902, Ellen White addressed the members of the Sanitarium church, urging the establishment of a church school, and as an incentive offered to provide the use of a nearby portion of her land at Elmshaven for the project. Excerpts from the timely address she gave open this section.

The Sanitarium church accepted Ellen White's proposal, but when the school opened in the fall no provision was made for small children, because it was reasoned that those under eight or ten years of age should be taught at home in harmony with Ellen White's instruction given earlier.

Not all parents were prepared to meet the ideal she set forth in her earlier writings, and this left not a few children to drift without discipline or proper training during their childhood years. The one deterrent to the church's making provision for the younger children was the oft-quoted E. G. White statement written in 1872 that "Parents should be the only teachers of their children until they have reached eight or ten years of age."—*Testimonies*, vol. 3, p. 137.

There seemed to be a marked division of thinking on the part of church officers and members on this important question.

As time went on the church school board arranged for an interview with Ellen White at her home early Thursday morning, January 14, 1904, to discuss this question of school-age attendance and the responsibility of the church for the education of young children. W. C. White saw it as rather a landmark meeting that would set a pattern for other church schools across the land.

Ellen White was informed in advance of the issue to be discussed and so was prepared to speak to the question in its several aspects. Minutes of the meeting were made and a copy of them was introduced into the general Document File in the Elmshaven vault. However, through some oversight no copy was placed in the regular E. G. White letter and manuscript file. Being minutes of a school board meeting, they were lost sight of for many years. During a thorough search in 1975 for all materials relating to the early training of children, the minutes of this enlightening interview came to light on April 24, 1975, and were published in full in the *Review and Herald* (now the *Adventist Review*) of April 24, 1975.

Brief excerpts from the 1902 appeal for a church school and that portion of the board minutes of January 14, 1904, which relate directly to the appropriate school age for the children of Adventist parents, are presented in chapters 23 and 24.

Chapter 25 brings together a few miscellaneous choice statements under the title of "General Guiding Principles."

In 1887 Ellen White suggested in *Testimonies*, volume 5, on pages 583, 584, that "strong young men, rooted and grounded in the faith" could "if so counseled by our leading brethren, enter the higher colleges in our land, where they would have a wider field for study and observation," and who like the Waldenses "might do a good work, even while gaining their education." These sentiments were repeated several times during the next decade, emphasizing the opportunities this would give for effective witness in non-Seventh-day Adventist schools, at the same time sounding timely cautions. Chapter 26 closes with a selection of these counsels.— WHITE TRUSTEES.

23.

Appeal for a Church School *

I promised that I would speak this morning in regard to the necessity of withdrawing our children from the public schools, and of providing suitable places where they can be educated aright. I have felt surprised at the apparently indifferent attitude of some, notwithstanding the oft-repeated warnings given that parents must provide for their families not merely with reference to their present interests, but especially with reference to their future, eternal interests. The characters that we form in this life are to decide our destiny. If we choose, we may live a life that measures with the life of God.

Every Christian family is a church in itself. The members of the family are to be Christlike in every action. The father is to sustain so close a relation to God that he realizes his duty to make provision for the members of his family to receive an education and training that will fit them for the future, immortal life. His children are to be taught the principles of heaven. He is the priest of the household, accountable to God for the influence that he exerts over every member of his

---

* Portion of an appeal for a church school to serve the Sanitarium [Deer Park], California, church, Monday morning, July 14, 1902.

family. He is to place his family under the most favorable circumstances possible, so that they shall not be tempted to conform to the habits and customs, the evil practices and lax principles, that they would find in the world. . . .

Upon fathers and mothers devolves the responsibility of giving a Christian education to the children entrusted to them. They are never to neglect their children. In no case are they to let any line of business to so absorb mind and time and talents that their children, who should be led in harmony with God, are allowed to drift until they are separated far from Him. They are not to allow their children to slip out of their grasp into the hands of unbelievers. They are to do all in their power to keep them from imbibing the spirit of the world. They are to train them to become helpers together with God. They are God's human hand, fitting themselves and their children for an endless life in the heavenly home.

The education of our children begins in the home. The mother is their first teacher. When they become old enough to attend school, shall we permit them to enter the public schools?

The Public School or Church School?—Many years ago, in Oakland, my husband and I conversed with a public school teacher in regard to the public schools in the city. He said to us: "If parents knew of the iniquity that is to our certain knowledge practised in these schools, there would be a furor raised in regard to these schools such as neither you nor I can imagine. The young people are rotten; and what kind of homes they have is more than our teachers can tell." This statement was made over twenty years ago. Have the conditions in our public schools improved since that time?

Some fathers and mothers are so indifferent, so careless, that they think it makes no difference whether their children attend a church school or a public school. "We are in the world," they say, "and we cannot get out of it." But, parents, we can get a good way out of the world, if we choose to do so. We can avoid seeing many of the evils that are multiplying so fast in these last days. We can avoid hearing about much of the wickedness and crime that exist.

Everything that can be done should be done to place ourselves and our children where we shall not see the iniquity that is practised in the world. We should carefully guard the sight of our eyes and the hearing of our ears, so that these awful things shall not enter our minds. When the daily newspaper comes into the house, I feel as if I wanted to hide it, that the ridiculous, sensational things in it may not be seen. It seems as if the enemy is at the foundation of the publishing of many things that appear in newspapers. Every sinful thing that can be found is uncovered and laid bare before the world.

The line of demarcation between those who serve God and those who serve Him not, is ever to remain distinct. The difference between believers and unbelievers should be as great as the difference between light and darkness. When God's people take the position that they are the temple of the Holy Ghost, Christ Himself abiding within, they will so clearly reveal Him in spirit, words, and actions, that there will be an unmistakable distinction between them and Satan's followers. . . .

Educating Children in Bible Principles.—Some of God's people permit their children to attend the public schools, where they mingle with those who are corrupt in morals. In these schools their children can neither study the Bible nor learn its principles. Christian parents, you must make provision for your children to be educated in Bible principles. And do not rest satisfied merely with having them study the Word in the church school. Teach the Scriptures to your children yourselves when you sit down, when you go out, when you come in, and when you walk by the way. Walk with your children much oftener than you do. Talk with them. Set their minds running in a right channel. As you do this, you will find that the light and the glory of God will come into your homes. But how can you expect His blessing when you do not teach your children aright?

I am merely touching upon a few points on a number of subjects relating to the training and education of children. Sometime I hope to treat upon these points more fully, for I have been thoroughly aroused to realize that these matters must be presented before our people. Seventh-day Adventists must move in a way altogether different from the way in which they have been moving, if they expect the approval of God to rest upon them in their homes.

Every faithful parent will hear from the lips of the Master the words, "Well done, good and faithful servant . . . enter thou into the joy of thy Lord." May the Lord help us to be good and faithful servants in our dealings with one another. He tells us to "consider one another to provoke unto love and to good works," helping and strengthening one another.

Church School Needed at Crystal Springs.—We are almost home. We are standing on the borders of the eternal world. Those who prove worthy will soon be introduced into the kingdom of God. We have no time to lose. We should establish the work in right lines here at Crystal Springs. Here are our children. Shall we allow them to be contaminated by the world—by its iniquity, its disregard of God's commandments? I ask those who are planning to send their children to the public school, where they are liable to be contaminated, How can you take such a risk?

We desire to erect a church school building for our children. Because of the many calls made for means, it seems a difficult matter to secure sufficient money or to arouse an interest great enough to build a small, convenient schoolhouse. I have told the school committee that I will lease to them some land for as long a time as they care to use it for school purposes. I hope that interest enough will be aroused to enable us to erect a building where our children can be taught the word of God, which is the lifeblood and the flesh of the Son of God. . . .

Will you not take an interest in the erection of this

school building, in which the word of God is to be taught? . . . We expect to have a school building, in which the Bible can be taught, in which prayers can be offered to God, and in which the children can be instructed in Bible principles. We expect that every one who can take hold with us will want to have a share in erecting this building. We expect to train a little army of workers on this hillside. . . .

There is no reason why this matter should drag. Let every one take hold to help, persevering with unflagging interest until the building is completed. Let every one do something. Some may have to get up as early as four o'clock in the morning, in order to help. . . .

Brethren and sisters, what will you do to help build a church school? We believe that every one will regard it as a privilege and a blessing to have this school building. Let us catch the spirit of the work, saying, "We will arise and build." If all will take hold of the work unitedly, we shall soon have a schoolhouse in which from day to day our children will be taught the way of the Lord. As we do our best, the blessing of God will rest upon us. Shall we not arise and build?—Manuscript 100, 1902.

24.

Counsel Regarding Age
of School Entrance

Report of Interview

Report of a meeting of the Sanitarium [Cal.] Church School Board, held at "Elmshaven," Sanitarium, Cal., Thursday morning, January 14, 1904.

Sister White spoke for a time, as follows:

For years, much instruction has been given me in regard to the importance of maintaining firm discipline in the home. I have tried to write out this instruction, and to give it to others. In one of the forthcoming volumes of my writings [*Education*] will be published considerable additional matter on the training of children.

Those who assume the responsibilities of parenthood should first consider whether they will be able to surround their children with proper influences. The home is both a family church and a family school. The atmosphere of the home should be so spiritual that all the members of the family, parents and children, will be blessed and strengthened by their association with one another. Heavenly influences are educational. Those who are surrounded by such influences are being prepared for entrance into the school above.

Mothers should be able to instruct their little ones

wisely during the earlier years of childhood. If every mother were capable of doing this, and would take time to teach her children the lessons they should learn in early life, then all children could be kept in the home school until they are eight, or nine, or ten years old.

But many who enter the marriage relation fail of realizing all the sacred responsibilities that motherhood brings. Many are sadly lacking in disciplinary power. In many homes there is but little discipline, and the children are allowed to do as they please. Such children drift hither and thither; there is nobody in the home capable of guiding them aright, nobody who with wise tact can teach them how to help father and mother, nobody who can properly lay the foundation that should underlie their future education. Children who are surrounded by these unfortunate conditions are indeed to be pitied. If not afforded an opportunity for proper training outside the home, they are debarred from many privileges that, by right, every child should enjoy. This is the light that has been presented to me.

Those who are unable to train their children aright, should never have assumed the responsibilities of parents. But because of their mistaken judgment, shall we make no effort to help their little ones to form right characters? God desires us to deal with these problems sensibly.

Church Schools to Be Connected With Sanitariums.—In all our sanitariums the standard is to be kept high. With these institutions should be connected, as physicians, managers, and helpers, only those who keep their households in order. The conduct of the children has an influence that tells upon all who come to these sanitariums. God desires that this influence shall be reformatory. And this can be; but care is required. The father and the mother must give special attention to the training of each child. But you know how the families are up on this hillside. The patients understand how it is. The way it is presented to me is that it is a shame that there is not the influence over the young children that there should be. Every one of them should be employed in doing something that is useful. They have been told what to do. If the father cannot be with them, the mother should be instructed how to teach them.

But since I have been here, the light has been given me that the very best thing that can be done is to have a school. I had no thought that the very little ones would be embraced in the school—not the very little ones. But it would be best to have this school for those who can be instructed and have the restraining influence upon them which a schoolteacher should exert. We have a school here because the Word of God could not be taught in the other [public] school. Our brother [Anthony] that teaches that school is fully capable of carrying a school with teaching the Word. He is fully capable of doing that. He has his position, they have hired him, and as long as they let him stay undisturbed, he had better stay there.

School Privileges for Younger Children.—But here is a work that must be done for the families, and for the children that are as old as seven years and eight years and nine years. We should have a lower department, that is a second department, where these children could be instructed. They will learn in school that which they frequently do not learn out of school, except by association. . . .

Now, it seems that the question is about these children going to school. I want to know from the parents, every one of them, who it is that feels perfectly satisfied with their children, as they are, without sending them to the school—to a school that has Bible lessons, has order, has discipline, and is trying to find something for them to do to occupy their time. I do not think there is anyone, if they come to understand it, who will have objections.

The Setting of the Early Counsel.—But when I heard what the objections were, that the children could not go to school till they were ten years old, I wanted to tell you that there was not a Sabbathkeeping school when the light was given to me that the children should not attend school until they were old enough to be instructed. They should be taught at home to know what proper manners were when they went to school, and not be led astray. The wickedness carried on in the common schools is almost beyond conception.

That is how it is, and my mind has been greatly stirred in regard to the idea, "Why, Sister White has said so and so, and Sister White has said so and so; and therefore we are going right up to it."

God wants us all to have common sense, and He wants us to reason from common sense. Circumstances alter conditions. Circumstances change the relation of things.

A Church School Versus Poor Home Management.—Here is a Sanitarium, and that sanitarium must carry the highest possible influence inside and out. Then, if they see children who come there—sharp-eyed, lynx-eyed, wandering about, with nothing to do, getting into mischief, and all these things—it is painful to the senses of those that want to keep the reputation of the school. Therefore, I, from the light that God has given me, [declare that] if there is a family that has not the capabilities of educating, nor discipline and government over their children, requiring obedience, the very best thing is to put them in some place where they will obey. Put them in some place where they will be required to obey, because obedience is better than sacrifice. Good behavior is to be carried out in every family.

We are educating God's little ones in our homes. Now what kind of an education are we giving them? Our words, are they loose and careless and slack? Is there an overbearing disposition? Is there a scolding and fretting because parents have not the powers to manage? The Lord wants us to take all things into consideration. Every parent has on his hands a sum to prove: How are my children? Where are they? Are they coming up for God or for the devil? All these things are to be considered.

The book that is coming out will have much to say in

regard to the great principles that are to be carried out in training the children, from the very baby in arms. The enemy will work right through those children, unless they are disciplined. Someone disciplines them. If the mother or the father does not do it, the devil does. That is how it is. He has the control. . . .

I shall not say so much now, because I want to understand just what I should speak on. I want the objections brought forth, why children should not have an education.

The Kindergarten at Battle Creek

We could do the same as they have in Battle Creek. They took me from place to place in the orphan asylum [Haskell Home] in Battle Creek. There were their little tables, there were their little children from five years old and upward. They were being educated on the kindergarten plan: how to work and how to manage. They had a great pile of sand of a proper quality, and they were teaching the children how to work together, how to make Noah's ark, and how to make the animals that enter into the Noah's ark. They were all doing this kind of work. It takes something. . . .

Now, I have perfect confidence in Sister Peck's teaching, but if she carries on what she has carried on—and I am satisfied it is just the thing that ought to be done—there would have to be an extra teacher; don't you think so?

*Sister Peck:** I think if we did the work in a satisfactory manner, and if we have any more children, we ought to have some extra help.

Light Given on "These Things"

Sister White: My ideas have come out in a crude way, just a jot here and a jot there. I have it written out, but not all. I have more to write. I want you to take care of

---

* One of Ellen G. White's literary assistants serving as the church school teacher.

what I have said. First, understand this. This is the light that has been given me in regard to these things.

Here are children that are quick. There are children five years old that can be educated as well as many children ten years old, as far as capabilities are concerned, to take in the mother's matters and subjects.

Now I want that just as long as Willie's children* are here, and they live here, I want they should have the discipline of a school. If it can be connected with this school by putting on an addition to the building, one room say, for such students, every one of us ought to feel a responsibility to provide that room. Those mothers that want to keep their children at home, and are fully competent and would prefer to discipline them herself, why, no one has any objection to that. They can do that. But provision is to be made so that the children of all who have any connection with this food factory and sanitarium and these things that are being carried on here, should be educated. We must have it stand to reach the highest standards.

Elder C. L. Taylor: Sister White, there is one question that I should like to raise, regarding the responsibility of parents and the relation of that responsibility to the church school. Now, suppose I have a little boy—I have one—seven years old. We are perfectly capable of training him, we have fitted ourselves to do that work. Now suppose we choose not to take that responsibility, to neglect the boy, let him drift around. Then does it become the responsibility of the church to do what I could do if I would do? That is the question. If I don't take care of my boy when I can, when I am able to do it, would I ask the church to do it in my place?

Sister White: You can take care of them, but do you?

Elder W. C. White: She refuses to take your isolated experience.

Sister White: The church here on this hill is a

---

* Ages: Henry and Herbert, twins, 7 years; Grace, 3 years. In time, all attended this school.

responsible church. It is connected with outside influences. These influences are constantly brought in to testify of us. The question is, Shall it be united, and shall it, if it is necessary, prepare a room—which won't cost everlastingly too much—a room that these children should come to and have discipline, and have a teacher, and get brought up where they are prepared for the higher school? Now that is the question.

The Kind of Education the Children Need

I say, these little children that are small ought to have education, just what they would get in school. They ought to have the school discipline under a person who understands how to deal with children in accordance with their different temperaments. They should try to have these children understand their responsibilities to one another, and their responsibility to God. They should have fastened in their minds the very principles that are going to fit them for the higher grade and the higher school.

There is a higher school that we are all going to, and unless these children are brought up with the right habits and the right thoughts, and the right discipline, I wonder how they will ever enter that school above? Where is their reverence? Where are their choice ideas that they should cultivate? And all these things. It must be an everyday experience.

The mother, as she goes around, is not to fret and to scold, and to say, "You are in my way, and I wish you would get away, I wish you would go outdoors," or any such thing. She is to treat her children just as God should treat His older children. He calls us children in His family. He wants us educated and trained according to the principles of the Word of God. He wants this education to commence with the little ones. If the mother has not the tact, the ingenuity, if she does not know how to treat human minds, she must put them under somebody that will discipline them and mold and fashion their minds.

Now, have I presented it so that it can be understood? Is there any point, Willie, that I have in the book that I have not touched here?

W. C. White: I don't know. I find, Mother, that our people throughout the States and throughout the world, I must say, sometimes make very far-reaching rulings based on an isolated statement.

Now, in my study of the Bible and in my study of your writings, I have come to believe that there is a principle underlying every precept, and that we cannot understand properly the precept without grasping the principle.

I have believed that in some of the statements which have created a good deal of controversy—like your counsels concerning the use of butter, and your statement that the only teacher that a child should have until it was eight or ten years old—it was our privilege to grasp the principle. I have believed that in the study of those statements that we should recognize that every precept of God is given in mercy, and in consideration of the circumstances.

God said, "What God hath joined together let no man put asunder"; and yet Christ explains the law of divorce as given because of the hardness of their hearts. Because of the degeneracy of the people a divorce law which was not in God's original plan was permitted. I believe that the principle should be understood in regard to such isolated statements as your protest against the use of butter, and the statement that the child should have no other teacher than the mother until it was eight or ten years old.

Now, when that view was given you about butter, there was presented to you the condition of things—people using butter full of germs. They were frying and cooking in it, and its use was deleterious. But later on, when our people studied into the principle of things, they found that while butter is not best, it may not be so bad as some other evils; and so in some cases they are using it.

I have supposed that this school question was the same. The ideal plan is that the mother should be the teacher—an intelligent teacher such an one as you have described this morning. But I have felt that it was a great misfortune to our cause from Maine to California, and from Manitoba to Florida, that our people should take that statement that the child should have no teacher but the parent until it is eight or ten years old, as a definite forbidding of those children to have school privileges. If I understand it, that is really the question before us this morning.

When the brethren study this matter from the standpoint of the good of the child, from the standpoint of fairness to the parents, as far as I can see, they all acknowledge that there are conditions in which it would be better for the child to have some school privilege than to be ruled out. But there is the precept, A child shall have no teacher but the parents until it is eight or ten years old; that settles it. . . .

Sister White: Well, if parents have not got it in them you might just as well stop where you are. Therefore, we have got to make provision, because there are a good many parents that have not taken it upon themselves to discipline themselves. . . .

I believe that the people about here that have advantages can each do a little something to support a school for the others. I am willing to do it. I do not think that should be a consideration that should come in at all. [We talk of] "the expense," "the expense," "the expense"—it is nothing at all to have the weight of a thimbleful of expense.

Setting a Pattern

W. C. White: As my children have been mentioned, I should like to say a word about this. My interest in the outcome of this interview is not now at all with reference to my own children. My interest in the outcome of this interview is with reference to its influence upon our work throughout the world. My interest for this school from the beginning until now has not been principally with reference to my children. . . .

It is known by everybody that Sister Peck has had a broad experience in teaching, and that she has had four years' experience with Mother, dealing with her writings, helping to prepare the book *Education*. My greatest interest for the school has not been my own family, neither has it been simply the St. Helena church.

My interest in this school lies in the fact that it is our privilege to set a pattern. The successes and failures and the rulings of this school will affect our church school work throughout California and much farther, because of Sister Peck's long experience as a teacher, and her work with you, Mother, in helping to prepare the book on education. All these things have put this school where it is a city set on a hill.

Now, my distress at the ruling with reference to the younger children has been not principally because my children were ruled out, but to build up a ruling which I consider is very cruel. It is being used in a way to do our younger children a great deal of harm.

The Question of Kindergarten

The world is doing a great work for the children through kindergartens. In places where we have institutions, and both parents are employed, they would gladly send children to a kindergarten. I have been convinced that in many of our churches a kindergarten properly conducted for a few hours a day, would be a great blessing. I have not found anything in your teachings or rulings, Mother, or advice to our people that would be contrary to it. But the rulings of our school superintendents have killed, completely killed, in most parts of the country any effort toward providing kindergarten work for our children.

There are a few instances where they stand to carry it forward. Dr. Kellogg does it in his orphans' school that you have seen and praised, and in a few other places they are doing it. At Berrien Springs they ventured last summer to bring in a kindergarten teacher and to permit that part of the work to have a little consideration; but generally, in about nine tenths of the field, this ruling of our school superintendents kills that part of the work completely.

Sister White: Well, there has got to be a reformation in that line.

W. C. White: And the ruling in this school here, and the reasons that have always been given me for this ruling have been based on your statement that a child's mother is to be its only teacher until it is eight or ten years old. I have believed that for the best interests of our school work throughout the world, that it is our privilege to have such an interview as we have had this morning, and also to study into the principle which underlies such things.

Sister White: Yes, it is right that it should stand before the people right. Now you will never find a better opportunity to have Sister Peck have the supervision over even the younger children. There has got to be a blending in some way.

As for a room, and there should be room, I question which is best, whether it should be connected right with the building, or whether it should be separate. It seemed to me that it might be a building by itself. I do not know which would be best. That must be considered—the advantages and disadvantages. I think Sister Peck, as well or better than any of the rest of us, could tell how that should be. . . .

Could the School Constitute a Disservice?

C. L. Taylor: We have talked this: That the church school will not be a blessing to a community, when it comes to take a responsibility that the parents themselves can carry. And when we go ahead and put our money into a building, it does not make any difference whether it is a building or a room. But when we take the responsibility that could be carried by the parents, then the church school becomes a curse or a hindrance, rather than a blessing. Now that is all I have ever heard when we have come to the point. . . .

Sister Peck: It has been a question in my mind on that point, Sister White, what our duty as teachers is— whether it was to try to help the parents to see and to take up their responsibility, or to take it away from them by taking their children into the school.

Sister White: If they have not felt their responsibility from all the books and writings and sermons, you might roll it onto them from now till the Lord comes, and they would not have any burden. It is no use talking about responsibility, when they have never felt it.

A School That Makes a Favorable Impression

We want to have a school in connection with the Sanitarium. It is presented to me that wherever there is a sanitarium, there must be a school, and that school must be carried on in such a way that it makes an impression on all who shall visit the Sanitarium. People will come into that school. They will see how that school is managed. It should not be far from the Sanitarium, so that they can understand.

In the management of the school there is to be the very best kind of discipline. In learning, the students cannot have their own way. They have got to give up their own way to discipline. This is a lesson that is yet to be learned by a good many families. But we hear, "Oh, let them do this. They are nothing but children. They will learn when they get older."

Well, just as soon as a child in my care would begin to show passion, and throw himself on the floor, he never did it but once, I want to tell you. I would not let the devil work right through that child and take possession of it.

The Lord wants us to understand things. He says, Abraham commanded his children and his household after him, and we want to understand what it means to command, and we want to understand that we have got to take hold of the work if we resist the devil.

Well, I do not know whether we are any farther along than when we began.

C. L. Taylor: Yes, I think we are.

Sister White: But some things have been said.

I. M. Bowen: I think we know what we will have to do.

Sister Gotzian: Enough has been said to set us thinking, and to do something.

Sister White: The Lord is in earnest with us. Yes; we have got to be an example. And now you see there are so many sanitariums, and so many schools, that must be connected with them. We have got to come to our senses and recognize that we have to carry an influence—that is an influence in regard to the children. . . .

Your school is to be a sample school. It is not to be a sample after the schools of the day. It is not to be any such thing. Your school is to be according to a plan that is far ahead of these other schools. It is to be a practical thing. The lessons are to be put into practice, and not merely a recitation of [theory].

C. L. Taylor: I am satisfied that when we begin to move in that direction, we will see real light come in.

—Manuscript 7, 1904

25.

General Guiding Principles

In Every Place Where There Is a Church

In every place where there is a church, large or small, there a school should be established.—Letter 108, 1899.

Not the Maxims of Men, but God's Word

The feeding upon the divine Word of God is the divine element which the soul needs in order to secure a healthy development of all its spiritual powers. In all our schools this word is to be made the essence of education; it is this that will give sanctified strength, wisdom, integrity, and moral power, if it is brought into the experience. It is not the words of worldly wisdom, it is not the maxims of men, not the theory of human beings, but it is the Word of God.—Manuscript 41a, 1896.

No Stereotyped Plan in Education

The Lord requires every person who shall take up responsibility to carry into work intelligent, trained capabilities, and work out his ideas conscientiously according to his previous knowledge and service in schools. The Lord has not designed any one, special, exact plan in education. It is the fear of the Lord that is the beginning of wisdom. When men with their varied traits of character shall take up their appointed work as teachers and follow a plan of teaching according to their own capabilities, they are not to suppose they must be a facsimile of those teachers who served before them, lest they spoil their own record.—Manuscript 170, 1901.

A Definition of True Education

True education is the preparation of the mental, moral, and physical powers for the performance of every duty, pleasant or otherwise, the training of every habit and practice, of heart, mind, and soul for divine service. Then of you it can be said in the heavenly courts, "Ye are laborers together with God" (see 1 Cor. 3:9).—Letter 189, 1899.

Commendable Qualities of the Swiss Schools

I see some things here in Switzerland that I think are worthy of imitation. The teachers of the schools always go out with their pupils while they are at play, and teach them how to amuse themselves and repress any disorder or any wrong. This is an invariable law, and includes children from five to fifteen years of age.

As a reward for good behavior and studious habits the teachers take their scholars out and have a long walk with them, dismissing the school earlier than usual. I like this; I think there is less opportunity for the children to yield to temptation. The teachers seem to enter into the sports of the children and to regulate them.

Love Versus Strict, Unbending Rules.—I cannot in any way sanction the idea that children must feel that they are under a constant distrust, and must be watched, and cannot act as children. But let the teachers join in the amusements of the children, be one with them, and show they want them to be happy, and it will give the children confidence. They can be controlled by love, but not by a stern, strict, unbending rule, to follow them in their meals and in their amusements.—Letter 42, 1886.

Our talents are lent us in trust, to use and increase by

their use. Oh, if parents would only realize that the families on earth may be symbols of the family in heaven. If they would realize their accountability to keep their homes free from every taint of moral evil. God designs that we shall have far more of heaven in our families than we now enjoy.

Pleasant Scenes and Interesting Work.—From their earliest years the children are learners, and if pleasant scenes are kept before them in the home, they will become familiar with Christian courtesy, kindness, and love. Their minds are built up by what they see and hear, and parents are sowing the seed which will reap a harvest either for weal or woe. If parents are Christians in name only, if they are not doers of the Word, they are placing their own superscription on their children, and not the superscription of God. Children long for something to impress the mind. For Christ's sake, parents, give their hungering, thirsting souls something upon which to feed.

Children are naturally active, and if parents do not furnish them with employment, Satan will invent something to keep them busy in an evil work. Therefore train your children to useful work. You can clothe all work with a dignity which will make it profitable and elevating.

Bring Pleasure in Relationship With Children.—Do not feel it your duty to make the lives of your children unpleasant. The unpleasantness will come fast enough. Bring all the pleasure possible into your exercises as teacher and educator of your children. Encourage them to make a companion of you. Sinful impulses, sinful inclinations, and objectionable habits you will surely find in your children; but if you encourage them to seek your society, you can give a right mold to their tastes and feelings, and banish discontent, repining, and rebellion. Overcome their pride by living before them an example of meekness and lowliness of heart.

We need to weed out from our conversation everything that is harsh and condemnatory. When we have put on Christ in meekness and lowliness of heart we shall represent Christ in all our dealings with our children. To all who labor in Christ's lines for the salvation of souls, the Saviour says, "Ye are laborers together with God. Ye are God's husbandry; ye are God's building."—Manuscript 143, 1899.

26.

Attending Colleges and Universities of the Land

It would be perfectly safe for our youth to enter the colleges of our land if they were converted every day; but if they feel at liberty to be off guard one day, that very day Satan is ready with his snares, and they are overcome and led to walk in false paths—forbidden paths, paths that the Lord has not cast up.

Now, shall professed Christians refuse to associate with the unconverted, and seek to have no communication with them? No, they are to be with them, in the world and not of the world, but not to partake of their ways, not to be impressed by them, not to have a heart open to their customs and practices. Their associations are to be for the purpose of drawing others to Christ.

The Influence of Error Repeatedly Presented.— Here is the danger of our youth. The attractions in these institutions are such, and the teaching so intermixed with error and sophistry, that they cannot discern the poison of sentiment mingled with the useful and precious. There is such an undercurrent, and it works in such a manner that many do not perceive it, but it is constantly at work. Certain ideas are constantly advanced by the professors, and repeated over and over, and at last the mind begins to assimilate and conform to these ideas.

Just so when infidel authors are studied. These men have sharp intellects, and their sharp ideas are presented, and the mind of the student is influenced by them; they are pleased with their brilliance.

But where did those men obtain their powers of intellect? Where did they get their sharpness? From the fountain of all knowledge. But they have prostituted their powers; they have given them as a contribution to the devil, and don't you think the devil is smart? Many are traveling in the devil's tracks by reading infidel authors. Satan is a sharp being, and they fall in love with his learning and smartness.—Manuscript 8b, 1891.

The Perils of Listening to the World's Great Men

To many of our youth there is great danger in listening to the discourses that are given by those who in the world are called great men. These discourses are often of a highly intellectual nature, and prevailing errors of science falsely so-called and of popular religious doctrine are mingled with wise sayings and observations, but they undermine the statements of the Bible and give the impression that there is reason for questioning the truth of the inspired Word. In this way the seeds of skepticism are sown by great and professedly wise men, but their names are registered in the books of record in heaven as fools, and they are an offense to God. They repeat the falsehoods that Satan put into the mouth of the serpent, and educate the youth in delusions.

This is the kind of education the enemy delights in. It is sorcery. The great apostle inquired, "Who hath bewitched you that ye should not obey the truth?" Those who receive and admire the sentiments of these so-called great men are in danger, for through the subtlety of the enemy the sophistical reasoning of these false teachers takes root in the heart of our youth, and almost imperceptibly they are converted from truth to error. But the conversion should be just the other way. Our young men who have seen the evidences of the verity of truth should be firmly established and able to win souls to Christ from the darkness of error.

The youth who go to Ann Arbor* must receive Jesus as their personal Saviour or they will build upon the sand, and their foundation will be swept away. The Spirit of Christ must regenerate and sanctify the soul, and pure affection for Christ must be kept alive by humble, daily trust in God. Christ must be formed within, the hope of glory. Let Jesus be revealed to those with whom you associate.—Letter 26, 1891.

Seventh-day Adventist Students

The Waldensians entered the schools of the world as students. They made no pretensions; apparently they paid no attention to anyone; but they lived out what they believed. They never sacrificed principle, and their principles soon became known. This was different from anything the other students had seen, and they began to ask themselves, What does this all mean? Why cannot these men be induced to swerve from their principles? While they were considering this, they heard them praying in their rooms, not to the virgin Mary, but to the Saviour, whom they addressed as the only mediator between God and man. The worldly students were encouraged to make inquiries, and as the simple story of the truth as it is in Jesus was told, their minds grasped it.

These things I tried to present at Harbor Heights [at an educational convention in 1891]. Those who have the spirit of God, who have the truth wrought into their very being, should be encouraged to enter colleges, and live the truth, as Daniel and Paul did. Each one should study to see what is the best way to get the truth into the school, that the light may shine forth. Let them show that they respect all the rules and regulations of the school. The leaven will begin to work; for we can depend much more upon the power of God manifested in the

* The University of Michigan was located at Ann Arbor, some 65 miles east of Battle Creek; in 1891 Adventist youth seeking medical training studied there.—COMPILERS.

lives of His children than upon any words that can be spoken. But they should also tell inquirers, in as simple language as they can, of the simple Bible doctrines.

Dropping Seeds of Truth Into Minds and Hearts

There are those who, after becoming established, rooted and grounded in the truth, should enter these institutions of learning as students. They can keep the living principles of the truth, and observe the Sabbath, and yet they will have opportunity to work for the Master by dropping seeds of truth in minds and hearts. Under the influence of the Holy Spirit, these seeds will spring up to bear fruit for the glory of God, and will result in the saving of souls. The students need not go to these institutions of learning in order to become enlightened upon theological subjects; for the teachers of the school need themselves to become Bible students. No open controversies should be started, yet opportunity will be given to ask questions upon Bible doctrines, and light will be flashed into many minds. A spirit of investigation will be aroused.

A Procedure Fraught With Great Danger.—But I scarcely dare present this method of labor; for there is danger that those who have no connection with God will place themselves in these schools, and instead of correcting error and diffusing light, will themselves be led astray. But this work must be done, and it will be done by those who are led and taught of God.—Manuscript 22a, 1895.

SECTION VII

Standards

INTRODUCTION

The Christian must keep a continuous watch on the standards he or she holds. As we face the vicissitudes of living in a world with declining standards, and associate with church members who may be measuring themselves among themselves, our own standards, once held high, may imperceptibly slip.

If we are to look at the messages God has sent His people in times of old and in our time, we see how He found it necessary to repeat and repeat encouragements to His people to walk in harmony with His will. In our time this is particularly true of acceptable Sabbath observance, dress and adornment, and health reform. Some valuable materials, along these lines, found here and there in Ellen White's manuscripts and letters of counsel have, since the issuance of the two preceding volumes of this series, been published in the *Adventist Review* and are now put into book form here. Some materials from published sources have also been included in the four chapters of this section.

The chapter presenting a grouping of materials on "The Propriety of Varying Attitudes in Prayer" seemed appropriate because some would strain applications of the counsel found in *Gospel Workers*, pages 178, 179, and *Selected Messages*, book 2, pages 311-316, calling upon Seventh-day Adventists to kneel in prayer as a sign of reverence and humility. While the instruction calls for supplicants to kneel in both public worship and private devotions, Ellen White's clear-cut counsel and her example indicate that kneeling is not required in every instance when the heart and voice are lifted in prayer. The materials presented are drawn from a wide span of Ellen White's ministry.—WHITE TRUSTEES.

27.

The Grace of Courtesy

Those who work for Christ are to be pure, upright, and trustworthy, and they are also to be tenderhearted, compassionate, and courteous. There is a charm in the intercourse of those who are truly courteous. Kind words, pleasant looks, a courteous demeanor, are of inestimable value. Uncourteous Christians, by their neglect of others, show that they are not in union with Christ. It is impossible to be in union with Christ and yet be uncourteous.

What Christ was in His life on this earth, that every Christian should be. He is our example, not only in His spotless purity but in His patience, gentleness, and winsomeness of disposition. He was as firm as a rock where truth and duty were concerned, but He was invariably kind and courteous. His life was a perfect illustration of true courtesy. He had ever a kind look and a word of comfort for the needy and oppressed.

His presence brought a purer atmosphere into the home, and His life was as leaven working amid the elements of society. Harmless and undefiled, He walked among the thoughtless, the rude, the uncourteous; amid the unjust publicans, the unrighteous Samaritans, the heathen soldiers, the rough peasants, and the mixed multitude. He spoke a word of sympathy here, and a word there, as He saw men weary, and compelled to bear heavy burdens. He shared their burdens, and repeated to them the lessons He had learned from nature of the love, the kindness, the goodness of God.

He sought to inspire with hope the most rough and unpromising, setting before them the assurance that they might become blameless and harmless, attaining such a character as would make them manifest as children of God.

In Ministering to Unbelievers.—Though He was a Jew, Christ mingled with the Samaritans, setting at naught the Pharisaic customs of His nation. In face of their prejudices, He accepted the hospitality of this despised people. He slept under their roofs, ate with them at their tables, partaking of the food prepared and served by their hands—and taught in their streets, and treated them with the utmost kindness and courtesy.

Jesus sat as an honored guest at the table of the publicans, by His sympathy and social kindliness showing that He recognized the dignity of humanity; and men longed to become worthy of His confidence. Upon their thirsty souls His words fell with blessed, life-giving power. New impulses were awakened, and the possibility of a new life opened to these outcasts of society.

A Powerful Argument for the Gospel.—The love of Christ mellows the heart and smooths all roughness from the disposition. Let us learn from Him how to combine a high sense of purity and integrity with sunniness of temperament. A kind, courteous Christian is the most powerful argument in favor of the gospel that can be produced.

The conduct of some professing Christians is so lacking in kindness and courtesy that their good is evil spoken of. Their sincerity may not be doubted, their uprightness may not be questioned. But sincerity and uprightness will not atone for a lack of kindness and courtesy. Such ones need to realize that the plan of redemption is a plan of mercy, set in operation to soften whatever is hard and rugged in human nature. They need to cultivate that rare Christian courtesy which makes men kind and considerate to all. The Christian is to be sympathetic as well as true, pitiful and courteous as well as upright and honest.

Men of the world study to be courteous, to make themselves as pleasing as possible. They study to render their address and manners such that they will have the greatest influence over those with whom they associate. They use their knowledge and abilities as skillfully as possible in order to gain this object. "The children of this world are in their generation wiser than the children of light."

As you go through life, you will meet with those whose lot is far from easy. Toil and deprivation, with no hope for better things in the future, make their burden very heavy. And when pain and sickness is added, the burden is almost greater than they can bear. Careworn and oppressed, they know not where to turn for relief. When you meet with such ones, put your whole heart into the work of helping them. It is not God's purpose that His children shall shut themselves up to themselves. Remember that for them as well as for you Christ died. In your dealing with them, be pitiful and courteous. This will open the way for you to help them, to win their confidence, to inspire them with hope and courage.

Christ's Grace Changes the Whole Man.—The apostle exhorts us, "As he which hath called you is holy, so be ye holy in all manner of conversation; because it is written, Be ye holy; for I am holy." The grace of Christ changes the whole man, making the coarse refined, the rough gentle, the selfish generous. It controls the temper and the voice. Its outworking is seen in politeness and tender regard shown by brother for brother, in kind, encouraging words and unselfish actions. An angel-presence is in the home. The life breathes forth a sweet perfume, which as holy incense ascends to God.

Love is manifested in kindness, gentleness, forbearance, and longsuffering. The expression of the countenance is changed. The peace of heaven is revealed. There is seen a habitual gentleness, a more than human love. Humanity becomes a partaker of divinity. Christ is honored by perfection of character. As these changes are perfected, angels break forth in rapturous song, and God and Christ rejoice over souls fashioned after the divine similitude.

Pleasant Tones and Correct Language.—We should accustom ourselves to speak in pleasant tones; to use pure, correct language, and words that are kind and courteous. Kind words are as dew and gentle showers to the soul. The scripture says of Christ that grace was poured into His lips, that He might "know how to speak a word in season to him that is weary." And the Lord bids us, "Let your speech be alway with grace," "that it may minister grace unto the hearers."

Some with whom you are brought in contact will be rough and uncourteous, but because of this, do not be less courteous yourself. He who wishes to preserve his own self-respect must be careful not to wound needlessly the self-respect of others. This rule should be sacredly observed toward the dullest, the most blundering.

What God intends to do with these apparently unpromising ones, you do not know. He has in the past accepted persons no more promising or attractive to do a great work for Him. His Spirit, moving upon the heart, has aroused every faculty to vigorous action. The Lord saw in those rough, unhewn stones precious material that would stand the test of storm and heat and pressure. God sees not as man sees. He does not judge from appearances, but He searches the heart, and judges righteously.

Let us be self-forgetful, ever on the watch to cheer others, to lighten their burdens by acts of tender kindness and deeds of unselfish love. These thoughtful courtesies, beginning in the home, and extending far beyond the home circle, go far to make up the sum of life's happiness, and the neglect of them constitutes no small share of life's wretchedness."—Manuscript 69, 1902. (Published in *Review and Herald*, Aug. 20, 1959.)

28.

Dress and Adornment

Blessings of Proper Attire

Appropriate, Modest, and Becoming.—In dress, as in all things else, it is our privilege to honor our Creator. He desires our clothing to be not only neat and healthful, but appropriate and becoming.—*Education,* p. 248.

We should seek to make the best of our appearance. In the tabernacle service, God specified every detail concerning the garments of those who ministered before Him. Thus we are taught that He has a preference in regard to the dress of those who serve Him. Very specific were the directions given in regard to Aaron's robes, for his dress was symbolic. So the dress of Christ's followers should be symbolic. In all things we are to be representatives of Him. Our appearance in every respect should be characterized by neatness, modesty, and purity.—*Testimonies,* vol. 6, p. 96.

By the things of nature [the flowers, the lily] Christ illustrates the beauty that Heaven values, the modest grace, the simplicity, the purity, the appropriateness, that would make our attire pleasing to Him.—*The Ministry of Healing,* p. 289.

The dress and its arrangement upon the person is generally found to be the index of the man or the woman.—*The Review and Herald,* Jan. 30, 1900.

We judge of a person's character by the style of dress worn. A modest, godly woman will dress modestly. A refined taste, a cultivated mind, will be revealed in the choice of a simple, appropriate attire. . . . The one who is simple and unpretending in her dress and in her manners shows that she understands that a true woman is characterized by moral worth. How charming, how interesting, is simplicity in dress, which in comeliness can be compared with the flowers of the field.—*The Review and Herald,* Nov. 17, 1904.

Sound Guiding Principles

If the world introduce a modest, convenient, and healthful mode of dress, which is in accordance with the Bible, it will not change our relation to God or to the world to adopt such a style of dress. Christians should follow Christ and make their dress conform to God's Word. They should shun extremes. They should humbly pursue a straightforward course, irrespective of applause or of censure, and should cling to the right because of its own merits.—*Testimonies,* vol. 1, pp. 458, 459.

I beg of our people to walk carefully and circumspectly before God. Follow the customs in dress so far as they conform to health principles. Let our sisters dress plainly, as many do, having the dress of good, durable material, appropriate for this age, and let not the dress question fill the mind. Our sisters should dress with simplicity. They should clothe themselves in modest apparel, with shamefacedness and sobriety. Give to the world a living illustration of the inward adorning of the grace of God.—*Manuscript 167, 1897.* (Published in *Child Guidance,* p. 414.)

Independence and the Courage to Be Right

Christians should not take pains to make themselves

a gazingstock by dressing differently from the world. But if, when following out their convictions of duty in respect to dressing modestly and healthfully, they find themselves out of fashion, they should not change their dress in order to be like the world; but they should manifest a noble independence and moral courage to be right, if all the world differ from them.—*Testimonies,* vol. 1, p. 458.

Refining the Tastes

Truth never makes men or women coarse, or rough or uncourteous. It takes men in all their sin and commonness, separates them from the world, and refines their tastes, even if they are poor and uneducated. Under Christ's discipline, a constant work of refinement goes on, sanctifying them through the truth. If they are tempted to exert one particle of influence that would lead away from Christ into the way of the world, in pride, or fashion, or display, they speak words of resistance that will turn aside the enemy's power. "I am not my own," they say. "I am bought with a price. I am a son, a daughter of God."—Letter 26, 1900.

Simplicity in Dress

As I have seen many Sabbathkeeping Adventists becoming worldly in thought, conversation, and dress, my heart has been saddened. The people who claim to believe that they have the last message of mercy to give to the world, are attracted by worldly fashions, and make great exertions to follow them as far as they think their profession of faith allows them to go. Worldly dress among our people is so noticeable that unbelievers frequently remark, "In their dress you cannot distinguish them from the world." This we know to be true, although there are many exceptions.

Those who meet the world's standard are not few in numbers. We are grieved to see that they are exerting an influence, leading others to follow their example. When

I see those who have named the name of Christ, aping the fashions introduced by worldlings, I have the most painful reflections. Their lack of Christlikeness is apparent to all. In the outward adorning there is revealed to worldlings as well as to Christians an absence of the inward adorning, the ornament of a meek and quiet spirit, which in the sight of God is of great price. . . .

Heart Condition Indicated.—We warn our Christian sisters against the tendency to make their dresses according to worldly styles, thus attracting attention. The house of God is profaned by the dress of professedly Christian women of today. A fantastic dress, a display of gold chains and gaudy laces, is a certain indication of a weak head and a proud heart.

In order to follow in the wake of fashion, many of our youth incur expenses which their condition in life does not justify. Children of poor parents seek to dress as do those who are wealthy. Parents tax their purses and their God-given time and strength in making and remodeling clothing to satisfy the vanity of their children. If our sisters who have abundance of means would regulate their expenditures, not in accordance with their wealth, but with regard to their responsibility to God, as wise stewards of the means entrusted to them, their example would do much to stay this evil now existing among us.

Satan's Tactics.—Satan stands in the background, devising the fashions which lead to extravagance in the outlay of means. In forming the fashions of the day, he has a fixed purpose. He knows that time and money which are devoted to meet the demands of fashion will not be used for higher, holier objects. Precious time is wasted in keeping pace with ever-changing and never-satisfying fashions. No sooner is one style introduced than new styles are devised, and then, in order for fashionable persons to remain fashionable, the dress must be remodeled. Thus professing Christians, with divided hearts, waste their time, giving to the world nearly all their energies.

This entirely unnecessary burden is taken up and willingly borne by our sisters. Half of their burdens come from an attempt to follow the fashions; yet they eagerly accept the yoke, because fashion is the god they worship. They are as truly held in shackles of bondage as is the veriest slave; and yet they talk of independence! They do not know the first principles of independence. They have no mind or taste or judgment of their own.

Satan is wonderfully successful in infatuating minds with the ever-varying styles of dress. He knows that while the minds of women are continually filled with a feverish desire to follow fashion, their moral sensibilities are weak, and they cannot be aroused to realize their true spiritual condition. They are worldly, without God, without hope.

Taste and Fitness and Durability.—We do not discourage taste and neatness in dress. Correct taste in dress is not to be despised or condemned. While needless ruffles, trimmings, and ornaments should be left off, we encourage our sisters to obtain good, durable material. Nothing is gained in trying to save means by purchasing cheap fabrics. Let the clothing be plain and neat, without extravagance of display.

Young ladies who break away from slavery to fashion will be ornaments in society. The one who is simple and unpretending in her dress and in her manners shows that she understands that a true lady is characterized by moral worth.—Manuscript 106, 1901. (Republished in *The Review and Herald,* March 20, 1958.)

Self-denial in dress is a part of our Christian duty. To dress plainly, abstaining from display of jewelry and ornaments of every kind, is in keeping with our faith. Are we of the number who see the folly of worldlings in indulging in extravagance of dress as well as in love of amusements? If so, we should be of that class who shun everything that gives sanction to this spirit which takes possession of the minds and hearts of those who live for this world only and who have no thought or care for the next.—*Testimonies*, vol. 3, p. 366.

Where Are We Drifting?

A sister who had spent some weeks at one of our institutions in Battle Creek said that she felt much disappointed in what she saw and heard there. She had thought to find a people far in advance of the younger churches, both in knowledge of the truth and in religious experience. Here she hoped to gain much instruction which she could carry to her sisters in the faith in a distant State. But she was surprised and pained at the lightness, the worldliness, and lack of devotion which she met on every hand.

Before accepting the truth, she had followed the fashions of the world in her dress, and had worn costly jewelry and other ornaments; but upon deciding to obey the word of God, she felt that its teachings required her to lay aside all extravagant and superfluous adorning. She was taught that Seventh-day Adventists did not wear jewelry, gold, silver, or precious stones, and that they did not conform to worldly fashions in their dress.

When she saw among those who profess the faith such a wide departure from Bible simplicity, she felt bewildered. Had they not the same Bible which she had been studying, and to which she had endeavored to conform her life? Had her past experience been mere fanaticism? Had she misinterpreted the words of the apostle, "The friendship of the world is enmity with God, for whosoever will be a friend of the world is the enemy of God"?

Mrs. D., a lady occupying a position in the institution, was visiting at Sister ————'s room one day, when the latter took out of her trunk a gold necklace and chain, and said she wished to dispose of this jewelry and put the proceeds into the Lord's treasury. Said the other, "Why do you sell it? I would wear it if it were mine." "Why," replied Sister ————, "when I received the truth, I was taught that all these things must be laid aside. Surely they are contrary to the teachings of God's Word." And she cited her hearer to the words of the apostles, Paul and Peter, upon this point, "In like manner, also, that women adorn themselves in modest apparel, with shamefacedness and sobriety; not with broidered hair, or gold, or pearls, or costly array; but (which becometh women professing godliness) with good works." "Whose adorning let it not be that outward adorning of plaiting the hair, and of wearing of gold, or of putting on of apparel. But let it be the hidden man of the heart, in that which is not corruptible, even the ornament of a meek and quiet spirit."

In answer, the lady displayed a gold ring on her finger, given her by an unbeliever, and said she thought it no harm to wear such ornaments. "We are not so particular," said she, "as formerly. Our people have been over-scrupulous in their opinions upon the subject of dress. The ladies of this institution wear gold watches and gold chains, and dress like other people. It is not good policy to be singular in our dress; for we cannot exert so much influence."

Conformity to Christ or the World.—We inquire, Is this in accordance with the teachings of Christ? Are we to follow the word of God or the customs of the world? Our sister decided that it was safest to adhere to the Bible standard. Will Mrs. D. and others who pursue a similar course be pleased to meet the result of their influence in that day when every man shall receive according to his works?

God's word is plain. Its teachings cannot be mistaken. Shall we obey it, just as He has given it to us, or shall we seek to find how far we can digress and yet be saved? Would that all connected with our institutions would receive and follow the divine light, and thus be enabled to transmit light to those who walk in darkness.

Conformity to the world is a sin which is sapping the spirituality of our people, and seriously interfering with their usefulness. It is idle to proclaim the warning message to the world, while we deny it in the transactions of daily life.—*The Review and Herald*, March 28, 1882.

"Self, Self, Self, Must Be Served"

Those who have bracelets, and wear gold and ornaments, had better take these idols from their persons and sell them, even if it should be for much less than they gave for them, and thus practice self-denial. Time is too short to adorn the body with gold or silver or costly apparel. I know a good work can be done in this line. Jesus, the Commander in the heavenly courts, laid aside His crown of royalty and His royal robe and stepped down from His royal throne, and clothed His divinity with the habiliments of humanity, and for our sakes became poor, that we through His poverty might come into possession of eternal riches, and yet the very ones for whom Christ has done everything that was possible to do to save perishing souls from eternal ruin feel so little disposition to deny themselves anything that they have money to buy.

The Lord is soon to come, and His reward is with Him and His work before Him to give every man according to his work. I try to set before the people that we are handling the Lord's money to accomplish the most important work that can be done. They can, individually, through denial of self, do much more if all do a little, and the many little rivulets will make quite a current sent flowing heavenward.

True, it is difficult for all to take in the situation. Self, self, self, must be served and glorified, and how hard it is for all to become laborers together with God. Oh, that a spirit of self-sacrifice might come to every church, and thus every soul nigh and afar off might learn the value of money, and use it while they can, and say, "Of Thine own, Lord, we give Thee" (See 1 Chronicles 29:14).—Letter 110, 1896.

We have not time to give anxious thought as to what we shall eat and drink, and wherewithal we shall be clothed. Let us live simply, and work in simplicity. Let us dress in such a modest, becoming way that we will be received wherever we go. Jewelry and expensive dress will not give us influence, but the ornament of a meek and quiet spirit—the result of devotion to the service of Christ—will give us power with God. Kindness and forethought for those about us are qualities precious in the sight of heaven. If you have not given attention to the acquirement of these graces, do so now, for you have no time to lose.—Manuscript 83, 1909.

The Clothes Seventh-day Adventist Ministers Wear*

EPHESIANS 3:6, 7: "That the Gentiles should be fellow heirs, and of the same body, and partakers of his promise in Christ by the gospel: whereof I was made a minister, according to the gift of the grace of God given unto me by the effectual working of his power."

"Whereof I was made a minister," not merely to present the truth to the people, but to carry it out in the life. . . . But it is not this only. There are other things to be considered, in which some have been negligent, but which are of consequence, in the light in which they have been presented before me. . . .

Carefulness in dress is an important item. There has been a lack here with ministers who believe present truth. The dress of some has been even untidy. Not only has there been a lack of taste and order in arranging the dress in a becoming manner upon the person, and in having the color suitable and becoming for a minister of Christ, but the apparel of some has been even slovenly. Some ministers wear a vest of a light color, while their pants are dark, or a dark vest and light pants, with no taste or orderly arrangement of the dress upon the person when they come before the people. These things are preaching to the people. The minister gives them an example of order, and sets before them the propriety of

---

* Reported as spoken before the General Conference of 1871.

neatness and taste in their apparel, or he gives them lessons in slackness and lack of taste which they will be in danger of following.

Attire Appropriate for the Pulpit.—Black or dark material is more becoming to a minister in the desk and will make a better impression upon the people than would be made by a combination of two or three different colors in his apparel.

I was pointed back to the children of Israel anciently, and was shown that God had given specific directions in regard to the material and style of dress to be worn by those who ministered before Him. The God of heaven, whose arm moves the world, who sustains us and gives us life and health, has given us evidence that He may be honored or dishonored by the apparel of those who officiate before Him. He gave special directions to Moses in regard to everything connected with His service. He gave instruction even in regard to the arrangement of their houses and specified the dress which those should wear who were to minister in His service. They were to maintain order in everything. . . .

That Right Impressions Might Be Made.—There was to be nothing slack and untidy about those who appeared before Him when they came into His holy presence. And why was this? What was the object of all this carefulness? Was it merely to recommend the people to God? Was it merely to gain His approbation?

The reason that was given me was this, that a right impression might be made upon the people. If those who ministered in sacred office should fail to manifest care, and reverence for God, in their apparel and their deportment, the people would lose their awe and their reverence for God and His sacred service.

If the priests showed great reverence for God by being very careful and very particular as they came into His presence, it gave the people an exalted idea of God and His requirements. It showed them that God was holy, that His work was sacred, and that everything in connection with His work must be holy; that it must be free from everything like impurity and uncleanness; and that all defilement must be put away from those who approach nigh to God.

The Minister's Dress and the Truth.—From the light that has been given me, there has been a carelessness in this respect. I might speak of it as Paul presents it. It is carried out in will-worship and neglecting of the body. But this voluntary humility, this will-worship and neglecting of the body, is not the humility that savors of heaven. That humility will be particular to have the person and actions and apparel of all who preach the holy truth of God, right and perfectly proper, so that every item connected with us will recommend our holy religion. The very dress will be a recommendation of the truth to unbelievers. It will be a sermon in itself. . . .

A minister who is negligent in his apparel often wounds those of good taste and refined sensibilities. Those who are faulty in this respect should correct their errors and be more circumspect. The loss of some souls at last will be traced to the untidiness of the minister. The first appearance affected the people unfavorably because they could not in any way link his appearance with the truths he presented. His dress was against him; and the impression given was that the people whom he represented were a careless set who cared nothing about their dress, and his hearers did not want anything to do with such a class of people. . . .

The Plane of Minister's Work Judged by His Dress.—Some who minister in sacred things so arrange their dress upon their persons that, to some extent at least, it destroys the influence of their labor. There is an apparent lack of taste in color and neatness of fit. What is the impression given by such a manner of dress? It is that the work in which they are engaged is considered no more sacred or elevated than common labor, as plowing in the field. The minister by his example brings down sacred things upon a level with common things. The influence of such preachers is not pleasing to God.—*Testimonies,* vol. 2, pp. 609-614.

On Making the Dress Question a Test

Your letter has been received and read. . . . The subject that you place before me for counsel [the proposal to return to the reform dress advocated and worn in the late 1860's] is one that needs to be carefully considered. Our sisters whose minds are agitated upon the subject of again resuming the reform dress, should be prayerfully cautious in every move they make. We have now the most solemn, important tests given to us from the Word of God for this special period of time. This test is for the whole world. The Lord does not require that any tests of human inventions shall be brought in to divert the minds of the people or create controversy in any line.

It may be that some are thirsting for distinction in some way. If they are thirsting for a battle with satanic agencies, let them be sure that they first have on every piece of the armor of God. If they have not, they will surely be worsted, and make for themselves grievous trials and disappointments which they are not prepared to meet. Let all seek the Lord most earnestly for that deep and rich experience that is to be found in the subject of heart preparedness to follow Christ where He shall lead the way.

"If any man will come after me," He says, "let him deny himself, and take up his cross, and follow me." These words are to be weighed well. The man who wishes to follow Christ, who chooses to walk in His footsteps, will find self-denial and the cross in that path. All who follow Christ will understand what this involves.

Dress Not to Be the Test Question.—God's tests are now to stand out plain and unmistakable. There are storms before us, conflicts of which few dream. There is no need now for any special alteration in our dress. The plain simple style of dress now worn, made in the most healthful way, demands no hoops, and no long trails and is presentable anywhere, and these things should not come in to divert our minds from the grand test which is to decide the eternal destiny of a world—the commandments of God and the faith of Jesus.

We are nearing the close of this world's history. A plain, direct testimony is now needed, as given in the Word of God, in regard to the plainness of dress. This should be our burden. But it is too late now to become enthusiastic in making a test of this matter. The desire to follow Christ in all humility of mind, preparing the heart, purifying the character, is by no means an easy work. Our sisters may be assured that the Lord has not inspired them to make a test of that which was once given as a blessing, but which by many was hated and despised as a curse.

The Reform Dress.—The reform dress, which was once advocated,* proved a battle at every step. Members of the church, refusing to adopt this healthful style of dress, caused dissension and discord. With some there was no uniformity and taste in the preparation of the dress as it had been plainly set before them. This was food for talk. The result was that the objectionable features, the pants, were left off. The burden of advocating the reform dress was removed because that which was given as a blessing was turned into a curse.

There were some things that made the reform dress a decided blessing. With it the ridiculous hoops which were then the fashion, could not possibly be worn. The long dress skirts trailing on the ground and sweeping up the filth of the streets could not be patronized. But a more sensible style of dress has now been adopted which does not embrace these objectionable features. The fashionable style of dress may be discarded and should be

* The "reform dress" advocated and adopted in the 1860's was designed by a group of SDA women in an attempt to provide a healthful, modest, comfortable, and neat attire in harmony with the light given Ellen White, which was much needed at the time. See pp. 252-255. It called for loose-fitting garments hung from the shoulders with a hemline about nine inches from the floor. The lower limbs were clothed with a trouserlike garment providing comfort and warmth. See *Story of Our Health Message*, pp. 112-130.—COMPILERS.

by all who will read the Word of God. The time spent in advocating the dress reform should be devoted to the study of the Word of God.

The dress of our people should be made most simple. The skirt and sacque I have mentioned may be used—not that just that pattern and nothing else should be established, but a simple style as was represented in that dress. Some have supposed that the very pattern given was the pattern that all were to adopt. This is not so. But something as simple as this would be the best we could adopt under the circumstances. No one precise style has been given me as the exact rule to guide all in their dress. . . .

Simple dresses should be worn. Try your talent, my sisters, in this essential reform.

The people of God will have all the test that they can bear.

The Sabbath question is a test that will come to the whole world. We need nothing to come in now to make a test for God's people that shall make more severe for them the test they already have. The enemy would be pleased to get up issues now to divert the minds of the people and get them into controversy over the subject of dress. Let our sisters dress plainly, as many do, having the dress of good material, durable, modest, appropriate for this age, and let not the dress question fill the mind. . . .

The Example Some Set.—There are those who with all the light of the Word of God will not obey His directions. They will follow their own tastes and do as they please. These give a wrong example to the youth, and to those who have newly come to the truth who have made it a practise to copy every new style of dress in trimmings that take time and money, and there is little difference between their apparel and that of the world-ling.

Let our sisters conscientiously heed the word of God for themselves. Do not begin the work of reform for others until you do; for you will have no success; you cannot possibly change the heart. The working of the Spirit of God inwardly will show a change outwardly. Those who venture to disobey the plainest statements of inspiration will not hear and receive and act upon all the human efforts made to bring these idolaters to a plain, unadorned, simple, neat, proper dress that does not in any way make them odd or singular. They continue to expose themselves by hanging out the colors of the world. . . .

Our whole term of probation is very brief, and a short work will be done on the earth. God's own tests will come; His proving will be sharp and decisive. Let every soul humble himself before God, and prepare for what is before us.—Letter 19, 1897.

29.

The Sabbath:

Guiding Principles in Sabbath

Observance

The Sabbath a Sign to the World of Loyalty.—
From the pillar of cloud Jesus "spake unto Moses,
saying, Speak thou also unto the children of Israel,
saying, Verily my sabbaths ye shall keep: for it is a sign
between me and you throughout your generations; that
ye may know that I am the Lord that doth sanctify you"
(Ex. 31:12, 13). The Sabbath is a pledge given by God
to man—a sign of the relation existing between the
Creator and His created beings. By observing the memorial of the creation of the world in six days and the
rest of the Creator on the seventh day, by keeping the
Sabbath holy, according to His directions, the Israelites
were to declare to the world their loyalty to the only true
and living God, the Sovereign of the universe.

By observing the true Sabbath Christians are ever to
bear to the world faithful witness of their knowledge of
the true and living God as distinguished from all false
gods, for the Lord of the Sabbath is the Creator of the
heavens and the earth, the One exalted above all other
gods.

"Ye shall keep the sabbath therefore; for it is holy
unto you. . . . Six days may work be done; but in the
seventh is the sabbath of rest, holy to the Lord: who-

soever doeth any work in the Sabbath day, he shall surely be put to death. Wherefore the children of Israel shall keep the sabbath, to observe the sabbath throughout their generations, for a perpetual covenant. It is a sign between me and the children of Israel for ever: for in six days the Lord made heaven and earth, and on the seventh day he rested, and was refreshed" (verses 14-17).— Manuscript 122, 1901.

Early Counsel on the Sabbath and the Children.—The house of God is desecrated and the Sabbath violated by Sabbath believers' children. They run about the house, play, talk, and manifest their evil tempers in the very meetings where the saints have met together to glorify God and to worship Him in the beauty of holiness. The place that should be holy, where a holy stillness should reign, and where there should be perfect order, neatness, and humility, is made to be a perfect Babylon and a place where confusion, disorder, and untidiness reign. This is enough to shut out God from our assemblies and cause His wrath to be kindled, that He will not be pleased to go out with the armies of Israel to battle against our enemies.

God would not give the victory in the ———— meeting. The enemies of our faith triumphed. God was displeased. His anger is kindled that His house should be made like Babylon. . . .

Above everything, take care of your children upon the Sabbath. Do not let them violate it, for you may just as well violate it yourself as to let your children do it. When you suffer your children to play upon the Sabbath, God looks upon you as a commandment breaker. You transgress His Sabbath.—Manuscript 3, 1854.

No Boisterous Noise and Confusion.—Then [the entire family] come to the table without levity. Boisterous noise and contention should not be allowed any day of the week; but on the Sabbath all should observe quietness. No loud-toned commands should be heard at any time; but on the Sabbath it is entirely out of place. This is God's holy day, the day He has set apart to commemorate His creative works, a day He has sanctified and hallowed.—Manuscript 57, 1897.

Seeking Our Own Pleasure.—I say to those who claim to be Seventh-day Adventists, Can you claim the seal of the living God? Can you claim that you are sanctified by the truth? We have not, as a people, given the law of God the preeminence as we should. We are in danger of doing our own pleasure on the Sabbath day.—Letter 258, 1907.

No Day for Pleasure Seeking, Swimming, or Ball Playing.—God would have all His gifts appreciated. All fragments, jots, and tittles are to be treasured carefully, and we are carefully to become acquainted with the necessities of others. All that we have of Bible truth is not merely for our benefit, but to impart to other souls, and this is to be impressed upon human minds, and every kindly word spoken to prepare the way to make a channel through which the truth will flow forth in rich currents to other souls.

Every working of Christ in miracles was essential, and was to reveal to the world that there was a great work to be done on the Sabbath day for the relief of suffering humanity, but the common work was not to be done. Pleasure seeking, ball playing, swimming, was not a necessity, but a sinful neglect of the sacred day sanctified by Jehovah. Christ did not perform miracles merely to display His power, but always to meet Satan in afflicting suffering humanity. Christ came to our world to meet the needs of the suffering, whom Satan was torturing.—Letter 252, 1906.

Sabbath Dishes.—We would charge all not to wash their dishes on the Sabbath if this can possibly be avoided. God is dishonored by any unnecessary work done on His holy day. It is not inconsistent, but proper, that the dishes should be left unwashed till the close of the Sabbath, if this can be managed.—Letter 104, 1901.

The Sabbath a Day of Service.—The first Sabbath of the week of prayer was a day of earnest activity. From

"Sunnyside" and the school, two teams and a boat were sent to Dora Creek to bring to the meetings those who were not able to walk so far. The people had been invited to bring their lunch, and come to the meeting prepared to spend the day, and they responded freely to the invitation.

Some were much surprised that we would exert ourselves on the Sabbath to bring them to the meeting. They had been taught that Sundaykeeping consisted largely in physical inactivity; and they thought that because we were zealous in the matter of Sabbathkeeping, we would keep it according to the teachings of the Pharisees.

We told our friends that in the matter of keeping the Sabbath, we studied the example and teachings of Christ whose Sabbaths were often spent in earnest effort to heal and to teach; that we believed that one of our sisters who was nursing a sick family was keeping the Sabbath as much as the one who was leading a division in the Sabbath school; that Christ could not please the Pharisees of His day, and that we did not expect that our efforts to serve the Lord would satisfy the Pharisees of our day.—*The Review and Herald*, Oct. 18, 1898.

Sacred and Secular Activities.—The priests in the temple performed greater labor on the Sabbath than upon other days. The same labor in secular business would be sinful; but the work of the priests was in the service of God.—*The Desire of Ages,* p. 285.

Far-reaching Example of a Headquarters Church.—My mind has been burdened in regard to the condition of the church in this place. . . . There was much need of exalting the standard in this place in many respects before a correct and saving influence could go forth to other places. As the truth has been presented here it has taken persons from the world and from the churches and brought them together in church capacity; but not all who have professed to believe the truth are sanctified through it. . . .

God calls upon the workers in this mission to elevate

the standard, and to show their regard for His requirements by honoring the Sabbath. . . . From this place the publications are sent out, and the laborers go forth to proclaim the commandments of God; and it is of the greatest importance that a right influence be exerted by this church, both by precept and example. The standard must not be placed so low that those who accept the truth shall transgress God's commandments while professing to obey them. Better, far better, would it be to leave them in darkness until they could receive the truth in its purity.

Seventh-day Adventists Being Watched.—There are those who are watching this people to see what is the influence of the truth upon them. The children of this world are wiser in their generation than the children of light; when the claims of the fourth commandment are set before them, they look to see how it is regarded by those who profess to obey it. They study the life and character of its advocates, to learn whether these are in harmony with their profession of faith; and upon the opinions thus formed many are influenced very largely in the acceptance or rejection of the truth. If this people will conform their lives to the Bible standard, they will be indeed a light in the world, a city set upon a hill.—Manuscript 3, 1885.

The Importance and Glory of the Sabbath.— Yesterday [August 10, 1851], which was Sabbath, we had a sweet, glorious time. The Lord met with us and the glory of God was shed upon us and we were made to rejoice and glorify God for His exceeding goodness unto us. . . . I was taken off in vision. . . .

I saw that we sensed and realized but little of the importance of the Sabbath, to what we yet should realize and know of its importance and glory. I saw we knew not what it was yet to ride upon the high places of the earth and to be fed with the heritage of Jacob. But when the refreshing and latter rain shall come from the presence of the Lord and the glory of His power we shall know what it is to be fed with the heritage of Jacob and ride upon the high places of the earth. Then shall we see the Sabbath more in its importance and glory. But we shall not see it in all its glory and importance until the covenant of peace is made with us at the voice of God, and the pearly gates of the New Jerusalem are thrown open and swing back on their glittering hinges and the glad and joyful voice of the lovely Jesus is heard richer than any music that ever fell on mortal ear bidding us enter. [I saw] that we had a perfect right in the city for we had kept the commandments of God, and heaven, sweet heaven is our home, for we have kept the commandments of God.—Letter 3, 1851.

A Few Sabbaths With the White Family

[Battle Creek, Michigan] Sabbath, January 1, 1859. Attended Preaching, a Baptism, and the Ordinances.—It is the commencement of the new year. The Lord gave James liberty Sabbath afternoon in preaching upon the necessary preparation for baptism, and to partake of the Lord's Supper. There was much feeling in the congregation. At intermission, all repaired to the water, where seven followed their Lord in baptism. It was a powerful season and of the deepest interest. Two little sisters about eleven years old were baptized. One, Cornelia C., prayed in the water to be kept unspotted from the world.

In the eve the church followed the example of their Lord and washed one another's feet, and then partook of the Lord's Supper. There was rejoicing and weeping in that house. The place was awful, and yet glorious, on account of the presence of the Lord.—Manuscript 5, 1859.

[Otsego, Michigan] Sabbath, January 8, 1859. Traveled to Meeting by Sleigh and Spoke Some.—It is the holy Sabbath. May we honor and glorify God today. We went with Brother Leighton in his sleigh to Otsego, four miles. It was very cold; could hardly keep comfortable. Found the meetinghouse not very warm. All were so cold. Must take time to get warm.

Brother Loughborough preached upon the judgment. Then I said a few words. Not very free. Then the church readily gave in their testimonies.—Manuscript 5, 1859.

[Battle Creek] Sabbath, March 5, 1859. **Stayed Home to Nurse James White.**—Did not attend meeting today. My husband was sick. Have remained with him to wait upon him. The Lord met with us and blessed us this morn. I had unusual liberty in prayer. Brother John Andrews preached twice today. He spent the eve and night with us. We enjoyed the visit much.—Manuscript 5, 1859.

[Battle Creek] Sabbath, March 19, 1859. **Attended Meeting and Read to the Children.**—Attended meeting in the forenoon. Brother Loughborough preached with great liberty upon the sleep of the dead and the inheritance of the saints. Tarried at home in the afternoon. Read to my children,* wrote a letter to Brother Newton and wife, encouraging them in spiritual things. In the evening attended meeting for communion and washing feet. Was not as free as I wished to be on such occasions.—Manuscript 5, 1859.

[Convis, Michigan] Sabbath, April 9, 1859. **Watched and Ministered at Convis.**—Rose early and rode about twelve miles to Convis to meet with the saints there. The ride was refreshing. Called at Brother Brackett's. They accompanied us to the place of meeting, about two miles distant from his house. A little company of Sabbathkeepers were collected in a large, commodious schoolhouse. James had great freedom

---

* Adelia Patten, for several years an assistant in the White home in Battle Creek, in her "Narrative of the Life, Experience, and Last Illness of Henry N. White," who died in December, 1863, made the following statement in regard to Ellen White's dealing with her children:

For a number of years past their mother has spent much time in reading to them on the Sabbath from her large amount of choice selections of moral and religious matter, a portion of which she has recently published in the work entitled, *Sabbath Readings.* Reading to them before they could readily read themselves, gave them a love for useful reading, and they have spent many leisure hours, especially the Sabbath hours, when not at Sabbath School and meeting, in perusing good books, with which they were well supplied.—*Appeal to Youth*, p. 19.

speaking to the people. I said a few words. Meeting held until about two o'clock. Nearly all bore testimony to the truth. After supper as the hours of holy time were closing, we had a refreshing season of prayer. James talked with the children before bowing to pray.—Manuscript 6, 1859.

[Battle Creek] Sabbath, April 23, 1859. Attended Meeting and Entertained Company.—Sister Brackett, Sister Lane and her daughter, Sister Scott, and Sister Smith came from Convis to the meeting at Battle Creek. They took dinner at our house.* Meeting was interesting through the day. Brother Waggoner preached in the forenoon. His discourse was appropriate. At intermission four were baptized—Sisters Hide, Scott, and Agnes Irving, and Brother Pratt. Our afternoon meeting was very interesting. My husband never had greater liberty. The Lord's Spirit was in the meeting. The Lord gave me freedom in exhortation. In the eve the ordinances of the Lord's house were attended to. It was a solemn, interesting occasion. I was unable to attend, being much exhausted.—Manuscript 6, 1859.

[Denver] Sabbath, July 20, 1872. Took a Walk, Wrote, and Read.—It is a beautiful morning. This is the Lord's rest day and we desire to keep the Sabbath that God may accept our efforts and that our own souls may be refreshed. We walked out, seeking a retired place in a grove where we could pray and read, but we were not successful. We spent the day in conversing upon reli-

---

* Sabbath meals in the White home in later years are described by her daughter-in-law in a statement dated October 16, 1949:

"As Mrs. E. G. White's daughter-in-law, I was a member of her household for a little more than a year, and was often in her home and travelled with her over a period of twenty years. I have been asked concerning the Sabbath meals in the White home.

"As full preparation as was possible was made on Friday, the preparation day, for the Sabbath meals. On Sabbath the food for both breakfast and dinner was served hot, it having been heated immediately preceding the meal. All unnecessary work was avoided on the Sabbath but at no time did Mrs. White consider it a violation of proper Sabbath observance to provide for the ordinary comforts of life such as the building of a fire for the heating of the house or the heating of the food for the meals."—(Signed) Mrs. W. C. White.

gious subjects, writing, and reading.—Manuscript 4, 1872.

[Battle Creek] Sabbath, April 12, 1873. Made Many Missionary Visits.—My husband spoke to the people in the forenoon. I remained at home because I did not feel able to attend. In the afternoon I attended meeting. . . .

After the meeting closed I visited Ella Belden. Had a sweet season of prayer with her. I then visited Brother and Sister W. Salisbury. We had a precious season of prayer with the family. Brother and Sister Salisbury united their prayers with mine. We all felt that the Lord blessed us. I then called upon aged Brother and Sister Morse. . . . I visited Brother and Sister Gardner. He is nearing the close of his journey. Disease has made him very weak. He was overjoyed to see me. We united our prayers together and the hearts of these afflicted ones were comforted and blessed.—Manuscript 6, 1873.

[Battle Creek] Sabbath, May 17, 1873. Rode a Few Miles, Slept Some.—We rode out a few miles in the oak grove. Rested about an hour. We slept some. . . . We had a season of prayer before returning home. In the afternoon we went to the meeting.—Manuscript 7, 1873.

[Washington, Iowa] Saturday, June 21, 1873. Wrote on Sufferings of Christ.—A beautiful day; rather warm. Took a pack. Felt better. Wrote fifteen pages on sufferings of Christ. I became much interested in my subject. Brother Wheeler, Hester, and Brother Van Ostrand went to the meeting. We had some prospect of rain. Called the family together and read the matter I had written. All seemed interested.—Manuscript 8, 1873.

[Walling's Mills] Friday, September 12, 1873. Entertained a Non-Adventist.—We arrived home a little before sundown. Received letters from Brother Canright, also Mary Gaskill and Daniel Bourdeau, giving us an account of camp meeting. When we reached home we found John Cranson there. We felt sorry that he should come to see us on the Sabbath. We do not like to have visitors to entertain upon the Sabbath who have no respect for God or His holy day.—Manuscript 11, 1873.

[En route from Colorado to Battle Creek] Sabbath, November 8, 1873. Traveled on Sabbath, Regretfully.*—We rested well on the car during the night. We were unwilling to report ourselves on the cars this morning, but circumstances connected with the cause and work of God demand our presence at the General Conference. We could not delay. If we were doing our own business we should feel it a breach of the fourth commandment to travel on the Sabbath. We engaged in no common conversation. We endeavored to keep our minds in a devotional frame and we enjoyed some of the presence of God while we deeply regretted the necessity of traveling upon the Sabbath.—Manuscript 13, 1873.

[Sydney, N.S.W., Australia] February 4, 1893. Spoke in the Morning, Boarded Ship in the Afternoon.—We rode in the cab to the church in Sydney, and I spoke from Hebrews 11 upon faith. The Lord strengthened me by His grace. I felt much strengthened and blessed. The Holy Spirit was upon me. Strength, both physical and spiritual, was given me in large measure. . . .

In the afternoon at two o'clock we stepped on board the steamer to take the journey we long dreaded. All our luggage had been stored away on Friday. We dislike very much to travel on the Sabbath but the work must be done in giving the message to the world and we can keep our minds and hearts uplifted to God and can hide in Jesus. When we cannot control these matters we must leave all with our heavenly Father. If our trust be in God He will help us.—Manuscript 76, 1893.

---

* See *Testimonies*, vol. 6, p. 360.

30.

The Propriety of Varying Postures in Prayer

Need Not Always Kneel

We must pray constantly, with a humble mind and a meek and lowly spirit. We need not wait for an opportunity to kneel before God. We can pray and talk with the Lord wherever we may be.*—Letter 342, 1906.

No Place Inappropriate for Prayer at Any Time or Place.—There is no time or place in which it is inappropriate to offer up a petition to God. . . . In the crowds of the street, in the midst of a business engagement, we may send up a petition to God, and plead for divine guidance, as did Nehemiah when he made his request before King Artaxerxes.—*Steps to Christ*, p. 99.

Communing With God in Our Hearts as We Walk and Work.—We may speak with Jesus as we walk by the way, and He says, I am at thy right hand. We may commune with God in our hearts; we may walk in companionship with Christ. When engaged in our

---

* Elder D. E. Robinson, one of Ellen White's secretaries from 1902 to 1915, reported:

"I have been present repeatedly at camp meetings and General Conference sessions in which Sister White herself has offered prayer with the congregation standing, and she herself standing."—D. E. Robinson letter, March 4, 1934.

daily labor, we may breathe out our heart's desire, inaudible to any human ear; but that word cannot die away into silence, nor can it be lost. Nothing can drown the soul's desire. It rises above the din of the street, above the noise of machinery. It is God to whom we are speaking, and our prayer is heard.—*Gospel Workers*, p. 258.

Not Always Necessary to Bow.—It is not always necessary to bow upon your knees in order to pray. Cultivate the habit of talking with the Saviour when you are alone, when you are walking, and when you are busy with your daily labor.—*The Ministry of Healing*, pp. 510, 511.

Congregation Kneels After Standing in Consecration.—The Spirit of the Lord rested upon me, and was revealed in the words that were given me to speak. I asked those present who felt the urgency of the Spirit of God, and who were willing to pledge themselves to live the truth and to teach the truth to others, and to work for their salvation, to make it manifest by rising to their feet. I was surprised to see the whole congregation rise. I then asked all to kneel down, and I sent up my petition to heaven for that people. I was deeply impressed by this experience. I felt the deep moving of the Spirit of God upon me, and I know that the Lord gave me a special message for His people at this time.—*The Review and Herald*, March 11, 1909.

Crowded Congregation in Europe Remained Seated.—I invited those who desired the prayers of the servants of God to come forward. All who had been backslidden, all who wished to return to the Lord and seek Him diligently, could improve the opportunity. Several seats were quickly filled and the whole congregation was on the move. We told them the best they could do was to be seated right where they were and we would all seek the Lord together by confessing our sins, and the Lord had pledged His word, "if we confess our sins, he is faithful, and just to forgive us our sins, and to cleanse us from all unrighteousness" (1 John 1:9).— Diary, Feb. 20, 1887. (Published in *Selected Messages*, book 1, p. 147.)

Congregation Rises to Feet for Consecration Prayer.—I invited all who wanted to give themselves to God in a sacred covenant, and to serve Him with their whole hearts, to rise to their feet. The house was full, and nearly all rose. Quite a number not of our faith were present, and some of these arose. I presented them to the Lord in earnest prayer, and we know that we had the manifestation of the Spirit of God. We felt that a victory had indeed been gained.—Manuscript 30a, 1896. (Published in *Selected Messages*, book 1, p. 150.)

Congregation Kneels for Consecration Prayer.—At the close of my discourse, I felt impressed by the Spirit of God to extend an invitation for all those to come forward who desired to give themselves fully to the Lord. Those who felt the need of the prayers of the servants of God were invited to make it manifest. About thirty came forward. . . .

At first I had hesitated, wondering if it were best to do so when my son and I were the only ones whom I could see who would give us any help on that occasion. But as though someone had spoken to me, the thought passed through my mind, "Cannot you trust in the Lord?" I said, "I will, Lord." Although my son was much surprised that I should make such a call on this occasion, he was equal to the emergency. I never heard him speak with greater power or deeper feeling than at that time. . . .

We knelt in prayer. My son took the lead, and the Lord surely indited his petition; for he seemed to pray as though in the presence of God.—*The Review and Herald*, July 30, 1895. (Republished in *Selected Messages*, book 1, pp. 148, 149.)

At a Workers Institute in Oakland, California.—Now we ask you to seek the Lord with all the heart. Will those who are determined to cut loose from every temptation of the enemy, and to seek for heaven above, signify such determination by rising to their feet. [Nearly all of the congregation present responded.]

We desire that every one of you shall be saved. We desire that for you the gates of the city of God shall swing back on their glittering hinges, and that you, with all the nations who have kept the truth, may enter in. There we shall give praise and thanksgiving and glory to Christ and to the Father evermore, even forever and ever. May God help us to be faithful in His service during the conflict, and overcome at last, and win the crown of life eternal.

[Praying] My heavenly Father, I come to Thee at this time, just as I am, poor and needy, and dependent upon Thee. I ask Thee to give me and give this people the grace that perfects Christian character, et cetera.—*The Review and Herald,* July 16, 1908.

Ellen White and Audience Standing for Consecration Prayer.—Who now, I ask, will make a determined effort to obtain the higher education? Those who will, make it manifest by rising to your feet. [The congregation rose.] Here is the whole congregation. May God help you to keep your pledge. Let us pray.

[Praying] Heavenly Father, I come to Thee at this time, just as I am, poor, weak, unworthy, and I ask Thee to impress the hearts of this people gathered here to-day. I have spoken to them Thy words, but, O Lord, Thou alone canst make the word effective, et cetera.—*The Review and Herald,* April 8, 1909. (Sermon at Oakland, California, Feb. 8, 1909.)

At the Close of a General Conference Sermon in Washington, D.C. *—May the Lord help you to take

---

* The sincere Christian is often in prayer in public and in private. He prays while walking on the street, while engaged in his work, and in the wakeful hours of the night. Ellen White counseled in a statement appearing in *Gospel Workers,* p. 178, that "both in public and in private worship, it is our privilege to bow on our knees before the Lord when we offer our petitions to

hold of this work as you have never yet taken hold of it. Will you do this? Will you here rise to your feet and testify that you will make God your trust and your helper? [Congregation rises.]

[Praying] I thank Thee, Lord God of Israel. Accept this pledge of this Thy people. Put Thy Spirit upon them. Let Thy glory be seen in them. As they shall speak the word of truth, let us see the salvation of God. Amen.—*General Conference Bulletin*, May 18, 1909.

Him." The following statement on this point, written in Australia and found in *Selected Messages*, book 2, p. 312, is more emphatic: "Both in public and private worship it is our duty to bow down upon our knees before God when we offer our petitions to Him. This act shows our dependence upon God." It is also a sign of reverence: "There should be an intelligent knowledge of how to come to God in reverence and godly fear with devotional love. There is a growing lack of reverence for our Maker, a growing disregard of His greatness and His majesty."—Manuscript 84b, 1897. (Quoted in *Selected Messages*, book 2, p. 312.)

That Ellen White did not intend to teach that on every prayer occasion we must kneel is made clear both by her words and her example. To her there was no time or place where prayer was not appropriate. Her family testified that in her home those at the dining table bowed their heads and not their knees. She was not known to kneel for the benediction at the close of services she attended. The earnest counsel on kneeling would seem to have its principal application in the worship services in the house of God and in family and private devotions at home. In public ministry there were times when she stood for prayer.—Compilers.

SECTION VIII

The Health Reform

INTRODUCTION

While there is much in the E. G. White published works dealing with health and health reform, no one statement from her pen recounts the giving of the early visions on this subject. These may be noted as coming to her in 1848, 1854, and 1863. For information that there was a vision touching health points in 1848 we must turn to a James White statement in the *Review and Herald,* November 8, 1870, in which he declares:

"It was twenty-two years ago the present autumn, that our minds were called to the injurious effects of tobacco, tea, and coffee, through the testimony of Mrs. W[hite]. . . .

"When we had gained a good victory over these things, and when the Lord saw that we were able to bear it, light was given relative to food and dress."

The broadening counsel on cleanliness and diet is found in a testimony written in 1854. Specific reference to the June 6, 1863, health-reform vision is given in E. G. White answers to certain questions published in the *Review and Herald* of October 8, 1867.

The growing interest in such details as are here revealed justifies the inclusion of these items in this volume, even though they are somewhat irregular in form.

The repeated statements of her nondependence on contemporary health writers are significant not only in a discussion of how the light came to her on health reform but in a study of her work generally.

The 1881 statement on the proper use of the testimonies on health reform shows a careful balance in her work in teaching health principles.—White Trustees.

31.

Visions That Early Called for Reforms

Attention Called to Tobacco, Tea, and Coffee in 1848 and 1851

I have seen in vision that tobacco was a filthy weed, and that it must be laid aside or given up. . . . Unless it is given up, the frown of God will be upon the one that uses it, and he cannot be sealed with the seal of the living God.—Letter 5, 1851. [James White in *Review and Herald,* November 8, 1870, puts the time of the vision in the fall of 1848. See Introduction.]

Important Principles Revealed in 1854

I then saw a lack of cleanliness among Sabbath-keepers. . . . I saw that God was purifying unto Himself a peculiar people. He will have a clean and a holy people in whom He can delight. I saw that the camp must be cleansed, or God would pass by and see the uncleanness of Israel and would not go forth with their armies to battle. He would turn from them in displeasure, and our enemies would triumph over us and we be left weak, in shame and disgrace.

I saw that God would not acknowledge an untidy, unclean person as a Christian. His frown was upon such. Our souls, bodies, and spirits are to be presented blameless by Jesus to His Father, and unless we are clean in person, and pure, we cannot be presented blameless to God.

I saw that the houses of the saints should be kept tidy and neat, free from dirt and filth and all uncleanness. I saw that the house of God had been desecrated by the carelessness of parents with their children and by the untidiness and uncleanness there. I saw that these things should meet with an open rebuke, and if there was not an immediate change in some that profess the truth in these things they should be put out of the camp. . . .

The Appetite and Proper Food.—I then saw that the appetite must be denied, that rich food should not be prepared, and that which is spent upon the appetite should be put into the treasury of God. It would tell there and those that denied themselves would lay up a reward in heaven. I saw that God was purifying His people.

Pride and idols must be laid aside. I saw that rich food was destroying the health of bodies, was ruining constitutions, destroying minds, and was a great waste of means.

I saw that many were sickly among the remnant who have made themselves so by indulging their appetites. If we wish good health, we must take special care of the health that God has given us, deny the unhealthy appetite, eat less fine food, eat coarse food free from grease.* Then as you sit at the table to eat you can from the heart ask God's blessing upon the food and can derive strength from coarse, wholesome food. God will be pleased to graciously bless it and it will be a benefit to the receiver.

I saw that we should pray as Solomon did—"Feed me with food convenient for me" (Prov. 30:8)—and as we make the prayer, act it out. Get food that is plain and that is essential to health, free from grease. Such food will be convenient for us.

---

* Careful examination and comparison of her writings seems to indicate that by "grease" she meant animal fat such as lard and suet. See *Counsels on Diet and Foods,* pp. 353-355.

There are some Sabbathkeepers who make a god of their bellies. They waste their means in obtaining rich food. Such, I saw, if saved at all, will know what pinching want is unless they deny their appetites and eat to the glory of God. There are but few who eat to the glory of God.

How can those who have cake and piecrust filled with grease ask God's blessing upon it and then eat with an eye single to God's glory? We are commanded to do all to the glory of God. We must eat and drink to His glory.—Manuscript 3, 1854.

32.

The 1863 Health Reform Vision

Pointed Questions Answered

Question on the Vision.—Did you receive your views upon health reform before visiting the Health Institute at Dansville, New York,* or before you had read works on the subject?

Answer.—It was at the house of Bro. A. Hilliard, at Otsego, Mich., June 6, 1863, that the great subject of Health Reform was opened before me in vision.

I did not visit Dansville till August, 1864, fourteen months after I had the view. I did not read any works upon health until I had written *Spiritual Gifts*, volumes 3 and 4, *Appeal to Mothers*, and had sketched out most of my six articles in the six numbers of *How to Live.*

I did not know that such a paper existed as *The Laws of Life*, published at Dansville, N.Y. I had not heard of the several works upon health, written by Dr. J. C. Jackson, and other publications at Dansville, at the time I had the view named above. I did not know that such works existed until September, 1863, when in Boston,

---

* The most prominent of medical institutions in the United States featuring reforms in diet and in the treatment of the sick was at this time operated by Dr. James C. Jackson at Dansville, New York.—COMPILERS.

Mass., my husband saw them advertised in a periodical called the *Voice of the Prophets*, published by Eld. J. V. Himes. My husband ordered the works from Dansville and received them at Topsham, Maine. His business gave him no time to peruse them, and as I determined not to read them until I had written out my views, the books remained in their wrappers.

As I introduced the subject of health to friends where I labored in Michigan, New England, and in the State of New York, and spoke against drugs and flesh meats, and in favor of water, pure air, and a proper diet, the reply was often made, "You speak very nearly the opinions taught in the *Laws of Life*, and other publications, by Drs. Trall, Jackson, and others. Have you read that paper and those works?"

My reply was that I had not, neither should I read them till I had fully written out my views, lest it should be said that I have received my light upon the subject of health from physicians, and not from the Lord.

And after I had written my six articles for *How to Live*, I then searched the various works on hygiene and was surprised to find them so nearly in harmony with what the Lord had revealed to me. And to show this harmony, and to set before my brethren and sisters the subject as brought out by able writers, I determined to publish *How to Live*, in which I largely extracted from the works referred to.

How the Dress Reform Was Revealed*

Question.—Does not the practice of the sisters in wearing their dresses nine inches from the floor contradict Testimony No. 11, which says they should reach somewhat below the top of a lady's gaiter boot?

Answer.—The proper distance from the bottom of the dress to the floor was not given to me in inches. . . .

---

* For an informative presentation on the "reform dress" adopted in response to this vision, and prevailing conditions which made such a change desirable, see *Story of Our Health Message*, pp. 112-130.

But three companies of females passed before me, with their dresses as follows with respect to length:

The first were of fashionable length, burdening the limbs, impeding the step, and sweeping the street and gathering its filth; the evil results of which I have fully stated. This class, who were slaves to fashion, appeared feeble and languid.

The dress of the second class which passed before me was in many respects as it should be. The limbs were well clad. They were free from the burdens which the tyrant, Fashion, had imposed upon the first class; but had gone to that extreme in the short dress as to disgust and prejudice good people, and destroy in a great measure their own influence. This is the style and influence of the "American Costume," taught and worn by many at "Our Home," Dansville, N.Y. It does not reach to the knee. I need not say that this style of dress was shown me to be too short.

A third class passed before me with cheerful countenances, and free, elastic step. Their dress was the length I have described as proper, modest, and healthful. It cleared the filth of the street and sidewalk a few inches under all circumstances, such as ascending and descending steps, et cetera.

As I have before stated, the length was not given me in inches. . . .

Relation of the Vision to Writing and Practice

And here I would state that although I am as dependent upon the Spirit of the Lord in writing my views as I am in receiving them, yet the words I employ in describing what I have seen are my own, unless they be those spoken to me by an angel, which I always enclose in marks of quotation.

As I wrote upon the subject of dress, the view of those three companies revived in my mind as plain as when I was viewing them in vision; but I was left to describe the length of the proper dress in my own language as best I could, which I have done by stating that the bottom of the dress should reach near the top of a lady's boot, which would be necessary in order to clear the filth of the street under the circumstances before named.

I put on the dress, in length as near as I had seen and described as I could judge. My sisters in northern Michigan also adopted it. And when the subject of inches came up in order to secure uniformity as to length everywhere, a rule was brought and it was found that the length of our dresses ranged from eight to ten inches from the floor. Some of these were a little longer than the sample shown me, while others were a little shorter.—*The Review and Herald,* Oct. 8, 1867.

Health Writings on June 6, the Day of the Vision*

I saw that now we should take special care of the health God has given us, for our work was not yet done. Our testimony must yet be borne and would have influence. I saw that I had spent too much time and strength in sewing and waiting upon and entertaining company. I saw that home cares should be thrown off. The preparing of garments is a snare; others can do that. God has not given me strength for such labor. We should preserve our strength to labor in His cause, and bear our testimony when it is needed. I saw that we should be careful of our strength and not take upon ourselves burdens that others can and should bear.

I saw that we should encourage a cheerful, hopeful, peaceful frame of mind, for our health depends upon our doing this. I saw that it was duty for everyone to have a care for his health, but especially should we turn our attention to our health, and take time to devote to our health that we may in a degree recover from the effects of overdoing and overtaxing the mind. The work God requires of us will not shut us away from caring for our health. The more perfect our health, the more perfect will be our labor.

---

* See *Testimonies,* vol. 3, p. 13 for a portion of this.

To Observe and Teach Health Reform Principles.—I saw that when we tax our strength, overlabor and weary ourselves much, then we take colds and at such times are in danger of diseases taking a dangerous form. We must not leave the care of ourselves for God to see to and to take care of that which He has left for us to watch and care for. It is not safe nor pleasing to God to violate the laws of health and then ask Him to take care of our health and keep us from disease when we are living directly contrary to our prayers.

I saw that it was a sacred duty to attend to our health, and arouse others to their duty, and yet not take the burden of their case upon us. Yet we have a duty to speak, to come out against intemperance of every kind,—intemperance in working, in eating, in drinking, and in drugging—and then point them to God's great medicine, water, pure soft water, for diseases, for health, for cleanliness, and for a luxury.

A Cheerful, Grateful Attitude.—I saw that my husband should not suffer his mind to dwell upon the wrong side—the dark, gloomy side. He should put from him saddening thoughts and saddening subjects, and be cheerful, happy, grateful, and should have a firm reliance upon God and an unshaken confidence and trust in Him. His health will be much better if he can control his mind. I saw that of all others my husband should have all the rest he can get [on] Sabbath, when not preaching. . . .

I saw that we should not be silent upon the subject of health but should wake up minds to the subject.—Manuscript 1, 1863.

A Review in 1867 of the Writing on Health Reform

Diseased minds have a diseased, sickly experience while a healthy, pure, sound mind, with the intellectual faculties unclouded, will have a sound experience which will be of inestimable worth. The happiness attending a life of well-doing will be a daily reward and will of itself be health and joy.

I was astonished at the things shown me in vision. Many things came directly across my own ideas. The matter was upon my mind continually. I talked it to all with whom I had opportunity to converse. My first writing of the vision was the substance of the matter contained in [Spiritual Gifts] Volume IV and in [my six articles in] How to Live, headed, "Disease and Its Causes."

We were unexpectedly called to visit Allegan to attend a funeral [June 23, 1863], and then soon left for our eastern journey [Aug. 19], intending to finish my book upon the journey. As we visited the churches, things which had been shown to me in relation to existing wrongs required nearly all my time out of meeting in writing out the matter for them. Before I returned home from the East I had written out about 500 pages for individuals and for churches.

After we returned from the East [Dec. 21, 1863], I commenced to write [Spiritual Gifts] Volume III, expecting to have a book of a size to bind in with the testimonies which help compose [Spiritual Gifts] Volume IV. As I wrote, the matter opened before me and I saw it was impossible to get all I had to write in as few pages as I at first designed. The matter opened and Volume III was full. Then I commenced on Volume IV,* but before I had my work finished, while preparing the health matter for the printers, I was called to go to Monterey. We went, and could not finish the work there as soon as we expected. I was obliged to return to finish the matter for the printers, and we left an appointment for the next week.

These two journeys in hot weather were too much for my strength. I had written almost constantly for above one year. I generally commenced writing at seven in the

---

* Volume IV continued the Old Testament history from the building of the sanctuary to Solomon, 119 pages, followed by a 40-page chapter entitled "Health" and then selections from the Testimonies, being a reprint of a major portion of Nos. 1 to 10, in all 160 pages.

morning and continued until seven at night, and then left writing to read proof sheets. My mind had been too severely taxed, and for three weeks I had not been able to sleep more than two hours in the night. My head ached constantly.

I therefore crowded into Volume IV the most essential points in the vision in regard to health, intending to get out another testimony in which I could more freely speak upon the happiness and miseries of married life. With this consideration, I closed up Volume IV [Aug. 23, 1864], that it might be scattered among the people. I reserved some important matter in regard to health, which I had not strength or time to prepare for that volume, and get it out in season for our [1864] Eastern journey.

Written Independent of Books or Opinions of Others

That which I have written in regard to health was not taken from books or papers. As I related to others the things which I had been shown, the question was asked, "Have you seen the paper, *The Laws of Life* or the *Water Cure Journal?*" I told them No, I had not seen either of the papers. Said they, "What you have seen agrees very much with much of their teachings." I talked freely with Dr. Lay and many others upon the things which had been shown me in reference to health. I had never seen a paper treating upon health.

After the vision was given me, my husband was aroused upon the health questions. He obtained books, upon our Eastern journey, but I would not read them. My view was clear, and I did not want to read anything until I had fully completed my books. My views were written independent of books or of the opinions of others.—Manuscript 7, 1867.

33.

Proper Use of the Testimonies on Health Reform *

I fully believe that the end of all things is at hand, and every power that God has given us should be employed in the very wisest and highest service to God. The Lord has brought out a people from the world to fit them not only for a pure and holy heaven, but to prepare them through the wisdom He shall give them to be co-laborers with God in preparing a people to stand in the day of God.

Great light has been given upon health reform, but it is essential for all to treat this subject with candor and to advocate it with wisdom. In our experience we have seen many who have not presented health reform in a manner to make the best impression upon those whom they wish would receive their views. The Bible is full of wise counsel, and even the eating and drinking receive proper attention. The highest privilege that man can enjoy is to be a partaker of the divine nature, and faith that binds us in strong relationship to God will so fashion and mold mind and conduct that we become one with Christ. No one should through intemperate appe-

* Written at Battle Creek, Michigan, March 23, 1881, and published in *The Review and Herald*, June 25, 1959.

tite so indulge his taste as to weaken any of the fine
works of the human machinery and thus impair the
mind or the body. Man is the Lord's purchased possession.

If we are partakers of the divine nature, we will live
in communion with our Creator and value all of God's
work which led David to exclaim, "I am fearfully and
wonderfully made" (Ps. 139:14). We will not consider
the organs of the body our own property, as if we had
created them. All the faculties God has given to the
human body are to be appreciated. "Ye are not your
own," "for ye are bought with a price: therefore glorify
God in your body, and in your spirit, which are God's"
(1 Cor. 6:19, 20).

We are not to treat unwisely one faculty of mind,
soul, or body. We cannot abuse any of the delicate
organs of the human body without having to pay the
penalty because of transgression of nature's laws. Bible
religion brought into practical life ensures the highest
culture of the intellect.

Temperance is exalted to a high level in the Word of
God. Obeying His Word we can rise higher and still
higher. The danger of intemperance is specified. The
advantage to be gained by temperance is laid open before
us all through the Scriptures. The voice of God is
addressing us, "Be ye therefore perfect, even as your
Father which is in heaven is perfect" (Matt. 5:48).

The example of Daniel is presented for us to study
carefully and learn the lessons that God has for us to
learn in this example given us in sacred history.

Guard Against Extremes

We wish to present temperance and health reform
from a Bible standpoint, and to be very cautious not to
go to extremes in abruptly advocating health reform. Let
us be careful not to graft into health reform one false
shoot according to our own peculiar overstrained ideas
and weave into it our own strong traits of character
making these as the voice of God, and passing judgment

on all who do not see as we do. It takes time to educate away from wrong habits.

Questions are coming in from brethren and sisters making inquiries in regard to health reform. Statements are made that some are taking the light in the testimonies upon health reform and making it a test. They select statements made in regard to some articles of diet that are presented as objectionable—statements written in warning and instruction to certain individuals who were entering or had entered on an evil path. They dwell on these things and make them as strong as possible, weaving their own peculiar, objectionable traits of character in with these statements and carry them with great force, thus making them a test, and driving them where they do only harm.

Need of Moderation and Caution

The meekness and lowliness of Christ is wanting. Moderation and caution are greatly needed, but they have not these desirable traits of character. They need the mold of God upon them. And such persons may take health reform and do great harm with it in prejudicing minds so that ears will be closed to the truth.

Health reform, wisely treated, will prove an entering wedge where the truth may follow with marked success. But to present health reform unwisely, making that subject the burden of the message, has served to create prejudice with unbelievers and to bar the way to the truth, leaving the impression that we are extremists. Now the Lord would have us wise and understanding as to what is His will. We must not give occasion for us to be regarded extremists. This will place us and the truth God has given us to bear to the people at a great disadvantage. Through weaving in unconsecrated self, that which we are ever to present as a blessing becomes a stumbling block.

We see those who will select from the testimonies the strongest expressions and, without bringing in or making any account of the circumstances under which the cautions and warnings are given, make them of force in every case. Thus they produce unhealthy impressions upon the minds of the people. There are always those who are ready to grasp anything of a character which they can use to rein up people to a close, severe test, and who will work elements of their own characters into the reforms. This, at the very outset, raises the combativeness of the very ones they might help if they dealt carefully, bearing a healthful influence which would carry the people with them. They will go at the work, making a raid upon the people. Picking out some things in the testimonies they drive them upon every one, and disgust rather than win souls. They make divisions when they might and should make peace.

Danger of Families Shown to Ellen White

I have been shown the danger of families that are of an excitable temperament, the animal predominating. Their children should not be allowed to make eggs their diet, for this kind of food—eggs and animal flesh—feeds and inflames the animal passions. This makes it very difficult for them to overcome the temptation to indulge in the sinful practice of self-abuse which in this age is almost universally practiced. This practice weakens the physical, mental, and moral powers and bars the way to everlasting life.

Some families were shown me as in a deplorable condition. Because of this debasing sin, they are where the truth of God cannot find access to heart or mind. This practice leads to deception, to falsehood, to licentious practices, and to the corrupting and polluting of other minds, even of very young children. The habit once formed is more difficult to overcome than the appetite for liquor or for tobacco.

These evils, so prevalent, led me to make the statements that I have made. The special reproofs were presented in warning to others; thus they come before other families than the very individuals corrected and reproved. But let the testimonies speak for themselves.

Let not individuals gather up the very strongest statements, given for individuals and families, and drive these things because they want to use the whip and to have something to drive. Let these active, determined temperaments take the Word of God and the testimonies, which present the necessity of forbearance and love and perfect unity, and labor zealously and perseveringly. With their own hearts softened and subdued by the grace of Christ, with their own spirits humble and full of the milk of human kindness, they will not create prejudice, neither will they cause dissension and weaken the churches.

Butter, Meat, and Cheese

The question whether we shall eat butter, meat, or cheese, is not to be presented to anyone as a test, but we are to educate and to show the evils of the things that are objectionable. Those who gather up these things and drive them upon others do not know what work they are doing. The Word of God has given tests to His people. The keeping of God's holy law, the Sabbath, is a test, a sign between God and His people throughout their generations forever. Forever this is the burden of the third angel's message—the commandments of God and the testimony of Jesus Christ.

Tea, Coffee, Tobacco, and Alcohol

Tea, coffee, tobacco, and alcohol we must present as sinful indulgences. We cannot place on the same ground, meat, eggs, butter, cheese, and such articles placed upon the table. These are not to be borne in front, as the burden of our work. The former—tea, coffee, tobacco, beer, wine, and all spiritous liquors—are not to be taken moderately, but discarded. The poisonous narcotics are not to be treated in the same way as the subject of eggs, butter, and cheese.

In the beginning animal food was not designed to be the diet of man. We have every evidence that the flesh of

dead animals is dangerous because of disease that is fast
becoming universal, because of the curse resting more
heavily in consequence of the habits and crimes of man.
We are to present the truth. We are to be guarded how
to use reason and select those articles of food that will
make the very best blood and keep the blood in an
unfevered condition.—Manuscript 5, 1881.

A Work Which Discredits Health Reform

There will be some who will not leave the best and
most correct impression upon minds. They will be
inclined to narrow ideas and plans, and have not the least
idea of what constitutes health reform. They will take
the testimonies which have been given for special individuals under peculiar circumstances, and make these
testimonies general and to apply in all cases, and in this
way they bring discredit upon my work and the influence of the testimonies upon health reform.—Letter 57,
1886.

34.

Spiritual and Physical Hazards of Indulged Appetite

Changes Because of Use of Flesh Food

The flesh of dead animals was not the original food for man. Man was permitted to eat it after the Flood because all vegetation had been destroyed. But the curse pronounced upon man and the earth and every living thing has made strange and wonderful changes. Since the Flood the human race has been shortening its period of existence. Physical, mental, and moral degeneracy is rapidly increasing in these latter days.—Manuscript 3, 1897.

Taste in Judgment Corrupted

You know not the danger of eating meat merely because your appetite craves it. By partaking of this diet, man places in his mouth that which stimulates unholy passions. Unhallowed emotions fill the mind, and the spiritual eyesight is beclouded; for the tendency of self-gratification is to corrupt the taste and the judgment. By furnishing your table with this kind of food, you go counter to the will of God. A condition of things is brought about which will lead to a disregard of the precepts of God's law. . . .

But it is not an easy matter to overcome hereditary

and cultivated tendencies to wrong. Self is masterful, and strives for the victory. But to "him that overcometh" the promises are given. The Lord presents the right way, but He compels no one to obey. He leaves those to whom He has given the light to receive or despise it, but their course of action is followed by sure results. Cause must produce effect. . . .

Parents have a most solemn obligation resting upon them to conform to right habits of eating and drinking. Set before your children simple, wholesome food, avoiding everything of a stimulating nature. The effect which a meat diet has upon nervous children is not to make them sweet tempered and patient, but peevish, irritable, passionate, and impatient of restraint. Virtuous practices are lost, and corruption destroys mind, soul, and body.—Manuscript 47, 1896.

Spiritual Health Sacrificed

Eating the flesh of dead animals is deleterious to the health of the body, and all who use a meat diet are increasing their animal passions and are lessening their susceptibility of the soul to realize the force of truth and the necessity of its being brought into their practical life.—Letter 54, 1896.

Religious and Physical Life Related

Eating the flesh of dead animals has an injurious effect upon spirituality. When meat is made the staple article of food, the higher faculties are overborne by the lower passions. These things are an offense to God, and are the cause of a decline in spiritual life. . . . Whatever we do in the line of eating and drinking should be done with the special purpose of nourishing the body, that we may serve God to His name's glory. The whole body is the property of God, and we must give strict attention to our physical well-being, for the religious life is closely related to physical habits and practices.—Letter 69, 1896.

The Lord has been teaching His people that it is for their spiritual and physical good to abstain from flesh eating. There is no need to eat the flesh of dead animals.—Letter 83, 1901.

The Peril of Willing Ignorance

What we eat and drink has an important bearing on our lives, and Christians should bring their habits of eating and drinking into conformity with the laws of nature. We must sense our obligations toward God in these matters. Obedience to the laws of health should be made a matter of earnest study; for willing ignorance on this subject is sin. Each one should feel a personal obligation to carry out the laws of healthful living.

To Whom Do We Belong?

Many turn away from the light, provoked because a word of caution is given, and ask, "May we not do as we please with ourselves?" Did you create yourselves? Did you pay the redemption price for your souls and bodies? If so, you belong to yourselves. But the Word of God declares, "Ye are bought with a price," "the precious blood of Christ." The Word of God tells us plainly that our natural habits are to be strictly guarded and controlled. "Abstain from fleshly lusts, which war against the soul." Shall we do this? The Word of God is perfect, converting the soul. If we diligently heed its precepts, we shall be conformed, physically and spiritually, into the image of God.—Letter 103, 1896.

Hindrances to Mental Improvement and Soul Sanctification

God requires continual advancement from His people. They need to learn that indulged appetite is the greatest hindrance to mental improvement and soul sanctification. As a people, with all our profession of health reform, we eat too much. Indulgence of appetite is the greatest cause of physical and mental debility, and lies largely at the foundation of feebleness and premature death. Intemperance begins at our tables when we use an unwise combination of foods. Let the individual who is seeking to possess purity of spirit bear in mind that in Christ there is power to control the appetite.—Manuscript 73, 1908.

As we approach the close of this earth's history, selfishness, violence, and crime prevail, as in the days of Noah. And the cause is the same—the excessive indulgence of the appetites and passions. A reform in the habits of life is especially needed at this time, in order to fit a people for the coming of Christ. The Saviour Himself warns the church: "Take heed to yourselves, lest at any time your hearts be overcharged with surfeiting and drunkenness, and cares of this life, and so that day come upon you unawares."

Hygienic reform is a subject that we need to understand in order to be prepared for the events that are close upon us. It is a branch of the Lord's work which has not received the attention it deserves, and much has been lost through neglect. It should have a prominent place; it is not a matter to be trifled with, to be passed over as non-essential, or to be treated as a jest. If the church would manifest a greater interest in this reform, their influence for good would be greatly increased.

For those who are looking for the coming of the Lord, for those who are called to be laborers in His vineyard—for all who are fitting themselves for a place in the everlasting kingdom—how important that the brain be clear, and the body as free as possible from disease.—Undated Manuscript 9.

35.

Teaching Health Reform in the Family

Consistency of Parents With Children at the Dining Table

Our work now is a very solemn, earnest work. We cannot evade it. There is the greatest necessity of education in more lines than one. The one great need with you both is to feel that you must be under supervision to God. You are His property. Your children are His property to be trained as younger members of the Lord's family, not to consider themselves to be especially indulged in any whim and denied nothing. Were you an observer of the same plan of discipline you see others pursuing in managing their children, you would criticize them severely.

And again, do not indulge yourselves in sitting at the table spread with a large variety of food, and because you enjoy these things, eat them before your children and say, No, you cannot have this. You cannot have that, it will hurt you, while you eat largely of the very things you forbid them to touch. Your discipline in this line needs the reformation and the principle of practice.

It is cruelty to sit down yourself to the third meal, and take satisfaction in talking and enjoying yourselves while you have your children sit by and eat nothing, representing the excellent discipline your children are under to let them watch your eating and not rebel against your authority. They do rebel. They are young now, but to continue this kind of discipline will spoil your authority.

Urging Children to Overeat

Then again you seem to fear when your children are at the table that they will not eat enough and urge them to eat and to drink. You need not have the slightest concern and show the anxiety you have manifested lest they shall not eat sufficiently. Their little stomachs are small and cannot hold a large amount. Better far let them have three meals than two for this reason. You let them have a large amount of food at one meal. The foundation is being laid for distention of the stomach, which results in dyspepsia.

To eat and to drink that which is not agreeable to them is not wisdom. And again, be sure and set before them the very food you desire they shall eat. That which is of a healthful quality of food for them is healthful for you. But the quantity of even healthful food should be carefully studied, so as not to introduce into the stomach too large a quantity at one meal. We must ourselves be temperate in all things, if we would give the proper lessons to our children. When they are older any inconsideration on your part is marked.—Letter 12, 1884.

Establish No One Rule

No eating should be allowed between our meals. I have eaten two meals each day for the last twenty-five years. I do not use butter myself, but some of my workers who sit at my table eat butter. They cannot take care of milk; it sours on the stomach, while they can take care of a small quantity of butter.

We cannot regulate the diet question by making any rule. Some can eat beans and dried peas, but to me this diet is painful. It is like poison. Some have appetites and taste for certain things, and assimilate them well. Others have no appetite for these articles. So one rule cannot be made for everyone.—Manuscript 15, 1889.

36.

Sister White and Prayer for the Sick

The question has been asked by some, "Has Sister White healed the sick?" I answer, "No, no; Sister White has often been called to pray for the sick, and to anoint them with oil in the name of the Lord Jesus, and with them she has claimed the fulfillment of the promise, 'The prayer of faith shall save the sick.'" No human power can save the sick, but, through the prayer of faith, the Mighty Healer has fulfilled His promise to those who have called upon His name. No human power can pardon sin or save the sinner. None can do this but Christ, the merciful physician of body and soul.

It has often been my privilege to pray with the sick. We should do this much more often than we do. If more prayer were offered in our sanitariums for the healing of the sick, the mighty power of the Healer would be seen. Many more would be strengthened and blessed, and many more acute sicknesses would be healed.

The power of Christ to stay disease has been revealed in the past in a remarkable manner. Before we were blessed with institutions where the sick could get help from suffering, by diligent treatment and earnest prayer in faith to God, we carried the most seemingly hopeless cases through successfully. Today the Lord invites the suffering ones to have faith in Him. Man's necessity is God's opportunity [Mark 6:1-5 quoted]. . . .

Simple Fervent Prayer to Accompany Treatment

With all our treatments given to the sick, simple fervent prayer should be offered for the blessing of healing. We are to point the sick to the compassionate Saviour, and His power to forgive and to heal. Through His gracious providence they may be restored. Point the sufferers to their Advocate in the heavenly courts. Tell them that Christ will heal the sick, if they will repent and cease to transgress the laws of God. There is a Saviour who will reveal Himself in our sanitariums to save those who will submit themselves to Him. The suffering ones can unite with you in prayer, confessing their sin, and receiving pardon.

It Is Christ Who Heals.—Sister White has never claimed to heal the sick. It is Christ who has healed in every instance, as it was Christ who in the days of His ministry raised the dead to life. It is Christ who performs every mighty work through the ministry of His servants. This Christ is to be trusted and believed in. His blessing upon the means used for restoration to health will bring success. The mercy of Christ delights to manifest itself in behalf of suffering humanity. It is He who imparts the ministration of healing to the sick, and physicians are to give to Him the glory for the wonderful works performed.—Letter 158, 1908.

Counsels on Many Matters

~~~~~~

INTRODUCTION

For one reason or another various lines of Ellen White's counsel have through the years come to the front and demanded our attention. These range from light on a few points of gardening to sinlessness and salvation. All seemed appropriate for inclusion in a book of *Selected Messages*. They fill this section but can be given no more than the barest touch of organization.

While most of the items will interest and be of service to nearly all readers, attention is called particularly to several of the last items, including "Disparaging the Pioneers" and "Attacks on Ellen White and Her Work." Had space allowed, other items might have been included.—WHITE TRUSTEES.

37.

Seventh-day Adventists and

Lawsuits

Opening Church Difficulties to Unbelievers.—
When troubles arise in the church we should not go for
help to lawyers not of our faith. God does not desire us
to open church difficulties before those who do not fear
Him. He would not have us depend for help on those
who do not obey His requirements. Those who trust in
such counselors show that they have not faith in God. By
their lack of faith the Lord is greatly dishonored, and
their course works great injury to themselves. In appealing to unbelievers to settle difficulties in the church
they are biting and devouring one another, to be "consumed one of another" (Gal. 5:15).

These men cast aside the counsel God has given, and
do the very things He has bidden them not to do. They
show that they have chosen the world as their judge, and
in heaven their names are registered as one with unbelievers. Christ is crucified afresh, and put to open shame.
Let these men know that God does not hear their
prayers. They insult His holy name, and He will leave
them to the buffetings of Satan until they shall see their
folly and seek the Lord by confession of their sin.

Matters connected with the church are to be kept

within its own borders. If a Christian is abused, he is to take it patiently; if defrauded, he is not to appeal to courts of justice. Rather let him suffer loss and wrong.

God will deal with the unworthy church member who defrauds his brother or the cause of God; the Christian need not contend for his rights. God will deal with the one who violates these rights. "Vengeance is mine, I will repay, saith the Lord." Rom. 12:19. An account is kept of all these matters, and for all the Lord declares that He will avenge. He will bring every work into judgment.

Unsafe Counselors

The interests of the cause of God are not to be committed to men who have no connection with heaven. Those who are disloyal to God cannot be safe counselors. They have not that wisdom which comes from above. They are not to be trusted to pass judgment in matters connected with God's cause, matters upon which such great results depend. If we follow their judgment, we shall surely be brought into very difficult places, and shall retard the work of God.

Those who are not connected with God are connected with the enemy of God, and while they may be honest in the advice they give, they themselves are blinded and deceived. Satan puts suggestions into the mind and words into the mouth that are entirely contrary to the mind and will of God. Thus he works through them to allure us into false paths. He will mislead, entangle, and ruin us if he can.

Anciently it was a great sin for the people of God to give themselves away to the enemy, and open before them either their perplexity or their prosperity. Under the ancient economy it was a sin to offer sacrifice upon the wrong altar. It was a sin to offer incense kindled by the wrong fire.

We are in danger of mingling the sacred and the common. The holy fire from God is to be used in our efforts. The true altar is Christ; the true fire is the Holy

Spirit. This is our inspiration. It is only as the Holy Spirit leads and guides a man that he is a safe counselor. If we turn aside from God and from His chosen ones to inquire at strange altars we shall be answered according to our works.

Let us show perfect trust in our Leader. Let us seek wisdom from the Fountain of wisdom. In every perplexing or trying situation, let God's people agree as touching the thing they desire, and then let them unite in offering prayer to God, and persevere in asking for the help they need. We are to acknowledge God in all our counsel, and when we ask of Him, we are to believe that we receive the very blessings sought.—Undated Manuscript 112.

Counsel to a Believer Threatening Lawsuits

When you engaged in that lawsuit against R, I said if S has gone so far as to enter into that business, it will be a blot upon his life. I have sorrowed because of your course in this; I know that it is not right, and will not in the least relieve the situation for you in any way. It is only a manifestation of that wisdom which is not from above.

I was informed that you intended to institute a suit against me, on the ground that you had been wronged by the testimonies given in your case. A letter came to me, threatening that if I did not acknowledge that I had wronged you, the suit would be entered upon. Now, I could hardly believe that you had gone so decidedly on the enemy's ground, knowing my lifework as well as you do.

All that I have written to you, every word of it, was the truth. I have no retractions to make. I have done only that which I know to be my duty to do. My only motive in publishing the matter was the hope of saving you. I had no thought but of sincere pity and love for your soul. You yourself know that I have great interest for your soul. . . .

If anyone shall seek to hinder me in this work by

appealing to the law, I shall not abate one jot of the testimonies given. The work in which I am engaged is not my work. It is the work of God, which He has given me to do. I did not believe that you would do so terrible a thing as to lift your finite hand against the God of heaven. Whoever shall do this work, let it not be you.
. . .

I want to say to you. Do not extort money from anyone because of words spoken against you or yours. You harm yourself by so doing. If we are looking unto Jesus, the Author and Finisher of our faith, we shall be able to pray, "Lord, forgive us our trespasses, as we forgive those who trespass against us." Jesus did not appeal to the law for redress when He was unjustly accused. When He was reviled, He reviled not again; when He was threatened, He did not retaliate.—Letter 38, 1891.

The Very Thing God Told Them Not to Do.—I have written largely in regard to Christians who believe the truth placing their cases in courts of law to obtain redress. In doing this, they are biting and devouring one another in every sense of the word, "to be consumed one of another." They cast aside the inspired counsel God has given, and in the face of the message He gives they do the very thing He has told them not to do. Such men may as well stop praying to God, for He will not hear their prayers. They insult Jehovah, and He will leave them to become the subjects of Satan until they shall see their folly and seek the Lord by confession of their sins.
. . .

What Appeals to the Courts Reveal.—The world and unconverted church members are in sympathy. Some when God reproves them for wanting their own way, make the world their confidence, and bring church matters before the world for decision. Then there is collision and strife, and Christ is crucified afresh, and put to open shame. Those church members who appeal to the courts of the world show that they have chosen the world as their judge, and their names are registered in heaven as one with unbelievers. How eagerly the world seizes the statements of those who betray sacred trusts!

This action, of appealing to human courts, never before entered into by Seventh-day Adventists, has now been done. God has permitted this that you who have been deceived may understand what power is controlling those who had entrusted to them great responsibilities. Where are God's sentinels? Where are the men who will stand shoulder to shoulder, heart to heart, with the truth, present truth for this time, in possession of the heart?—Manuscript 64, 1898.

The Saints to Judge the World

The saints are to judge the world. Then are they to depend upon the world, and upon the world's lawyers to settle their difficulties? God does not want them to take their troubles to the subjects of the enemy for decision. Let us have confidence in one another.—Manuscript 71, 1903.

Lawyers and Laodiceans

To lean upon the arm of the law is a disgrace to Christians; yet this evil has been brought in and cherished among the Lord's chosen people. Worldly principles have been stealthily introduced, until in practice many of our workers are becoming like the Laodiceans—half-hearted, because so much dependence is placed on lawyers and legal documents and agreements. Such a condition of things is abhorrent to God.—Manuscript 128, 1903.

A Lawsuit Against the Publishing House

"Dare any of you, having a matter against another, go to law before the unjust, and not before the saints? Do ye not know that the saints shall judge the world? and if the world shall be judged by you, are ye unworthy to judge the smallest matters? Know ye not that we shall judge angels? how much more the things that pertain to this life? If then ye have judgments of things pertaining to this life, set them to judge who are least esteemed in the church. I speak to your shame. Is it so that there is not a wise man among you? no, not one that shall be able to judge between his brethren? But brother goeth to law with brother, and that before the unbelievers. Now therefore there is utterly a fault among you, because ye go to law one with another. Why do ye not rather take wrong? why do ye not rather suffer yourselves to be defrauded? Nay, ye do wrong, and defraud, and that your brethren. Know ye not that the unrighteous shall not inherit the kingdom of God?" (1 Cor. 6:1-9). . . . When church members have this knowledge, their practice will be of a character to recommend their faith. By a well-ordered life, and godly conversation, they will reveal Christ. There will be no lawsuits between neighbors or brothers.

I call upon you in the name of Christ to withdraw the suit that you have begun and never bring another into court. God forbids you thus to dishonor His name. You have had great light and many opportunities, and you cannot afford to unite with worldlings and follow their methods. Remember that the Lord will treat you according to the stand that you take in this life. . . .

I tell you solemnly that if you take the action which you now purpose to take, you will never recover from the result of it. If you open before the world the wrongs that you suppose your brethren have done you, there will be some things that will have to be said on the other side. I have a caution to give you.

In regard to the case of those who shared large responsibilities with you in the Review and Herald, and who have turned to be enemies of the work, you will not wish to hear the verdict that shall be passed upon them when the judgment shall sit and the books shall be opened, and every man shall be judged according to the things written in the books. I want to save you from following a course that would link you up with those who have linked themselves up with fallen angels, to do all the harm they possibly can to those who love God, and who, under great difficulty, are striving to proclaim present truth to the world.

The Publishing House Not Blameless.—Those against whom you bring your charges know that I have not approved of their manner of dealing with you, and that I have reproved them for their unfeeling management of your case. There are those who have not acted honorably. They have not done as they would be done by. But because of this, should you, in the face of the warnings given, move so manifestly against the instruction given? I beg of you not to cut yourself off from the confidence of your brethren and from taking a part in the publishing work.

I would rather share your loss than to have you push this matter through to the injury of your soul, giving Satan an opportunity to present your case before unbelievers in a most ridiculous light, and to hold up the office of publication in a disparaging light. . . .

God's Cause Injured

Take this case out of the lawyers' hands. It seems awful to me to think that you will go directly contrary to the plain word of God, and will open to the world your cruel work against God's commandment-keeping people. If this action of yours were to tell only against those who have done injustice, the harm would not be so far-reaching; but can you not see that it will arouse prejudice against God's people as a body? Thus you will bruise and wound Christ in the person of His saints, and cause Satan to exult because through you he could work against God's people and against His institutions, doing them great harm.—Letter 301, 1905.

38.

Science and Revelation

"The fool hath said in his heart, There is no God." The mightiest intellects of earth cannot comprehend God. If He reveals Himself at all to men, it is by veiling Himself in mystery. His ways are past finding out. Men must be ever searching, ever learning; and yet there is an infinity beyond. Could they fully understand the purposes, wisdom, love, and character of God, they would not believe in Him as an infinite being, and trust Him with the interests of their souls. If they could fathom Him, He would no longer stand supreme.

There are men who think they have made wonderful discoveries in science. They quote the opinions of learned men as though they considered them infallible, and teach the deductions of science as truths that cannot be controverted. And the Word of God, which is given as a lamp to the feet of the world-weary traveler, is judged by this standard, and pronounced wanting.

The scientific research in which these men have indulged has proved a snare to them. It has clouded their minds, and they have drifted into skepticism. They have a consciousness of power; and instead of looking to the Source of all wisdom, they triumph in the smattering of knowledge they may have gained. They have exalted their human wisdom in opposition to the wisdom of the great and mighty God, and have dared to enter into controversy with Him. The word of inspiration pronounces these men "fools."

The Fruitage of Skepticism

God has permitted a flood of light to be poured upon the world in discoveries in science and art; but when professedly scientific men lecture and write upon these subjects from a merely human standpoint, they will assuredly come to wrong conclusions. The greatest minds, if not guided by the Word of God in their research, become bewildered in their attempts to investigate the relations of science and revelation. The Creator and His works are beyond their comprehension; and because they cannot explain these by natural laws, Bible history is considered unreliable. Those who doubt the reliability of the records of the Old and New Testaments, will be led to go a step farther, and doubt the existence of God; and then, having let go their anchor, they are left to beat about upon the rocks of infidelity.

Moses wrote under the guidance of the Spirit of God, and a correct theory of geology will never claim discoveries that cannot be reconciled with his statements. The idea that many stumble over, that God did not create matter when He brought the world into existence, limits the power of the Holy One of Israel.

Test Science by God's Word.—Many, when they find themselves incapable of measuring the Creator and His works by their own imperfect knowledge of science, doubt the existence of God and attribute infinite power to nature. These persons have lost the simplicity of faith, and are removed far from God in mind and spirit. There should be a settled faith in the divinity of God's Holy Word. The Bible is not to be tested by men's idea of science, but science is to be brought to the test of this unerring standard. When the Bible makes statements of facts in nature, science may be compared with the Written Word, and a correct understanding of both will always prove them to be in harmony. One does not contradict the other. All truth, whether in nature or revelation, agrees.

Scientific research will open to the minds of the really wise vast fields of thought and information. They will see God in His works, and will praise Him. He will be to them first and best, and the mind will be centered upon Him. Skeptics, who read the Bible for the sake of caviling, through ignorance claim to find decided contradictions between science and revelation. But man's measurement of God will never be correct. The mind unenlightened by God's Spirit will ever be in darkness in regard to His power.

Spiritual things are spiritually discerned. Those who have no vital union with God are swayed one way and another; they put men's opinions in the front, and God's Word in the background. They grasp human assertions, that judgment against sin is contrary to God's benevolent character, and, while dwelling upon infinite benevolence, try to forget that there is such a thing as infinite justice.

When we have right views of the power, greatness, and majesty of God, and of the weakness of man, we shall despise the assumptions of wisdom made by earth's so-called great men, who have none of Heaven's nobility in their characters. There is nothing for which men should be praised or exalted. There is no reason why the opinions of the learned should be trusted, when they are disposed to measure divine things by their own perverted conceptions. Those who serve God are the only ones whose opinion and example it is safe to follow. A sanctified heart quickens and intensifies the mental powers. A living faith in God imparts energy; it gives calmness and repose of spirit, and strength and nobility of character.

God Can Work Above His Laws.—Men of science think that with their enlarged conceptions they can comprehend the wisdom of God, that which He has done or can do. The idea largely prevails that He is bounded and restricted by His own laws. Men either deny and ignore His existence, or think to explain everything, even the operations of His Spirit upon the human heart, by natural laws; and they no longer reverence His name or fear His power. While they think they are gaining everything, they are chasing bubbles, and losing precious opportunities to become acquainted with God. They do not believe in the supernatural, not realizing that the Author of nature's laws can work above those laws. They deny the claims of God, and neglect the interests of their own souls; but His existence, His character, His laws, are facts that the reasoning of men of the highest attainments cannot overthrow.

The pen of inspiration thus describes the power and majesty of God: "Who hath measured the waters in the hollow of his hand, and meted out heaven with the span, and comprehended the dust of the earth in a measure, and weighed the mountains in scales, and the hills in a balance? . . . Behold, the nations are as a drop of a bucket, and are counted as the small dust of the balance: behold, he taketh up the isles as a very little thing. And Lebanon is not sufficient to burn, nor the beasts thereof sufficient for a burnt offering. All nations before him are as nothing; and they are counted to him less than nothing, and vanity. . . . It is he that sitteth upon the circle of the earth, and the inhabitants thereof are as grasshoppers; that stretcheth out the heavens as a curtain, and spreadeth them out as a tent to dwell in" (Isa. 40:12-22).

God's Character Interpreted by His Works.— Nature is a power, but the God of nature is unlimited in power. His works interpret His character. Those who judge Him from His handiworks, and not from the suppositions of great men, will see His presence in everything. They behold His smile in the glad sunshine, and His love and care for man in the rich fields of autumn. Even the adornments of the earth, as seen in the grass of living green, the lovely flowers of every hue, and the lofty and varied trees of the forest, testify to the tender, fatherly care of our God, and to His desire to make His children happy.

The power of the great God will be exerted in behalf of those that fear Him. Listen to the words of the prophet: "Hast thou not known? hast thou not heard, that the everlasting God, the Lord, the Creator of the ends of the earth, fainteth not, neither is weary? there is no searching of his understanding. He giveth power to the faint; and to them that have no might he increaseth strength. Even the youths shall faint and be weary, and the young men shall utterly fall. But they that wait upon the Lord shall renew their strength; they shall mount up with wings as eagles; they shall run, and not be weary; and they shall walk, and not faint" (verses 28-31).

In the Word of God many queries are raised that the most profound scholars can never answer. Attention is called to these subjects to show us how many things there are, even among the common things of everyday life, that finite minds, with all their boasted wisdom, can never fully comprehend.

Science an Aid to Understand God.—All the systems of philosophy devised by men have led to confusion and shame when God has not been recognized and honored. To lose faith in God is terrible. Prosperity cannot be a great blessing to nations or individuals, when once faith in His Word is lost. Nothing is truly great but that which is eternal in its tendencies. Truth, justice, mercy, purity, and the love of God, are imperishable. When men possess these qualities, they are brought into close relationship to God, and are candidates for the highest exaltation to which the race can aspire. They will disregard human praise, and will be superior to disappointment, weariness, the strife of tongues, and contentions for supremacy.

He whose soul is imbued with the Spirit of God will learn the lesson of confiding trust. Taking the Written Word as his counselor and guide, he will find in science an aid to understand God, but he will not become exalted, till, in his blind self-conceit, he is a fool in his ideas of God.—*Signs of the Times*, March 13, 1884.

The precepts and principles of religion are the first steps in the acquisition of knowledge, and lie at the very foundation of true education. Knowledge and science must be vitalized by the Spirit of God in order to serve the noblest purposes. The Christian alone can make the right use of knowledge. Science, in order to be fully appreciated, must be viewed from a religious standpoint. Then all will worship the God of science."—Manuscript 30, 1896.

God the Designer and Creator

We need more to be shut in the audience with God. There is need of guarding our own thoughts. We are surely living amid the perils of the last days. We must walk before God meekly, with deep humility; for it is only such that will be exalted.

O how little man can comprehend the perfection of God, His omnipresence united with His almighty power. A human artist receives his intelligence from God. He can only fashion his work in any line to perfection from materials already prepared for his work. In his finite power he could not create and make his materials to serve his purpose if the Great Designer had not been before him, giving him the very improvements first in his imagination.

The Lord God commands things into being. He was the first designer. He is not dependent on man, but graciously invites man's attention, and cooperates with him in progressive and higher designs. Then man takes all the glory to himself, and is extolled by his fellow men as a very remarkable genius. He looks no higher than man. The one first cause is forgotten. . . .

I am afraid we have altogether too cheap and common ideas. "Behold, the heaven and heaven of heavens cannot contain thee." Let not any one venture to limit the power of the Holy One of Israel. There are conjectures and questions in regard to God's work. "Put off thy shoes from off thy feet, for the place whereon thou standest is holy ground." Yes, angels are the ministers of God upon the earth, doing His will.

All Things Stood Up Before Him at His Voice.—In the formation of our world, God was not beholden to preexistent substance or matter. For the "things which are seen were not made of things which do appear." On the contrary, all things, material or spiritual, stood up before the Lord Jehovah at His voice, and were created for His own purpose. The heavens and all the host of them, the earth and all things that are therein, are not only the work of His hand, they came into existence by the breath of His mouth.

The Lord had given evidence that by His power He could in one short hour dissolve the whole frame of nature. He can turn things upside down, and destroy the things that man has built up in his most firm and substantial manner. He "removeth the mountains," He "overturneth them in his anger," He "shaketh the earth out of her place, and the pillars thereof tremble." "The pillars of heaven tremble and are astonished at his reproof." "The mountains quake at him, and the hills melt, and the earth is burned at his presence."—Manuscript 127, 1897.

39.

Questions About the Saved

Will Children of Unbelieving Parents Be Saved?*

I had some conversation with Elder [J.G.] Matteson in regard to whether children of unbelieving parents would be saved. I related that a sister had with great anxiety asked me this question, stating that some had told her that the little children of unbelieving parents would not be saved.

This we should consider as one of the questions we are not at liberty to express a position or an opinion upon, for the simple reason that God has not told us definitely about this matter in His Word. If He thought it was essential for us to know, He would have told us plainly.

The things He has revealed are for us and for our children. There are things we do not now understand. We are ignorant of many things that are plainly revealed. When these subjects which have close relation to our eternal welfare are exhausted, then it will be ample time to consider some of these points that some are unnecessarily perplexing their minds about.

Children of Believing Parents. —I know that some

---

* See "Children in the Resurrection" in *Selected Messages*, book 2, pp. 259, 260, and "Comfort for a Bereaved Mother," in *Child Guidance*, pp. 565, 566.

questioned whether the little children of even believing parents should be saved, because they have had no test of character and all must be tested and their character determined by trial. The question is asked, "How can little children have this test and trial?" I answer that the faith of the believing parents covers the children, as when God sent His judgments upon the first-born of the Egyptians.

The word of God came to the Israelites in bondage to gather their children into their houses and to mark the doorposts of their houses with blood from a lamb, slain. This prefigured the slaying of the Son of God and the efficacy of His blood, which was shed for the salvation of the sinner. It was a sign that the household accepted Christ as the promised Redeemer. It was shielded from the destroyer's power. The parents evidenced their faith in implicitly obeying the directions given them, and the faith of the parents covered themselves and their children. They showed their faith in Jesus, the great Sacrifice, whose blood was prefigured in the slain lamb. The destroying angel passed over every house that had this mark upon it. This is a symbol to show that the faith of the parents extends to their children and covers them from the destroying angel.

God sent a word of comfort to the bereaved mothers of Bethlehem that the weeping Rachels should see their children coming from the land of the enemy. Christ took little children in His arms and blessed them and rebuked the disciples who would send away the mothers, saying, "Suffer little children, and forbid them not, to come unto me: for of such is the kingdom of heaven" (Matt. 19:14).

Christ blessed the children brought to Him by the faithful mothers. He will do this now if mothers will do their duty to their children and teach their children and educate them in obedience and submission. Then they will bear the test and will be obedient to the will of God, for parents stand in the place of God to their children.

Unruly Children of Adventist Parents.—Some

parents allow Satan to control their children, and their children are not restrained, but are allowed to have wicked tempers, to be passionate, selfish, and disobedient. Should they die these children would not be taken to heaven. The parents' course of action is determining the future welfare of their children. If they allow them to be disobedient and passionate they are allowing Satan to take them in charge and work through them as shall please his satanic majesty, and these children, never educated to obedience and to lovely traits of character, will not be taken to heaven, for the same temper and disposition would be revealed in them.

I said to Brother Matteson, "Whether all the children of unbelieving parents will be saved we cannot tell, because God has not made known His purpose in regard to this matter, and we had better leave it where God has left it and dwell upon subjects made plain in His Word."

This is a most delicate subject. Many unbelieving parents manage their children with greater wisdom than many of those who claim to be children of God. They take much pains with their children, to make them kind, courteous, unselfish and to teach them to obey, and in this the unbelieving show greater wisdom than those parents who have the great light of truth but whose works do not in any wise correspond with their faith.

Will There Be a Certain Number?—Another question upon which we had some conversation was in regard to the elect of God—that the Lord would have a certain number, and when that number was made up then probation would cease. These are questions you or I have no right to talk about. The Lord Jesus will receive all who come unto Him. He died for the ungodly and every man who will come, may come.

Certain conditions are to be complied with on the part of man, and if he refuses to comply with the conditions, he cannot become the elect of God. If he will comply, he is a child of God, and Christ says if he will continue in faithfulness, steadfast and immovable in his obedience, He will not blot out his name out of the book of life but will confess his name before His Father and before His angels. God would have us think and talk and present to others those truths which are plainly revealed, and all have naught to do with these subjects of speculation, for they have no special reference to the salvation of our souls.—Manuscript 26, 1885.

Will the Resurrected Recognize One Another?

God's greatest gift is Christ, whose life is ours, given for us. He died for us, and was raised for us, that we might come forth from the tomb to a glorious companionship with heavenly angels, to meet our loved ones and to recognize their faces, for the Christlikeness does not destroy their image, but transforms it into His glorious image. Every saint connected in family relationship here will know each other there.

When we are redeemed, the Bible will be understood in a higher, broader, and clearer sense than it now is. The veil that has hung between mortality and immortality will be rent away. We shall see His face.—Letter 79, 1898.

40.

The Question of the Date Line

The Sabbath Made for a Round World

God rested on the seventh day, and set it apart for man to observe in honor of His creation of the heavens and the earth in six literal days. He blessed and sanctified and made holy the day of rest. When men are so careful to search and dig to see in regard to the precise period of time, we are to say, God made His Sabbath for a round world; and when the seventh day comes to us in that round world, controlled by the sun that rules the day, it is the time in all countries and lands to observe the Sabbath. In the countries where there is no sunset for months, and again no sunrise for months, the period of time will be calculated by records kept. . . .

The Lord accepts all the obedience of every creature He has made, according to the circumstances of time in the sun-rising and sun-setting world. . . . The Sabbath was made for a round world, and therefore obedience is required of the people that are in perfect consistency with the Lord's created world.—Letter 167, 1900.

The Date Line Problem

Sister T has been speaking of you to me. She says that you are in some confusion in regard to the day line. Now, my dear sister, this talk about the day line is only

a something that Satan has devised as a snare. He seeks
to bewitch the senses, as he does in saying, "Lo, here is
Christ, or there." There will be every fiction and devising of Satan to lead persons astray, but the word is,
"Believe it not. For there shall arise false Christs, and
false prophets, and shall shew great signs and wonders;
insomuch that, if it were possible, they shall deceive the
very elect. Behold, I have told you before. Wherefore if
they shall say unto you, Behold, he is in the desert; go
not forth: behold, he is in the secret chambers; believe it
not" (Matt. 24:23-26).

Seventh-day Sabbath Left in No Uncertainty.—
We have the positive word of God in regard to the
Sabbath [Ex. 31:12-18 quoted].

Is it possible that so much importance can be clus-
tered about those who observe the Sabbath, and yet no
one can tell when the Sabbath comes? Then where is the
people who bear the badge or sign of God? What is the
sign? The seventh-day Sabbath, which the Lord blessed
and sanctified, and pronounced holy, with great penal-
ties for its violation.

The seventh-day Sabbath is in no uncertainty. It is
God's memorial of His work of creation. It is set up as a
heaven-given memorial, to be observed as a sign of
obedience. God wrote the whole law with His finger on
two tables of stone. . . .

Now, my sister, . . . I write . . . to tell you that we
are not to give the least credence to the day line theory.
It is a snare of Satan brought in by his own agents to
confuse minds. You see how utterly impossible for this
thing to be, that the world is all right observing Sunday,
and God's remnant people are all wrong. This theory of
the day line would make all our history for the past
fifty-five years a complete fallacy. But we know where
we stand. . . .

To Stand Fast by Our Colors.—My sister, let not
your faith fail. We are to stand fast by our colors, the
commandments of God and the faith of Jesus. All those
who hold the beginning of their confidence firm unto the

end will keep the seventh-day Sabbath, which comes to us as marked by the sun. The fallacy of the day line is a trap of Satan to discourage. I know what I am speaking about. Have faith in God. Shine where you are, as a living stone in God's building.

The children of God will be triumphant. They will come off conquerors and more than conquerors over all the opposing, persecuting elements. Fear not. By the power of Bible truth and love exemplified in the cross, and set home by the Holy Spirit, we shall have the victory. The whole battle before us hinges upon the observance of the true Sabbath of Jehovah. . . .

I can write no more now, but I say, Give no ear to heresy. Cling to a plain "Thus saith the Lord." He will comfort and bless you, and will give you joy in your heart. Praise the Lord that we have clear light, and a plain, distinct message to bear.—Letter 118, 1900.

41.

Memorials, Are They Proper?

Memorials to Remind Us of Our History

When Israel obtained special victories after leaving Egypt, memorials were preserved of these victories. Moses and Joshua were commanded of God to do this, to build up remembrances. When the Israelites had won a special victory over the Philistines, Samuel set up a commemorative stone and called it Ebenezer, saying, "Hitherto hath the Lord helped us" (1 Samuel 7:12).

Oh, where, as a people, are our commemorative stones? Where are set up our monumental pillars carved with letters expressing the precious story of what God has done for us in our experience? Can we not, in view of the past, look on new trials and increased perplexities— even afflictions, privations, and bereavements—and not be dismayed, but look upon the past and say, "'Hitherto hath the Lord helped us.' I will commit the keeping of my soul unto Him as unto a faithful Creator. He will keep that which I have committed to His trust against that day. 'As thy days, so shall thy strength be.'"— Manuscript 22, 1889.

Call to Remember the Former Days

The dealings of God with His people should be often repeated. How frequently were the waymarks set up by the Lord in His dealings with ancient Israel! Lest they should forget the history of the past, He commanded Moses to frame these events into song, that parents might teach them to their children. They were to gather up memorials and to lay them up in sight. Special pains were taken to preserve them, that when the children should inquire concerning these things, the whole story might be repeated. Thus the providential dealings and the marked goodness and mercy of God in His care and deliverance of His people were kept in mind. We are exhorted to "call to remembrance the former days, in which, after ye were illuminated, ye endured a great fight of afflictions." Hebrews 10:32. For His people in this generation the Lord has wrought as a wonder-working God. The past history of the cause of God needs to be often brought before the people, young and old. We need often to recount God's goodness and to praise Him for His wonderful works.—*Testimonies,* vol. 6, pp. 364, 365.

42.

Renting Our Churches to Other Denominations

One week ago last Sabbath, I filled an appointment to speak in the church in San Francisco. We had an excellent meeting. There seemed to be an earnest desire to hear, and an interest in the words spoken.

This is the first time I had spoken in the San Francisco church since long before the earthquake and fire. The building was in a much better condition than I expected to find it. The meeting room is large, and well kept. On the platform, and in front the floor is carpeted with red Brussels. The carpet is well preserved and is kept looking nice. The pulpit is well arranged.

Your grandfather and I were the ones who worked up the plans for erecting this building. A few others united with us, and we all worked together as best we could.

There are large, stained glass windows, which help to give a good appearance. The baptistry is nicely arranged. Back of the pulpit the wall swings back on hinges and the baptistry is thus brought into full view of the audience. I cannot express my thankfulness that the Lord preserved this large meetinghouse through the earthquake and the fire. We appreciate it now very much.

The church is rented to the Presbyterians for services

on Sunday. This makes it a little inconvenient for us at times, but as their meetinghouse was destroyed, they feel very grateful for the privilege of using ours.

In some of the lower rooms dispensary work is carried on, and there are well-equipped treatment rooms. The work that has been done here has been a blessing to many, especially since the fire.—Letter 18a, 1906.

43.

Feelings of Despondency

Ellen White Suffered Desponding Feelings

You ask me why it is that you awake in the night and feel enclosed in darkness? I often feel the same way myself; but these desponding feelings are no evidence that God has forsaken you or me. . . . Gloomy feelings are no evidence that the promises of God are of no effect.

You look at your feelings, and because your outlook is not all brightness, you begin to draw more closely the garment of heaviness about your soul. You look within yourself and think that God is forsaking you. You are to look to Christ. . . .

Entering into communion with our Saviour, we enter the region of peace. . . . We must put faith into constant exercise, and trust in God whatever our feelings may be. . . . We are to be of good cheer, knowing that Christ has overcome the world. We will have tribulation in the world, but peace in Jesus Christ. My brother, turn your eyes from within, and look to Jesus who is your only helper.—Letter 26, 1895.

Counsel to a Despondent Sister

In my Christian experience I have passed over the ground where you are now traveling. It seemed that I was bound in chains of despair. When quite young, only about 12 years old, I was for months utterly helpless. But the Lord did not suffer me to remain in this condition. He attracted me by His own mercy and grace, and brought me to the light. He will help you.

Look away from yourself. Do not think or talk of yourself. You cannot save yourself by any good work that you may do. The Lord Jesus has not made you a sin-bearer. He has not been able to find any human or angelic being to be a sin-bearer. He says, "Come unto me, all ye that labour and are heavy laden, and I will give you rest." Do you not believe the words of Christ? He bids you, "Take my yoke upon you, and learn of me; for I am meek and lowly in heart; and ye shall find rest unto your souls. For my yoke is easy, and my burden is light."

Think of the Saviour. Lay your sins, both of omission and of commission, upon the Sin-bearer. You know that you love the Lord; then do not worry away your life because Satan harasses you with his falsehoods. Believe that Jesus will and does pardon your transgression. He bore the sins of the whole world. He loves to have the weak and troubled soul come to Him and rely upon Him. Seek God in simple faith, saying, "I believe; help thou mine unbelief."

Angels Minister to Trusting Souls.—The Lord does not readily cast off His erring children. He bears long with them. His angels minister to every believing, trusting soul. Now, when you read these words, believe that the Lord accepts you just as you are, erring and sinful. He knows that you cannot blot out one sin; He knows that His precious blood, shed for the sinner, makes that one who is troubled, worried, and perplexed, a child of God.

The Word of God is like a garden filled with beautiful, fragrant flowers. My sister, will you not pluck the flowers, the roses, the lilies, and the pinks of His promises? Rest in His love. No tongue can express or finite mind conceive the greatness and richness of His promises for just such weak and trembling souls as you are. Simple faith and trust is your part; the Lord's part He never fails to fulfill. By faith draw close to the precious Sin-bearer, and then cling to Him by faith. Do not worry; this will not help the matter at all. Believe that Christ Himself rebukes the enemy, and that he can have no more control over you. Believe that Satan has been rebuked. When the enemy comes in like a flood, the Spirit of the Lord will lift up for you a standard against him.

Take Hold of Jesus and Never Let Go.—Again I bid you to look away from yourself. Look to Jesus. Take hold of the Mighty One, and never let go. Our Lord Jesus has expressed His love for you in that He gave His own life that you might be saved; you must not distrust that love. Do not look on the dark side. Be hopeful in God. By beholding Jesus as your sin-pardoning Saviour you become changed into His image. Say, "I have asked my Saviour, He has set me free, and I am free indeed. I am the Lord's, and the Lord is mine. I will not fear. I know that He loves me in my infirmities, and I will not make Him sorry by showing that I distrust Him. I break with the enemy. Christ has cut the cords that bound me, and I will praise the Lord."

Thus you can educate and strengthen your mind. May the Lord help and bless you every moment. Be free, yes, be free in the Lord just now. Rejoice in your freedom.—Letter 36, 1900.

Look Beyond the Shadows

Jesus lives; He has risen, He has risen, He is alive forevermore. Do not feel that you carry the load. It is true you wear the yoke, but whom are you yoked up with?—No less a personage than your Redeemer. Satan will cast his hellish shadow athwart your pathway; you cannot expect anything else; but he cast the same dark shadow athwart the pathway of Christ. Now all you have to do is to look beyond the shadow to the brightness of Christ. . . . Do not look at the discouragements; think of how precious is Jesus.

Your memory will be renewed by the Holy Spirit. Can you forget what Jesus has done for you? . . . You were taken away from yourself; your deepest, sweetest thoughts were upon your precious Saviour, His care, His assurance, His love. How your desires went out to Him!

All your hopes rested upon Him, all your expectations were associated with Him. Well, He loves you still; He has the balm that can heal every wound and you can repose in Him. . . .

The Comforter will be to you all that you desire. You will be weighted with the Spirit of God, and the importance of the message, and the work. I know that the Lord is willing to reveal to you wondrous things out of His law. Oh, let all take knowledge of you, that you have been with Jesus.—Letter 30a, 1892.

Face the Light.—I will not allow my mind to dwell on the dark side. Jesus has light and comfort and hope and joy for me. I want to face the light, that the brightness of the Sun of Righteousness may shine into my heart, and be reflected to others. It is the duty of every Christian to shine—to shed abroad the light of the grace that Christ imparts. God would have me, even in my pain, praise Him, showing that I realize that His presence is with me. (Rom. 5:1; 1 John 5:11 quoted.)—Manuscript 19, 1892.

44.

Specific Light on Gardening

Ellen G. White Instructed in Planting Fruit Trees

While we were in Australia, we adopted the . . . plan . . . of digging deep trenches and filling them in with dressing that would create good soil. This we did in the cultivation of tomatoes, oranges, lemons, peaches, and grapes.

The man of whom we purchased our peach trees told me that he would be pleased to have me observe the way they were planted. I then asked him to let me show him how it had been represented in the night season that they should be planted. I ordered my hired man to dig a deep cavity in the ground, then put in rich dirt, then stones, then rich dirt. After this he put in layers of earth and dressing until the hole was filled. I told the nurseryman that I had planted in this way in the rocky soil in America. I invited him to visit me when these fruits should be ripe. He said to me, "You need no lesson from me to teach you how to plant the trees."

Our crops were very successful. The peaches were the most beautiful in coloring, and the most delicious in flavor of any that I had tasted. We grew the large yellow Crawford and other varieties, grapes, apricots, nectarines, and plums.—Letter 350, 1907.

The Spraying of Fruit Trees

There are those who say that nothing, not even insects, should be killed. God has not entrusted any such message to His people. It is possible to stretch the command "Thou shalt not kill" to any limit; but it is not according to sound reasoning to do this. Those who do it have not learned in the school of Christ.

This earth has been cursed because of sin, and in these last days vermin of every kind will multiply. These pests must be killed, or they will annoy and torment and even kill us, and destroy the work of our hands and the fruit of our land. In places there are ants [termites] which entirely destroy the woodwork of houses. Should not these be destroyed? Fruit trees must be sprayed, that the insects which would spoil the fruit may be killed. God has given us a part to act, and this part we must act with faithfulness. Then we can leave the rest with the Lord.

God has given no man the message, Kill not ant or flea or moth. Troublesome and harmful insects and reptiles we must guard against and destroy, to preserve ourselves and our possessions from harm. And even if we do our best to exterminate these pests, they will still multiply.—Manuscript 70, 1901. *(Review and Herald,* Aug. 31, 1961.)

45.

*Balanced Counsel on Picture-making and Idolatry**

It is a difficult matter for men and women to draw the line in the matter of picture-making. Some have made a raid against pictures, daguerreo-types, and pictures of every kind. Everything must be burned up, they say, urging that the making of all pictures is prohibited by the second commandment; that they are an idol.

An idol is anything that human beings love and trust in instead of loving and trusting in the Lord their Maker. Whatever earthly thing men desire and trust in as having power to help them and do them good, leads them away from God, and is to them an idol. Whatever divides the affections, or takes away from the soul the supreme love of God, or interposes to prevent unlimited confidence and entire trust in God, assumes the character and takes the form of an idol in the soul temple.

The first great commandment is, "Thou shalt love the Lord thy God with all thy heart, and with all thy soul, and with all thy mind" (Matt. 22:37). Here is allowed no separation of the affections from God. In 1 John 2:15-17 we read, "Love not the world, neither the things that are in the world. If any man love the world,

* See *Selected Messages*, book 2, pp. 318-320.

the love of the Father is not in him. For all that is in the world, the lust of the flesh, and the lust of the eyes, and the pride of life, is not of the Father, but is of the world. And the world passeth away, and the lust thereof: but he that doeth the will of God abideth forever." Now if the pictures made have a tendency to separate the affections from God, and are worshiped in the place of God, they are idols. Have those who claim to be followers of Jesus Christ exalted these things above God, and given their affections to them? Has their love for treasures filled a place in their hearts that Jesus should occupy?

Have those who have burned up all their pictures of friends and any kind of pictures they happened to have, come up to a higher state of consecration for this act, and do they seem in words, in deportment, and in soul, to be ennobled, elevated, more heavenly-minded? Is their experience richer than before? Do they pray more, and believe with a more perfect faith after this consuming sacrifice which they have made? Have they come up into the mount? Has the holy fire been kindled in their hearts, giving new zeal and greater devotion to God and His work than before? Has a live coal from off the altar of sacrifice touched their hearts and their lips? By their fruits you can tell the character of the work.—Manuscript 50, 1886.

46.

Music and the Music Director

Singing Drives Powers of Darkness Away

I saw we must be daily rising and keep the ascendancy above the powers of darkness. Our God is mighty. I saw singing to the glory of God often drove the enemy [away], and praising God would beat him back and give us the victory.—Manuscript 5, 1850.

Worldliness in Musical Lines

It is not safe for the Lord's workers to take part in worldly entertainments. Association with worldliness in musical lines is looked upon as harmless by some Sabbathkeepers. But such ones are on dangerous ground. Thus Satan seeks to lead men and women astray, and thus he has gained control of souls. So smooth, so plausible is the working of the enemy that his wiles are not suspected, and many church members become lovers of pleasure more than lovers of God.—Manuscript 82, 1900.

I was shown the case of Brother U—that he would be a burden to the church unless he comes into a closer relation with God. He is self-conceited. If his course is questioned he feels hurt. If he thinks another is preferred before him, he feels that it is an injury done to him. . . .

Brother U has a good knowledge of music, but his education in music was of a character to suit the stage rather than the solemn worship of God. Singing is just as much the worship of God in a religious meeting as speaking, and any oddity or peculiarity cultivated attracts the attention of the people and destroys the serious, solemn impression which should be the result of sacred music. Anything strange and eccentric in singing detracts from the seriousness and sacredness of religious service.

Dignified, Solemn, Impressive Music.—Bodily exercise profiteth little. Everything that is connected in any way with religious worship should be dignified, solemn, and impressive. God is not pleased when ministers professing to be Christ's representatives so misrepresent Christ as to throw the body into acting attitudes, making undignified and coarse gestures, unrefined, coarse gesticulations. All this amuses, and will excite the curiosity of those who wish to see strange, odd, and exciting things, but these things will not elevate the minds and hearts of those who witness them.

The very same may be said of singing. You assume undignified attitudes. You put in all the power and volume of the voice you can. You drown the finer strains and notes of voices more musical than your own. This bodily exercise and the harsh, loud voice makes no melody to those who hear on earth and those who listen in heaven. This singing is defective and not acceptable to God as perfect, softened, sweet strains of music. There are no such exhibitions among the angels as I have sometimes seen in our meetings. Such harsh notes and gesticulations are not exhibited among the angel choir. Their singing does not grate upon the ear. It is soft and melodious and comes without this great effort I have witnessed. It is not forced and strained, requiring physical exercise.

The Feelings Not Touched, the Heart Not Subdued.—Brother U is not aware how many are amused and disgusted. Some cannot repress thoughts not very sacred and feelings of levity to see the unrefined motions made in the singing. Brother U exhibits himself. His singing does not have an influence to subdue the heart and touch the feelings. Many have attended the meetings and listened to the words of truth spoken from the pulpit, which have convicted and solemnized their minds; but many times the way the singing has been conducted has not deepened the impression made. The demonstrations and bodily contortions, the unpleasant appearance of the strained, forced effort has appeared so out of place for the house of God, so comical, that the serious impressions made upon the minds have been removed. Those who believe the truth are not as highly thought of as before the singing.

It Must Be "All in His Way."—Brother U's case has been a difficult one to manage. He has been like a child undisciplined and uneducated. When his course has been questioned, instead of taking reproof as a blessing, he has let his feelings get the better of his judgment and he has become discouraged and would do nothing. If he could not do in everything as he wanted to do, all in his way, he would not help at all. He has not taken hold of the work earnestly to reform his manners but has given up to mulish feelings that separate the angels from him and bring evil angels around him. The truth of God received in the heart commences its refining, sanctifying influence upon the life. . . .

Brother U has thought that singing was about the greatest thing to be done in this world and that he had a very large and grand way of doing it.

Your singing is far from pleasing to the angel choir. Imagine yourself standing in the angel band elevating your shoulders, emphasizing the words, motioning your body and putting in the full volume of your voice. What kind of concert and harmony would there be with such an exhibition before the angels?

The Power of Music.—Music is of heavenly origin. There is great power in music. It was music from the angelic throng that thrilled the hearts of the shepherds on Bethlehem's plains and swept round the world. It is in music that our praises rise to Him who is the embodiment of purity and harmony. It is with music and songs of victory that the redeemed shall finally enter upon the immortal reward.

There is something peculiarly sacred in the human voice. Its harmony and its subdued and heaven-inspired pathos exceeds every musical instrument. Vocal music is one of God's gifts to men, an instrument that cannot be surpassed or equaled when God's love abounds in the soul. Singing with the spirit and the understanding also is a great addition to devotional services in the house of God.

How this gift has been debased! When sanctified and refined it would accomplish great good in breaking down the barriers of prejudice and hardhearted unbelief, and would be the means of converting souls. It is not enough to understand the rudiments of singing, but with the understanding, with the knowledge, must be such a connection with heaven that angels can sing through us.

Softer, Silvery Strains Drowned Out.—Your voice has been heard in church so loud, so harsh, accompanied or set off with your gesticulations not the most graceful, that the softer and more silvery strains, more like angel music, could not be heard. You have sung more to men than to God. As your voice has been elevated in loud strains above all the congregation, you have been thoughtful of the admiration you were exciting. You have really had such high ideas of your singing, that you have had some thoughts that you should be remunerated for the exercise of this gift.

The love of praise has been the mainspring of your life. This is a poor motive for a Christian. You have wanted to be petted and praised like a child. You have had much to contend with in your own nature. It has been hard for you to overcome your natural besetments and live a self-denying, holy life.—Manuscript 5, 1874.

47.

Work in the Spirit of Prayer

I feel an intense desire that this [the 1901 General Conference session] shall be a meeting where God can preside. This is an important time, a very important time. There is a great work to do. But whether the meeting shall be a success depends on us individually. We can make a heaven here during this meeting. . . .

There are solemn and important decisions to be made at this meeting, and God wants every one of us to stand in right relation to Him. He wants us to do a great deal more praying and a great deal less talking. He wants us to keep the windows of the soul opened heavenward. The threshold of heaven is flooded with the light of God's glory, and God will let this light shine into the heart of everyone who at this meeting will stand in right relation to Him.

Some have said that they thought that at this meeting several days ought to be spent in prayer to God for the Holy Spirit, as at the day of Pentecost. I wish to say to you that the business which may be carried on at this meeting is just as much a part of the service of God as is prayer. The business meeting is to be just as much under the dictation of the Spirit as the prayer meeting. There is danger of our getting a sentimental, impulsive religion.

Let the business transacted at this meeting stand forth in such sacredness that the heavenly host can approve of it. We are to guard most sacredly the business lines of our work. Every line of business carried on here is to be in accordance with the principles of heaven.

God wants you to stand in position where He can breathe upon you the Holy Spirit, where Christ can abide in the heart. He wants you at the beginning of this meeting to lay off whatever of controversy, of strife, of dissension, of murmuring, you have been carrying. What we need is a great deal more of Christ and none of self. The Saviour says, "Without me ye can do nothing." . . .

We have come to a point where God is going to work for His people. He wishes them to be a representative people, distinct from all other peoples in our world. He wants them to stand on vantage ground, because He gave His life that they might stand there. Do not disappoint the Lord.—Manuscript 29, 1901.

Too Many Resolutions

Your very many resolutions need to be reduced to one third their number, and great care should be taken as to what resolutions are framed.—Letter 21-a, 1888.

I have been shown that our conferences have been overburdened with resolutions. One tenth as many would be of far greater value than a larger number. I stated these things clearly, but still you urged that the resolution should be carried into effect.—Letter 22, 1889.

48.

The Bible Prophets Wrote for Our Time

Never are we absent from the mind of God. God is our joy and our salvation. Each of the ancient prophets spoke less for their own time than for ours, so that their prophesying is in force for us. "Now all these things happened unto them for ensamples: and they are written for our admonition, upon whom the ends of the world are come" (1 Cor. 10:11). "Not unto themselves, but unto us they did minister the things, which are now reported unto you by them that have preached the gospel unto you with the Holy Ghost sent down from heaven; which things the angels desire to look into" (1 Peter 1:12).

The Bible has been your study-book. It is well thus, for it is the true counsel of God, and it is the conductor of all the holy influences that the world has contained since its creation. We have the encouraging record that Enoch walked with God. If Enoch walked with God, in that degenerate age just prior to the destruction of the world by a flood, we are to receive courage and be stimulated with his example that we need not be contaminated with the world but, amid all its corrupting influences and tendencies, we may walk with God. We may have the mind of Christ.

Treasures for the Last Generation

Enoch, the seventh from Adam, was ever prophesying the coming of the Lord. This great event had been revealed to him in vision. Abel, though dead, is ever speaking of the blood of Christ which alone can make our offerings and gifts perfect. The Bible has accumulated and bound up together its treasures for this last generation. All the great events and solemn transactions of Old Testament history have been, and are, repeating themselves in the church in these last days. There is Moses still speaking, teaching self-renunciation by wishing himself blotted from the Book of Life for his fellow men, that they might be saved. David is leading the intercession of the church for the salvation of souls to the ends of the earth. The prophets are still testifying of the sufferings of Christ and the glory that should follow. There the whole accumulated truths are presented in force to us that we may profit by their teachings. We are under the influence of the whole. What manner of persons ought we to be to whom all this rich light of inheritance has been given. Concentrating all the influence of the past with new and increased light of the present, accrued power is given to all who will follow the light. Their faith will increase, and be brought into exercise at the present time, awakening an energy and an intensely increased earnestness, and through dependence upon God for His power to replenish the world and send the light of the Sun of Righteousness to the ends of the earth.

God has enriched the world in these last days proportionately with the increase of ungodliness, if His people will only lay hold of His priceless gift and bind up their every interest with Him. There should be no cherished idols, and we need not dread what will come, but commit the keeping of our souls to God, as unto our faithful Creator. He will keep that which is committed to His trust.—Letter 74a, 1897.

49.

Can All Have the Gift of Prophecy?

From time to time reports come to me concerning statements that Sister White is said to have made but which are entirely new to me, and which cannot fail to mislead the people as to my real views and teaching. A sister, in a letter to her friends speaks with much enthusiasm of a statement by Brother Jones that Sister White has seen that the time has come when, if we hold the right relation to God, all can have the gift of prophecy to the same extent as do those who are now having visions.

Where is the authority for this statement? I must believe that the sister failed to understand Brother Jones, for I cannot think that he made the statement. The writer continues: "Brother Jones said last night that is the case, not that God will speak to all for the benefit of every one else but to each for his own benefit, and this will fulfill the prophecy of Joel." He stated that this is already being developed in numerous instances.

He spoke as if he thought none would hold such a leading position as Sister White had done and will still do. Referred to Moses as a parallel. He was a leader, but many others are referred to as prophesying, though their prophecies are not published. He (Brother Jones) will not give permission to have the matter copied for general circulation, that has been read here from some sister.

. . .

These ideas in relation to prophesying, I do not hesitate to say, might better never have been expressed. Such statements prepare the way for a state of things that Satan will surely take advantage of to bring in spurious exercises. There is danger, not only that unbalanced minds will be led into fanaticism, but that designing persons will take advantage of this excitement to further their own selfish purposes.

Jesus has raised His voice in warning: "Beware of false prophets, which come to you in sheep's clothing, but inwardly they are ravening wolves. Ye shall know them by their fruits" (Matt. 7:15, 16). "Thus saith the Lord of hosts, hearken not unto the words of the prophets that prophesy unto you: they make you vain: they speak a vision of their own heart, and not out of the mouth of the Lord" (Jer. 23:16). "If any man shall say to you, Lo here is Christ, or lo, he is there, believe him not; for false Christs and false prophets shall arise, and shall shew signs and wonders to seduce, if it were possible, even the elect. But take ye heed; behold, I have foretold you all things" (Mark 13:21-23).—Letter 6a, 1894.

50.

Disparaging the Pioneers

It is possible to relate that which has happened in connection with the past experience of the people of God, and so relate it as to make their experience assume a ludicrous and objectionable appearance. It is not fair to take certain features of the work and set them apart from the great whole. A mixture of truth and error may be presented in so doing, which our enemies would handle greatly to the disadvantage of the truth and to the hindrance of the work and cause of God. . . .

Let none of our brethren imagine that they are doing God's service in presenting the deficiencies of men who have done good, grand, acceptable work in laboring to unfold the message of mercy to fallen men, for the salvation of perishing souls. Suppose that these brethren have weak traits of character which they have inherited from their deficient ancestors, shall these deficiencies be hunted up and made prominent?

Shall men whom God has chosen to carry out the reformation against the papacy and idolatry be presented in an objectionable light? The banner of the ruler of the synagogue of Satan was lifted high, and error apparently marched in triumph, and the reformers through the grace given them of God, waged a successful warfare against the host of darkness. Events in the history of the reformers have been presented before me. I know that the Lord Jesus and His angels have with intense interest watched the battle against the power of Satan, who combined his hosts with evil men for the purpose of extinguishing the divine light, the fire of God's kingdom. They suffered for Christ's sake scorn, derision, and the hatred of men who knew not God. They were maligned and persecuted even unto death, because they would not renounce their faith. If anyone presumes to take these men in hand, and to lay before the world their errors and mistakes, let him remember that he is dealing with Christ in the person of His saints. . . .

A Rebuke to an Adventist Author.—You have made public the errors and defects of the people of God, and in so doing have dishonored God and Jesus Christ. I would not for my right arm have given to the world that which you have written. You have not been conscious of what would be the influence of your work. . . .

The Lord did not call upon you to present these things to the public as a correct history of our people. Your work will make it necessary for us to put forth labor to show why these brethren took the extreme position that they did, and call up the circumstances that vindicate those upon whom your articles have laid suspicion and reproach.

You Have Given a Distorted View.—You were not in the early experience of the people of whom you have written, and who have been laid to rest from their labors. You have given but a partial view; for you have not presented the fact that the power of God worked in connection with their labors, even though they made some mistakes. You have made prominent before the world the errors of the brethren, but have not represented the fact that God worked to correct those errors, and to set the objectionable matters right. Opposers will be glad to multiply the matter which has been furnished to their hand by our people. You have arrayed the errors of the early apostles, the errors of those who were precious in the eyes of the Lord in the days of Christ.

In presenting the extreme positions that have been taken by the messengers of God, do you think that confidence will be inspired in the work of God for this time? Let God by inspiration trace the errors of His people for their instruction and admonition; but let not finite lips or pens dwell upon those features of the experience of God's people that will have a tendency to confuse and cloud the mind. Let no one call attention to the errors of those whose general work has been accepted of God. The articles you have presented are not of a character to leave a true and fair impression upon the minds of those who read them concerning our work and our workers. . . .

God's children are very precious in His sight, and those who by pen or voice weaken the influence of even the least of those who believe in Jesus Christ, are registered in heaven as injurers of the Lord Himself. "Inasmuch as ye have done it unto one of the least of these my brethren, ye have done it unto me." We need to remember that we should guard carefully our thoughts, our feelings, our words, our actions, lest we wound and bruise the Saviour in the person of His saints; for He has told us plainly that He identifies Himself with suffering humanity. Not one of God's faithful ones will receive the honor of a crown of life in the kingdom of glory, who has not passed through severe conflicts and trials. Every one who wins in running the race for the immortal crown, will have striven lawfully.

Turn Not Weapons on Christ's Soldiers.—We are to direct the weapons of our warfare against our foes, but never to turn them toward those who are under marching orders from the King of kings, who are fighting manfully the battles of the Lord of lords. Let no one aim at a soldier whom God recognizes, whom God has sent forth to bear a special message to the world and to do a special work.

The soldiers of Christ may not always reveal perfection in their step, but their mistakes should call out from their fellow comrades not words that will weaken, but words that will strengthen, and will help them recover their lost ground. They should not turn the glory of God into dishonor, and give an advantage to the bitterest foes of their King.

Let not fellow soldiers be severe, unreasonable judges of their comrades, and make the most of every defect. Let them not manifest satanic attributes in becoming accusers of the brethren. We shall find ourselves misrepresented and falsified by the world, while we are maintaining the truth and vindicating God's downtrodden law; but let no one dishonor the cause of God by making public some mistake that the soldiers of Christ may make, when that mistake is seen and corrected by [the] ones who have taken some false position. . . .

God will charge those who unwisely expose the mistakes of their brethren with sin of far greater magnitude than He will charge the one who makes a misstep. Criticism and condemnation of the brethren are counted as criticism and condemnation of Christ.—Letter 48, 1894.

Increased Light Imposes Increased Responsibility

In this day we have been privileged to have increased light and large opportunities, and we are held responsible for the improvement of light. This will be manifested by increased piety and devotion. Our loyalty to God should be proportionate to the light which shines upon us in this age.

But the fact that we have increased light does not justify us in dissecting and judging the character of men whom God raised up in former times to do a certain work and to penetrate the moral darkness of the world.

In the past the servants of God wrestled with principalities and powers, and with the rulers of the darkness of this world, and with spiritual wickedness in high places, the same as we, who bear aloft the banner of truth, do today. These men were God's noblemen, His living agencies, through whom He wrought in a won-

derful manner. They were depositaries of divine truth to
the extent that the Lord saw fit to reveal the truth that
the world could bear to hear. They proclaimed the truth
at a time when false, corrupt religion was magnifying
itself in the world.

**No Occasion to Depreciate Character or Excuse
Sin.**—I could wish that the curtain could be rolled back,
and that those who have not spiritual eyesight might see
these men as they appear in the sight of God; for now
they see them as trees walking. They would not then put
their human construction upon the experience and works
of the men who parted the darkness from the track and
prepared the way for future generations.

Living down in our own generation, we may pronounce judgment upon the men whom God raised up to
do a special work, according to the light given to them
in their day. Though they may have been overcome with
temptation, they repented of their sins; and no opportunity is left for us to depreciate their characters or to
excuse sin. Their history is a beacon of warning to us,
and points out a safe path for our feet if we will but shun
their mistakes. These noble men sought the mercy seat
and humbled their souls before God.

Let not our voices or pens show that we are disre-
garding the solemn injunctions of the Lord. Let no one
depreciate those who have been chosen of God, who have
fought manfully the battles of the Lord, who have woven
heart and soul and life into the cause and work of God,
who have died in faith, and who are partakers of the
great salvation purchased for us through our precious
sin-bearing, sin-pardoning Saviour.

Speak Not of Mistakes of Living or Dead.—God
has inspired no man to reproduce their mistakes, and to
present their errors to a world that is lying in wickedness, and to a church composed of many who are weak in
faith. The Lord has not laid the burden upon men to
revive the mistakes and errors of the living or the dead.
He would have His laborers present the truth for this
time. Speak not of the errors of your brethren who are

living, and be silent as to the mistakes of the dead.

Let their mistakes and errors remain where God has put them—cast into the depths of the sea. The less that is said by those who profess to believe present truth, in regard to the past mistakes and errors of the servants of God, the better it will be for their own souls, and for the souls of those whom Christ has purchased with His own blood. Let every voice proclaim the words of the first and the last, the Alpha and Omega, the beginning and the end. John heard a voice saying, "Blessed are the dead which die in the Lord from henceforth: Yea, saith the Spirit, that they may rest from their labours; and their works do follow them" (Rev. 14:13).—*The Review and Herald,* Nov. 30, 1897.*

---

* This counsel was written to a worker who had published two articles in the *Review and Herald* (April 3 and 10, 1894) under the title "Danger of Adopting Extreme Views."—COMPILERS.

51.

Attacks on Ellen White and Her Work

Should We Keep Silent?

When man assails his fellow men, and presents in a ridiculous light those whom God has appointed to do work for him, we would not be doing justice to the accusers, or to those who are misled by their accusations should we keep silent, leaving the people to think that their brethren and sisters, in whom they have had confidence, are no longer worthy of their love and fellowship. This work, arising in our very midst, and resembling the work of Korah, Dathan, and Abiram, is an offence to God, and should be met. And on every point the accusers* should be called upon to bring their proof. Every charge should be carefully investigated; it should not be left in any uncertain way, the people should not be left to think that it may be or it may not be. The accusers should do all in their power to lift every sign of reproach that cannot be substantiated.

Leave Not the People to Believe a Lie.—This should be done in the case of every church. And when there is a servant of God, whom He has appointed to do a certain work, and who for half a century has been an

---

* Addressed to certain accusers in Australia who had had special evidence of Ellen White's work.—COMPILERS.

accepted worker, laboring for the people of our faith, and before God's workers as one whom the Lord has appointed; when for some reason one of the brethren falls under temptation, and because of the messages of warning given him becomes offended, as did the disciples of Christ, and walks no more with Christ; when he begins to work against the truth, and make his disaffection public, declaring things untrue which are true, these things must be met. The people must not be left to believe a lie. They must be undeceived. The filthy garments with which the servant of God has been clothed must be removed.

If those who have done this work take shelter in the statement that they are led by the Holy Spirit, it is as Satan clothing himself with the heavenly garments of purity, while still working out his own attributes.—Letter 98a, 1897.

So-called Discrepancies and Contradictions in the Testimonies.—Those who have chosen to follow their own way, have begun to publish the discrepancies and contradictions, so-called, that they claim to find in connection with the Testimonies; and they are misstating some matters by using their own words instead of the words found in my writings. These charges will have to be met, that truth may take the place of falsehood.—Letter 162, 1906.

To Meet and Correct Falsehoods

I have no controversy with V. My life mission is before the world. It is not my work. It is the Lord's work. I take no credit to myself; for the Lord will deliver me from the strife of tongues. "By their fruits ye shall know them."

We shall now have to meet and correct the falsehoods that have gone forth from V and his wife, in order that our brethren may know from whence they come. I must know what he charges against them. To bring before the public a tirade against a woman is not a result of the working of the Holy Spirit, but an inspiration of the spirit of the enemy, to which we shall give no place. Shall we leave souls to drink in temptation because of misrepresentation? No, never; I would be an unfaithful steward did I do this. There now needs to be a true statement placed before the people; and then my work is done. I enter into no arguments, but I cannot allow the work of God, which has borne fruit that has been before the people during almost my whole lifetime, to be brushed away as a cobweb, by whom? A human being, subject to temptation, whom Satan is now sifting as wheat.—Letter 65, 1897.

The Church Paper to Speak

(A Message to the Editor in 1883.)

I have been waiting to see what you would do in putting something in the paper to vindicate the right. You have had ample time. . . .

Why do you not do justice by my husband's name and reputation, and why do you keep entirely silent and let the dragon roar?

For myself I care not, my peace is not disturbed, but I do care for the watchmen whom God has placed on the walls of Zion who ought to give the trumpet a certain sound. You certainly ought to do something for your own sake, for Christ's sake, for the truth's sake. Why do you not let the right appear? Why do you remain as silent as the dead? Is this the way you defend the truth? . . .

Mrs. White the Text of Every Opposer.—Truth will triumph. I expect that the raid will be made against me till Christ comes. Every opposer to our faith makes Mrs. White his text. They begin to oppose the truth and then make a raid against me. What have I done, if evil, then let them bear witness of the evil. . . .

Well, Long's and also Green's books* came out, these most weak and contemptible productions. I waited

---

* The products of a breakaway, apostate movement.

for you and others to speak of these, as you stood in the responsible position you did as watchmen on the walls of Zion and should warn the people. . . .

Why All This Zeal Against Me?—Things move rapidly, and there are strange and startling developments made in quick succession. We are nearing the end. Why, I ask, is all this zeal against me? I have attended to my business given me of God. I have injured no one. I have spoken to the erring the words God has given me. Of course, I could not compel them to hear. Those who had the benefit of Christ's labors were just as enraged against Him as the enemies are against me.

I have only done my duty. I have spoken because compelled to speak. They have not rejected me, but Him who sent me. He has given me my work. . . .

I am watched, every word I write is criticised, every move I make is commented upon. . . .

I leave my work and its results until we gather about the great white throne. Do you see the Spirit of Christ in this watching, in these suspicions, in these conjectures, these suppositions? What right have they to suppose, to conjecture, to misinterpret my words? to misstate me as they do?

There is a class that love just this kind of food. They are scavengers not looking candidly to see what good my writings and my testimonies have done, but like Satan, the accuser of the brethren, see what evil they can find, what mischief they can work, what word they can twist, and put their wicked construction upon it, to make a false prophet. . . .

I see the satanic spirit more plainly developed than has been manifested the last forty years.—Letter 3, 1883.

Communicated Like Leaven.—If Satan can excite criticism among any of the Lord's professed people, then it is communicated like leaven from one to another. Give the spirit of criticism no quarter, for it is Satan's science. Accept it, and envy, jealousy, and evil surmisings of one another follow.

Press together, is the command I hear from the Captain of our salvation. Press together. Where there is unity, there is strength. All who are on the Lord's side will press together. There is need of perfect unity and love among believers in the truth, and anything that leads to dissension is of the devil. The Lord designs that His people shall be one with Him as the branches are one with the vine. Then they will be one with each other.—Letter 6, 1899.

A Long List of False Statements Expected.—I expect now that a long list of false statements will be presented to the world, and that lie upon lie, misstatement upon misstatement, which Satan has originated in the minds of individuals, will by some be accepted as truth. But I leave my case in the hands of God, and those who know my life practice will not receive the lies that are spoken.—Letter 22, 1906.

52.

Sinlessness and Salvation

_____

The Claim to Sinlessness*

Says John, in speaking of the deceiver that doeth
great wonders: He shall make an image to the beast, and
shall cause all to receive his mark. Will you please to
consider this matter? Search the Scriptures, and see.
There is a wonder-working power to appear: and it will
be when men are claiming sanctification, and holiness,
lifting themselves up higher and higher and boasting of
themselves.

Look at Moses and the prophets; look at Daniel and
Joseph and Elijah. Look at these men, and find me one
sentence where they ever claimed to be sinless. The very
soul that is in close relation to Christ, beholding His
purity and excellency, will fall before Him with shamefacedness.

Daniel was a man to whom God had given great skill
and learning, and when he fasted the angel came to him
and said, "Thou art greatly beloved." And he fell
prostrate before the angel. He did not say, "Lord, I have
been very faithful to You and I have done everything to
honor You and defend Your word and name. Lord, You

_____

* Excerpt from a sermon preached by Ellen G. White at Santa Rosa,
California, March 7, 1885.

know how faithful I was at the king's table, and how I maintained my integrity when they cast me into the den of lions." Was that the way Daniel prayed to God?

No; he prayed and confessed his sins, and said, Hear O Lord, and deliver; we have departed from Thy Word and have sinned. And when he saw the angel, he said, My comeliness was turned into corruption. He could not look upon the angel's face, and he had no strength; it was all gone. So the angel came to him and set him upon his knees. He could not behold him then. And then the angel came to him with the appearance of a man. Then he could bear the sight.

Only Those Far From Christ Claim Sinlessness.—Why is it that so many claim to be holy and sinless? It is because they are so far from Christ. I have never dared to claim any such a thing. From the time that I was 14 years old, if I knew what the will of God was, I was willing to do it. You never have heard me say I am sinless. Those that get sight of the loveliness and exalted character of Jesus Christ, who was holy and lifted up and His train fills the temple, will never say it. Yet we are to meet with those that will say such things more and more.—Manuscript 5, 1885.

Let God, Not Men, Declare It

I want to say to whomsoever the glory of God has been revealed, "You will never have the least inclination to say, 'I am holy, I am sanctified.'"

After my first vision of glory, I could not discern the brightest light. It was thought that my eyesight was gone, but when I again became accustomed to the things of this world I could see again. This is why I tell you never to boast, saying, "I am holy, I am sanctified," for it is the surest evidence that you know not the Scripture or the power of God. Let God write it in His books if He will, but you should never utter it.

I have never dared to say, "I am holy, I am sinless," but whatever I have thought was the will of God I have tried to do it with all my heart, and I have the sweet peace of God in my soul. I can commit the keeping of my soul to God as unto a faithful Creator, and know that He will keep that which is committed to His trust. It is my meat and drink to do my Master's will.—Manuscript 6a, 1886.

Not Until This Vile Body Is Changed

We must establish an unyielding enmity between our souls and our foe; but we must open our hearts to the power and influence of the Holy Spirit. . . . We want to become so sensitive to holy influences, that the lightest whisper of Jesus will move our souls, till He is in us, and we in Him, living by the faith of the Son of God.

We need to be refined, cleansed from all earthliness, till we reflect the image of our Saviour, and become "partakers of the divine nature, having escaped the corruption that is in the world through lust." Then we shall delight to do the will of God, and Christ can own us before the Father and before the holy angels as those who abide in Him, and He will not be ashamed to call us brethren.

But we shall not boast of our holiness. As we have clearer views of Christ's spotlessness and infinite purity, we shall feel as did Daniel, when he beheld the glory of the Lord, and said, "My comeliness was turned in me into corruption."

We cannot say, "I am sinless," till this vile body is changed and fashioned like unto His glorious body. But if we constantly seek to follow Jesus, the blessed hope is ours of standing before the throne of God without spot or wrinkle, or any such thing; complete in Christ, robed in His righteousness and perfection.—*Signs of the Times,* March 23, 1888.

When the Conflict Is Ended

When the times of refreshing shall come from the presence of the Lord, then the sins of the repentant soul who has received the grace of Christ and has overcome

through the blood of the Lamb, will be removed from
the records of heaven, and will be placed upon Satan, the
scapegoat, the originator of sin, and be remembered no
more against him forever. . . . When the conflict of life
is ended, when the armor is laid off at the feet of Jesus,
when the saints of God are glorified, then and then only
will it be safe to claim that we are saved, and sinless.—
Signs of the Times, May 16, 1895.

The Assurance of Salvation Now

The perishing sinner may say: "I am a lost sinner;
but Christ came to seek and to save that which was lost.
He says, 'I came not to call the righteous, but sinners to
repentance' (Mark 2:17). I am a sinner, and He died
upon Calvary's cross to save me. I need not remain a
moment longer unsaved. He died and rose again for my
justification, and He will save me now. I accept the
forgiveness He has promised."—"Justified by Faith" (a
pamphlet published in 1893), p. 7. Reprinted in *Selected
Messages*, book 1, p. 392.

He who repents of his sin and accepts the gift of the
life of the Son of God, cannot be overcome. Laying hold
by faith of the divine nature, he becomes a child of God.
He prays, he believes. When tempted and tried, he
claims the power that Christ died to give, and overcomes
through His grace. This every sinner needs to understand. He must repent of his sin, he must believe in
the power of Christ, and accept that power to save and to
keep him from sin. How thankful ought we to be for the
gift of Christ's example.—*The Review and Herald*, Jan.
28, 1909.

Don't Worry, Your Hope Is in Christ

A life in Christ is a life of restfulness. There may be
no ecstasy of feeling, but there should be an abiding,
peaceful trust. Your hope is not in yourself; it is in
Christ. Your weakness is united to His strength, your

ignorance to His wisdom, your frailty to His enduring might. . . .

We should not make self the center and indulge anxiety and fear as to whether we shall be saved. All this turns the soul away from the Source of our strength. Commit the keeping of your soul to God, and trust in Him. Talk and think of Jesus. Let self be lost in Him. Put away all doubt; dismiss your fears. Say with the apostle Paul, "I live; yet not I, but Christ liveth in me: and the life which I now live in the flesh I live by the faith of the Son of God, who loved me, and gave himself for me" (Gal. 2:20). Rest in God. He is able to keep that which you have committed to Him. If you will leave yourself in His hands, He will bring you off more than conqueror through Him that has loved you.—*Steps to Christ,* pp. 70-72.

53.

Study the Testimonies

Light Will Condemn Those Who Do Not Choose to Study and Obey

Precious instruction has been given to our people in the books I have been charged to write. How many read and study these books? The light that God has given may be regarded with indifference and unbelief, but this light will condemn all who have not chosen to accept and obey it.—Letter 258, 1907.

Ellen G. White Urged to Call for Testimony Study

I am instructed to say to our churches, Study the Testimonies. They are written for our admonition and encouragement, upon whom the ends of the world are come. If God's people will not study these messages that are sent to them from time to time, they are guilty of rejecting light. Line upon line, precept upon precept, here a little and there a little, God is sending instruction to His people. Heed the instruction; follow the light. The Lord has a controversy with His people because in the past they have not heeded His instruction and followed His guidance.

I have been reading Volume Six of the *Testimonies*, and I find in this little book instruction that will help us to meet many perplexing questions. How many have read the article "Evangelistic Work" in this volume? I

advise that these directions and warnings and cautions be
read to our people at some time when they are gathered
together. By far too small a portion of our people are in
possession of these books.—Letter 292, 1907.

Personal Study Would Answer Questions

We receive many letters from our brethren and
sisters, asking for advice on a great variety of subjects. If
they would study the published *Testimonies* for themselves, they would find the enlightenment they need. Let
us urge our people to study these books, and circulate
them. Let their teachings strengthen our faith.

Let us study more diligently the Word of God. The
Bible is so plain and clear that all who will may
understand. Let us thank the Lord for His precious
Word, and for the messages of His Spirit that give so
much light. I am instructed that the more we study the
Old and New Testaments, the more we shall have
impressed on our mind the fact that each sustains a very
close relation to the other, and the more evidence we
shall receive of their divine inspiration. We shall see
clearly that they have but one Author. The study of these
precious volumes will teach us how to form characters
that will reveal the attributes of Christ.—Manuscript
81, 1908.

Read the Testimonies for Yourselves

I am at times made very sad as I think of the use
made of the Testimonies. Men and women report everything that strikes them or that they hear as a testimony from Sister White, when Sister White never heard
of such a thing. . . .

The only safety for any of us is to plant our feet upon
the Word of God and study the Scriptures, making
God's Word our constant meditation. Tell the people to
take no man's word regarding the Testimonies, but to
read them and study them for themselves, and then they
will know that they are in harmony with the truth. The
Word of God is the truth.—Letter 132, 1900.

Testimonies *Our Protection*

I urged our brethren to become acquainted with the teachings that are in the *Testimonies*. God has given us light that we cannot disregard or treat with indifference or contempt. He has let light shine upon us in reproofs, in warnings, that we may, if we will, take hold upon it and escape the dangers that beset our pathway. When temptations arise, we may be guarded and we may discern them because the Lord has pointed them out to us, that we shall not be deceived.—Manuscript 23, 1889.

The humility that bears fruit, filling the soul with a sense of the love of God, will speak for the one who has cherished it, in the great day when men will be rewarded according as their works have been. Happy will be the one of whom it can be said, "The Spirit of God never stirred this man's soul in vain. He went forward and upward from strength to strength. Self was not woven into his life.

"Each message of correction, warning, and counsel he received as a blessing from God. Thus the way was prepared for him to receive still greater blessings, because God did not speak to him in vain. Each step upward on the ladder of progress prepared him to climb still higher. From the top of the ladder the bright beams of God's glory shone upon him. He did not think of resting, but sought constantly to attain the wisdom and righteousness of Christ. Ever he pressed toward the mark for the prize of the high calling of God in Christ Jesus."

This experience every one who is saved must have. In the day of judgment, the course of the man who has retained the frailty and imperfection of humanity will not be vindicated. For him there will be no place in heaven. He could not enjoy the perfection of the saints in light. He who has not sufficient faith in Christ to believe that He can keep him from sinning, has not the faith that will give him an entrance into the kingdom of God.—Manuscript 161, 1897.

SECTION X

Meeting Fanaticism

INTRODUCTION

God's church has often been threatened by fanaticism and extremes of one kind or another. It was so in Reformation times and has been so in the days of the remnant church. The section "Fanaticism and Deceptive Teachings" in *Selected Messages*, book 2, contains an abundance of timely warnings on problems of this nature. Two matters, however, that were not particularly emphasized in that section are false speaking in tongues, and demon possession and the casting out of demons.

In 1908, Mr. and Mrs. Ralph Mackin called on Ellen White. As she gave counsel then and in the days that followed, these two subjects became quite prominent. The report of the interview and the letters of counsel written after Ellen White was given instruction on these matters in vision were published in the *Review and Herald* of August 10, 17, and 24, 1972. Major portions are included here to make the record available in book form.—WHITE TRUSTEES.

54.

The Mackin Case

On Thursday morning, November 12, 1908, Ellen White was at her Elmshaven home busy in her writing room. Here her son, W. C. White, found her and told her there were two persons in the living room below who wished to talk with her. Joining him, she went downstairs to meet Ralph Mackin and his wife. She found a well-dressed and seemingly very sincere couple in their middle thirties. Mrs. White soon learned that her visitors were earnest students of the Bible and the Testimonies and had come to California from Ohio for the express purpose of learning whether their unusual experience of a few months past was endorsed by the Lord.

The conversation with the Mackins was taken down stenographically at the time of the interview by Clarence C. Crisler, Ellen G. White's leading secretary.—COM-PILERS.

Report of the Interview

Brother and Sister Mackin stated that they had felt impressed by the Holy Spirit to make a special trip West in order to interview Sister White regarding some unusual experiences through which they had been passing. During the Week of Prayer nearly three years before they had united with their little church at Findlay, Ohio, in a special season of seeking God for the outpouring of the Holy Spirit.

Ralph Mackin: In the Week of Prayer reading for that year, every article was directed to the people to seek for the Holy Spirit. We set aside in our little church three days for fasting and prayer, and we fasted and prayed for three days—that is, not constantly together, but we felt the need of a deeper work and felt the necessity of coming into possession of more of the Spirit of God. We began to study from that time on the work of the Holy Spirit, from the Bible and the *Testimonies,* and especially from volume 8 and volume 7, and *Early Writings,* and also the little book made up of a collection of leaflets and entitled, *Special Testimonies to Ministers and Workers.* This we found to be a most precious volume to us. It shows how in times past men who had been called of God were treated, et cetera.

The message that the Lord gave me particularly was to follow the life of the apostles. . . .

Several scriptures were then read, including Luke 24 to the close of the chapter, ending with these words:

"And they worshipped him, and returned to Jerusalem with great joy: and were continually in the temple, praising and blessing God. Amen."

Now, I teach that this blessing is the blessing of sanctification that they received, that He bestowed upon them; and when we seek God—if we are a sinner, until we are converted; if we are converted, then we put up the prayer for the power of sanctification to live clean, wholesome lives. *Not* that it is the work of an instant; *not* "once sanctified, always sanctified"; that is not true. But we should so firmly and eagerly put up our petition that we receive the blessing. It has the same physiological effect on us—oh, we just want to praise Jesus, and it makes us so loving and gentle and kind. But we notice that the disciples were not ready yet to go out with that blessing to do work for the Master. He told them to tarry until they were endued with power from on high.

Then we put up our petition and hold right on by faith, and that which encouraged us to do this was the chapter entitled "The Shaking Time" in *Early Writings*—we hung right on by faith, until great drops of sweat stood on our brow. Believing that the same power that the disciples had was for us today, we were encouraged to hold on.

Experience Recorded in Acts 2 Repeated.— When that promised blessing came on us, as we put up our petitions to God, we had the same experience as recorded here in Acts 2 in regard to the apostles. When that promised power came upon us we spake in other tongues as the Spirit gave us utterance.

In Toledo, when we were bearing our message on the street, a man who was a Polish Catholic stood on the street when Mrs. Mackin was speaking; and as the Spirit of God came upon her, and spoke to them through her in another language that she could not understand, this Polish gentleman exclaimed, "I know what that lady is speaking. She is speaking in my own tongue of a calamity which is soon to be visited on this city."

Alleged Foreign Tongue.—In other instances, when one comes into this blessing of speaking with tongues, the Lord may give me the same tongue, and we may hold a conversation in the language that the Spirit of God may have given us utterance in. Even three or four may take part in the conversation, and yet it is a foreign tongue to them, and one waits on the other until the other is through; and it is all in order. This is the experience we received, according to the promised blessing. . . .

If we are in a delusion, we are honestly there. But if this is from the Spirit of God, we want to follow it. . . .

This Spirit tells us to search the Word: tells us to be earnest; and tells us to be careful about our diet; tells us exactly what you have said.

Gift of Prophecy Claimed.—Now, my wife, the Spirit operates through her, and we believe that this is the gift of prophecy that is to be poured out onto all flesh. This Spirit leads us into kindness and purity of life, and we can't understand it—why—only that as the Word of God has said, that these experiences come as the result of receiving the blessing of the Spirit of God. . . .

The Camp Meeting Experience.—Before we went onto the campground—we did not go until Friday—my wife and two other ladies (my mother, and another lady, Sister Edwards, a sister-in-law to the president of the conference)—before we went upon the campground this last year, they three were seeking the Lord. I had gone downtown on an errand; and the Spirit of God told her (Mrs. Mackin) to go on the campground, and there sing; and there He would tell her what to sing.

And she wept just like a child, and just seemed like she could not stand it because that the Lord showed her the condition of our people—soon the plagues would fall, and they were unready. There was no meeting in progress, and the Spirit of the Lord came upon her as she went onto the campground, and (turning to Mrs. Mackin) you may tell her what words you sang.

Mrs. Mackin: The Lord put this burden upon me. I could not stand it. I wanted to tell it so bad, and sing that song so bad. And I could not get rid of it till I would do it. "Oh, pray," says I to Sister Edwards; and so I stood on the campground, and I sang just what the Lord gave me. The Lord—this is what I sang:—

"He is coming; He is coming;
Get ready; Get ready."

And then that statement in *Early Writings*—

"How many I saw coming up to the falling of the plagues without a shelter. Receive ye the Holy Ghost." These are the words I sang. I sang them over and over again. They could hear it all over the campground, and they came together; but before that, the Lord showed me how they would wring their hands as the plagues were falling. The Lord can show anything in just a moment, better than He could tell it to us. And so He showed me how they would wring their hands, and that put on me a greater burden than ever. Well, that is when they arrested us. . . .

It is when the singing is extemporaneous—dictated by the Spirit—that it is the most wonderful.

If you have any light for us . . .

Ellen G. White: I do not know that I have anything special that I could say. There will be things that will transpire at the very close of this earth's history, it has been presented to me, similar to some of the things that you have represented; but I cannot say anything on these points now.

R. Mackin: Is there any question, Brother White, or anything now?

W. C. White: I do not know as there is anything more than to pray that the Lord will give Mother some word, and then take time for matters to develop. It is better, in presenting anything to her, to present the subject briefly and clearly, and then perhaps have another interview with her later on.

R. Mackin: We are fasting and praying. If we are in a delusion, we want to know it, just as much as if we were in the right.

Mrs. Mackin: Our brethren certainly think that we are in a delusion.

Ellen G. White: What place was this that you speak of, where this singing was?

R. Mackin: Mansfield, Ohio, at the camp meeting.

Ellen G. White: Our people—Sabbathkeeping people?

R. Mackin: Yes, our own people.

W. C. White: Was that verse that Mrs. Mackin sang last night extemporaneous or a known hymn? [At the prayer meeting in the sanitarium chapel Brother Mackin had given his testimony in the praise service and was followed by Mrs. Mackin, who sang.]

Mrs. R. Mackin: Oh, that was one of our published hymns. It is in the new *Christ in Song.*

R. Mackin: From hearing that you could scarcely gain an idea of her singing when the words are given to her by the Holy Spirit. The most wonderful thing is when she sings "Glory!" She says when she sings it she seems to be in the presence of Jesus, with the angels. She repeats the word "Glory!" over and over again. She has been tested with the piano, and musicians say it is a freak—the lowness and the highness with which she does it. She cannot do it only as she prays in the Spirit and special power comes upon her.

Mrs. Mackin: We don't have this power, only as we seek Jesus.

Casting Out Demons.—*R. Mackin:* The Lord has given us power, Sister White, to cast out demons. Many people are possessed with demons. I remember a statement you wrote a few years ago that many were possessed with demons as verily as they were in the days of Christ. When we are in a meeting, and these demons are in a meeting, they may cause people to do queer things. I noticed in the Bible when Jesus was in the Temple that demons at once came out. "Hold thy peace, and come out of him." The Lord instructs us to lay the people down, lest the demons throw them when they come out. We found in the beginning that when we begin to rebuke these demons they oftentimes close the eyes of these people, and will sometimes cause them to bark like a dog, and stick out their tongue; but as we continue to rebuke them, why, the eyes open and they become calm, and the demons——

Now it is through the gift of the Spirit that the Lord tells us when the demons are gone, that they are all gone. One lady in particular had six demons, and she said she just felt them when they came out—it just seemed to pull her in every part of the body.

But our brethren say that they can't be in the last days; but we find that it coincides with just what the Saviour said in the last chapter of Mark, in that great commission: "And these signs shall follow them that believe; In my name shall they cast out devils; they shall speak with new tongues;" and so on.

Mrs. Mackin: We did not get this all at once, either.

R. Mackin: Read the remaining verses of Mark: "And these signs shall follow them that believe; In my name shall they cast out devils; they shall speak with new tongues; they shall take up serpents; and if they drink any deadly thing, it shall not hurt them; they shall lay hands on the sick, and they shall recover. So then after the Lord had spoken unto them, he was received up into heaven, and sat on the right hand of God. And they went forth, and preached every where, the Lord working with them, and confirming the word with signs following. Amen." Our experience, so far as we are able to discern, corroborates with the Bible. Here is something that I would like to read [here Brother Mackin read extracts, including the following, from an article in the *Review and Herald*, by Sister White, published in the issue for April 11, 1899, and entitled, "The Newcastle Camp Meeting"]:

"During the night of the first Sabbath of the Newcastle meeting, I seemed to be in meeting, presenting the necessity and importance of our receiving the Spirit. This was the burden of my labor—the opening of our hearts to the Holy Spirit."

[No record was made by the stenographer as to the exact place where Brother Mackin began reading this article, and where he ceased reading; but at least a considerable portion was read.]

What Is the Evidence?—*R. Mackin:* In connection with the receiving of power from on high there is a question, it seems to me, just as pertinent now as in the days of the apostles—What is the evidence? If we receive it, will it not have the same physiological effect on us as it did back there? It can be expected that we shall speak as the Spirit gives us utterance.

Ellen G. White: In the future we shall have special tokens of the influence of the Spirit of God—especially at times when our enemies are the strongest against us. The time will come when we shall see some strange things; but just in what way—whether similar to some of the experiences of the disciples after they received the

Holy Spirit following the ascension of Christ—I cannot say.

R. Mackin: We will continually pray to the Lord about this, and ask Him to give you light in regard to it. So I leave you our address, and if you have anything for us after this, we shall be glad to receive it.

W. C. White: You will probably spend a few days here, will you not?

R. Mackin: If the Holy Spirit tells us that our work is done now, we will go; if He tells us to tarry, we will tarry. It leads us. As I have presented this message to different congregations the Spirit of God has witnessed to it, and many weep, and they say, "Oh, we need power, we need help, and this is the power promised, and let us seek God."

Mrs. Mackin: The real test is love—1 Corinthians 13. . . .

R. Mackin: Satan wants to hinder this work. We are sealed by the Holy Spirit of promise. I present it from *Early Writings* when the angels are about to loose the four winds, Jesus gazes in pity on the remnant, and with uplifted hands cries, "My blood, Father, My blood, My blood, My blood!" He repeats it four times; for His people are still unsealed. He commissions an angel to fly swiftly to the four angels holding the four winds, with the message, "Hold! Hold! Hold! Hold! until the servants of God are sealed in their foreheads." And as I bring these things before the congregation it is the most earnest and devoted ones that it seems to affect, mostly.

Ellen White Recounts Early Experiences.—Sister White then began talking, and continued for about half an hour. She told incident after incident connected with her early labors shortly after the passing of the time in 1844. Her experiences with unusual forms of error in those days in later years led her to be fearful of anything savoring of a spirit of fanaticism.

As Sister White continued, she told of some who had strange exercisings of the body and of others who were governed largely by their own impressions. Some thought it wrong to work. Still others believed that the righteous dead had been raised to eternal life. A few sought to cultivate a spirit of humility by creeping on the floor, like little children. Some would dance, and sing "Glory, glory, glory, glory, glory, glory," over and over again. Sometimes a person would jump up and down on the floor, with hands uplifted, praising God; and this would be kept up for as long as half an hour at a time.

Among those who took part in these extraordinary forms of fanaticism were some who had once been faithful, God-fearing brethren and sisters. The strange exercisings of body and mind were carried to such lengths that in a few places the officers of the law felt compelled to restrain them by casting them into prison. The cause of God was thus brought into disrepute and it took years to outlive the influence that these exhibitions of fanaticism had upon the general public.

Sister White further told of how she was called upon repeatedly to meet this fanaticism squarely and to rebuke it sternly in the name of the Lord. She emphasized the fact that we have a great work to do in the world, that our strength with the people lies in the power that accompanies a clear presentation of the Word of the living God. The law of Jehovah is to be exalted and made honorable; and the various features of the third angel's message are to be plainly outlined before the people that all may have an opportunity to hear the truth for this time and to decide whether to obey God rather than man.

If we as a church were to give place to any form of fanaticism, the minds of unbelievers would be diverted from the living Word to the doings of mortal men, and there would appear more of the human than the divine. Besides, many would be disgusted by that which to their minds seemed unnatural and bordering on the fanatical. Thus the proclamation of the message for this time would be sadly hindered. The Holy Spirit works in a manner that commends itself to the good judgment of the people.

An Interesting Proposal.—In the midst of Sister White's account of her early experiences with fanaticism Brother Mackin made the following proposal:

R. Mackin: If we would now have the spirit of prayer, and this power would come upon my wife, would you be able to discern whether this was of the Lord or not?

Ellen G. White: I could not tell you anything about it. But I am telling you these experiences in order that you may know what we have passed through. We tried in every way possible to rid the church of this evil. We declared in the name of the Lord God of Israel that God does not work through His children in a way that brings the truth into disrepute, and that unnecessarily creates deep-seated prejudice and bitter opposition. In our work we must take a straightforward course and seek to reach the people where they are.

Rebuking Fanaticism.—*R. Mackin:* I remember reading very much of this in volume 1 of *Testimonies for the Church*—your experience in rebuking fanaticism, and of the cause in the East when they set the time, in 1855, I believe.

Ellen G. White: Some would dance up and down, singing, "Glory, glory, glory, glory, glory." Sometimes I would sit still until they got through, and then I would rise and say: This is not the way the Lord works. He does not make impressions in this way. We must direct the minds of the people to the Word as the foundation of our faith.

I was but a mere child at that time; and yet I had to bear my testimony repeatedly against these strange workings. And ever since that time I have sought to be very, very careful lest something of this sort should come in again among our people. Any manifestation of fanaticism takes the mind away from the evidence of truth—the Word itself.

You might take a consistent course, but those who would be influenced by you might take a very inconsistent course, and as a result we should very soon have our hands full of something that would make it almost impossible to give unbelievers the right impression of our message and work. We must go to the people with the solid Word of God; and when they receive that Word, the Holy Spirit may come, but it always comes, as I have stated before, in a way that commends itself to the judgment of the people. In our speaking, our singing, and in all our spiritual exercises, we are to reveal that calmness and dignity and godly fear that actuates every true child of God.

Dangers That Threaten Now.—There is constant danger of allowing something to come into our midst that we may regard as the working of the Holy Spirit, but that in reality is the fruit of a spirit of fanaticism. So long as we allow the enemy of truth to lead us into a wrong way we cannot hope to reach the honest in heart with the third angel's message. We are to be sanctified through obedience to the truth.

I am afraid of anything that would have a tendency to turn the mind away from the solid evidences of the truth as revealed in God's Word. I am afraid of it; I am afraid of it. We must bring our minds within the bounds of reason, lest the enemy so come in as to set everything in a disorderly way. There are persons of an excitable temperament who are easily led into fanaticism; and should we allow anything to come into our churches that would lead such persons into error we would soon see these errors carried to extreme lengths; and then because of the course of these disorderly elements a stigma would rest upon the whole body of Seventh-day Adventists.

I have been studying how to get some of these early experiences into print again, so that more of our people may be informed; for I have long known that fanaticism will be manifest again, in different ways. We are to strengthen our position by dwelling on the Word, and by avoiding all oddities and strange exercisings that some would be very quick to catch up and practice. If we were to allow confusion to come into our ranks, we could not bind off our work as we should. We are trying to bind it off now, in every way possible.

I thought I must relate these things to you.

R. Mackin: Well, now, that which you have stated does not correspond with our experience. We have been very cautious in this matter, and we find that the experience through which we have passed, and which we have endeavored to outline briefly to you this morning, tallies exactly with the experience of God's servants of old as given in the Word.

Ellen G. White: During the years of Christ's ministry on earth godly women assisted in the work that the Saviour and His disciples were carrying forward. If those who were opposing this work could have found anything out of the regular order in the conduct of these women, it would have closed the work at once. But while women were laboring with Christ and the apostles, the entire work was conducted on so high a plane as to be above the shadow of a suspicion. No occasion for any accusation could be found. The minds of all were directed to the Scriptures rather than to individuals. The truth was proclaimed intelligently, and so plainly that all could understand.

Now I am afraid to have anything of a fanatical nature brought in among our people. There are many, many who must be sanctified; but they are to be sanctified through obedience to the message of truth. I am writing on this subject today. In this message there is a beautiful consistency that appeals to the judgment. We cannot allow excitable elements among us to display themselves in a way that would destroy our influence with those whom we wish to reach with the truth. It took us years to outlive the unfavorable impression that unbelievers gained of Adventists through their knowledge of the strange and wicked workings of fanatical elements among us during the early years of our existence as a separate people.

Be Guarded.—*R. Mackin:* Well, now, this that you are giving us, would this be considered testimony under the Spirit, or is it simply counsel—of relating your experience?

Ellen G. White: I am giving you history.

R. Mackin: But you do not say that that applies to our case now, until you have further light on it?

Ellen G. White: I could not say; but it appears to be along that line, as I am afraid of it. It appears to be along that line that I have met again and again.

W. C. White: It is now twelve o'clock. Would you not like to rest before dinner?

Ellen G. White: Well, I could not let you go before I had said what I have said. I would say: Be guarded. Do not let anything appear that savors of fanaticism, and that others would act out. There are some who are eager to make a show, and they will act out whatever you may do—whether it be of the same tenor or not. I have been very careful not to stir up anything like strangeness among our people.

R. Mackin: But it is true that when the Holy Spirit does come, as is stated in your works, that many will turn against it, and declare that it is fanaticism?

Ellen G. White: Of course they will; and for this reason we ought to be very guarded. It is through the Word—not feeling, not excitement—that we want to influence the people to obey the truth. On the platform of God's Word we can stand with safety. The living Word is replete with evidence, and a wonderful power accompanies its proclamation in our world.

R. Mackin: Well, we must not tire you.

Mrs. Mackin: Praise the Lord!

Ellen G. White (rising, and shaking hands): I want the Spirit of the Lord to be with you, and you, and me. We are to be just like God's little children. The power of His grace must not be misunderstood. We must have it in all meekness and humility and lowliness of mind, that God may make the impression Himself upon the minds of the people. I hope the Lord will bless you and give you a solid foundation, which foundation is the Word of the living God.—Manuscript 115, 1908. (Published in *The Review and Herald,* Aug. 10, 17, 24, 1972.)

The Lord Did Give Light

Mr. and Mrs. Ralph Mackin:

Dear Brother and Sister: Recently, in visions of the night, [December 10] there were opened before me some matters that I must communicate to you. I have been shown that you are making some sad mistakes. In your study of the Scriptures and of the Testimonies, you have come to wrong conclusions. The Lord's work would be greatly misunderstood if you should continue to labor as you have begun. You place a false interpretation upon the Word of God, and upon the printed Testimonies; and then you seek to carry on a strange work in accordance with your conception of their meaning. You suppose that all you do is for the glory of God, but you are deceiving yourselves and deceiving others.

Your wife, in speech, in song, and in strange exhibitions that are not in accordance with the genuine work of the Holy Spirit, is helping to bring in a phase of fanaticism that would do great injury to the cause of God, if allowed any place in our churches.

On Casting Out Demons.—You have even supposed that power is given you to cast out devils. Through your influence over the human mind men and women are led to believe that they are possessed of devils, and that the Lord has appointed you as His agents for casting out these evil spirits.

I have been shown that just such phases of error as I was compelled to meet among Advent believers after the passing of the time in 1844, will be repeated in these last days. In our early experience, I had to go from place to place and bear message after message to disappointed companies of believers. The evidences accompanying my messages were so great that the honest in heart received as truth the words that were spoken. The power of God was revealed in a marked manner, and men and women were freed from the baleful influence of fanaticism and disorder, and were brought into the unity of the faith.—Letter 358, 1908.

Call a Halt.—My brother and sister, I have a message for you: you are starting on a false supposition. There is much of self woven into your exhibitions. Satan will come in with bewitching power, through these exhibitions. It is high time that you call a halt. If God had given you a special message for His people, you would walk and work in all humility—not as if you were on the stage of a theater, but in the meekness of a follower of the lowly Jesus of Nazareth. You would carry an influence altogether different from that which you have been carrying. You would be anchored on the Rock, Christ Jesus.

My dear young friends, your souls are precious in the sight of Heaven. Christ has bought you with His own precious blood, and I do not want you to be indulging a false hope, and working in false lines. You are certainly on a false track now, and I beg of you, for your souls' sake, to imperil no longer the cause of truth for these last days. For your own souls' sake, consider that the manner in which you are working is not the way God's cause is to be advanced. The sincere desire to do others good will lead the Christian worker to put away all thought of bringing into the message of present truth any strange teachings leading men and women into fanaticism. At this period of the world's history, we must exercise the greatest of care in this respect.

Some of the phases of experience through which you are passing, not only endanger your own souls, but the souls of many others; because you appeal to the precious words of Christ as recorded in the Scriptures, and to the Testimonies, to vouch for the genuineness of your message. In supposing that the precious Word, which is verity and truth, and the Testimonies that the Lord has given for His people, are your authority, you are deceived. You are moved by wrong impulses, and are bracing up yourselves with declarations that mislead. You attempt to make the truth of God sustain false sentiments and incorrect actions that are inconsistent and fanatical. This makes tenfold, yes, twentyfold harder the work of the church in acquainting the people with the truths of the third angel's message.—Letter 358, 1908. (Published in part in *Selected Messages*, book 2, pp. 44-46.)

Another Reference to Demon Possession

Last night instruction was given me for our people. I seemed to be in a meeting where representations were being made of the strange work of Brother Mackin and wife. I was instructed that it was a work similar to that which was carried on in Orrington, in the State of Maine, and in various other places after the passing of the time in 1844. I was bidden to speak decidedly against this fanatical work.

I was shown that it was not the Spirit of the Lord that was inspiring Brother and Sister Mackin, but the same spirit of fanaticism that is ever seeking entrance into the remnant church. Their application of Scripture to their peculiar exercises is Scripture misapplied. The work of declaring persons possessed of the devil, and then praying with them and pretending to cast out the evil spirits, is fanaticism which will bring into disrepute any church which sanctions such work.

I was shown that we must give no encouragement to these demonstrations, but must guard the people with a decided testimony against that which would bring a stain upon the name of Seventh-day Adventists, and destroy the confidence of the people in the message of truth which they must bear to the world.*—*Pacific Union Recorder*, Dec. 31, 1908. (Republished in *Selected Messages*, book 2, p. 46.)—Letter 354, 1908.

---

* Several communications regarding the Mackin experience are published in *Selected Messages*, book 2, pp. 41-47.

SECTION XI

Last-Day Events

INTRODUCTION

With the focus of Adventism on the return of Christ, the climactic last-day events associated with His second coming have ever been a theme of major interest to Seventh-day Adventists. It could not be otherwise, for Seventh-day Adventism sprang from a religious milieu, the Millerite Movement, which stressed eschatological events—the resurrection, the last judgment, the punishment of sin and sinners.

The visions given to Ellen White at the outset of her mission brought the importance of the seventh-day Sabbath prominently into view as the testing truth, which in the last days would divide the inhabitants of the earth into two classes—those who obey God and will be eternally saved and those who reject His law and will be eternally lost. The attitude of the individual toward the seventh-day Sabbath would be the determining factor.

The closing events of this earth's history highlighted the little 219-page *Great Controversy* published in 1858, and were the crucial, climactic issue of the great controversy depictions in the books bearing that title issued in 1884, 1888, and 1911.

How carefully Adventists have studied the closing chapters of this book, and have thrilled at the inspired picture of what is before the church and the world! With no abating of interest they have scrutinized all the published Ellen G. White writings for kindred statements that might throw some added light on coming events. In this section we present for the first time a number of heretofore unpublished eschatological statements, which help to round out the picture of the final events of earth's history.

As Sunday law issues intensified in the late 1800's and agitation for a national Sunday law in the United States increased, Ellen White wrote perceptively of "The Impending Conflict" in *Testimonies,* volume 5, pages 711-718, discussing the significance of the issues then facing Seventh-day Adventists, declaring that the church was not ready for the issue, and conjecturing that God might yet, "in answer to the prayers of His people, hold in check the workings of those who are making void His law" (p. 714).

As the laws calling for Sunday observance in certain of the Southern States were enforced and Adventists were arrested, imprisoned, and forced to labor in chain gangs for not observing these laws, the Sabbath-Sunday issue took on greater significance and came in for earnest study at the 1889 General Conference session. Carefully reviewing the principles involved, Ellen White counseled caution in any action that might be taken by the delegates.

Agitation for Sunday legislation gradually waned, but in succeeding years Ellen White kept the issues of the final conflict before church leaders. Times might have changed, so far as actual persecution for Sabbath observance was concerned, but the issues and the principles involved remained the same. Since Ellen White's death further changes have taken place, but we believe that the same principles and the same issues will be revived in the coming conflict, present appearances to the contrary not withstanding.

The major portion of this section includes eschatological statements which frequently parallel the presentation given in *The Great Controversy,* but which just as often provide new details and new insights. These materials have been divided into three main areas, namely:

1. Lessons from meeting the Sunday law crisis of the late 1880's and early 1890's.

2. General counsels appropriate for a people approaching the end.

3. Involvements of "the last great struggle," with the Sabbath-Sunday issue as the crucial factor.

The reader will note that, while Ellen White calls our attention to trying experiences ahead, which will doubtless include martyrdoms, and predicts apostasies in our ranks, she also forecasts large accessions to the church and gives encouraging assurance of Heaven's sustaining grace to God's loyal people.—WHITE TRUSTEES.

55.

Lessons From Meeting the Sunday Law Crisis of the Late 1880's and Early 1890's

---

Assurance as the Clouds Darken in 1884

Great things are before us, and we want to call the people from their indifference to get ready. . . . We are not now to cast away our confidence, but to have firm assurance, firmer than ever before. Hitherto hath the Lord helped us, and He will help us to the end. We will look to the monumental pillars, reminders of what the Lord hath done for us, to comfort and to save us from the hand of the destroyer. . . .

We can but look onward to new perplexities in the coming conflict, but we may well look on what is past as well as what is to come, and say, "Hitherto hath the Lord helped us" (1 Sam. 7:12). "As thy days, so shall thy strength be" (Deut. 33:25). The trial will not exceed the strength which shall be given us to bear it. Then, let us take up our work just where we find it, without one word of repining, imagining nothing can come, but that strength will come proportionate to the trials. . . .

Our present peace must not be disturbed by anticipated trials, for God will never leave nor forsake one soul who trusts in Him. God is better unto us than our fears. . . .

Don't Borrow Trouble for a Future Crisis.—Many will look away from present duties, present comfort and blessings, and be borrowing trouble in regard to the future crisis. This will be making a time of trouble beforehand, and we will receive no grace for any such anticipated troubles. . . . When the scene of sore conflict comes, we have learned the lesson of holy confidence, of blessed trust, and we place our hands in the hands of Christ, our feet on the Rock of Ages, and we are secure from storm, from tempest. We are to wait on our Lord. Jesus will be an ever-present help in every time of need.—Letter 11a, 1884.

You inquire in regard to the course which should be pursued to secure the rights of our people to worship according to the dictates of our own conscience. This has been a burden on my soul for some time, whether it would be a denial of our faith, and an evidence that our trust was not fully in God. But I call to mind many things God has shown me in the past in regard to things of a similar character, as the draft [during the American Civil War] and other things. I can speak in the fear of God, it is right we should use every power we can to avert pressure that is being brought to bear upon our people. . . .

[We are] not to provoke those who have accepted the spurious sabbath, an institution of the Papacy, in the place of God's holy Sabbath. Their not having the Bible arguments in their favor makes them all the more angry and determined to supply the place of arguments that are wanting in the Word of God by the power of their might. The force of persecution follows the steps of the dragon. Therefore great care should be exercised to give no provocation. And again, let us as a people, as far as possible, cleanse the camp of moral defilement and aggravating sins. . . .

All the policy in the world cannot save us from a terrible sifting, and all the efforts made with high authorities will not lift from us the scourging of God, just because sin is cherished. If as a people we do not keep ourselves in the faith and not only advocate with pen and voice the commandments of God, but keep them every one, not violating a single precept knowingly, then weakness and ruin will come upon us. . . .

Appeals of No Avail Without Working of the Holy Spirit.—All the struggles to carry our appeals to the highest authorities in our land, however earnest and strong and eloquent may be the pleas in our favor, will not bring about that which we desire, unless the Lord works by His Holy Spirit in the hearts of those who claim to believe the truth. We may struggle as a mighty man in swimming against the current of Niagara, but we shall fail unless the Lord pleads in our behalf. God will be honored among His people. They must be pure, they must be divested of self, steadfast, unmovable, always abounding in the work of the Lord. . . .

Laws to Exalt the False Sabbath.—We are to be ready and waiting for the orders of God. Nations will be stirred to their very center. Support will be withdrawn from those who proclaim God's only standard of righteousness, the only sure test of character. And all who will not bow to the decree of the national councils, and obey the national laws to exalt the sabbath instituted by the man of sin to the disregard of God's holy day, will feel, not the oppressive power of popery alone, but of the Protestant world, the image of the beast. . . .

The great issue so near at hand will weed out those whom God has not appointed and He will have a pure, true, sanctified ministry prepared for the latter rain. . . .

A new life is proceeding from satanic agencies to work with a power we have not hitherto realized. And shall not a new power from above take possession of God's people?—Letter 55, 1886.

We must soon wrestle with the powers of the land, and we have every reason to fear that falsehood will gain the mastery. We shall call upon our churches in the name of the Lord to view this struggle in its true light.* It is a contest between the Christianity of the Old and

---

* See *Testimonies*, vol. 5, pp. 711-718, "The Impending Conflict" (1889).—COMPILERS.

New Testaments, and the Christianity of human tradition and corrupt fables.

This contest is to decide whether the pure gospel shall have the field in our nation, or whether the popery of past ages shall receive the right hand of fellowship from Protestantism, and this power prevail to restrict religious liberty. . . . The message must go broadcast, that those who have been imperceptibly tampering with popery, not knowing what they were doing, may hear. They are fraternizing with popery by compromises and by concessions which surprise the adherents of the papacy. . . .

God's Children in Other Churches.—God has children, many of them, in the Protestant churches, and a large number in the Catholic churches, who are more true to obey the light and to do [to] the very best of their knowledge than a large number among Sabbathkeeping Adventists who do not walk in the light. The Lord will have the message of truth proclaimed, that Protestants may be warned and awakened to the true state of things, and consider the worth of the privilege of religious freedom which they have long enjoyed.

Sunday Amendment in the United States.—This land has been the home of the oppressed, the witness for liberty of conscience, and the great center of scriptural light. God has sent messengers* who have studied their Bibles to find what is truth, and studied the movements of those who are acting their part in the fulfilling prophecy in bringing about the religious amendment which is making void the law of God and thus giving ascendancy to the man of sin. And shall no voice be raised of direct warning to arouse the churches to their danger? Shall we let things drift, and let Satan have the victory without a protest? God forbid. . . .

Many Not in Our Ranks to Come to the Front.—There are many souls to come out of the ranks of the world, out of the churches—even the Catholic

---

* A. T. Jones and others.

Church—whose zeal will far exceed that of those who have stood in rank and file to proclaim the truth heretofore. For this reason the eleventh hour laborers will receive their penny. These will see the battle coming and will give the trumpet a certain sound. When the crisis is upon us, when the season of calamity shall come, they will come to the front, gird themselves with the whole armor of God, and exalt His law, adhere to the faith of Jesus, and maintain the cause of religious liberty which reformers defended with toil and for which they sacrificed their lives. . . .

A Spurious Sabbath the Issue.—A spurious sabbath is presented to be legislated into power, compelling the observance of a sabbath which God has not enjoined upon man. The persecutions of Protestants by Romanism, by which the religion of Jesus Christ was almost annihilated, will be more than rivaled, when Protestantism and popery are combined. . . .

Our own land is to become a battlefield on which is to be carried on the struggle for religious liberty—to worship God according to the dictates of our own conscience. Then can we not discern the work of the enemy in keeping men asleep who ought to be awake, whose influence shall not be neutral, but wholly and entirely on the Lord's side? Shall men cry, Peace and safety, now, when sudden destruction is coming upon the world, when God's wrath shall be poured out?—Manuscript 30, 1889.

America Can Become the Place of Greatest Peril

America, . . . where the greatest light from heaven has been shining upon the people, can become the place of greatest peril and darkness because the people do not continue to practice the truth and walk in the light. . . .

The more nearly we approach the closing scenes of this earth's history, the more pronounced will be the work of Satan. Every species of deception will take the lead to divert the mind from God through Satan's devices.—Letter 23c, 1894.

*An Early View of Sabbath Importance**

I saw that we sensed and realized but little of the importance of the Sabbath, to what we yet should realize and know of its importance and glory. I saw we knew not what it was yet to ride upon the high places of the earth and to be fed with the heritage of Jacob. But when the refreshing and latter rain shall come from the presence of the Lord and the glory of His power, we shall know what it is to be fed with the heritage of Jacob and ride upon the high places of the earth. Then shall we see the Sabbath more in its importance and glory.

But we shall not see it in all its glory and importance until the covenant of peace is made with us at the voice of God, and the pearly gates of the New Jerusalem are thrown open and swing back on their glittering hinges, and the glad and joyful voice of the lovely Jesus is heard richer than any music that ever fell on mortal ear bidding us enter.—Letter 3, 1851.

We must take a firm stand that we will not reverence the first day of the week as the Sabbath, for it is not the day that was blessed and sanctified by Jehovah, and in reverencing Sunday we should place ourselves on the side of the great deceiver. The controversy for the Sabbath will open the subject to the people, and an opportunity will be given that the claims of the genuine Sabbath may be presented. . . .

The God-fearing, commandment-keeping people should be diligent, not only in prayer, but in action, and this will bring the truth before those who have never heard it. . . .

When the law of God has been made void, and apostasy becomes a national sin, the Lord will work in behalf of His people. Their extremity will be His opportunity. He will manifest His power in behalf of His church. . . .

A Time to Witness.—The Lord has enlightened us

---

* See also *Early Writings*, pp. 32-34, for the vision in 1847 on the importance of the Sabbath.

in regard to what is coming upon the earth that we may enlighten others, and we shall not be held guiltless if we are content to sit at ease, with folded hands, and quibble over matters of minor importance. . . .

The people must not be left to stumble their way along in darkness, not knowing what is before them, and unprepared for the great issues that are coming. There is a work to be done for this time in fitting a people to stand in the day of trouble, and all must act their part in this work. They must be clothed with the righteousness of Christ, and be so fortified by the truth that the delusions of Satan shall not be accepted by them as genuine manifestations of the power of God. . . .

It is a solemn time for God's people, but if they stand close by the bleeding side of Jesus, He will be their defense. He will open ways that the message of light may come to the great men, to authors and lawmakers. They will have opportunities of which you do not now dream, and some of them will boldly advocate the claims of God's downtrodden law. . . .

Satan's Strategy in the Final Conflict.—There is now need of earnest working men and women who will seek for the salvation of souls, for Satan as a powerful general has taken the field, and in this last remnant of time he is working through all conceivable methods to close the door against light that God would have come to His people. He is sweeping the whole world into his ranks, and the few who are faithful to God's requirements are the only ones who can ever withstand him, and even these he is trying to overcome. . . .

Go to God for yourselves; pray for divine enlightenment, that you may know that you do know what is truth, that when the wonderful miracle-working power shall be displayed, and the enemy shall come as an angel of light, you may distinguish between the genuine work of God and the imitative work or the powers of darkness. . . .

A world is to be warned, and when the third angel's message goes forth with a loud cry, minds will be fully prepared to make decisions for or against the truth. The great change is to be made by Satan and his evil angels, united with evil men who will fix their destiny by making void the law of God in the face of convincing evidence from His Word that it is unchangeable and eternal.

Loud Cry of Third Angel's Message.—The very time of which the prophet has written will come, and the mighty cry of the third angel will be heard in the earth, his glory will lighten the world, and the message will triumph, but those who do not walk in its light will not triumph with it. . . .

The solemn time has come when ministers should be weeping between the porch and the altar, crying, "Spare thy people, O Lord, and give not thine heritage to reproach" (Joel 2:17). It is a day when, instead of lifting up their souls in self-sufficiency, ministers and people should be confessing their sins before God and one another.

An Army of Believers Who Stand the Last Test.—The law of God is made void, and even among those who advocate its binding claims are some who break its sacred precepts. The Bible will be opened from house to house, and men and women will find access to these homes, and minds will be opened to receive the Word of God; and, when the crisis comes, many will be prepared to make right decisions, even in the face of the formidable difficulties that will be brought about through the deceptive miracles of Satan. Although these will confess the truth and become workers with Christ at the eleventh hour, they will receive equal wages with those who have wrought through the whole day. There will be an army of steadfast believers who will stand as firm as a rock through the last test. . . .

Increased light will shine upon all the grand truths of prophecy, and they will be seen in freshness and brilliancy, because the bright beams of the Sun of Righteousness will illuminate the whole. . . .

When the angel was about to unfold to Daniel the

intensely interesting prophecies to be recorded for us who are to witness their fulfillment, the angel said, "Be strong, yea, be strong" (Dan. 10:19). We are to receive the very same glory that was revealed to Daniel, because it is for God's people in these last days, that they may give the trumpet a certain sound.—Manuscript 18, 1888.

When Christ shall come the second time, the whole world will be represented by two classes, the just and the unjust, the righteous and the unrighteous. Preceding the great sign of the coming of the Son of man, there will be signs and wonders in the heavens. . . .

Already sprinklings from the vials of God's wrath have been let fall upon land and sea, affecting the elements of the air. The causes of these unusual conditions are being searched for, but in vain.

God has not restrained the powers of darkness from carrying forward their deadly work of vitiating the air, one of the sources of life and nutrition, with a deadly miasma. Not only is vegetable life affected, but man suffers from pestilence. . . .

Physical and Religious World to Be Shaken.—These things are the result of drops from the vials of God's wrath being sprinkled on the earth, and are but faint representations of what will be in the near future.

Earthquakes in various places have been felt, but these disturbances have been very limited. . . . Terrible shocks will come upon the earth, and the lordly palaces erected at great expense will certainly become heaps of ruins.

The earth's crust will be rent by the outbursts of the elements concealed in the bowels of the earth. These elements, once broken loose, will sweep away the treasures of those who for years have been adding to their wealth by securing large possessions at starvation prices from those in their employ.

And the religious world too, is to be terribly shaken, for the end of all things is at hand. . . . All society is ranging into two great classes, the obedient and the disobedient. . . .

There Will Be Laws Controlling Conscience.— The so-called Christian world is to be the theater of great and decisive actions. Men in authority will enact laws controlling the conscience, after the example of the papacy. Babylon will make all nations drink of the wine of the wrath of her fornication. Every nation will be involved. Of this time John the Revelator declares:

"The merchants of the earth are waxed rich through the abundance of her delicacies. And I heard another voice from heaven, saying, Come out of her, my people, that ye be not partakers of her sins, and that ye receive not of her plagues. For her sins have reached unto heaven, and God hath remembered her iniquities. Reward her even as she rewarded you, and double unto her double according to her works: in the cup which she hath filled fill to her double. How much she hath glorified herself, and lived deliciously, so much torment and sorrow give her: for she saith in her heart, I sit a queen, and am no widow, and shall see no sorrow" (Rev. 18:3-7).

One Universal Confederacy.—"These have one mind, and shall give their power and strength unto the beast. These shall make war with the Lamb, and the Lamb shall overcome them: for he is Lord of lords, and King of kings: and they that are with him are called, and chosen, and faithful" (Rev. 17:13, 14).

"These have one mind." There will be a universal bond of union, one great harmony, a confederacy of Satan's forces. "And shall give their power and strength unto the beast." Thus is manifested the same arbitrary, oppressive power against religious liberty, freedom to worship God according to the dictates of conscience, as was manifested by the papacy, when in the past it persecuted those who dared to refuse to conform with the religious rites and ceremonies of Romanists.

In the warfare to be waged in the last days there will be united, in opposition to God's people, all the corrupt powers that have apostatized from allegiance to the law of Jehovah. In this warfare the Sabbath of the fourth commandment will be the great point at issue, for in the Sabbath commandment the great Lawgiver identifies Himself as the Creator of the heavens and the earth. . . .

In Revelation we read concerning Satan: "And he doeth great wonders, so that he maketh fire come down from heaven on the earth in the sight of men, and deceiveth them that dwell on the earth by the means of those miracles which he had power to do in the sight of the beast; saying to them that dwell on the earth, that they should make an image to the beast, which had the wound by a sword, and did live. And he had power to give life unto the image of the beast, that the image of the beast should both speak, and cause that as many as would not worship the image of the beast should be killed. And he causeth all, both small and great, rich and poor, free and bond, to receive a mark in their right hand, or in their foreheads: and that no man might buy or sell, save he that had the mark, or the name of the beast, or the number of his name" (Rev. 13:13-17). . . .

"And I saw three unclean spirits like frogs come out of the mouth of the dragon, and out of the mouth of the beast, and out of the mouth of the false prophet. For they are the spirits of devils, working miracles, which go forth unto the kings of the earth and of the whole world, to gather them to the battle of that great day of God Almighty. Behold, I come as a thief. Blessed is he that watcheth, and keepeth his garments, lest he walk naked, and they see his shame" (chap. 16:13-15). . . .

Satan Will Appear to Succeed.—All things in nature and in the world at large are charged with intense earnestness. Satan, in cooperation with his angels and with evil men, will put forth every effort to gain the victory, and will appear to succeed. But from this conflict, truth and righteousness will come forth triumphant in victory. Those who have believed a lie will be defeated, for the days of apostasy will be ended.—Manuscript 24, 1891.

Counsel Relating to Sunday Law Issues

There have arisen in our conference questions that need to have careful attention, whether the Sabbath-keepers in the Southern States, where they are liable to feel the oppressive power of their State laws if they labor on Sunday, shall rest on Sunday to avoid the persecution which must come if they do any labor.* Some of our brethren seem anxious that a resolution shall be passed by the General Conference advising our Sabbathkeeping brethren liable to imprisonment and fines, to refrain from labor on that day. Such resolutions should not be placed before this conference, requiring their action.

There are questions about which it is far better to have as little notoriety given as possible, in either case—for or against. . . .

God Will Give Light and Knowledge When Needed.—When the Sunday question is legislated to become a law, there will not be so great a danger of taking steps that are not of a character to receive the sanction of Heaven . . . for the reason that the Lord gives light and knowledge just when it is most needed. . . .

While all Sabbathkeepers are anxious and troubled, seeking to penetrate the mysteries of the future, and to learn all they can in regard to the correct position they shall take, be careful that they are advised correctly in regard to Sunday observance. . . . There will ever be danger of going to extremes. . . .

If the decision is made that our people shall not labor on Sunday and that our brethren in the Southern States† shall appear to harmonize with the Sunday law, because

---

* The 1889 General Conference session was held in Battle Creek, October 18 to November 5. On Sabbath, November 2, Ellen White spoke in the morning on Revelation 13, "laying out in clear lines the position of the people of God for this time in regard to Sunday laws." Sabbath afternoon she read from the *Testimonies* and an 1883 General Conference sermon relating to the same subject. Neither presentation was reported.—COMPILERS.

† At the time this manuscript was written Seventh-day Adventists in some of the Southern States were being persecuted because of violation of State Sunday laws. Some of these Adventists refusing to pay fines imposed were put in chain gangs.

of oppression, how long before all over the world [our people] shall be in like circumstances as they are in the South. The decision is to be a universal one. If it comes to the light of day as it will in degrees and there will be concessions and servile bowing to an idol god by those who claim to be Sabbathkeepers, there will be a yielding of principles until all is lost to them.

If we counsel them not to respect the idol sabbath exalted to take the place of the Sabbath of the Lord our God, then instruct them in this matter in a quiet way and encourage no defying of the law powers in words or actions unless called to do this for the honor of God to vindicate His downtrodden law. Let there be no unnecessary act of arousing the combative spirit or passions of opponents. . . .

There should be no just occasion to our enemies to charge us with being lawless and defying the laws through any imprudence of our own.* We should not feel it enjoined upon us to irritate our neighbors who idolize Sunday by making determined efforts to bring labor on that day before them purposely to exhibit an independence. . . .

There should be no noisy demonstration. Let us consider how fearful and terribly sad is the delusion that has taken the world captive and by every means in our power seek to enlighten those who are our bitterest enemies. If there is the acceptance of the principles of the inworking of the Holy Ghost which he [the Christian] must have to fit him for heaven, he will do nothing rashly or presumptuously to create wrath and blasphemy against God. . . .

How You Treat the Sabbath Question Is Decisive. —There are some trying testimonies to be manfully borne by Sabbathkeepers and some bitter persecution finally endured. . . . Let no resolutions be passed here which will encourage half-hearted service or cowardly hiding our light under a bushel or under a bed, for we

---

* See *Testimonies*, vol. 9, pp. 232-238, "Sunday Labor."

will certainly be tried and tested. . . . Be sure the Sabbath is a test question, and how you treat this question places you either on God's side or Satan's side. The mark of the beast is to be presented in some shape to every institution and every individual. . . .

Every move from the first made by Satan was the beginning of his work to continue to the end to exalt the false, to take the place of the genuine Sabbath of Jehovah. He is just as intent now and more determined to do this than ever before. He has come down with great power to deceive them who dwell on the earth with his satanic delusions. . . .

As we meet the emergency, the law of God becomes more precious, more sacred, and as it is more manifestly made void and set aside, in proportion should arise our respect and reverence for the law. . . .

In the exercise of the longsuffering of God, He gives to nations a certain period of probation, but there is a point which, if they pass, there will be the visitation of God in His indignation. He will punish. The world has been advancing from one degree of contempt for God's law to another, and the prayer may be appropriate at this time, "It is time for thee, Lord, to work: for they have made void thy law" (Ps. 119:126). . . .

Individuals to Take Responsibility.—Let not anyone make any proud boast, either by precept or example, to show that he is defying the laws of the land. Make no resolutions as to what persons in different states may do, or may not do. Let nothing be done to lessen individual responsibility. To their God they must stand or fall. Let none feel it is his duty to make speeches in the presence of our own people, or of our enemies, that will arouse their combativeness, and they take your words and construe them in such a way that you are charged with being rebellious to the government, for this will close the door of access to the people. . . .

While we cannot bow to an arbitrary power to lift up the Sunday by bowing to it, while we will not violate the Sabbath, which a despotic power will seek to compel us to do, we will be wise in Christ. . . . We must say no words that will do ourselves harm, for this would be bad enough, but when you speak words, and when you do presumptuous things that imperil the cause of God, you are doing a cruel work, for you give Satan advantage. We are not to be rash and impetuous, but always learning of Jesus, how to act in His spirit, presenting the truth as it is in Jesus. . . .

Danger of Hasty, Ill-advised Moves.—One indiscreet, high-tempered, stubborn-willed man will, in the great question introduced before us, do much harm. Yes, he will leave such an impression that all the force of Seventh-day Adventists could not counteract his acts of presumption because Satan, the arch deceiver, the great rebel, is deluding minds to the true issue of the great question, and its eternal bearing. . . .

There are those who will, through hasty, ill-advised moves, betray the cause of God into the enemy's power. There will be men who will seek to be revenged, who will become apostates and betray Christ in the person of His saints. All need to learn discretion; then there is danger on the other hand of being conservative, of giving away to the enemy in concessions. . . .

Anything we may do that lifts up the spurious to take the place of the true and genuine Sabbath, is disloyal to God, and we must move very carefully, lest we exalt the decisions of the man of sin. We are not to be found in a neutral position on this matter of so great consequence. . . .

Persecution in the Battle Before the Last Closing Conflict.—The two armies will stand distinct and separate, and this distinction will be so marked that many who shall be convinced of the truth will come on the side of God's commandment-keeping people. When this grand work is to take place in the battle, prior to the last closing conflict, many will be imprisoned, many will flee for their lives from cities and towns, and many will be martyrs for Christ's sake in standing in defense of the truth. . . . You will not be tempted above what you are able to bear. Jesus bore all this and far more. . . .

Work of Wolves in Sheep's Clothing.—There will be, even among us, hirelings and wolves in sheep's clothing who will persuade [some of] the flock of God to sacrifice unto other gods before the Lord. . . . Youth who are not established, rooted and grounded in the truth, will be corrupted and drawn away by the blind leaders of the blind; and the ungodly, the despisers that wonder and perish, who despise the sovereignty of the Ancient of Days, and place on the throne a false god, a being of their own defining, a being altogether such an one as themselves—these agents will be in Satan's hands to corrupt the faith of the unwary.

Self-indulgent Will Scorn Faithful Ones

Those who have been self-indulgent and ready to yield to pride and fashion and display, will sneer at the conscientious, truth-loving, God-fearing people, and will in this work sneer at the God of heaven Himself. . . .

In the name of the Lord I advise all His people to have trust in God and not begin now to prepare to find an easy position for any emergency in the future, but to let God prepare for the emergency. . . .

As Our Day Will Be Our Strength.—When the Christian is looking forward to duties and severe trials that he anticipates are to be brought upon him, because of his Christian profession of faith, it is human nature to contemplate the consequences, and shrink from the prospects, and this will be decidedly so as we near the close of this earth's history. We may be encouraged by the truthfulness of God's word, that Christ never failed His children as their safe Leader in the hour of their trial; for we have the truthful record of those who have been under the oppressive powers of Satan, that His grace is according to their day. God is faithful who will not suffer us to be tempted above that we are able. . . .

There may be large mountains of difficulties in regard to how to meet the claims of God and not stand in

defiance of the laws of the land. He [the believer] must
not be making ample provisions for himself to shield
himself from trial, for he is only God's instrument and
he is to go forward in singleness of purpose with his
mind and soul garrisoned day by day, that he will not
sacrifice one principle of his integrity, but he will make
no boasts, issue no threats, or tell what he will or will
not do. For he does not know what he will do until
tested. . . .

**We Are Not to Irritate Sundaykeeping Neigh-
bors.**—There should be a constant walking in all humility. There should be no just occasion for our enemies
to charge us with being lawless and defying the laws
through any imprudence of our own. We should not feel
it enjoined upon us to irritate our neighbors who idolize
Sunday by making determined efforts to bring labor on
that day before them purposely to exhibit an independence. Our sisters need not select Sunday as the day to
exhibit their washing. There should be no noisy demonstration. Let us consider how fearful and terribly sad is
the delusion that has taken the world captive and by
every means in our power seek to enlighten those who are
our bitterest enemies. If there is the acceptance of the
principles of the inworking of the Holy Ghost which he
[the Christian] must have to fit him for heaven, he will
do nothing rashly or presumptuously to create wrath and
blasphemy against God. . . .

**No Deaths Among God's People After Probation
Closes.**—After Jesus rises up from the mediatorial
throne, every case will be decided, and oppression and
death coming to God's people will not then be a testimony in favor of the truth. . . .

We urge you to consider this danger: That which we
have most to fear is nominal Christianity. We have many
who profess the truth who will be overcome because they
are not acquainted with the Lord Jesus Christ. They
cannot distinguish His voice from that of a stranger.
There is to be no dread of anyone being borne down even
in a widespread apostasy, who has a living experience in

the knowledge of our Lord and Saviour Jesus Christ. If Jesus be formed within, the hope of glory, the illiterate as well as the educated can bear the testimony of our faith, saying, "I know in whom I have believed." Some will not, in argument, be able to show wherein their adversary is wrong, having never had any advantages that others have had, yet these are not overborne by the apostasy, because they have the evidence in their own heart that they have the truth, and the most subtle reasoning and assaults of Satan cannot move them from their knowledge of the truth, and they have not a doubt or fear that they are themselves in error. . . .

When profligacy and heresy and infidelity fill the land, there will be many humble homes where prayer, sincere and contrite prayer, will be offered from those who have never heard the truth, and there will be many hearts that will carry a weight of oppression for the dishonor done to God. We are too narrow in our ideas, we are poor judges, for many of these will be accepted of God because they cherish every ray of light that shone upon them.—Manuscript 6, 1889.

Pay Fine if It Will Deliver From the Oppressor

Men are inspired by Satan to execute his purposes against God. The Lord has said, "Verily my sabbaths ye shall keep: for it is a sign between me and you throughout your generations" (Ex. 31:13). None should disobey this command in order to escape persecution. But let all consider the words of Christ, "When they persecute you in this city, flee ye into another" (Matt. 10:23). If it can be avoided, do not put yourselves into the power of men who are worked by the spirit of Antichrist. If the payment of a fine will deliver our brethren from the hands of these oppressors, let it be paid, rather than to be pressed and made to work on the Sabbath. Everything that we can do should be done that those who are willing to suffer for the truth's sake may be saved from oppression and cruelty. . . .

When men under conviction resist light, follow

their own inclinations, and regard the favor of men above the favor of God, they do as did many in Christ's day. . . .

Commandments Not to Be Ignored in Order to Have an Easy Time.—Christ is our example. The determination of Antichrist to carry out the rebellion he began in heaven will continue to work in the children of disobedience. Their envy and hatred against those who obey the fourth commandment will wax more and more bitter. But the people of God are not to hide their banner. They are not to ignore the commandments of God, and in order to have an easy time go with the multitude to do evil. They should be careful not to condemn their brethren in the faith who are steadfast, immovable, always abounding in the work of the Lord. . . .

Those who forsake God in order to save their lives will be forsaken by Him. In seeking to save their lives by yielding the truth, they will lose eternal life.

Natural affection for relatives and friends should not lead any soul who sees the light to reject the light, to dishonor God the Father and Jesus Christ, His only begotten Son. Every possible excuse for disobedience will be framed by men who choose, as many did in Christ's day, the favor of men rather than the favor of God. If one chooses wife or children, father or mother, before Christ, that choice will stand through eternal ages, with all its weight of responsibility. . . .

The soul that has had light in regard to the Lord's Sabbath, His memorial of creation, and to save himself from inconvenience and reproach has chosen to remain disloyal, has sold his Lord. He has dishonored the name of Christ. He has taken his stand with the armies of Antichrist; with them at the last great day, he will be found outside the city of God, not with the loyal, the true and righteous, in the heavenly kingdom.

All who have genuine faith will be tested and tried. They may have to forsake houses and lands, and even their own relatives, because of bitter opposition. "But when they persecute you in this city, flee ye into another," Christ said. "Ye shall not have gone over the cities of Israel, till the Son of man be come" (Matt. 10:23).

Antichrist—Those Who Exalt Themselves Against God—Will Feel His Wrath.—The greater man's influence for good, under the control of the Spirit of God, the more determined will be the enemy to indulge his envy and jealousy toward him by religious persecution. But all heaven is on the side of Christ, not of Antichrist. Those who love God and are willing to be partakers with Christ in His sufferings, God will honor. Antichrist, meaning all who exalt themselves against the will and work of God, will at the appointed time feel the wrath of Him who gave Himself that they might not perish but have eternal life. All who persevere in obedience, all who will not sell their souls for money or for the favor of men, God will register in the book of life.—Manuscript 9, 1900.

56.

As We Near the End

Misleading Messages Will Be Accepted by Many

Test everything before it shall be presented to the flock of God. . . . In messages that profess to be from Heaven, expressions will be made that are misleading, and if the influence of these things be accepted, it will lead to exaggerated movements, plans, and devising that will bring in the very things that Satan would have current—a strange spirit, an unclean spirit, under the garments of sanctity; a strong spirit to overbear everything. Fanaticism will come in, and will so mingle and interweave itself with the workings of the Spirit of God, that many will accept it all as from God, and will be deceived and misled thereby.

There are strong statements often made by our brethren who bear the message of mercy and warning to our world, that would better be repressed. . . . Let not one word be expressed to stir up the spirit of retaliation in opposers of the truth. Let nothing be done to arouse the dragonlike spirit, for it will reveal itself soon enough, and in all its dragon character, against those who keep the commandments of God and have the faith of Jesus. . . .

Confronted by Our Carelessly Spoken Words.—The time will come when we shall be called to stand before kings and rulers, magistrates and powers, in vindication of the truth. Then it will be a surprise to those witnesses to learn that their positions, their words, the very expressions made in a careless manner or thoughtless way, when attacking error or advancing truth—expressions that they had not thought would be remembered—will be reproduced, and they will be confronted with them, and their enemies will have the advantage, putting their own construction on these words that were spoken unadvisedly. . . .

How Satan Will Work to Deceive.—Many things intended to deceive us will come, bearing some of the marks of truth. Just as soon as these shall be set forth as the great power of God, Satan is all ready to weave in that which he has prepared to lead souls from the truth for this time.

Some will accept and promulgate the error, and when the reproof comes that will place matters in the true light, those who have had little experience and who are ignorant of the oft-repeated workings of Satan, will cast away with the rubbish of error that which has been before them as truth. Thus the light and warnings which God gives for this time will be made of no effect. . . .

False Messages Will Be Charged Upon Ellen White.—Every conceivable message is coming to counterfeit the work of God, and always bearing the inscription of truth upon its banner. And those who are prepared for anything new and sensational, will handle these things in such a manner that our enemies will charge all that is inconsistent and overdone upon Mrs. E. G. White, the prophetess. . . .

There will be counterfeit messages coming from persons in all directions. One after another will rise up, appearing to be inspired, when they have not the inspiration of heaven, but are under the deception of the enemy. All who receive their messages will be led astray. Then let us walk carefully, and not open wide the door for the enemy to enter through impressions, dreams, and visions. God help us to look in faith to Jesus, and be guided by the words He has spoken.—Letter 66, 1894.

Steadfastness, but No Defiance

We are to fix the eye of faith steadfastly upon Jesus. When the days come, as they surely will, in which the law of God is made void, the zeal of the true and loyal should rise with the emergency, and should be the more warm and decided, and their testimony should be the more positive and unflinching. But we are to do nothing in a defiant spirit, and we shall not, if our hearts are fully surrendered to God. . . .

Satan's Wrath Against the Three Angels' Messages.—The third angel is represented as flying in the midst of heaven, symbolizing the work of those who proclaim the first, second, and third angel's messages; all are linked together. The evidences of the abiding, ever-living truth of these grand messages that mean so much to us, that have awakened such intense opposition from the religious world, are not extinct. Satan is constantly seeking to cast his hellish shadow about these messages, so that the remnant people of God shall not clearly discern their import—their time and place—but they live, and are to exert their power upon our religious experience while time shall last. . . .

The Revelator says, "I saw another angel come down from heaven, having great power; and the earth was lightened with his glory. And he cried mightily with a strong voice, saying, Babylon the great is fallen, is fallen" (Rev. 18:1, 2). This is the same message that was given by the second angel—Babylon is fallen, "because she made all nations drink of the wine of the wrath of her fornication" (chap. 14:8). What is that wine? Her false doctrines. She has given to the world a false sabbath instead of the Sabbath of the fourth commandment, and has repeated the lie Satan first told to Eve in Eden—the natural immortality of the soul. Many kindred errors she has spread far and wide, "teaching for doctrines the commandments of men."

Two Distinct Calls to the Churches.—When

Jesus began His public ministry, He cleansed the temple from its sacrilegious profanation. Almost the last act of His ministry was to cleanse the Temple again. So in the last work for the warning of the world, two distinct calls are made to the churches; the second angel's message, and the voice heard in heaven, "Come out of her, my people. . . . For her sins have reached unto heaven, and God hath remembered her iniquities" (Rev. 18:4, 5).

As God called the children of Israel out of Egypt, that they might keep His Sabbath, so He calls His people out of Babylon that they may not worship the beast nor his image. The man of sin, who thought to change times and laws, has exalted himself above God by presenting this spurious sabbath to the world; the Christian world has accepted this child of the Papacy, and cradled and nourished it, thus defying God by removing His memorial and setting up a rival sabbath.

A More Decided Effort to Exalt Sunday.—After the truth has been proclaimed as a witness to all nations, at a time when every conceivable power of evil is set in operation, when minds are confused by the many voices crying, "Lo, here is Christ," "Lo, He is there," "This is truth," "I have a message from God," "He has sent me with great light," and there is a removing of the landmarks, and an attempt to tear down the pillars of our faith—then a more decided effort is made to exalt the false sabbath, and to cast contempt upon God Himself by supplanting the day He has blessed and sanctified.

While Satan Works the Angel of Revelation 18 Proclaims His Message.—This false sabbath is to be enforced by an oppressive law. Satan and his angels are wide awake and intensely active, working with energy and perseverance through human instrumentalities to bring about his purpose of obliterating the knowledge of God. While Satan is working with his lying wonders, the time has come [that was] foretold in the Revelation, when the mighty angel that shall lighten the earth with his glory will proclaim the fall of Babylon and call upon

God's people to forsake her. . . .

Repairers of the Breach.—As the end approaches, the testimonies of God's servants will become more decided and more powerful, flashing the light of truth upon the systems of error and oppression that have so long held the supremacy. The Lord has sent us messages for this time to establish Christianity upon an eternal basis, and all who believe present truth must stand, not in their own wisdom, but in God; and raise up the foundation of many generations. These will be registered in the books of heaven as repairers of the breach, the restorers of paths to dwell in. We are to maintain the truth because it is truth, in the face of the bitterest opposition. . . .

Temptations will come upon us. Iniquity abounds where you least expect it. Dark chapters will open that are most terrible, to weigh down the soul; but we need not fail nor be discouraged while we know that the bow of promise is above the throne of God.

We shall be subject to heavy trials, opposition, bereavement, affliction; but we know that Jesus passed through all these. These experiences are valuable to us. The advantages are not by any means confined to this short life. They reach into eternal ages. . . .

As we near the close of this earth's history, we advance more and more rapidly in Christian growth, or we retrograde just as decidedly.—Letter 1f, 1890.

Backsliding SDA's Unite With Unbelievers

Satan is Christ's personal enemy. . . . Long has he deceived mankind, and great is his power over the human family; and his rage against the people of God increases as he finds that the knowledge of God's requirements is extending to all parts of the world, and that the light of present truth is shining to those who have long sat in darkness. . . .

The Word of God . . . is to be our defense when Satan works with such lying wonders that, if it were possible, he would deceive the very elect. It is then that those who have not stood firmly for the truth will unite with the unbelieving, who love and make a lie. When these wonders are performed, when the sick are healed and other marvels are wrought, they will be deceived. Are we prepared for the perilous times that are right upon us? Or arc wc standing where we will fall an easy prey to the wiles of the devil?—Manuscript 81, 1908.

A Science of the Devil

What is soon coming upon us? Seducing spirits are coming in. If God has ever spoken by me, you will before long hear of a wonderful science—a science of the devil. Its aim will be to make of no account God and Jesus Christ whom He has sent. Some will exalt this false science, and through them Satan will seek to make void the law of God. Great miracles will be performed in the sight of men in behalf of this wonderful science.— Letter 48, 1907.

The Time of Apostasy Is Here

The end of all things is near at hand. The signs are rapidly fulfilling, yet it would seem that but few realize that the day of the Lord is coming, swiftly, silently, as a thief in the night. Many are saying, "Peace and safety." Unless they are watching and waiting for their Lord, they will be taken as in a snare. . . .

"Now the Spirit speaketh expressly, that in the latter times some shall depart from the faith, giving heed to seducing spirits, and doctrines of devils" (1 Tim. 4:1). The time of this apostasy is here. Every conceivable effort will be made to throw doubt upon the positions that we have occupied for over half a century. . . .

Fire From Heaven.—Those who look for miracles as a sign of divine guidance are in grave danger of deception. It is stated in the Word that the enemy will work through his agents who have departed from the faith, and they will seemingly work miracles, even to the bringing down of fire out of heaven in the sight of men. By means of "lying wonders" Satan would deceive, if possible, the very elect.—Letter 410, 1907.

Angels Will Hold Four Winds Until After Sealing

Angels are holding the four winds, represented as an angry horse seeking to break loose, and rush over the face of the whole earth, bearing destruction and death in its path. . . .

I tell you in the name of the Lord God of Israel that all injurious, discouraging influences are held in control by unseen angel hands, until everyone that works in the fear and love of God is sealed in his forehead.—Letter 138, 1897.

Satan and His Angels Mingle With Apostates

Satan and his angels will appear on this earth as men, and will mingle with those, of whom God's Word says, "Some shall depart from the faith, giving heed to seducing spirits, and doctrines of devils" (1 Tim. 4:1).—Letter 147, 1903.

The Work of Independent Teachers

From that which the Lord has been pleased to show me, there will arise just such ones all along, and many more of them, claiming to have new light, which is a side issue, an entering wedge. The widening will increase until there is a breach made between those who accept these views* and those who believe the third angel's message.

Just as soon as these new ideas are accepted, then there will be a drawing away from those whom God has used in this work, for the mind begins to doubt and withdraw from the leaders, because God has laid them aside and chosen "more humble" men to do His work.

---

* This concerns certain views on the prophecies held by "Brother D" (*Testimonies*, vol. 5, pp. 289-297), his negative position on the Spirit of Prophecy, and his position of impaired confidence in General Conference leadership.—COMPILERS.

This is the only interpretation they can give to this matter, as the leaders do not see this important light.

God is raising up a class to give the loud cry of the third angel's message. . . . It is Satan's object now to get up new theories to divert the mind from the true work and genuine message for this time. He stirs up minds to give false interpretation of Scripture, a spurious loud cry, that the real message may not have its effect when it does come. This is one of the greatest evidences that the loud cry will soon be heard and the earth will be lightened with the glory of God.—Letter 20, 1884.

Evil Angels in the Form of Believers Will Work in Our Ranks

I have been shown that evil angels in the form of believers will work in our ranks to bring in a strong spirit of unbelief. Let not even this discourage you, but bring a true heart to the help of the Lord against the powers of satanic agencies.

These powers of evil will assemble in our meetings, not to receive a blessing, but to counterwork the influences of the Spirit of God. Take up no remark that they may make, but repeat the rich promises of God, which are yea and amen in Christ Jesus.

We are never to catch up the words that human lips may speak to confirm the evil angels in their work, but we should repeat the words of Christ. Christ was the Instructor in the assemblies of these angels before they fell from their high estate.—Letter 46, 1909.

We have great and solemn truths to give to the world, and they are to be proclaimed in no hesitating, limping style. The trumpet is to give a certain sound. Some will come to hear the strange message out of curiosity; others with a longing to receive true knowledge, asking the question, "What shall I do that I may inherit eternal life?" (Mark 10:17).

Thus men came to Christ. And mingling with His hearers were [evil] angels in the form of men, making their suggestions, criticizing, misapplying, and misinterpreting the Saviour's words. . . .

In this time evil angels in the form of men will talk with those who know the truth. They will misinterpret and misconstrue the statements of the messengers of God. . . .

Have Seventh-day Adventists forgotten the warning given in the sixth chapter of Ephesians? We are engaged in a warfare against the hosts of darkness. Unless we follow our Leader closely, Satan will obtain the victory over us.—Letter 140, 1903.

Apostasies That Will Surprise Us

We shall in the future, as we have in the past, see all kinds of character developed. We shall witness the apostasy of men in whom we have had confidence, in whom we trusted, who, we supposed, were as true as steel to principle.

Something comes to test them, and they are overthrown. If such men fall, some say, "Whom can we trust?" This is the temptation Satan brings to destroy the confidence of those who are striving to walk in the narrow way. Those who fall have evidently corrupted their way before the Lord, and they are beacons of warning, teaching those who profess to believe the truth that the Word of God alone can keep men steadfast in the way of holiness, or reclaim them from guilt. . . .

Let every soul, whatever may be his sphere of action, make sure that the truth is implanted in the heart by the power of the Spirit of God. Unless this is made certain, those who preach the Word will betray holy trust.

Physicians will be tempted and make shipwreck of faith. Lawyers, judges, senators, will become corrupted, and, yielding to bribery, will allow themselves to be bought and sold.—Manuscript 154, 1898.

Apostates Will Use Hypnotism

The time has come when even in the church and in our institutions, some will depart from the faith, giving heed to seducing spirits and doctrines of devils. But God will keep that which is committed to Him. Let us draw near to Him, that He may draw near to us. Let us bear a plain, clear testimony right to the point, that hypnotism is being used by those who have departed from the faith, and that we are not to link up with them. Through those who depart from the faith, the power of the enemy will be exercised to lead others astray.—Letter 237, 1904.

"Unify, Unify"

The last great conflict is before us, but help is to come to all who love God and obey His law, and the earth, the whole earth, is to be lighted with the glory of God. "Another angel" is to come down from heaven. This angel represents the giving of the loud cry, which is to come from those who are preparing to cry mightily, with a strong voice, "Babylon the great is fallen, is fallen, and is become the habitation of devils, and the hold of every foul spirit, and a cage of every unclean and hateful bird" (Rev. 18:1, 2).

We have a testing message to give, and I am instructed to say to our people, "Unify, unify." But we are not to unify with those who are departing from the faith, giving heed to seducing spirits and doctrines of devils. With our hearts sweet and kind and true, we are to go forth to proclaim the message, giving no heed to those who lead away from the truth.—Manuscript 31, 1906.

57.

The Last Great Struggle

I was moved by the Spirit of the Lord to write that book [*The Great Controversy*]. . . . I knew that time was short, and that the scenes which are soon to crowd upon us would at the last come very suddenly and swiftly, as represented in the words of Scripture, "The day of the Lord so cometh as a thief in the night" (1 Thess. 5:2).

The Lord has set before me matters which are of urgent importance for the present time, and which reach into the future. . . . I was assured that there was no time to lose. The appeals and warnings must be given. Our churches must be aroused, must be instructed, that they may give the warning to all whom they can possibly reach, declaring that the sword is coming, that the Lord's anger upon a profligate world will not long be deferred. I was shown that many would listen to the warning. Their minds would be prepared to discern the very things that it pointed out to them.

I was shown . . . that the warning must go where the living messenger could not go, and that it would call the attention of many to the important events to occur in the closing scenes of this world's history.

Coming Events Shown to Ellen White.—As the condition of the church and the world was open before me, and I beheld the fearful scenes that lie just before us, I was alarmed at the outlook; and night after night, while all in the house were sleeping, I wrote out the things given me of God. I was shown the heresies which are to arise, the delusions that will prevail, the miracle-working power of Satan—the false Christs that will appear—that will deceive the greater part, even of the religious world, and that would, if it were possible, draw away even the elect. . . .

The warning and instruction of this book are needed by all who profess to believe the present truth, and the book is adapted to go also to the world, calling their attention to the solemn scenes just before us.—Letter 1, 1890.

The Trouble Ahead

Oppressors Will Be Permitted to Triumph for a Time.—With pity and compassion, with tender yearning, the Lord is looking upon His tempted and tried people. For a time the oppressors will be permitted to triumph over those who know God's holy commandments. All are given the same opportunity that was granted to the first great rebel to demonstrate the spirit that moves them to action. It is God's purpose that everyone shall be tested and proved, to see whether he will be loyal or disloyal to the laws which govern the kingdom of heaven. To the last God permits Satan to reveal his character as a liar, an accuser, and a murderer. Thus the final triumph of His people is made more marked, more glorious, more full and complete. . . .

The people of God should be wide awake, not trusting in their own wisdom, but wholly in the wisdom of their Leader. They should set aside days for fasting and prayer. . . .

We Are Nearing the Crisis.—We are nearing the most important crisis that has ever come upon the world. If we are not wide awake and watching, it will steal upon us as a thief. Satan is preparing to work through his human agencies in secrecy. . . .

We must know the reasons of our faith. The importance and solemnity of the scenes opening before us demand this, and on no account must the spirit of complaining be encouraged. . . .

We may have to plead most earnestly before legislative councils for the right to exercise independent judgment, to worship God according to the dictates of our conscience. Thus in His providence God has designed that the claims of His holy law shall be brought before men in the highest authority. But as we do all we can as men and women who are not ignorant of Satan's devices, we are to manifest no bitterness of feeling. Constantly we are to offer prayer for divine aid. It is God alone who can hold the four winds until the angels shall seal the servants of God in their foreheads.

Satan's Determined Efforts.—The Lord will do a great work in the earth. Satan makes a determined effort to divide and scatter His people. He brings up side issues to divert minds from the important subjects which should engage our attention. . . .

Many are holding the truth only with the tips of their fingers. They have had great light and many privileges. Like Capernaum they have been exalted to heaven in this respect. In the time of test and trial that is approaching, they will become apostates unless they put away their pride and self-confidence, unless they have an entire transformation of character.—Letter 5, 1883.

A Law of Nations That Will Cause Men to Violate God's Law

The Lord will judge according to their works those who are seeking to establish a law of the nations that will cause men to violate the law of God. In proportion to their guilt will be their punishment.—Letter 90, 1908.

The World in Rebellion

Christ's Betrayal and Crucifixion Reenacted.—The scenes of the betrayal, rejection, and crucifixion of Christ have been reenacted, and will again be reenacted on an immense scale. People will be filled with the attributes of Satan. The delusions of the archenemy of God and man will have great power. Those who have given their affections to any leader but Christ will find themselves under the control, body, soul, and spirit of an infatuation that is so entrancing that under its power souls turn away from hearing the truth to believe a lie. They are ensnared and taken, and by their every action, they cry, "Release unto us Barabbas, but crucify Christ." . . .

In the churches which have departed from truth and righteousness, it is being revealed what human nature will be and do when the love of God is not an abiding principle in the soul. We need not be surprised at anything that may take place now. We need not marvel at any developments of horror. Those who trample under their unholy feet the law of God have the same spirit as had the men who insulted and betrayed Jesus. Without any compunctions of conscience they will do the deeds of their father the devil. . . .

Those who choose Satan as their ruler will reveal the spirit of their chosen master, who caused the fall of our first parents. By rejecting the divine Son of God, the personification of the only true God, who possessed goodness, mercy, and untiring love, whose heart was ever touched with human woe, and accepting a murderer in His place, the people showed what human nature can and will do, when the restraining Spirit of God is removed, and men are under the great apostate. Just to that degree that light is refused and rejected will there be misconception and misunderstanding. Those who reject Christ and choose Barabbas will work under a ruinous deception. Misrepresentation, the bearing of false witness, will grow under open rebellion. . . .

United in Desperate Companionship.—Christ shows that without the controlling power of the Spirit of God humanity is a terrible power for evil. Unbelief, hatred of reproof, will stir up satanic influences. Principalities and powers, the rulers of the darkness of this world, and spiritual wickedness in high places, will unite in a desperate companionship. They will be leagued against God in the person of His saints. By misrepresentation and falsehood they will demoralize both men and women who to all appearances believe the truth. False witnesses will not be wanting in this terrible work. . . .

After speaking of the end of the world, Jesus comes back to Jerusalem, the city then sitting in pride and arrogance, and saying, "I sit a queen, and shall see no sorrow" (see Rev. 18:7). As His prophetic eye rests upon Jerusalem, He sees that as she was given up to destruction, the world will be given up to its doom. The scenes that transpired at the destruction of Jerusalem will be repeated at the great and terrible day of the Lord, but in a more fearful manner. . . .

As men throw off all restraint, and make void His law themselves, as they establish their own perverted law, and try to force the consciences of those who honor God and keep His commandments to trample the law under their feet, they will find that the tenderness which they have mocked will be exhausted. . . .

Coming Calamities.—A world is represented in the destruction of Jerusalem, and the warning given then by Christ comes sounding down the line to our time: "And there shall be signs in the sun, and in the moon, and in the stars; and upon the earth distress of nations, with perplexity; the sea and the waves roaring" (Luke 21:25). Yes, they shall pass their borders, and destruction will be in their track. They will engulf the ships that sail upon their broad waters, and with the burden of their living freight, they will be hurried into eternity, without time to repent.

There will be calamities by land and by sea, "men's hearts failing them for fear, and for looking after those things which are coming on the earth: for the powers of heaven shall be shaken. And then shall they see the Son of man coming in a cloud with power and great glory" (verses 26, 27). In just the same manner as He ascended will He come the second time to our world. "And when these things begin to come to pass, then look up, and lift up your heads; for your redemption draweth nigh" (verse 28).—Manuscript 40, 1897.

The Breakdown of Society.—Those in the world, having lost their connection with God, are making desperate, insane efforts to make centers of themselves. This causes distrust of one another, which is followed by crime. The kingdoms of the world will be divided against themselves. Fewer and fewer will become the sympathetic cords which bind man in brotherhood to his fellow man. The natural egotism of the human heart will be worked upon by Satan. He will use the uncontrolled wills and violent passions which were never brought under the control of God's will. . . .

Every man's hand will be against his fellow man. Brother will rise against brother, sister against sister, parents against children, and children against parents. All will be in confusion. Relatives will betray one another. There will be secret plotting to destroy life. Destruction, misery, and death will be seen on every hand. Men will follow the unrestrained bent of their hereditary and cultivated tendency to evil. . . .

God's Retributive Judgments Seen in Vision.— God has a storehouse of retributive judgments, which He permits to fall upon those who have continued in sin in the face of great light. I have seen the most costly structures in buildings erected and supposed to be fireproof. And just as Sodom perished in the flames of God's vengeance, so will these proud structures become ashes. I have seen vessels which cost immense sums of money wrestling with the mighty waters, seeking to breast the angry billows. But with all their treasures of gold and silver, and with their human freight they sink into a watery grave. Man's pride will be buried with the treasures he has accumulated by fraud. God will avenge the widows and orphans who in hunger and nakedness have cried to Him for help from oppression and abuse.

The time is right upon us when there will be sorrow

in the world that no human balm can heal. The flattering monuments of men's greatness will be crumbled in the dust, even before the last great destruction comes upon the world. . . .

Only by being clothed with the robe of Christ's righteousness can we escape the judgments that are coming upon the earth.—Letter 20, 1901.

Many Children Will Be Taken Away

Ere long we are to be brought into strait and trying places, and the many children brought into the world will in mercy be taken away before the time of trouble comes.—Manuscript 152, 1899. (See *Child Guidance*, pp. 565, 566; *Counsels on Health*, p. 375.)

The Final Conflict Will Be Short but Terrible

We are standing on the threshold of great and solemn events. Prophecies are fulfilling. The last great conflict will be short, but terrible. Old controversies will be revived. New controversies will arise. We have a great work to do. Our ministerial work must not cease. The last warnings must be given to the world. There is a special power in the presentation of the truth at the present time. How long will it last? Only a little while.
. . .

The inquiry of everyone should be, "Whose am I? To whom do I owe allegiance? Is my heart renewed? Is my soul reformed? Are my sins forgiven? Will they be blotted out when the time of refreshing shall come?"
. . .

Prophets Wrote for Their Own and Our Day.—The last books of the Old Testament show us workers taken from the laborers in the field. Others were men of high ability and extensive learning, but the Lord gave them visions and messages. These men of the Old Testament spoke of things transpiring in their day, and Daniel, Isaiah, and Ezekiel not only spoke of things that concerned them as present truth, but their sights reached down to the future, and to what should occur in these last days.—Letter 132, 1898.

When Persecuted Flee to Another Place

In some places where the opposition is very pronounced, the lives of God's messengers may be endangered. It is then their privilege to follow the example of their Master and go to another place.—Letter 20, 1901.

Martyrdom God's Means of Bringing Many Into Truth

The worthies who refused to bow to the golden image were cast into a burning fiery furnace, but Christ was with them there, and the fire did not consume them. . . .

Now some of us may be brought to just as severe a test—will we obey the commandments of men or will we obey the commandments of God? This is the question that will be asked of many. The best thing for us is to come into close connection with God, and, if He would have us be martyrs for the truth's sake, it may be the means of bringing many more into the truth.— Manuscript 83, 1886.

Christ Stands by the Side of Persecuted Saints

Never is the tempest-tried soul more dearly loved by his Saviour than when he is suffering reproach for the truth's sake. When for the truth's sake the believer stands at the bar of unrighteous tribunals, Christ stands by his side. All the reproaches that fall upon the human believer fall upon Christ in the person of His saints. "I will love him," said Christ, "and will manifest myself to him" (John 14:21). Christ is condemned over again in the person of His believing disciples.

When for the truth's sake the believer is incarcerated in prison walls, Christ manifests Himself to him, and ravishes his heart with His love. When he suffers death for the sake of Christ, Christ says to him, "They may kill the body, but they cannot hurt the soul." "Be of good cheer; I have overcome the world." "They crucified Me, and if they put you to death, they crucify Me afresh in the person of My saints."

Persecution cannot do more than cause death, but the life is preserved to eternal life and glory. The persecuting power may take its stand, and command the disciples of Christ to deny the faith, to give heed to seducing spirits and doctrines of devils, by making void the law of God. But the disciples may ask, "Why should I do this? I love Jesus, and I will never deny His name." When the power says, "I will call you a disturber of the peace," they may answer, "Thus they called Jesus, who was truth, and grace and peace."—Letter 116, 1896.

Merchants and Princes Will Take Their Stand

Some who are numbered among merchants and princes will take their position to obey the truth. God's eye has been upon such as they have acted according to the light they have had, maintaining their integrity. Cornelius, a man of high position, maintained his religious experience, strictly walking in accordance with the light he had received. God had His eye upon him, and He sent His angel with a message to him. The heavenly messenger passed by the self-righteous ones, came to Cornelius, and called him by name. . . .

This record is made for the special benefit of those who are living in these last days. Many who have had great light have not appreciated and improved it as it was their privilege to do. They have not practiced the truth. And because of this the Lord will bring in those who have lived up to all the light they have had. And those who have been privileged with opportunities to understand the truth and who have not obeyed its principles will be swayed by Satan's temptations for self-advancement. They will deny the principles of truth in practice and bring reproach upon the cause of God.

Christ declares that He will spue these out of His mouth, and leave them to follow their own course of actions to distinguish themselves. This course of action does indeed make them prominent as men that are unfaithful householders.

God's Measurement of Those Who Walk in the Light They Have.—The Lord will give His message to those who have walked in accordance with the light they have had, and will recognize them as true and faithful, according to the measurement of God. These men will take the place of those who, having light and knowledge, have walked not in the way of the Lord, but in the imagination of their own unsanctified hearts.

We are now living in the last days, when the truth must be spoken, when in reproof and warning it must be given to the world, irrespective of consequences. If there are some who will become offended and turn from the truth, we must bear in mind that there were those who did the same in Christ's day. . . .

The Ranks Will Not Be Diminished.—But there are men who will receive the truth, and these will take the places made vacant by those who become offended and leave the truth. . . . The Lord will work so that the disaffected ones will be separated from the true and loyal ones. . . . The ranks will not be diminished. Those who are firm and true will close up the vacancies that are made by those who become offended and apostatize. . . .

Many will prize the wisdom of God above any earthly advantage, and will obey the Word of God as the supreme standard. These will be led to great light. These will come to the knowledge of the truth, and will seek to get this light of truth before those of their acquaintance who like themselves are anxious for the truth.—Manuscript 97, 1898.

Every Human Being Will Be Either in Christ's Army or Satan's Army

We are nearing the close of this earth's history, when two parties alone can exist, and every man, woman, and child will be in one of these armies. Jesus will be the General of one army; of the opposing army, Satan will be the leader. All who are breaking, and teaching others to break, the law of God, the foundation of His government in heaven and in earth, are marshaled under one superior chief, who directs them in opposition to the government of God. And "the angels which kept not their first estate, but left their own habitation" (Jude 6) are rebels against the law of God, and enemies to all who love and obey His commandments. These subjects, with Satan their leader, will gather others into their ranks through every possible means, to strengthen his forces and urge his claims.

Through his deception and delusion, Satan would, if possible, deceive the very elect. His is no minor deception. He will seek to annoy, to harass, to falsify, to accuse, and misrepresent all whom he cannot compel to give him honor and help him in his work. His great success lies in keeping men's minds confused, and ignorant of his devices, for then he can lead the unwary as it were, blindfolded. . . .

The Sabbath Is the Issue in the Final Conflict.—The Sabbath is the great test question. It is the line of demarkation between the loyal and true and the disloyal and transgressor. This Sabbath God has enjoined, and those who claim to be commandment keepers, who believe that they are now under the proclamation of the third angel's message, will see the important part the Sabbath of the fourth commandment holds in that message. It is the seal of the living God. They will not lessen the claims of the Sabbath to suit their business of convenience.—Manuscript 34, 1897.

John in the Revelation writes of the unity of those living on the earth to make void the law of God. "These have one mind, and shall give their power and strength unto the beast. These shall make war with the Lamb, and the Lamb shall overcome them: for he is Lord of lords, and King of kings: and they that are with him are called, and chosen, and faithful" (Rev. 17:13, 14). "And I saw three unclean spirits like frogs come out of the mouth of the dragon, and out of the mouth of the beast, and out of the mouth of the false prophet" (chap. 16:13).

All who will exalt and worship the idol Sabbath, a

day that God has not blessed, help the devil and his angels with all the power of their God-given ability, which they have perverted to a wrong use. Inspired by another spirit, which blinds their discernment, they cannot see that the exaltation of Sunday is entirely the institution of the Catholic Church. . . .

Sabbath Is the Issue That Divides the World.—The Lord of heaven permits the world to choose whom they will have as ruler. Let all read carefully the thirteenth chapter of Revelation, for it concerns every human agent, great and small. Every human being must take sides, either for the true and living God, who has given to the world the memorial of Creation in the seventh-day Sabbath, or for a false sabbath, instituted by men who have exalted themselves above all that is called God or that is worshiped, who have taken upon themselves the attributes of Satan, in oppressing the loyal and true who keep the commandments of God. This persecuting power will compel the worship of the beast by insisting on the observance of the sabbath he has instituted. Thus he blasphemes God, sitting "in the temple of God, shewing himself that he is God" (2 Thess. 2:4). . . .

The 144,000 Without Guile.—One of the marked features in the representation of the 144,000 is that in their mouth there was found no guile. The Lord has said, "Blessed is the man . . . in whose spirit there is no guile." They profess to be children of God, and are represented as following the Lamb whithersoever He goeth. They are prefigured before us as standing on Mount Zion, girt for holy service, clothed in white linen, which is the righteousness of the saints. But all who follow the Lamb in heaven will first have followed Him on earth, in trustful, loving, willing obedience, followed Him not fretfully and capriciously, but confidently, truthfully, as the flock follows the shepherd. . . .

Satan Making His Last Effort for the Mastery.—The world is in copartnership with the professed Christian churches in making void the law of Jehovah. God's law is set aside, it is trampled underfoot; and from all the loyal people of God, the prayer will ascend to heaven, "It is time, for thee, Lord, to work: for they have made void thy law" (Ps. 119:126). Satan is making his last and most powerful effort for the mastery, his last conflict against the principles of God's law. A defiant infidelity abounds.

After John's description in Revelation 16 of that miracle-working power which was to gather the world to the last great conflict, the symbols are dropped, and the trumpet voice once more gives a certain sound. "Behold, I come as a thief. Blessed is he that watcheth, and keepeth his garments, lest he walk naked, and they see his shame" (Rev. 16:15).—Manuscript 7a, 1896.

Christ Mingles in the Ranks in the Last Conflict

The agency of the Holy Spirit is to combine with human effort and all heaven is engaged in the work of preparing a people to stand in these last days. The end is near and we want to keep the future world in view. . . .

In this last conflict the Captain of the Lord's host [Joshua 5:15] is leading on the armies of heaven and mingling in the ranks and fighting our battles for us. We shall have apostasies, we expect them. "They will go out from us because they were not of us" (see 1 John 2:19). "Every plant, which my heavenly Father hath not planted, shall be rooted up" (Matt. 15:13).

The angel, the mighty angel from heaven, is to lighten the earth with His glory (Rev. 18:1), while he cries mightily with a loud voice, "Babylon the great is fallen, is fallen" (verse 2). . . . We would lose faith and courage in the conflict, if we were not sustained by the power of God.

Every form of evil is to spring into intense activity. Evil angels unite their powers with evil men, and as they have been in constant conflict and attained an experience in the best modes of deception and battle and have been strengthening for centuries, they will not yield the last great final contest without a desperate struggle and all the world will be on one side or the other of the question.

The battle of Armageddon will be fought. And that day must find none of us sleeping. Wide awake we must be, as wise virgins having oil in our vessels with our lamps. The power of the Holy Ghost must be upon us and the Captain of the Lord's host will stand at the head of the angels of heaven to direct the battle. Solemn events before us are yet to transpire. Trumpet after trumpet is to be sounded; vial after vial poured out one after another upon the inhabitants of the earth. Scenes of stupendous interest are right upon us and these things will be sure indications of the presence of Him who has directed in every aggressive movement, who has accompanied the march of His cause through all the ages, and who has graciously pledged Himself to be with His people in all their conflicts to the end of the world. He will vindicate His truth. He will cause it to triumph. He is ready to supply His faithful ones with motives and power of purpose, inspiring them with hope and courage and valor in increased activity as the time is at hand.

One Fierce Last Struggle.—Deceptions, delusions, impostures will increase. The cries will come in from every quarter, "Lo, here is Christ! Lo, there is Christ!" "But," said Christ, "Go ye not . . . after them" (Luke 21:8). There will be one fierce struggle before the man of sin shall be disclosed to this world—who he is and what has been his work.

While the Protestant world is becoming very tender and affectionate toward the man of sin (2 Thess. 2:3), shall [not] God's people take their place as bold and valiant soldiers of Jesus Christ to meet the issue which must come, their lives hid with Christ in God? Mystic Babylon has not been sparing in the blood of the saints and shall we [not] be wide awake to catch the beams of light which have been shining from the light of the angel who is to brighten the earth with his glory.— Letter 112, 1890.

Our Lives and the Final Preparation

God Will Try Us.—Before giving us the baptism

of the Holy Spirit, our heavenly Father will try us, to see if we can live without dishonoring Him.—Letter 22, 1902.

Everything Imperfect Will Be Put Away.— When our earthly labors are ended, and Christ shall come for His faithful children, we shall then shine forth as the sun in the kingdom of our Father. But before that time shall come, everything that is imperfect in us will have been seen and put away. All envy and jealousy and evil surmising and every selfish plan will have been banished from the life.—Letter 416, 1907.

When Perfection of Character Is Reached.—Are we striving with all our God-given powers to reach the measure of the stature of men and women in Christ? Are we seeking for His fullness, ever reaching higher and higher, trying to attain to the perfection of His character? When God's servants reach this point, they will be sealed in their foreheads. The recording angel will declare, "It is done." They will be complete in Him whose they are by creation and by redemption.—Manuscript 148, 1899.

We Shall Be Gifted With a Higher Nature.— When Christ comes, He takes those who have purified their souls by obeying the truth. . . . This mortal shall put on immortality, and these corruptible bodies, subject to disease, will be changed from mortal to immortal. We shall then be gifted with a higher nature. The bodies of all who purify their souls by obeying the truth shall be glorified. They will have fully received and believed in Jesus Christ.—Manuscript 36, 1906.

A Vivid View of Coming Events

Friday [Jan. 18, 1884] night several heard my voice exclaiming, "Look, Look!" Whether I was dreaming or in vision I cannot tell. I slept alone.

The time of trouble was upon us. I saw our people in great distress, weeping and praying, pleading the sure promises of God, while the wicked were all around us mocking us and threatening to destroy us. They ridiculed our feebleness, they mocked at the smallness of our numbers, and taunted us with words calculated to cut deep. They charged us with taking an independent position from all the rest of the world. They had cut off our resources so that we could not buy or sell, and they referred to our abject poverty and stricken condition. They could not see how we could live without the world. We were dependent on the world, and we must concede to the customs, practices, and laws of the world, or go out of it. If we were the only people in the world whom the Lord favored, the appearances were awfully against us.

They declared that they had the truth, that miracles were among them; that angels from heaven talked with them and walked with them, that great power and signs and wonders were performed among them, and that this was the temporal millennium they had been expecting so long. The whole world was converted and in harmony with the Sunday law, and this little feeble people stood out in defiance of the laws of the land and the law of God, and claimed to be the only ones right on the earth.
. . .

"Look Up! Look Up!"—But while anguish was upon the loyal and true who would not worship the beast or his image and accept and revere an idol sabbath, One said, "Look up! Look up!" Every eye was lifted, and the heavens seemed to part as a scroll when it is rolled together, and as Stephen looked into heaven, [so] we looked. The mockers were taunting and reviling us, and boasting of what they intended to do to us if we continued obstinate in holding fast our faith. But now we were as those who heard them not; we were gazing upon a scene that shut out everything else.

There stood revealed the throne of God. Around it were ten thousand times ten thousand and thousands upon thousands, and close about the throne were the martyrs. Among this number I saw the very ones who were so recently in such abject misery, whom the world knew not, whom the world hated and despised.

A voice said, "Jesus, who is seated upon the throne, has so loved man that He gave His life a sacrifice to redeem him from the power of Satan, and to exalt him to His throne. He who is above all powers, He who has the greatest influence in heaven and in earth, He to whom every soul is indebted for every favor he has received, was meek and lowly in disposition, holy, harmless, and undefiled in life.

"He was obedient to all His Father's commandments. Wickedness has filled the earth; it is defiled under the inhabitants thereof. The high places of the powers of earth have been polluted with corruption and base idolatries, but the time has come when righteousness shall receive the palm of victory and triumph. Those who were accounted by the world as weak and unworthy, those who were defenseless against the cruelty of men, shall be crowned conquerors and more than conquerors." [Rev. 7:9-17 quoted.]

They are before the throne enjoying the sunless splendors of eternal day, not as a scattered, feeble company, to suffer by the satanic passions of a rebellious world, expressing the sentiments, the doctrines, and the counsels of demons.

Now the Saints Have Nothing to Fear.—Strong and terrible have become the masters of iniquity in the world under the control of Satan, but strong is the Lord God who judgeth Babylon. The just have no longer anything to fear from force or fraud as long as they are loyal and true. A mightier than the strong man armed is set for their defense. All power and greatness and excellence of character will be given to those who have believed and stood in defense of the truth, standing up and firmly defending the laws of God.

Another heavenly being exclaimed with firm and musical voice, "They have come out of great tribulation. They have walked in the fiery furnace in the world, heated intensely by the passions and caprices of men who would enforce upon them the worship of the beast and his image, who would compel them to be disloyal to the

God of heaven.

"They have come from the mountains, from the rocks, from the dens and caves of the earth, from dungeons, from prisons, from secret councils, from the torture chamber, from hovels, from garrets. They have passed through sore affliction, deep self-denial, and deep disappointment. They are no longer to be the sport and ridicule of wicked men. They are to be no longer mean and sorrowful in the eyes of those who despise them.

"Remove the filthy garments from them, with which wicked men have delighted to clothe them. Give them a change of raiment, even the white robes of righteousness, and set a fair mitre upon their heads."

There They Stand Victors in the Great Conflict.—They were clothed in richer robes than earthly beings had ever worn. They were crowned with diadems of glory such as human beings had never seen. The days of suffering, of reproach, of want, of hunger, are no more; weeping is past. Then they break forth in songs, loud, clear, and musical. They wave the palm branches of victory, and exclaim, "Salvation to our God which sitteth upon the throne, and unto the Lamb" (Rev. 7:10).

Oh, may God endue us with His Spirit and make us strong in His strength! In that great day of supreme and final triumph it will be seen that the righteous were strong, and that wickedness in all its forms and with all its pride was a weak and miserable failure and defeat. We will cling close to Jesus, we will trust Him, we will seek His grace and His great salvation. We must hide in Jesus, for He is a covert from the storm, a present help in time of trouble.—Letter 6, 1884.

Two Columns of Angels Escort Saints to the City of God.—The Lifegiver is coming to break the fetters of the tomb. He is to bring forth the captives and proclaim, "I am the resurrection and the life." There stands the risen host. The last thought was of death and its pangs. The last thoughts they had were of the grave and the tomb, but now they proclaim, "O death, where is thy sting? O grave, where is thy victory" (1 Cor. 15:55). The pangs of death were the last things they felt. . . .

When they awake the pain is all gone. "O grave, where is thy victory?" Here they stand and the finishing touch of immortality is put upon them and they go up to meet their Lord in the air. The gates of the city of God swing back upon their hinges, and the nations that have kept the truth enter in.

There are the columns of angels on either side, and the ransomed of God walk in through the cherubim and seraphim. Christ bids them welcome and puts upon them His benediction: "Well done, thou good and faithful servant: . . . enter thou into the joy of thy lord" (Matt. 25:21). What is that joy? He sees of the travail of His soul, and is satisfied. That is what we labor for.

Here is one, who in the night season we pleaded with God on his behalf. There is one that we talked with on his dying bed, and he hung his helpless soul upon Jesus. Here is one who was a poor drunkard. We tried to get his eyes fixed upon Him who is mighty to save and we told him that Christ could give him the victory. There are the crowns of immortal glory upon their heads, and then the redeemed cast their glittering crowns at the feet of Jesus; and then the angelic choir strikes the note of victory and the angels in the two columns take up the song and the redeemed host join as though they had been singing the song on the earth, and they have been.

Celestial Music.—Oh, what music! There is not an inharmonious note. Every voice proclaims, "Worthy is the Lamb that was slain" (Rev. 5:12). He sees of the travail of His soul and is satisfied. Do you think anyone there will take time to tell of his trials and terrible difficulties? "The former shall not be remembered, nor come into mind" (Isa. 65:17). "God shall wipe away all tears from their eyes" (Rev. 21:4).—Manuscript 18, 1894.

APPENDIX A

The Great Controversy

—1911 Edition

A statement made by W. C. White before the General Conference Council, October 30, 1911.

Addressing the council, Elder W. C. White said:

"It is with pleasure that I present to you a statement regarding the latest English edition of *Great Controversy*.

"About two years ago, we were told that the electrotype plates for this book, in use at the Pacific Press, the Review and Herald, and the International Tract Society (London), were so worn that the book must be reset and new plates made. This work has been done at the Pacific Press. Four sets of plates were made—one for each of our offices in Washington, Mountain View, Nashville, and Watford.

"In a letter sent to the managers of our publishing houses, I wrote as follows, on July 24, 1911:*

"'After taking counsel with ministers, canvassers, and other friends of the book, we thought best to reset the text so that the new edition would correspond as nearly as possible with the old. And although we could not use exactly the same type, the matter runs nearly page for page. Every chapter in the new edition begins and ends on the same pages as does the corresponding

---

* This is the same as the letter of the same date that was addressed to "Our General Missionary Agents."

chapter in the old edition.

" 'The most noticeable change in the new edition is the improvement in the illustrations. Each of the forty-two chapters, together with the Preface, Introduction, Contents, and list of Illustrations, has a beautiful pictorial heading; and ten new full-page illustrations have been introduced, to take the place of those which were least attractive.

" 'The thirteen Appendix notes of the old edition, occupying thirteen pages, have been replaced by thirty-one notes occupying twelve pages. These are nearly all reference notes, intended to help the studious reader in finding historical proofs of the statements made in the book.

" 'The Biographical Notes have been omitted, and the general Index has been enlarged from twelve to twenty-two pages, thus greatly facilitating the finding of desired passages.

" 'In the body of the book, the most noticeable improvement is the introduction of historical references. In the old edition, over seven hundred Biblical references were given, but in only a few instances were there any historical references to the authorities quoted or referred to. In the new edition the reader will find more than four hundred references to eighty-eight authors and authorities.

" 'When we presented to Mother the request of some of our canvassers, that there should be given in the new edition not only scripture references but also references to the historians quoted, she instructed us to hunt up and insert the historical references. She also instructed us to verify the quotations, and to correct any inaccuracies found; and where quotations were made from passages that were rendered differently by different translators, to use that translation which was found to be most correct and authentic.

" 'The finding of the various passages quoted from historians has been a laborious task, and the verification of the passages quoted has led to some changes in the wording of the text. This is especially noticeable in the quotations from the *History of the Reformation*, by J. Merle D'Aubigné. It was found that there were six or more English translations, American and British, which varied much in wording, although almost identical in thought; and in the old edition of *Great Controversy* three of these had been used, according to the clearness and beauty of the language. But we learned that only one of these many translations had the approval of the author; that is the one used by the American Tract Society in its later editions. Therefore the quotations from D'Aubigné in this edition of *Great Controversy* have been made to conform in the main to this approved translation.

"'In a few instances, new quotations from historians, preachers, and present-day writers have been used in the place of the old, because they are more forceful or because we have been unable to find the old ones. In each case where there has been such a change, Mother has given faithful attention to the proposed substitution, and has approved of the change.

"'You will find that changes of this character have been made on pages 273, 277, 306-308, 334, 335, 387, 547, 580, and 581.

"'There are still some score or more quotations in the book whose authority we have so far been unable to trace. Fortunately, these relate to matters regarding which there is not a probability of there being any serious contention.

"'In spelling, punctuation, and capitalization, changes have been made to bring this book into uniformity of style with the other volumes of this series.

"'In eight or ten places, time references have been changed because of the lapse of time since the book was first published.

"'In several places, forms of expression have been changed to avoid giving unnecessary offense. An example of this will be found in the change of the word "Romish" to "Roman" or "Roman Catholic." In two places the phrase "divinity of Christ" is changed to "deity of Christ." And the words "religious toleration" have been changed to "religious liberty."

" 'The statements made on pages 285-287, regarding the action of the Assembly, in its blasphemous decrees against religion and the Bible, have been so worded as to show that the Assembly set aside, and afterward restored, not only the Bible but also God and His worship.

" 'In the new edition, the rise of the papacy in 538, and its fall in 1798, are spoken of as its "supremacy" and "downfall," instead of its "establishment" and "abolition," as in the old edition.

" 'In each of these places the more accurate form of expression has been duly considered and approved by the author of the book.

" 'On pages 50, 563, 564, 580, 581, and in a few other places where there were statements regarding the papacy which are strongly disputed by Roman Catholics, and which are difficult to prove from accessible histories, the wording in the new edition has been so changed that the statement falls easily within the range of evidence that is readily obtainable.

" 'Regarding these and similar passages, which might stir up bitter and unprofitable controversies, Mother has often said: "What I have written regarding the arrogance and the assumptions of the papacy is true. Much historical evidence regarding these matters has been designedly destroyed; nevertheless, that the book may be of the greatest benefit to Catholics and others, and that needless controversies may be avoided, it is better to have all statements regarding the assumptions of the pope and the claims of the papacy stated so moderately as to be easily and clearly proved from accepted histories that are within the reach of our ministers and students."

" 'If you hear reports that some of the work done on this latest edition was done contrary to Mother's wish or without her knowledge, you can be sure that such reports are false, and unworthy of consideration.' "

Passages from the old and the new editions were read

and compared, to illustrate the statement read from the speaker's letter of July 24. Then Brother White said:

"Since the printing of this new edition, Mother has taken great pleasure in looking over and rereading the book. Day after day, as I visited her in the morning, she spoke of it, saying that she enjoyed reading it again, and that she was glad that the work we have done to make this edition as perfect as possible was completed while she was living and could direct in what was done.

"Mother has never claimed to be authority on history. The things which she has written out, are descriptions of flashlight pictures and other representations given her regarding the actions of men, and the influence of these actions upon the work of God for the salvation of men, with views of past, present, and future history in its relation to this work. In connection with the writing out of these views, she has made use of good and clear historical statements to help make plain to the reader the things which she is endeavoring to present. When I was a mere boy, I heard her read D'Aubigné's *History of the Reformation* to my father. She read to him a large part, if not the whole, of the five volumes. She has read other histories of the Reformation. This has helped her to locate and describe many of the events and the movements presented to her in vision. This is somewhat similar to the way in which the study of the Bible helps her to locate and describe the many figurative representations given to her regarding the development of the great controversy in our day between truth and error.

"Mother has never laid claim to verbal inspiration, and I do not find that my father, or Elder Bates, Andrews, Smith, or Waggoner, put forth this claim. If there were verbal inspiration in writing her manuscripts, why should there be on her part the work of addition or adaptation? It is a fact that Mother often takes one of her manuscripts, and goes over it thoughtfully, making additions that develop the thought still further.

"The first edition of this book was published in California in 1884. When *Spirit of Prophecy,* Volume III was printed, there was some matter left over. A portion of this was printed in pamphlet form and circulated; and it was expected that Mother would proceed immediately to add to this matter and bring out Volume IV. Before Father's death he had advertised the book, *Spirit of Prophecy,* Volume IV.

"When Mother brought out Volume IV, she and those who had to do with its publication had in mind the fulfillment of Father's plan. We also had in mind that it was written for the Adventist people of the United States. Therefore with much difficulty the matter was compressed so as to bring this volume into about the same size as the other volumes of the series.

"Later on, when it was found that the book could be sold to all people, the publishers took the plates and printed an edition on larger paper. Illustrations were inserted, and an experiment made in selling it as a subscription book at $1.50.

"In 1885 Mother and I were sent to Europe, and there the question came up regarding its translation into German, French, Danish, and Swedish. As Mother considered this proposition, she decided to make additions to the matter.

"Mother's contact with European people had brought to her mind scores of things that had been presented to her in vision during past years, some of them two or three times, and other scenes many times. Her seeing of historic places and her contact with the people refreshed her memory with reference to these things, and so she desired to add much material to the book. This was done, and the manuscripts were prepared for translation.

"After our return to America, a new edition was brought out much enlarged. In this edition some of the matter used in the first English edition was left out. The reason for these changes was found in the fact that the new edition was intended for worldwide circulation.

"In her public ministry, Mother has shown an ability to select from the storehouse of truth, matter that is well adapted to the needs of the congregation before her; and she has always thought that, in the selection of matter for publication in her books, the best judgment should be shown in selecting that which is best suited to the needs of those who will read the book.

"Therefore, when the new edition of *Great Controversy* was brought out in 1888, there were left out about twenty pages of matter—four or five pages in a place—which was very instructive to the Adventists of America, but which was not appropriate for readers in other parts of the world.

"Much of the research for historical statements used in the new European and American editions of *Great Controversy* was done in Basel, where we had access to Elder Andrews' large library, and where the translators had access to the university libraries.

"When we came to go over this matter for the purpose of giving historical references, there were some quotations which we could not find. In some cases there were found other statements making the same point, from other historians. These were in books accessible in many public libraries. When we brought to Mother's attention a quotation that we could not find, and showed her that there was another quotation that we had found, which made the same point, she said, 'Use the one you can give reference to, so that the reader of the books, if he wishes to go to the source and find it, can do so.' In that way some historical data have been substituted.

"Now, with reference to the statement that the people at Washington, or the General Conference Committee men, have been doing this or that, right or wrong, in connection with this book, it is important that you should have a clear statement of facts regarding the matter.

"Our brethren at Washington and at Mountain View have done only that which we requested them to do. As stated in the beginning, we took counsel with the men of the Publishing Department, with State canvassing agents, and with members of the publishing committees, not only in Washington, but in California, and I asked them to kindly call our attention to any passages that needed to be considered in connection with the resetting of the book.

"When it was pointed out that some of the historical data were questioned and challenged, we asked them to give us a written statement that would help us in our research. They did as we requested and nothing more. All decisions as to what should be changed, and what should be printed word for word as in the old edition, were made in Mother's office, by persons in her employ and working under her direction. Therefore there is no occasion for any one to say a word against the General Conference Committee men or the literary men at Washington, or against the book, because of anything done by the brethren in Washington or elsewhere in connection with this work.

"We are very thankful to our brethren in Washington, and to many others, for kind and faithful painstaking labors in looking up those passages that were likely to be challenged by the Catholics and other critics. We were also profoundly thankful to our brethren in England and on the Continent, and also to brethren in Boston, New York, and Chicago, for helping to find in the great libraries, and verify, those quotations that were difficult to locate. They have done this work at our request, and to help us in what we thought ought to be done. The uses made of the results of this research, are seen in the historical references at the foot of the page and in the Appendix.

"The Appendix in the old book, as you remember, was partly explanatory, partly argumentative, and partly apologetic; but such notes seemed to us to be no longer necessary, and the thirty-one notes in the new edition are chiefly references to historical statements showing the correctness of the statements made in the book. We felt that it would be of value to the studious reader to have these definite references to the statements of well-known historians."

Copy of a Letter Written by Elder W. C. White:

Sanitarium, Calif., July 25, 1911

To the Members of the
Publication Committee

Dear Brethren:

In the accompanying letter to our State Missionary Agents, I have made a brief statement about the changes that appear in the new edition of *Great Controversy*.

A study of these changes may lead some to ask the question, "Has Sister White the authority and right to make changes in her published writings, either by addition, or by omission, or by any change whatever in the forms of expression, the manner of description, or the plan of the argument?"

The simple statement of some facts regarding the writing of her books, and the enlargement and development of the story of the great controversy between Christ and Satan, may of itself constitute an answer to this question.

It is generally admitted that in Sister White's discourses, spoken to the people, she uses great freedom and wisdom in the selection of proofs and illustrations, to make plain and forcible her presentation of the truths revealed to her in vision. Also, that she selects such facts and arguments as are adapted to the audience to whom she is speaking. This is essential to the attainment of the best results from her discourses.

And she has always felt and taught that it was her duty to use the same wisdom in the selection of matter for her books, that she does in the selection of matter for her discourses.

When Mother was writing *Great Controversy*, Volume IV, in 1882-1884, she was instructed regarding the general plan of the book. It was revealed to her that she should present an outline of the controversy between Christ and Satan as it developed in the first centuries of the Christian era, and in the great Reformation of the sixteenth century, in such a way as to prepare the mind of the reader to understand clearly the controversy as it is going on in our day.

While Mother was writing this book, many of the scenes were presented to her over and over again in visions of the night. The vision of the deliverance of God's people, as given in Chapter XL, was repeated three times; and on two occasions, once at her home in Healdsburg and once at the St. Helena Sanitarium, members of her family, sleeping in nearby rooms, were awakened from sleep by her clear, musical cry, "They come! They come!" (See page 636.)

Several times we thought that the manuscript of the book was all ready for the printer, and then a vision of some important feature of the controversy would be repeated, and Mother would again write upon the subject, bringing out the description more fully and clearly. Thus the publishing was delayed, and the book grew in size.

Mother regarded this new book as an expansion of the subject as first published in "Spiritual Gifts," Volume I (1858), and now found in *Early Writings,* pages 210-295.

And notwithstanding the divine instruction regarding the plan of the book, which has made it so useful to the general public, Mother felt that it was addressed chiefly to the Adventist people of the United States. Later, in preparing it for a wider circulation, she omitted a few portions that had appeared in the earlier edition. Examples of these may be found in the chapter entitled, "The Snares of Satan," pages 518-530. . . .

In her first visions the lives of the patriarchs, the mission and teachings of Christ and His apostles, and the controversy as carried forward by the church of Christ from the ascension to our day were at first presented to her in outline and were written out in brief, comprehensive articles as we find them in *Early Writings.*

In later years, one group of subjects after another was

shown her in vision repeatedly, and each time the revelation brought out more clearly the details of the whole or of some features of the subject.

Consequently Mother has written and published her views on the various phases of the great controversy several times, and each time more fully.

That which was published regarding the fall of Satan, the fall of man, and the plan of salvation, in *Early Writings* occupied eight pages. The same subjects as published in *Patriarchs and Prophets* occupied thirty larger pages.

That which was published in 1858 about the life of Christ, as found in *Early Writings,* occupied forty pages. The same as published in 1878 fills over six hundred pages of *Spirit of Prophecy,* Volumes II and III. And as now published in *Desire of Ages,* and in *Christ's Object Lessons,* it fills more than a thousand pages.

In *Great Controversy,* Volume IV, published in 1885, in the chapter "Snares of Satan," there are three pages or more of matter that was not used in the later editions, which were prepared to be sold to the multitudes by our canvassers. It is most excellent and interesting reading for Sabbathkeepers, as it points out the work that Satan will do in persuading popular ministers and church members to elevate the Sunday Sabbath, and to persecute Sabbathkeepers. [Currently found in *Testimonies to Ministers,* pp. 472-475.]

It was not left out because it was less true in 1888 than in 1885, but because Mother thought it was not wisdom to say these things to the multitudes to whom the book would be sold in future years. . . .

With reference to this, and to other passages in her writings which have been omitted in later editions, she has often said: "These statements are true, and they are useful to our people; but to the general public, for whom this book is now being prepared, they are out of place. Christ said, even to His disciples, 'I have many things to say unto you, but ye cannot bear them now.' And Christ taught His disciples to be 'wise as serpents, and harmless as doves.' Therefore, as it is probable that more souls will be won to Christ by the book without this passage than with it, let it be omitted." *

Regarding changes in forms of expression, Mother has often said: "Essential truths must be plainly told; but so far as possible they should be told in language that will win, rather than offend."—W. C. White letter, July 25, 1911.

---

* A Marian Davis statement.—COMPILERS.

APPENDIX B

W. C. White statement made to W. W. Eastman,* November 4, 1912.

It seems to me, Brother Eastman, that we must hold fast our confidence in the great Adventist movement of 1844, and we should not be easily moved from the positions held by the leaders in that movement and by the pioneers of our own denomination.

At the same time, I believe we should encourage our editors, our ministers, and the teachers in our schools, and the rank and file of our people, as far as they have time and opportunity, to be thorough Bible students and faithful students of history so that they may know for themselves and so that they can prove to people who do not accept our denominational books as authority, the points that we hold as a people. It is my conviction that those who write for our denominational papers regarding prophecy and its fulfillment ought to be encouraged to give deep and faithful study to the subjects about which they write, and to use in their arguments references and quotations from those historians which will be accepted by the readers as authority.

It may be all right for a preacher in presenting

---

* Publishing Department Secretary, Southwestern Union Conference.

Biblical expositions to his congregations to quote from *Daniel and Revelation* and *Great Controversy* as well expressed statement of his views; but it could hardly be wise for him to quote from them as authoritative histories to prove his points. I think you will discern the reasonableness of this proposition. A Presbyterian who was endeavoring to prove the soundness of his theories to a congregation of Methodists would not be expected to depend largely upon Presbyterian writers to prove his points, nor would a Methodist who was endeavoring to convince a Baptist of the soundness of the Methodist religion, make the greatest headway by using Methodist writers as his authority. In all our work we must study to follow methods that are most effective.

When it comes to the matter of writing out expositions of doctrine or of prophecy, still greater care must be taken by the writer than by the preacher to select those authorities which will be accepted as authorities by the critical and studious reader.

If I understand the matter correctly, Brother ———— has been writing articles on prophecy and its fulfillment in which he uses *Daniel and Revelation* and *Great Controversy* as authority to prove his points. This I should consider to be a very poor policy. Some readers will accept it as establishing the truth. Some readers will accept it as true, while questioning the authority. With others the use of these denominational books in such a way will constitute a challenge for them to endeavor to prove that there are errors in the books thus used as authority. Will it not be better for all classes if in our sermons and articles, we prove our points by references to authorities that are generally accepted?

Ellen G. White Writings on History

Regarding Mother's writings and their use as authority on points of history and chronology, Mother has never wished our brethren to treat them as authority regarding the details of history or historical dates. The great truths revealed to Mother regarding the controversy between good and evil, light and darkness, have been given to her in various ways, but chiefly as flashlight views of great events in the lives of individuals and in the experiences of churches, of bands of reformers, and of nations. What has thus been revealed to her she has written out first briefly in the *Early Writings,* then more fully as in *Spiritual Gifts* and in *Spirit of Prophecy,* and finally in the Great Controversy series.

When writing out the experiences of Reformers in the time of the Reformation and in the great Advent Movement of 1844, Mother often gave at first a partial description of some scene presented to her. Later on she would write it out more fully, and again still more fully. I have known her to write upon one subject four or five times, and then mourn because she could not command language to describe the matter more perfectly.

When writing out the chapters for *Great Controversy,* she sometimes gave a partial description of an important historical event, and when her copyist who was preparing the manuscripts for the printer, made inquiry regarding time and place, Mother would say that those things are recorded by conscientious historians. Let the dates used by those historians be inserted. At other times in writing out what has been presented to her, Mother found such perfect descriptions of events and presentations of facts and of doctrines written out in our denominational books, that she copied the words of these authorities.

When *Controversy* was written, Mother never thought that the readers would take it as authority on historical dates or use it to settle controversy regarding details of history, and she does not now feel that it should be used in that way. Mother regards with great respect the work of those faithful historians who devoted years of time to the study of God's great plan as presented in the prophecy, and the outworking of that plan as recorded in history.

In past years whenever definite proof has been found that the writers of our Adventist literature had come short of finding the exact proof regarding details, Mother has taken her position in favor of correcting those things that were clearly found to be in error. When she was consulted about the efforts that were being made to revise and correct the good book *Daniel and Revelation,* she has always opposed making many changes, and has always favored correcting those things that were plainly shown to be incorrect.

Chronology

It seems to me there is danger of placing altogether too much stress upon chronology. If it had been essential to the salvation of man that he should have a clear and harmonious understanding of the chronology of the world, the Lord would not have permitted the disagreements and discrepancies which we find in the writings of the Bible historians, and it seems to me that in these last days there ought not to be so much controversy regarding dates.

For myself, I will say this: That the more I study the experience of the Adventist people, the more I feel to honor and praise and magnify the wisdom of the God of heaven who gave to a plain man like William Miller an understanding of the great truths of the prophecies. It is evident to anyone who will study his explanation of prophecy that while he had the truth regarding the principal features, that he adopted at first many inaccurate and incorrect interpretations regarding details. At first these were accepted by his associates; but God raised up scholarly men who had enjoyed broader opportunities for study than Miller, and these men by their study of the prophecies and history found the truth regarding many points in which Miller's exposition was incorrect.

One who studies this experience from the standpoint of faith in that great Advent movement, as presented in *Daniel and Revelation,* and in *Great Controversy,* cannot fail to rejoice in the goodness of God as they see how He brought in truth and light through the study of many men and it seems to me that we who love the work that was built upon that foundation ought to treat very kindly, very considerately, very reverently the work which God helped Miller to do.

Make Only Modest Claims

But if we claim that Miller and his associates had a perfect and complete knowledge of the truth regarding the correspondence of history with prophecy, or if we claim for the pioneers in the third angel's message that their knowledge was complete and infallible, if we say, "Never in the history of this cause have we been obliged to confess ourselves in error," we shall unwisely and unnecessarily challenge criticism that will display to the world in a manifold and exaggerated light the imperfection and inaccuracies of some of our expositions which have been corrected by the results of faithful study in later years.

It seems to me, Brother Eastman, that there is great possibility of our weakening our influence by closing our eyes to the fact that we are all as little children learning from day to day from the great Teacher, and that it is our privilege to advance in knowledge and understanding. It seems to me that it is much wiser for us to convince the world that God has been leading us, and that He is leading us by presenting from time to time, unanswerable evidences regarding the soundness of our position by a clear presentation of the correspondence of prophecy and history through the use of historical data which the world cannot question, than by any efforts that we shall make to prove that the positions we held last year or ten years ago or twenty years ago or thirty years ago were infallible and unchangeable.

Regarding Mother's writings, I have overwhelming evidence and conviction that they are the description and delineation of what God has revealed to her in vision, and where she has followed the description of historians or the exposition of Adventist writers, I believe that God has given her discernment to use that which is correct and in harmony with truth regarding all matters essential to salvation. If it should be found by faithful study that she has followed some expositions of prophecy which in some detail regarding dates we cannot harmonize with our understanding of secular history, it does not influence my confidence in her writings as a whole any more than my confidence in the Bible is influenced by the fact that I cannot harmonize many of the statements regarding chronology.

APPENDIX C

W. C. White letter to L. E. Froom,* January 8, 1928

Dear Brother Froom:

Yesterday's mail brought me your letter of January 3. In it you present some queries calling for a reply from me.

You refer to a memory of a conversation with me in which you think I remarked that mother said with reference to some of her writings, "My work is to prepare; your work is to shape it up."

I do not remember of ever hearing mother make such a statement, and I do not think that any of her helpers ever heard her make such a statement. The thought which would prompt such a statement is not in harmony with her ideas regarding her work and the work of her copyists and secretaries.

There is a statement which I have made to several of our leading workers from which the idea conveyed in your query may have developed. I have told them that in the early days of our work, mother had written a testimony to an individual or to a group, containing information and counsel that would be valuable to others, and the brethren were questioning her as to how

---

* At that time Elder Froom was an associate secretary of the General Conference Ministerial Association.

it ought to be used. She said to my father often and sometimes to him and his associates—"I have done my part. I have written out what the Lord has revealed to me. Now it is for you to say how it shall be used."

You will readily see that such a proposition was very reasonable. My father and his associates were in contact with all the problems pertaining to the cause of present truth, which has since developed into the work of the General Conference, and it was a wise provision of *heaven that they should share* in the responsibility of saying how and in what manner the messages should be placed before whom they were intended to benefit.

You seem to think that if there was such a statement as referred to in your letter, it would be a benefit to some of our brethren. I cannot comprehend how it would benefit them. Possibly you can make it plain to me.

Regarding the two paragraphs which are to be found in *Spiritual Gifts* and also in the *Spirit of Prophecy* regarding amalgamation and the reason why they were left out of the later books, and the question as to who took the responsibility of leaving them out, I can speak with perfect clearness and assurance. They were left out by Ellen G. White. No one connected with her work had any authority over such a question, and I never heard of anyone offering to her counsel regarding this matter.

In all questions of this kind, you may set it down as a certainty that Sister White was responsible for leaving out or adding to matters of this sort in the later editions of our books.

Sister White not only had good judgment based upon a clear and comprehensive understanding of conditions and of the natural consequences of publishing what she wrote, but she had many times direct instruction from the angel of the Lord regarding what should be omitted and what should be added in new editions. . . .

Consider for a few moments the chapter in the first edition of *Great Controversy*, Volume IV, published by Pacific Press in 1884. In Chapter XXVII, "The Snares of Satan," you find that about four pages in the latter part of the chapter were omitted from the later editions of *Great Controversy*. These four pages are to be found in *Testimonies to Ministers*, pages 472 to 475. The information contained in these four pages is very valuable to Seventh-day Adventists and was very appropriately included in the first edition of *Great Controversy*, Volume IV, which when it was published was like the other volumes considered to be a message especially to Seventh-day Adventists, and to [all] Christian people sympathizing with them in beliefs and aims.

But when it was decided that *Great Controversy*, Volume IV should be republished in form for general circulation by subscription agents, Ellen G. White suggested that the pages be left out because of the likelihood that ministers of popular churches reading those statements would become angered and would array themselves against the circulation of the book.

Why will not our brethren study God's merciful dealings to us by imparting information to us by the Spirit of Prophecy in its beautiful, harmonious, and helpful features, instead of picking and criticizing and dissecting, trying to cut it up into little mechanical concrete blocks such as we buy for our children to play with and then ask somebody else to fit it together so that it will make a pattern that pleases them and leave out the particular parts of the pattern that they do not like? I pray the Lord to give us patience and guidance in doing what we can to help such ones to see the beauty of God's work.

You refer to other letters containing questions which I have not answered. I hope to get at them soon, but not this morning.

Yours faithfully,
W. C. White

W. C. White letter to L. E. Froom, **January 8, 1928**

Dear Brother Froom:

Since sending away a letter to you yesterday I have

found yours of December 22. In it you tell me that for two full years you have been encouraging Elder Daniells to prepare a book on the Spirit of Prophecy, but you failed to tell me what response he gives to these requests.

Referring to the statements that have been published by Elder Loughborough, you speak of the stress placed upon him by the physical manifestations and intimate that these do not appeal to you.

I fully agree with you that the great proof of the divine hand in the gift to the remnant church is in the internal evidence of the writings themselves. Nevertheless, I must believe that in the physical manifestations which have accompanied the bestowal of light and revelation, there is some real value; otherwise God would not have given them. Furthermore I am brought in contact with a great many people, earnest, sincere, and precious in the sight of the Lord, who do regard these physical manifestations as a matter of serious importance, and they testify that their faith has been greatly strengthened by a clear knowledge of the methods adopted by our heavenly Father for the confirmation of the receivers in the light He has given them.

You refer to the little statement which I sent you regarding verbal inspiration. This statement made by the General Conference of 1883 was in perfect harmony with the beliefs and positions of the pioneers in this cause, and it was, I think, the only position taken by any of our ministers and teachers until Prof. [W. W.] Prescott, president of Battle Creek College, presented in a very forceful way another view—the view held and presented by Professor Gausen.* The acceptance of that view by the students in the Battle Creek College and many others, including Elder Haskell, has resulted in bringing into our work questions and perplexities without end, and always increasing.

Sister White never accepted the Gausen theory re-

---

* Probably François Gaussen, a Swiss clergyman (1790-1863), who maintained that the Bible was verbally inspired.

garding verbal inspiration, either as applied to her own work or as applied to the Bible.

You say that in your endeavor to have a loyal and rational understanding of the background of this marvelous gift, you have been seeking to gain information concerning the various persons who helped Sister White in the literary phase of the work.

It is my conviction, Brother Froom, that you will never get light regarding the background of the gift of the Spirit of Prophecy by studying the characteristics and qualifications of the faithful copyist and the copy editors, whom Sister White called to her assistance in preparing for publication articles for our periodical and chapters for her books.

The foundation by which to fix faith in the messages which God has sent to His people, will be more readily found in the study of His dealings with His prophets in past ages. It seems to me that the study of the life and labors and writings of Saint Paul are more helpful and illuminating than any other line of study we might suggest, and I do not think we shall be greatly helped in establishing confidence in the writings of Paul by searching to make a list of his helpers and by study into their history and their experience. It is easy for me to believe that Jeremiah was directed of God in his selection of Baruch as a copyist; also that Paul had heavenly wisdom in selecting those who should act as his amanuensis from time to time according to his needs.

It is my belief that Sister Ellen G. White had heavenly guidance in choosing the persons who should act as copyists and those who should help to prepare articles for our periodicals and chapters for our books.

I am well acquainted with the circumstances which led her to select some of these workers and of the direct encouragements given her regarding their qualifications and trustworthiness for the work. I also know of instances where she was directed to instruct, to caution, and sometimes to dismiss from her employ those whose lack of spirituality disqualified them for satisfactory service. Regarding this, Elder Starr could give you an interesting chapter regarding Sister White's experience with Miss Fannie Bolton, and I could tell you of a circumstance under which she was separated from her own niece, Mary Clough, whom she greatly loved.

In the early '60's, Sister White was unaided, except by her husband, who would listen to her as she read chapters of manuscript and would suggest grammatical corrections as they occurred to his mind. As a little boy I remember witnessing circumstances like this—Elder White in his weariness would be lying on the sofa and Sister White would bring in a chapter written for *Spiritual Gifts* and would read to him and he would suggest, as stated above, grammatical corrections. Articles for the *Testimonies* were treated in a similar way.

Beside the few testimonies which were printed, many personal testimonies were sent to individuals and oftentimes Sister White would write saying, "I have no one to copy this Testimony. Please make a copy for yourself and send the original back to me." As a result of this method of work, we have in our manuscript vault many of the early testimonies in Sister White's handwriting.

In the earlier '60's, Sister Lucinda M. Hall acted as Sister White's housekeeper, secretary, and sometimes traveling companion. She was both timid and conscientious, and only the plainest grammatical errors were corrected by her. About 1862, Sister Adelia Patten connected with the White family and did some copying for Sister White. Later on she connected with the Review and Herald.

In the autumn of 1872 Sister White visited Colorado and became acquainted with her niece Mary C. Clough, and in '74, '75 and '76 Miss Clough assisted in preparing copy for *Spirit of Prophecy*, Volumes II and III. She also accompanied Elder and Mrs. White in their camp-meeting labors and acted as reporter for the public press. In so doing, she was the first publicity agent regularly employed by the denomination and may be looked up to as the grandmother of our publicity department.

Her experience as a newspaper reporter, the confidence that she thus gained and the praise that was heaped upon her work, unfitted her for the delicate and sacred work of being copy editor for *Review* articles and the chapters for the *Great Controversy*. In a vision it was presented to Sister White that she and Mary were looking at some wondrous developments in the sky. They meant much to Sister White, but to Mary they seemed to mean nothing; and the angel said, "Spiritual things are spiritually discerned," and then instructed Sister White that she should no longer employ her niece as her book editor.

During '68, '69, and '70, various ones were employed by Sister White to copy her testimonies. Among them were Miss Emma Sturgess, afterward the wife of Amos Prescott; Miss Anna Hale, afterward the wife of Irwin Royce; and others, whose names I do not now remember.

After the death of Elder [James] White in 1881, Sister White employed Sister Marian Davis. She had been for some years a proofreader in the Review and Herald, and Sister White received assurance through revelation that Sister Davis would be a conscientious and faithful helper. Later on Sister Eliza Burnham was employed by Sister White, and at one time Mrs. B. L. Whitney and Fannie Bolton were employed at Battle Creek as helpers when there was much work to do. Sister Davis was with Sister White in Europe in 1886 and 1887. She was also Sister White's principal helper in Australia.

As the work in Australia grew, Sister Burnham was called to assist in the book editing, and Maggie Hare and Minnie Hawkins were employed as copyists.

I had forgotten to mention that during the years when Sister White was in Healdsburg, Sister J. I. Ings did much copying of testimonies and of manuscripts.

At one time, while we were in Australia, it was proposed that the *Special Testimonies to Ministers* (i.e.,

Special Testimonies, Series A) published and sent out by
Elder [O. A.] Olsen* in the early '90's should be
reprinted—the matter to be grouped according to subjects. While this was under consideration, it happened
that Elder W. A. Colcord, who had once been secretary
of the General Conference and for many years a leading
writer on religious liberty topics, was out of employment, and at my solicitations Sister White employed
him to take the special testimonies and group the matter
according to subjects for republication. He spent several
weeks on this work and was paid by Sister White; but
the work was never used. If I remember correctly, this
was the extent of his connection with her literary work.

The last work done by Sister Davis was the selection
and arrangement of the matter used in *Ministry of
Healing.*

Elder C. C. Crisler assisted Sister White in selecting
and arranging the matter appearing in *Acts of the Apostles*
and *Prophets and Kings.*

This sketch of the work and the workers does not
claim to be complete. It was never considered by me or
by any of Sister White's helpers that the personnel of her
working force was of any primary interest to the readers
of her books. She wrote the matter. She wrote very fully.
There was always a controversy between her and the
publishers regarding the quantity of matter that should
be used. Sister White was best pleased when a subject
was presented very fully, and the publishers were always
bringing pressure to bear to have the matter condensed
or abbreviated so that the book would not be too large.
Consequently, after important chapters were prepared
for the printer, and sometimes after they were sent to the
printer, a new presentation of the subject would be given
Sister White, and she would write additional matter and
insist upon its being incorporated. This experience applied chiefly to the *Great Controversy,* Vol. IV.

A corresponding difficulty regarding the amount of

---

* General Conference president.

matter prepared for *Desire of Ages* was overcome in part by the setting apart of portions which were used in *Christ's Object Lessons* and *Thoughts From the Mount of Blessing.*

Regarding the reading of works of contemporary authors during the time of the preparation of these books, there is very little to be said, because, when Sister White was busily engaged in writing she had very little time to read. Previous to her work of writing on the life of Christ and during the time of her writing, to some extent, she read from the works of Hanna, Fleetwood, Farrar, and Geikie. I never knew of her reading Edersheim. She occasionally referred to Andrews, particularly with reference to chronology.

Why did she read any of these books? The great events of the conflict of the ages as brought out in the Great Controversy [i.e., Conflict] Series, were presented to her in part at many different times. In the first presentation a brief outline was given her as represented in the third section of the book now called *Early Writings.*

Later on the great events of the patriarchal age and the experience of the prophets were presented to her as brought out in her articles in *Testimonies for the Church,* and in her series of articles published in later years in the *Review, The Signs of the Times,* and the *Southern Watchman.* These series, you will remember, deal quite fully with the work of Ezra, Nehemiah, Jeremiah, and other of the prophets.

The great events occurring in the life of our Lord were presented to her in panoramic scenes as also were the other portions of the *Great Controversy.* In a few of these scenes chronology and geography were clearly presented, but in the greater part of the revelation the flashlight scenes, which were exceedingly vivid, and the conversations and the controversies, which she heard and was able to narrate, were not marked geographically or chronologically, and she was left to study the Bible and history, and the writings of men who had presented the

life of our Lord to get the chronological and geographical
connection.

Another purpose served by the reading of history and
the *Life of Our Lord* and the *Life of St. Paul*, was that in
so doing there was brought vividly to her mind scenes
presented clearly in vision, but which were through the
lapse of years and her strenuous ministry, dimmed in her
memory.

Many times in the reading of Hanna, Farrar, or
Fleetwood, she would run on to a description of a scene
which had been vividly presented to her, but forgotten,
and which she was able to describe more in detail than
that which she had read.

Notwithstanding all the power that God had given
her to present scenes in the lives of Christ and His
apostles and His prophets and His reformers in a
stronger and more telling way than other historians, yet
she always felt most keenly the results of her lack of
school education. She admired the language in which
other writers had presented to their readers the scenes
which God had presented to her in vision, and she found
it both a pleasure, and a convenience and an economy of
time to use their language fully or in part in presenting
those things which she knew through revelation, and
which she wished to pass on to her readers.

In many of her manuscripts as they come from her
hand quotation marks are used. In other cases they were
not used; and her habit of using parts of sentences found
in the writings of others and filling in a part of her own
composition, was not based upon any definite plan nor
was it questioned by her copyists and copy writers until
about 1885 and onward.

When critics pointed out this feature of her work as
a reason for questioning the gift which had enabled her
to write, she paid little attention to it. Later on, when
complaint was made that this was an injustice to other
publishers and writers, she made a decided change—a

---

* This may refer to William Hanna's *Life of Our Lord* (1863).

change which you are familiar with.

It is my belief, Brother Froom, that I cannot too frequently restate the fact that Sister White's mind was keenly active with reference to the contents of the articles published in our periodicals, and the chapters composing her books, and that she had help from Heaven and was remarkably acute in detecting any error made by copyists or by copy editors. This condition prevailed during all her busy years before the death of her husband and after the death of her husband, during her ministry in Europe and Australia and in the greater part of the years spent in America after her return from Australia.

In her very last years her supervision was not so comprehensive, but she was marvelously blessed in her intelligence in directing regarding the matter previously written which was being used in her last years and in pointing out those subjects which needed to be emphasized and those subjects which could be spared as we proceeded with the work of abridgment of the larger books in preparing copy for translation into foreign tongues.

Please read this statement to Elder Daniells, and if you observe that in my haste I have left matter so that it can be easily misunderstood, please point this out to me and give me an opportunity to strenthen the matter before it is placed by you before others of your brethren.

Yours truly,
W. C. WHITE

W. C. White letter to L. E. Froom, * December 13, 1934

Dear Brother Froom:

I hold in my hand your letter of December 3. The questions you ask are very comprehensive and rather difficult to answer.

---

* At this time secretary of the General Conference Ministerial Association.

It is a fact that during my thirty or more years of association with Ellen White I had the utmost confidence in her ministry. I know that she received revelations from God which were of untold value to the church and to the world. I did not enter as fully as some of our brethren wish to do in an analysis of the sources of information which enabled her to write her books.

The framework of the great temple of truth sustained by her writings was presented to her clearly in vision. In some features of this work, information was given in detail. Regarding some features of the revelation, such as the features of prophetic chronology, as regards the ministration in the sanctuary and the changes that took place in 1844, the matter was presented to her many times and in detail many times, and this enabled her to speak very clearly and very positively regarding the foundation pillars of our faith.

In some of the historical matters such as are brought out in *Patriarchs and Prophets* and in *Acts of the Apostles,* and in *Great Controversy,* the main outlines were made very clear and plain to her, and when she came to write up these topics, she was left to study the Bible and history to get dates and geographical relations and to perfect her description of details.

Ellen White was a rapid reader and had a very retentive memory. The revelations which she had received enabled her to grip subjects regarding which she read in a vigorous way. This enabled her to select and appropriate that which was true and to discard that which was erroneous or doubtful.

She read diligently the *History of the Reformation of the Sixteenth Century.* Much of D'Aubigné's history she read aloud to my father. She was an interested reader of religious journals, and during the many years that Uriah Smith was editor of the *Review,* it was her custom to request him after having made use of the religious exchanges, to pass them over to her and she would spend a portion of her time in scanning them in selecting precious things which sometimes appeared in the *Review.*

In these she also gathered information regarding what was going on in the religious world.

Regarding the study of books, there came a time shortly after the erection of the brick edifice which housed the Review and Herald plant that the large room facing the north end on the second floor was assigned to Elder and Mrs. White as their editorial and writing room. In this was located the Review and Herald library. To this Elder White made reference in his writings, and from the library Ellen White made selection of books which she considered profitable to read.

It was remarkable that in her reading and scanning of books that her mind was directed to the most helpful books and to the most helpful passages contained in those books. Occasionally she would mention to Father, and in my presence, her experience in being led to examine a book which she had never looked into before, and her experience in opening it to certain passages that helped her in describing that which she had seen and wished to present.

I am supposing that Bliss's *Memoirs* was in this library, but I have no knowledge as to whether she read it or not. I never heard her mention that book in connection with her work.

The explanatory notes found in her large subscription books were, some of them, written by herself, but most of them were written by J. H. Waggoner, Uriah Smith, and M. C. Wilcox in conjunction with Marian Davis.

You ask if James White brought to Ellen White books, the reading of which would help her in her writing. I do not remember of any such occurrence. I do remember that she occasionally brought interesting passages which she had been reading to the attention of her husband.

You ask if her helpers brought statements to her attention which they thought would help her in her writings. Nothing of this kind occurred previous to the writing of *Great Controversy*, Volume IV, at Healdsburg, in 1883 or 1884. Then it was seldom and related to minor details.

When we were in Basel, in 1886, we had a very interesting experience with a group of translators. We found that our brethren in Europe were very desirous of having *Great Controversy,* Volume IV, translated in the French and German languages. . . .

To provide this book for the French people, Elder Au Franc had been employed as translator and had put twenty or more chapters into what he considered his first-class French. Not everyone was satisfied with his translation and Elder Jean Vuilleumier had been employed to make a translation and had gotten through with a half dozen more chapters.

Regarding the German, there were three attempts at translation. Professor Kuhns, Madam Bach, and Henry Fry were the translators.

What should we do? Several persons were united in condemning each of these translations and it was difficult to find more than two persons who would speak a good word for either one.

Elder Whitney, manager of the Basel office, recognized the fact that Sister White's writing was difficult. The figures of speech were in some cases imperfectly understood by the translators, and in some cases where they were understood the translators did not know the religious phraseology of their own language well enough to give a correct translation.

Finally a way was arranged. Each morning at nine o'clock, two of the German translators, two of the French translators, Elder Whitney, Sister Davis, and myself met in the editorial room and chapter by chapter of the English book was read and commented upon. The translators recognizing a difficult passage, would stop the reading and discuss between themselves what the wording should be in French and in German. Frequently Elder Whitney would stop the reading and say, "John, how would you translate that?" Then he would appeal to Elder Au Franc saying, "Do you agree with that?"

Discerning that they did not understand in completeness the English text, Sister Davis and Brother Whitney would discuss its meaning and then the translators would again propose translation.

When we reached those chapters relating to the Reformation in Germany and France, the translators would comment on the appropriateness of the selection of historical events which Sister White had chosen, and in two instances which I remember, they suggested that there were other events of corresponding importance which she had not mentioned. When this was brought to her attention, she requested that the histories be brought to her that she might consider the importance of the events which had been mentioned. The reading of the history refreshed to her mind that which she had seen, after which she wrote a description of the event.

I was with Mother when we visited Zurich and I well remember how thoroughly her mind was aroused by seeing the old cathedral and the marketplace, and she spoke of them as they were in the days of Zwingle.

During her two years' residence in Basel, she visited many places where events of special importance occurred in the Reformation days. This refreshed her memory as to what she had been shown and this led to important enlargement in those portions of the book dealing with the Reformation days. . . .

With very kind regards, I remain,
Sincerely your brother,
W. C. White

Scripture Index

The following Scripture Index indicates where the author has quoted the passage of Scripture referred to or has said something having a bearing upon it.

EXODUS

5:1 122
24:12 122

NUMBERS

20:11 .... 121, 122

1 SAMUEL

7:12 110

2 KINGS

6:16 37
25:7 121

2 CHRONICLES

32:7 37

JOB

41:31 112

PSALMS

31:12 76
32:8 49

PROVERBS

3:6 49

ECCLESIASTES

12:13 95

ISAIAH

8:20 30
28:10, 13 33
30:21 .... 33, 122
42:4 72
58 64

JEREMIAH

39:6, 7 121
52:10, 11 121

EZEKIEL

2:5 75

DANIEL

7:10 122

MATTHEW

5:14 17
5:15 45
7:20 75
11:7 112
11:28-30 16
12:1 106
12:10-13 106
12:38 105
13:25 19
14:15-21 .... 105, 106
14:25, 26 .... 105, 106
16:1 105
16:27 122
18:18 22
18:19 24
24:24 .... 74, 114

MARK

2:23 106
3:1-5 106
4:21 45
6:35-44 .... 105, 106
7:13 86
8:11 105
13:22 .... 74, 114

LUKE

2:29 106
6:1 106
6:6-10 106
9:12-17 .... 105, 106
11:16 105
11:33 45
16:31 70

JOHN

3:16 118
5:39 31
6:5-13 .... 105, 106
6:35, 48 106
8:44 122
15 35
15:1 36
16:12 .... 56, 57
17 21
17:11 18
17:21, 22 24

ACTS

2:17 29
4:32 20

1 CORINTHIANS

4:9 16
6:19, 20 72
12:4-12 25

2 CORINTHIANS

2:16 115
12:4 57

EPHESIANS

2:14-16, 19-21 21
6:11 39

1 THESSALONIANS

5:2 113

1 TIMOTHY

4:1 37

2 TIMOTHY

1:12 37

HEBREWS

4:12 69
10:35 110

JAMES

4:8 122

2 PETER

1:21 30
3:16 82

REVELATION

1:3, 11 113
1:7 112
1:19 39
3:14-22 17
12:11 112
12:12 83
14:12 42
14:15 112

General Index

A

Abraham, faith of 194, 195
  saved by faith in Christ same as the sinner saved today 195
Acceptance, with God sure only through Jesus 199
Action, concerted, necessary for efficient service 24
Acts of the Apostles 458, 462 Appendix
  EGW felt perfect peace of mind while preparing 124
Adam, free from effects of sin when was tempted 141
Adornment, time is too short for, with gold or silver or costly apparel 247
Adulterer, who had been warned, counseled, and reproved, EGW refused to varnish over case of 53
Advent, Second, EGW heard God announce, but could not remember after vision 112
  ends soul preparation 155
Air, pure, beneficial 277
Amadon, George W. 94, footnote
Amalgamation, 452, 453 Appendix
America, can become place of greatest peril 387
  to become battlefield for religious liberty 387
American costume 278
Anarchy 418
Andrews, J. N. 262, 459, 464 Appendix
  library of, used by EGW in preparing *Great Controversy* (1888 ed.) 439 Appendix
  spent too much time perfecting *History of the Sabbath* 97
Angel, Daniel could not bear sight of until he came with appearance of a man 354
  of Revelation 18, lightens earth with glory 425
    proclaims his message while Satan works with his lying wonders 406
    represents giving of loud cry 412
  standing in the sun, is Christ 169
  words of, EGW always enclosed in quotation marks 278
Angels, evil, Christ was instructor of, before they fell 410
  in human form mingled with Christ's hearers 411
  in time of trouble wicked claim they walk, talk to angels from heaven 428
  will assemble in our meetings to

counteract work of God's Spirit 410
  will work in our ranks in form of believers 410
  ministered to Christ in His need, but this did not make His life free from conflict and temptation 131
  we will never gain strength by considering what we might do if we were 140
Ann Arbor, SDA youths who attend the University of Michigan at, to be converted 233
Answers, to questions put to EGW by G. A. Irwin, written out for benefit of SDA's 51
Anthony, Mr., SDA public school teacher at Crystal Springs public school 206, 216
Antichrist, he who takes stand with armies of, will be found outside city of God 401
  meaning all who exalt selves against will and work of God, will feel His wrath at appointed time 402
Appeal to Mothers 276
Appeal to Youth 262 footnote
Appearance, we should seek to make the best of our 241
Appearances, God does not judge by 240
Appetite, Christ began work of redemption just where the ruin began, on 128
  Christ's victory over, points us to way to overcome 129
  unhealthy, should be denied 274
Apostasy, even in our church and institutions some will depart from faith 411, 412
  every conceivable effort will be made to throw doubt on established SDA positions 408
  men in whom we have had confidence apostatize because corrupted their way before Lord 411
  physicians, lawyers, judges, senators will become corrupt 411
  ranks of God's people do not diminish; those who have lived up to light have had fill vacancies left by apostates 421
  time of, is here 408
  we shall witness of men in whom we have had confidence 411
Apostasies 381, 382
Apostates, hypnotism being used by 412
  Satan and his angels will appear on earth and mingle with 409
  those who are holding truth with tips of

fingers will become, in approaching test, unless characters transformed 415

those who have been self-indulgent will sneer at conscientious and even God Himself 397

we not to unify with those who departing from faith 412

See also Hirelings

Armageddon, battle of, will be fought 426

Captain of Lord's host will stand at head of angels of heaven to direct battle of 426

symbols dropped after revelator's description of miracle-working power that gathers world to last great conflict 425

See also Conflict, future

Army, church likened to, of well-disciplined soldiers 24

Articles, all EGW (up to 1894), fresh from her pen 117

Assurance, of favor with God, words expressing lack of, express unbelief 149

Atonement, Christ became sin for man 194

Christ's, had not been made plain to SDA's 183, 184

depend solely on merits of 145

mystery angels desire to look into 169

Atonement and Incarnation, dwell more upon 187

Attacks, on God's servants, from our very midst, should be met 348

Attribute(s), human beings possess reason, conscience, memory, will, affections 130

Au Franc, Brother 463 Appendix

Australia, EGW expressed the wish, but not a divine message, that Brother C. go to Australia 58, 59

B

Babylon, mystic, not been sparing of blood of saints 426

wine of, represents false doctrines 405

Bach, Madam 463 Appendix

Ball playing, pleasure seeking, and swimming on Sabbath, a sinful neglect of God's sacred day 257

Baptism 261, 263

James White baptized two 11-year-old sisters 261

Bates, Joseph 94, footnote

Beauty, that Heaven values, Christ used the things of nature to illustrate 241

Belden, Ella 264

Belief, may exist without trust, but confidence born of trust cannot exist without faith 191

Believe, only, an error 147

Believers, testimony of, must be one 20

Bible, and science, see Science, and Bible

and Spirit of Prophecy, have same author 30

God desires us to study 29

in public labor get proofs from, not EGW's writings 29, 30

many queries raised in, which most profound scholar can never answer 310

not contradicted by the Testimonies 32

not maxims of men, to be essence of education in our schools 227

not to be tested by men's ideas of science, but science to be brought to test of this unerring standard 307

present principles first, then the Testimonies 30

recommended as rule of faith, practice 29

Spirit of Prophecy is the lesser light leading to 30

Spirit was not given to supersede 30

the test, not feeling or excitement 375

See also Word of God

Blair Amendment to change U.S. Constitution 166

Bliss, Sylvester 463 Appendix

Bolton, Fannie 455, 457 Appendix

busy preparing EGW articles for papers and editing Testimonies and letters 117

EGW denied claim of, that she had made EGW's books 92

EGW strictly forbade, to change her wording 92

never was EGW's bookmaker 91, 92

sometimes made suggestions regarding arrangement of EGW material to be published 92

Books by EGW, statements on how they were prepared 88   introduction written by the help of Spirit 50

Bourdeau, Daniel F. 264

Bowen, L. M. 226

Brackett, Sister 263

Bread, of heaven, must be eaten and digested to become part of life 203

Burnham, Eliza 457 Appendix

Business meetings, care should be taken as to what resolutions framed 337

may be conducted in spirit of prayer 336, 337

Butler, G. I. 96 footnote, 165 footnote, 178 footnote

letter from, to EGW 165

sick man at the time of the Minneapolis GC session 178

Butter, principles involved in EGW statements on 221

Butter, meat, and cheese, not to be made a test, but we are to educate on 287

C

Cain, offerings 168, 169

Calamity, Mrs. Mackin predicted in Polish a, in Toledo, Ohio 365
  seasons of, in coming crisis 387

Calamities, before last great destruction, monuments to men's greatness crumbled in dust 419
  earth's crust will be rent by outburst of the elements 391
  EGW saw in vision costly vessels with human freight sink to watery grave 418
  powers of darkness are restrained from vitiating air 391
  terrible earthquakes will reduce lordly palaces to ruins 391
  time upon us when will be sorrow no human balm can heal 418, 419
  waves will engulf ships with passengers 417
  waves will pass their borders, destruction will be their trade 417
  will be, by land and sea 417

Canright, D. M. 264
  made bold assertions and misapplied Scriptures 83

Catholics, many, who come to truth will show greater zeal than many SDA's 386, 387

Catholic churches, God has a large number of children in 386

Centers, those who have lost their connection with God making desperate, insane efforts to make, of themselves 254

Change, outward, reveals working of Spirit inwardly 254

Character, Christian, cannot be claimed now without God's grace 150
  perfection of, we shall never see God unless we strive for 148
  righteous, Enoch and Elijah perfected 146, 147
  transformed through implantation of Christ's character in human nature 198

Charges, false, against EGW by false brethren should be met 348, 349, 350

Child-preaching, in Scandinavian countries, presented before EGW 110, 111

Children, allowed to run about, play, talk, and manifest evil tempers in Sabbath services desecrate the church and the Sabbath 257
  are younger members of God's household 293
  differences in, some 5-year-olds can be educated as well as many 10-year-olds 219
  discipline of, by parents 225

of believing parents, EGW deals with question of salvation of 313-315
  of God, united whole in Christ 21
  of unbelieving parents, EGW deals with question of whether saved 313-315
  of unbelieving parents, EGW stated we cannot tell whether, will be saved 315
  of unbelieving parents, many better trained than children of professed believers 315
  permitted by parents to be disobedient and passionate, who die in this condition, not taken to heaven 314, 315
  should not be permitted to violate the Sabbath 257
  wandering about, creating mischief, give Sanitarium visitors bad impression 217

Christ, alone could bear afflictions of all of human family 133
  angels ministered to in His need, but this did not make His life free from conflict and temptation 131
  arms are open to receive us 152
  as man belonged to human family, Jewish race 127
  as man could have yielded to temptation 129
  as man developed perfect character 133
  as man did not even possess angelic powers 129
  as man did not possess same sinful, corrupt, fallen disloyalty we possess or could not have been perfect offering 131
  as man passed through same test Adam and Eve passed through 129
  awakened impulses for new life in outcasts 238
  became sin for man 194
  became subject to sorrow, weariness, hunger, and thirst 141
  becomes our righteousness when we do our best 180
  began work of redemption just where ruin began, on appetite 128
  breathed same air we breathe, traveled in same world we inhabit 130
  came as a man, tempted as a man, rendering obedience of a man 139
  came, not only to be sacrifice for sin but example to man 138, 139
  came to earth, not only to atone for sin but to show man by example how to keep law 135
  came to earth to refute Satan's lie that not possible for human beings to keep God's law 130
  came to earth to stand as man before heaven and earth 127
  complete system of truth 198
  condescended to connect our fallen hu-

manity with His divinity 134
connects the finite with infinite 140
could have been born with face bright
with light, a form tall and beautiful, a personality that would
have changed all, but this not
God's plan 127
could have come to earth in such beauty
as to have been unlike sons of men
127
could, have fallen? EGW answers
question 129, 130
could have yielded to Satan's lying
suggestions as did Adam 130
courtesy, Christian's example in 237
death, as well as life, manifested God's
love, justice and immutability
132
desires unity in church 15
did not come to world to render obedience of a lesser God to a greater,
but as a man 139
did not have temptations as children
have, erroneous to say 134
died not only to expiate sin but to
restore human nature 154
endured Adam's test in our humanity
129
example ever to be kept before us 15
features of, like those of other human
beings 127
firm as a rock, yet invariably kind and
courteous 237
flee to, as soon as sin committed 196
free agent with liberty to yield to
temptation and work at cross-purposes with God 131
gives man moral power to overcome
153
had He not stood as our representative
His innocence would have exempted Him from all anguish,
but it was His very innocence that
made Him feel keenly Satan's assaults 129
had infinite power to overcome because
was perfectly obedient to Father's
will 142
has shown is possible for all humanity
to obey God's laws 135
having taken our fallen nature, showed
what it might become by our partaking of divine nature 134
helpless babe in the manger still the
divine Son of God 128
higher attributes of, it is our privilege
to have 130
how dealt with people while on earth
237, 238
human nature of, was created 129
human nature of, identical with ours
129
human nature of, when we give it a
power not possible for man to have
we destroy the completeness of

His humanity 139
if, could not have fallen, could not have
been tempted 131
if, had special powers man cannot have,
Satan would have made capital of
matter 139
in coming to this world, did not become sinner 133
influence of, to be felt through His
believing children 15
in flesh was God in humanity 128
in health of perfect manhood was as one
afflicted 133
instructor of evil angels before they fell
410
in synagogue at Nazareth 164
keeping of commandments disproved
Satan's claim that man cannot
keep 139
kept God's commandments in same
way humanity can keep 140
kept His Father's commandments as a
man 138
knew on cross, as no other can know,
awful power of Satan's temptations 132
ladder in Jacob's dream 154
laid hold of divine power to overcome
as we may 140
life of, testified that, with aid of same
divine power He received, man
may obey God's law 132
life of, was animated and regulated by
His Father's Spirit 134
lived life of perfect man for thirty years
136
look to and live 151
mediatorial work of, began with man's
Fall 194
mediatorial work of, for this time, we
should meditate upon 187
mingled with Samaritans though it was
contrary to Jewish custom 238
must know Him individually as Saviour
170
not only Sacrifice but Priest, as well
141
obedience of, not something for which
particularly adapted 139
obedience of, not to be put aside as
altogether different from obedience He requires of us 135
on cross felt wrath of God against
transgression 132
only one who walked the earth on
whom rested no taint of sin 134
our pattern 170
pardon by, means not only forgiveness
but renewal of mind 190
perfection of, atones for our shortcomings 180
performed miracles of healing on Sabbath, but not common work 258
power came directly from Father 128
proved by actual fact that command-

ments could be kept 139

recognized dignity of humanity 238

relied on His Father for wisdom and strength to resist and overcome tempter 134

resisted temptation same way we may resist 136, 137

"resisted unto blood" in Gethsemane 131

sacrifice of, failure to appreciate, leads to receiving unsound, perilous, theories 190

sacrifice of, failure to appreciate makes us fall short of our privileges 190

sacrifice of, sufficient, outward observances of no value 190

sat as honored guest at tables of publicans 238

sinless 134

sinlessness of, as a man greatly disturbed Satan 134

stood test as true human being 139

stood test of trial and temptation that might become owner of all humanity 142

subject to temptation but did not yield to sin 141

subject to trial and disappointment in His own home 130

temptation in wilderness stronger than any ever brought to bear on man 136

temptation in wilderness was, not God, but man, being tempted 140

temptations and sufferings proportionate to His exalted, sinless character 131

tempted in human nature 130

took on His divine soul the result of transgression 128

uniting link binding believers to God 21

was not situated in surroundings calculated to preserve life of purity, yet was uncontaminated 133, 134

yoke of, if men wear, will not pull apart 26

yoke of, wearers draw together 16

See also Incarnation

Christ-filled discourses needed 184, 185

Christian family, every, a church 209

Christians, in danger of changing leaders unconsciously 19

should be sympathetic, as well as true 239

should exhibit habitual gentleness 240

Christ's Object Lessons 458 Appendix

Chronology, danger of laying too much stress on 448 Appendix

Church, beware of those who have burden to denounce 17

children allowed to run about, play, talk, and manifest evil tempers in, desecrate 257

Christian society formed for its members 15

definition 15-19

denouncing, accusing, condemning, work of Satan 19

drawing apart from, frowned upon 21

enfeebled and defective, is only object on earth on which God bestows His supreme regard 14

God has, to whom He has delegated power 23

God never designed that, should be controlled by one man 16

inspire, not tear down 19

like army well-disciplined soldiers 24

model, Bible sets before us a 18

organization formed to increase usefulness in world 16

organized body through whom God will work 17

perfect order, neatness, and humility should reign in 257

ranks of God's people not diminish; those who have lived up to light have had will fill vacancies left by apostates 421

separate from world, heaven's greatest object in earth 17

still God's body, though may have Judases, Peters, and overzealous Johns 17

those who draw apart from, weighing church in human scales 18

to be representative God's family in another world 17

to present enemy with united front 20

united in fellowship 15

unity 15, 20-22

Christ desires to see 15

we not to join Satan in denouncing 19

wherever there is, a school should be established 227

Church members left in darkness as Jews, unless repent 17

need to be wide awake 19

not to turn weapons of warfare against own ranks 18

Satan gives restless, who look for new contrivances, something to do 18

to answer Christ's prayer for unity 17, 18

to be benefitted by grace, influence of other members 15, 16

to be separate from world 17

to bind selves to covenant of love, harmony 16

to seek to restore, not tear down, discourage, destroy church 19

weak, strengthened by mature Christians 16

Church membership, a covenant of agreement 16

Churches, SDA, renting of to other denominations 322, 323

Church school(s), for SDA children near

St. Helena Sanitarium, Calif., in 1902 206

Crystal Springs for younger children, EGW urges 225

to teach Bible, have prayers, instruct in Bible principles 212, 213

needed at Crystal Springs in 1902 212

question raised whether a curse when responsibility for education shed by parents 224

report of meeting of Sanitarium, Calif., board in 1904 214-226

responsibility of parents to send children to 210, 211

SDA Sanitariums should have, connected with 215, 216

Circumstances, alter conditions 217

City mission, undue familiarity in a 54, 55

Civil rights, should do all in power to maintain, as pertain to conscience 384

Civil War, draft in American 384

Cleanliness 272

Cleanliness, needed among God's people 273, 274

Cloud, great white, at Second Advent 112

Clough, Mary C., 455, 456 Appendix

best copyist EGW ever had 106

earnest Christian but not an SDA 103 footnote

EGW's copyist 103-107

EGW's niece, daughter of her sister Caroline 103 footnote

enthusiastic over Jesus' discourse on "Bread of Life" 106

enthusiastic over subjects in Spirit of Prophecy, vol. 2 105

not only copyist for EGW but also publicity agent 103 footnote

vision EGW had that led to her separation from 456, 457 Appendix

Coarseness, and roughness, must be removed from character before Jesus comes 155

Coffee 272

Colcord, W. A. 457 Appendix

Commandments, can be kept, Christ proved by actual fact 139

Commandments of God and faith of Jesus, both of equal importance 184

burden of our message 168

third angel's message 172

Common subjects, and inspired instruction, distinction 60, 61 footnote

and instruction from the Lord 59

discussed by EGW concerning houses, lands, trading, location for institution, not inspired 58

such as the number of rooms in particular sanitarium not derived from vision 59

See also Revelation-inspiration

Communion 262

See also Lord's supper, Footwashing

Complaining, spirit of, on no account to be encouraged 415

Confession, if you need to, lose no time 152

Conflict, coming: danger of either being too rash or too conservative in, 397

men who seek to be revenged, becoming apostates, betraying Christ 397

one indiscreet, high-tempered man will do much harm 397

people will not be left to stumble into coming crisis 389

some will betray God's cause through hasty, ill-advised moves 397

those who have living experience not overborne by apostasy 399, 400

we can look for new perplexities in 383

we not to be found in neutral position in, 397

Conflict, final, contest between Christianity of Bible and Christianity of human tradition 386

contest to be over whether popery receives the right hand of fellowship from Protestantism 386

contest to decide whether or not the pure gospel will have the field in U.S. 386

See Final conflict, Last days

Conflict, future, after Revelator's description of miracle-working power that gathers world to last great conflict, symbols are dropped 425

all world one side or other in 425

believers must not make ample provision for, to shield from trial 399

Captain of Lord's host leading armies of heaven and mingling in ranks 425

do not condemn brethren who are steadfast and immovable 401

every form of evil to spring into intense activity 425

every man, woman, child will be either in Christ's or Satan's army 421

forces of evil not yield up last great conflict without desperate struggle 425

God's people not to prepare to find easy position in any future emergency, but to let God prepare them 398

last great conflict, short, terrible 419

many will come to side of God's commandment-keeping people 397

two armies will stand distinct and separate 397

Conflict, last great, See Conflict; future; Armageddon

Conflict of the ages, events in, frequently appeared first as articles in Review, Signs, and Watchman 459, Appendix

scenes relating to, first given to EGW

in outline 442, Appendix
truths revealed to EGW regarding, given chiefly as flashlight views 446, 447 Appendix
Conflict of the Ages Series 459 Appendix
contain comforting light God gave EGW 50
EGW firm in her confidence in light given her 122
EGW not originator of 50
footnotes in 463 Appendix
origin of 99-102
reason EGW wrote more fully regarding, in her later books is that later vision brought out details more clearly 442, 443 Appendix
significant statements on how prepared 88ff
Conflict Series books, 121-124. See also Conflict of the Ages Series
Conformity to the world, sin 247
Confusion, result of misinterpreting the testimonies 80
Conversion, natural laws, some try to explain, by 309
Cornell, Merrit E. 94, footnote
Correcting, EGW tried to confine, error to smallest circle possible 65, 66
Cosmogony, all things material or spiritual stood up before Jehovah at His voice 312
    all things not only the work of God's hands, they come into existence by breath of His mouth 312
    God not beholden to preexistent substance or matter in formation of our 312
    idea of some that God did not create matter when He brought world into existence, limits His power 307
Cottrell, R. F., wrote introduction to Spiritual Gifts, vol. 1 100
Courtesy, Christian 237-240
Covenant, the Father and Son made covenant to rescue man 130
    most powerful argument in favor of gospel 238
Courtesies, thoughtful, beginning in home extend far beyond 240
Cranson, John 264
Creation, God commands things into being 311
    See also Cosmogony
Creed, of SDA Church, John 17 21
Crisis, final, as near will be more need of harmony than heretofore 26
Crisler, Clarence C. 363
Critics, those who expose sins of their brethren will be judged more severely than one criticized 345
Criticism, communicated like leaven 351
    Satan's science 351
    when people offer, praise that which good 120

Cross, Christ knew on, as no other can know, awful power of Satan's temptations 132
    Christ on, felt wrath of God against transgression 132
    Christ presents as center of attraction 21
Crown of life, not one of God's faithful ones receives, who has not passed through severe conflicts 344

D

Danger, of picking, criticizing, and dissecting EGW's writings 453 Appendix
Daniel and Revelation, by Uriah Smith 446 Appendix, 447 Appendix
Daniells, A. G. 453, 454 Appendix, 461 Appendix
Dansville, N.Y., health-reform establishment 276. See also footnote Our Home 278
Date line, controversy concerning, is Satan's device to divert attention 317, 318, 319
    EGW deals with matter of 317-319
D'Aubigne, J. Merle 435 Appendix, 437, 462 Appendix
Davis, Marian 457 Appendix, 458 Appendix, 463 Appendix, 464 Appendix
    abilities of as EGW's literary assistant increased with the years 93
    death of 91, 93, 93 footnote
    did not attempt to write transitions in EGW's gathered materials, but brought them to EGW 93
    EGW acknowledged she had a point regarding rock from which water flowed 121
    EGW acknowledged she had a point regarding Zedekiah having his eyes put out 121
    EGW felt she was irreplaceable 91
    EGW's chief worker 91
    EGW's literary assistant 88, 91ff
    EGW stated she was her bookmaker 91, 92
    enlightening statements concerning the relationshp of, to production of EGW's books 88, 444 Appendix
    gathered materials on life of Christ from all EGW's writings for manuscript, Desire of Ages 116, 117
    had a memory for locating pertinent materials in EGW's writings and the faculty for organizing 91, 93
    looked for sentences in EGW letters for use in Desire of Ages 117
    meticulousness of, in seeking guidance from W. C. White and EGW in preparing EGW's writings 92

never lost sense of sacredness of her work in preparing EGW's writings for publication 91

specified improvements for *Patriarchs and Prophets* 121

wanted EGW or W.C. White to see every little change of a word she made in EGW's writings 92

working on Spirit of Prophecy, vol. 4, in 1886 111

working under great difficulties while preparing *Desire of Ages* 116, 117

Deception, Satan's greatest, the idea that Christ did all and we can go on transgressing 153

Deceptions, brought in by some who repudiate testimonies, claim Scripture as evidence 83

Decision, of church, ratified when every specification Christ has given has been carried out in true Christian spirit 22

Defense, of God's servants against false accusations, there is a time for 348

Defiant spirit, God's people will be true and loyal to Him in last days, but will show no 405

Deficiencies, unavoidable, Christ makes up for 195

Degeneracy, physical, mental, and moral rapidly increasing 289

Delusions, EGW shown those that will prevail 114, 414

last-day, those who believe God has spoken through EGW will be safe from 83, 84

of Satan, God's people must be clothed with Christ's righteousness to see through 389

Demarcation, line of, between people of God and world, to remain distinct 211

Demons, casting out. See Exorcism

Demon possession 362

Ralph Mackin claimed demons closed eyes of possessed, made them bark and stick out tongues 368

Desire of Ages 109 footnote, 122, 458 Appendix

EGW resolved not to write certain chapters on life of Christ in, suggested by Marian Davis unless Spirit led her 116

interruptions in preparing manuscript for 116, 117

manuscript sent from Australia to America care of Brother Linden 116

Marian Davis gathered materials on life of Christ from all of EGW's writings for 116, 117

Marian Davis looked for sentences in EGW's letters to use for 117

portions of manuscript to be used as articles 116

significant statements on how prepared 88, 103ff

statements on the Incarnation 126

Desire of Ages and *Christ's Object Lessons* amplified *Spirit of Prophecy*, vols. 2, 3, which in turn amplified portions of *Early Writings* 443, Appendix

Despondency, do not look to self, but to Jesus 324-327

feelings of 324-327

feelings of, no evidence God has forsaken 324

how EGW handled 324, 325

Devil, helping the, those who specify what in the *Testimonies* is inspired and what is EGW's uninspired words are 70

Diary, EGW, meaning explained 32 footnote

Diet 272

has important bearing on our lives 291

parents have solemn obligation to feed their children wholesome 290

proper, beneficial 277

Differences, among brethren, Satan's devices to divert from issue between us 20

Discipline, Church guards rights of all 16

increases sense of mutual dependence 16

Discipline of children, need of, by parents 225

Discouragement, unbelief cherished brings 149

Discourteous, we not to be, because others rough and discourteous 240

Discourtesy, Christians revealing, not in union with Christ 237

Discrepancies, EGW's attitude toward, discovered in her writings 447, 448, Appendix

in William Miller's expositions of prophecy 448, Appendix

minor, regarding dates did not shake W. C. White's confidence in EGW's writings as a whole 449, 450, Appendix

and contradictions, so-called, in the *Testimonies* 349

Discrimination, between what is testimony from God and what is human production, a misconception 70

between what one regards in testimonies as inspired and what is EGW's own mind, tantamount to rejecting 68, 69

those persisting in, between inspired and uninspired, satanic agencies will choose for 70

Dishwashing, on Sabbath should be avoided if possible 258

Disorderly elements, license not to be

given to, that desire to control the work 26

Disorganization, Satan would rejoice if could introduce, among SDA's 26

Disparaging the pioneers 298

Distrust, teachers not to show, of students 228

Disunion, among brethren, not a good sign 26
　devising of unsanctified minds 21
　dishonoring to God 21
　See also Unity, Separation

Disunity. See Unity

Divine nature, partakers of, God has made provision for us to become 203
　partaking of, the only way of escape 197

Doctrines, basic, of SDA Church, gotten through Bible study followed by guidance through EGW visions 31, 32, 38

Doubt, every conceivable effort will be made to throw, on established SDA positions 408
　is sin to cherish 149

Doubts, Satan's hooks upon which to hang 69

Doubters, of Bible record, will doubt God's existence 307

Doubting, unprofitable 151

Dress 272
　and adornment 236, 241-255
　black or dark material more becoming to minister than two or three colors 250
　character is judged by one's style of 242
　Christian's, should conform to God's Word 242
　Christians should not make selves gazingstock 242, 243
　Christian's should shun extremes in 242
　Christian woman's, should be plain, of good durable material, appropriate for the age 353
　EGW cautioned against SDA's making their, according to worldly style 244
　EGW did not discourage good taste and neatness in 245
　EGW encouraged purchase of good durable material 245
　EGW explains her testimony concerning length of reform dress 277-279
　fantastic, gold chains, and gaudy laces, a sure indication of weak head and proud heart 244
　follow custom in, so far as conforms to health principles 242
　God desires that our clothing be neat, healthful, appropriate, and becoming 241
　gave specific directions regarding dress of priests 250
　has preference regarding, of those

who serve Him 241
　is honored is dishonored by apparel we wear 250
　good taste in a minister's 249
　if, when following convictions, Christians find selves out of fashion, should not change 243
　if world introduces modest, convenient, healthful mode of, we may adopt 242
　index of a man or woman 242
　it is our privilege to honor our Creator by our 241
　jewelry and expensive, not give us influence 249
　let it be made of good, durable material, modest, appropriate for the age 254
　Lord does not require any test of human invention 252
　new convert taught SDA's did not follow worldly fashions in 247
　of Christ's followers should be symbolic of His neatness, modesty and purity 241
　not dress reform, but Sabbath, the great test question in the coming conflict 252, 253, 254
　of SDA's, should be most simple 253, 254
　of some ministers untidy, even slovenly 249
　plain, simple style of, worn in 1897 acceptable 252, 253
　question of, should not be allowed to divert from grand test 252
　question of, should not fill mind 242, 254
　reform, EGW cautions regarding resuming 252
　representative attire worn by priests inspired reverence in Israelites 250
　Satan successful in infatuating minds regarding styles of 245
　self-denial in, part of Christian duty 245
　sensible style of in 1897, acceptable 253
　SDA's should, with simplicity and modesty 242
　should be plain and neat, without extravagance 245
　some SDA's thirsting for distinction in 252
　there is no need now (1897) for special alteration in our 252
　those who follow own tastes in, give youth wrong example 254
　to be nothing slack or untidy about those who appeared before God anciently 250
　true lady is shown by her simple, unpretending 245
　See also Reform dress, Fashions

Drugs 277

E

Early Writings 442, 443, 447, 459 Appendix

Earthquake, the mighty 112

Earthquakes. See Calamities

Eating, between meals, should not be allowed 294, 295

Eating and drinking. See Diet

Edersheim 459 Appendix

Education, begins in home 210

by worldly wise men, EGW called sorcery 232

EGW advocated, of children at home up to age 10, when SDA's had no church schools 216, 217

of children, because many homes not ideal, better for parents to send children to Christian schools 215

circumstances must be considered relative to school-age entrance 221, 222

EGW said need for reformation in SDA anti-kindergarten attitude 224

EGW states SDA's should be example in 226

EGW urges founding of Crystal Springs church school for younger children 225

ideally the mother the child's teacher until age 8 or 10 221, 222

if mother unable to train children, should be put under somebody who can 220

in Bible principles, importance of 211, 212

maternal influence 220

mother to instruct them until they 8 or 10 years of age 214, 215

pleasant scenes in home to be kept before children 229

school age 8 or 10 221, 222

W. C. White comments on question of school entrance at ages 8 to 10 224

of SDA youths, in worldly institutions, dangers of 231, 232

principles of religion the first steps to acquisition of knowledge and lie at foundation of true 311

SDA, Bible, not maxims of men, to be the essence of 227

God has not designed any one exact plan in 227, 228

true, the preparation of mental, moral, and physical powers for performance of every duty 228

the training of heart, mind, and soul for divine service 228

wherever there is a church a school should be established 227

Education 223

in preparation 214, 217, 218

Eggs and meat, excite to masterbation when made a child's diet 286

1888. See Minneapolis General Conference

Elect of God, conditions for becoming one of 315, 316

End, near the, false notion advanced that every child of God will act independent of religious organization 26

Enoch, and Elijah, correct representatives of what race might be through faith in Christ 146

if, walked with God in corrupt age, we may also 338

Eschatology. See Last days

Eternal life, conditions of, simple 150, 151

Eternity, our hope for now and our song in, "Saved by the blood of Christ" 173

Events in church history. See History, events in church

Events in history of reformers, presented before EGW 110

Evil, origin of, Satan in heaven claimed to be sanctified 199

Evil angels. See Angels, evil

Example, Christ our 138, 139

Excuse, if I were of different disposition, would serve God 136

Exorcism 362

Mackins claimed certain people possessed, then pretended cast out demons 378

Mackins claimed to have cast out six demons in one case 368

Mackins led people to believe they demon possessed 376

Extremes, will ever be danger of going to, in obeying Sunday law 394, 395

F

Failure, for those who flatter selves that doing God's work disconnected from His agencies 25

Faith, departers from, those following own independent judgment 23

fails to reach vital point if truth does not engage the heart, transform character 192

general, is not enough 194

implicit, importance of simple 200

work of righteousness cannot be carried forward without 201

important to understand its nature 191

individual, some find it hard to exercise 151

in heart, necessary 150

in Jesus as sinner's only hope, left out of discourses and religious experience 168

of Jesus, has been overlooked 168

what constitutes it 172
saving, is none that does not produce good fruit 195
so simple 145
to sanctify the life 146
Faith and Works 144, 148, 180 footnote
Falkhead, N. D., example of one who accepted personal testimony from EGW 84, 85
Fall, of man, broke golden chain of obedience 138
terrible by those who think they stand but have not the truth as it is in Jesus 154
Falling, we can be kept from, by accepting Christ's power to overcome 356
False Christs, deception, delusions, impostures will increase 426
EGW shown false Christs that will appear, the miracle-working power of Satan 414
voices will call attention to, after truth has been proclaimed as witness to all nations 406
False loud cry, Satan's object, to divert attention from the true loud cry through false interpretations of Scripture 410
False positions, danger of trying to maintain 449, Appendix
False statements, EGW expected long list of, against her to be presented to world 352
Familiarity, undue, at a city mission 54, 55
Family, on earth to be symbols of family in heaven 229
Fanatics, will handle heresies in such a way that enemies will charge upon EGW 404
Fanaticism, after 1844 brought God's cause into disrepute 371
creeping like children 371
dancing and shouting 371
EGW called to rebuke 376
EGW rebuked 372
no-work doctrine 370
some arrested by law officers 371
some believed resurrection of the just had taken place 370, 371
strange bodily exercises 370
strange work in Mackin case similar to fanaticism in Orrington, Maine 378
will be repeated in last days 376
and extremes 362, 363-378
any manifestation of, takes mind from evidences of Word 372
bringing into the message of present truth any strange teachings will lead to 377
claims that all may have gift of prophecy will lead to 341
constant danger of allowing, to come in

under guise of Spirit's work 373
demonstrations of, bring stain on SDA name 378
EGW afraid of anything that turns mind away from truth revealed in God's Word 373, 375
EGW cautioned regarding going to extremes in health reform 284, 285
EGW declared that Mackins claiming that certain people demon possessed, then pretending to exorcise them, was 379
excitable people who are easily led into 373
following disappointment of 1844, 370
if misleading messages accepted, they will bring in, so mingled with workings of Spirit as to deceive many 403
like that following 1844 will be manifest again 373
Machins claimed their experience tallied with God's Word 374
minds diverted from living Word to mortal man 371, 372
oddities and strange exercises, we are to avoid all 373, 375
permitted, would bring stigma against whole body of SDA's 373
spirit of, ever seeking entrance into remnant church 378
Farrar 459 Appendix
Fashions, worldly, many SDA's follow as far as think their profession of faith allows 243, 244
many SDA youths spend beyond their means to keep up with 244
rapid change of 244
Satan knows that women who feverishly follow, have weak moral sensibilities 245
Satan stands in background, devising 244
SDA's shackled by, yet talking of independence 245
See also Dress
Fasting, should set aside days for prayer and 414
Father, position of in home like that of priest 209
Feelings, danger of making criterion 151
depending on, weakens one's soul as well as souls of others 151
Feelings, human, will lead men to take work into own hands 21
Final conflict, events in church history selected and arranged to shed light on 111, 112
every nation will be involved in 392
whole battle hinges on keeping of true Sabbath 319
Final crisis. See Crisis, final
Firm, Christ obeyed as in partnership with the great, we to obey as in copartnership with Him 135

Five thousand, feeding of, EGW writing about 105
    Mary Clough reading back to EGW 106
Flashlight pictures, description of historical events and other representations EGW had seen in vision 437 Appendix
Fleetwood 459 Appendix
Flesh food. See Meat eating
Flesh, of animals, not part of man's original diet 289
Food 272
    coarse, wholesome is best 274
    eat less fine, and more coarse, free of grease 274
Footwashing 261
Forgiveness of sin, not the sole result of Christ's death 154
Form, Brother P made his religious experience too much of 146
Four winds, God alone can hold, until angels seal God's servants 415
    held until God's people sealed 409
    likened to angry horse seeking to break loose and wreak destruction 409
Fry, Henry 463 Appendix

G

Galatians, law in, E. J. Waggoner presented near close of Minneapolis GC session 158
    point of difference at Minneapolis GC session 167
    is what sparked the controversy at Minneapolis GC session 158
Gardening 298
Gardner, Brother and Sister 264
Gaskill, Mary 264
General Conference session, action of Nov. 16, 1883, regarding republication of the early Testimonies 96 footnote
    action stating the church's view regarding inspiration 96 footnote
Geology, Moses wrote under Spirit's guidance, and correct theory of, will never claim discoveries that cannot be reconciled with his statements 307
    See also Cosmogony, Creation
Giekie 459 Appendix
Gift of prophecy, claims that all may have, will lead to fanaticism 341
    is God's voice in our midst 83
Gifts, diversity of, combined, needed for success of work 24, 25
    given to make church symmetrical 21
God, can work above natural laws, skeptics fail to realize that 309
    could in one short hour destroy whole frame of nature 312

creative power of, contrasted with creative power of man 311
does not work through His children in a way that brings truth into disrepute 372
if men could fully understand His purposes, wisdom, love, and character, would not believe Him infinite 306
if men understood all about, He would no longer stand supreme 306
if, reveals Himself at all to men, is by veiling Himself in mystery 306
love, justice, and immutability of, manifested in Christ's death, as well as His life 132
mightiest intellect cannot comprehend 306
subordination to, only safety 20
we must ever search for, yet an infinity beyond 306
works of, interpret His character 309, 310
Gospel Workers 236, 269, 270
    1893 ed. 148 introd. note
Gotzian, Josephine 226
Grace, of Christ, changes the whole man 239
    of God may be claimed now 150
Grammarian, EGW conceded she was no grammarian 90
Grease, eating cake and pie crust filled with, dishonors God 275
    eat less fine food and more coarse food free of 274
    See also Rich foods
Great controversy, EGW permitted to behold (in vision) the working, in different ages, of 110
    vision first received in 1848, repeated March 14, 1858 99
    See also Conflict of the Ages
Great Controversy, 109 footnote, 119, 122, 448, 462 Appendix
Great Controversy, differences between 1888 and 1911 eds. 433-436 Appendix
    1888 ed., called "volume 4" by EGW 114 footnote
    1888 ed., decision regarding 1911 rev. made after counsel with ministers, canvassers, and friends of book 433 Appendix
    1888 ed., development of 438, 439 Appendix
    1888 ed., history of writing of 111-114
    1885 ed., portions of, omitted in later editions, appear in Testimonies to Ministers 443 Appendix
    1888 ed., reason for 1911 rev.—1888 plates worn out 433 Appendix
    1884 ed., see Spirit of Prophecy, vol. 4
    EGW acknowledged God impressed her to write 113

approved W. C. White's statement
regarding 1911 ed. 122
beheld fearful scenes just before us
which are described in 413, 414
bidden to write to shed light on final
conflict 111. See also Conflict,
final
difficulty with paralysis when began
writing 100
employed the best workers possible
113
gives reason 1911 revision made
123, 124
instructed those in charge of 1911
rev. to insert historical references,
verify quotations, correct inaccuracies 434, 439 Appendix
instructed those in charge of 1911
rev. to use most authentic and
approved translations 434, 435
Appendix
moved by Spirit to write 413, 414
shown heresies that will arise, delusions that will prevail, false
Christs that will appear 414
witnessed events described in 61
footnote
history of expansion of 109-114
how changes made in 1884, 1888, and
1911 editions 443, 444 Appendix
in writing, points forcibly impressed on
EGW's mind, as though God
spoke 113
later editions omitted statements that
might cause offense, that more
souls might be won 443, 444 Appendix
1911 ed., appendix to 440 Appendix
EGW appreciated above silver and
gold 123
EGW carefully examined changes in
wording in, and approved 124
EGW pleased with the revision 123,
124
EGW stated that what she had written regarding papacy true, but
much historical evidence destroyed 436 Appendix
EGW supervised revision of 437
Appendix
four sets of plates made 433 Appendix
historical quotations updated 434,
435, 439 Appendix
in eight or ten instances place and
time references changed because of
time lapse 435 Appendix
letter by W. C. White, dated July
25, 1911, concerning 441, 444
Appendix
more accurate terms substituted for
less accurate ones in 435, 436
Appendix
question of whether EGW had right
to make changes in 441 Appendix

score or more quotations in 1888 ed.
could not be traced to sources 435
Appendix
statements subject to dispute substituted by statements readily available 436, 439, 440 Appendix
unnecessarily offensive expressions
changed in 435, 436 Appendix
updating in spelling, punctuation,
and capitalization 435 Appendix
W. C. White averred rumors EGW
had not known or approved some
work done on, false 436, 437,
439, 440 Appendix
not to be quoted as history to prove
points 446 Appendix
portions of Spirit of Prophecy, vol. 4,
omitted in, included in Testimonies
to Ministers 452, 453 Appendix
primarily based on panoramic scenes
EGW saw in vision sometimes located in point of time and place,
but often not 459 Appendix
reasons for changes in 1911 edition
433, 444 Appendix
scenes EGW had witnessed in vision
repeated when wrote 112
scenes EGW previously shown presented anew in vision of night as
she was writing 123
scenes of past and future opened to
EGW's mind in writing 111
significant statements on how prepared
88, 99ff.
story, in EGW's mind all material
comprising agelong conflict part
of 109 footnote
See also Spirit of Prophecy, vol. 4; Spiritual Gifts, vol. 1

H

Hale, Anna 457 Appendix
Hall, Lucinda M. 456 Appendix
Hanna, William 459 Appendix
Happiness, the sum of life's, made up of
thoughtful courtesies 240
Harbor Heights, Mich., educational con-
vention 233
Hare, Maggie 457 Appendix
Hart, Josiah 94, footnote
Haskell, S. N. 96 footnote, 178
Haskell orphanage, in Battle Creek 218
Hawkins, Minnie 457 Appendix
Healing, sick desiring healing should be
pointed to Christ 296
simple fervent prayer to accompany
treatment 296
Healings, in early days of message 295
we would see more, if we prayed in our
sanitariums 295, 296
Health 272
Health, psychosomatic aspect in case of
James White 280

See also Health reform

Health laws, God not pleased when we violate, then ask to be kept from disease 280

willing ignorance of, sin 291

Health reform 236

better for small children to eat three meals, not two, a day 294

butter, meat, and cheese not to be made test but matter of education 287

caution needed not to go to extremes in 284, 285

certain children not to be allowed to make eggs and meat their diet 286

eating between meals should not be allowed 294, 295

eggs, butter, cheese not to be classed in same category with tea, coffee, tobacco, and spiritous liquors as things to be discarded 28

EGW advocates moderation in teaching 285

EGW counsels people to be careful in presenting 285

EGW not dependent on contemporary health writers 272

EGW warns against lifting statements regarding, out of context 285, 286

God requires advancement in 291

if given prominent place, will increase our influence for good 292

misuse of EGW statements regarding 286, 287

not to be trifled with, ignored, or treated in jest 292

parents make a serious mistake when they impose, on their children, but do not practice themselves 293, 294

primary reason for discarding meat in these last days is disease in animals 287, 288

proper use of testimonies on 283-288

purpose of, not only to prepare people for heaven but to stand in day of God 283

takes time to educate away from wrong habits 284, 285

tea, coffee, tobacco, and all spiritous liquors to be discarded 287

testimonies for special cases under special circumstances not to be applied to all cases 288

those who apply special-case testimony to all cases discredit EGW's works 288

visions calling for 272-282

we need to understand, to be prepared for coming events 292

wisdom and candor needed in presenting 283

See also Health

Health reform vision of June 6, 1863, EGW describes in detail the process of writing out 280-282

EGW maintained she did not get information from contemporaries 276

EGW's perceptions of her health on day she received 279, 280

Health reform visions of 1848, 1854, 1863 272-282

Heaven, as saints ascend to, two columns angels on either side 431

bread of, must be eaten and digested to become part of life 203

character we take to, that which imparted to us through Christ's righteousness 191

EGW saw in vision some saints seen suffering in time of trouble 428

envy, jealousy, hatred cannot exist in 155

joys of redeemed over souls helped save 431

no one will take time to tell of trials on earth 431

nothing but love, joy, and harmony will exist in 155

redeemed cast crowns at Jesus' feet 431

saints in, come from mountains, rocks, dens and caves of earth, dungeons, prisons, secret councils, torture chambers, hovels, garrets 430

those who would be saints in, must first be saints on earth 191

vision of throne of God seen by saints in time of trouble 428, 429

we shall not see Sabbath in all its importance and glory until the voice of God, and gates of New Jerusalem opened 261

would not be a place of joy for those with sinful propensities 191

Heresies, EGW shown, that will arise 114, 414

every conceivable counterfeit message coming 404

if misleading messages accepted, will bring in strange, unclean spirit under garments of sanctity 403

many things intended to deceive will come bearing some marks of truth 404

misleading messages will be accepted by many in last days 403

will bear inscription of truth on banner 404

will be counterfeit messages from all directions 404

Heretical sentence, EGW declared that her writings did not contain one 52

Hester, Brother 264

Hide, Sister 263

Higher education: attendance of SDA's at non-SDA universities 207

Hilliard, A., Brother 276

Hines, J. V. 277

Hirelings, there will be, who will persuade some sacrifice to false gods 398

History, EGW's use of, in published writings 445-450 Appendix

events in church, selected and arranged to shed light on final conflict in *Great Controversy* 111, 112

question of EGW as authority on 445-450 Appendix

Histories, EGW's use of 447, 465
    Bible 122
    books in Review library 462 Appendix
    to find dates and geographical locations 462 Appendix

Historians, sacred, guided by power of Christ's Spirit to record His words and works 137

W. C. White explains EGW given discernment to use descriptions of historians in harmony with truths essential to salvation 449 Appendix

History of the Reformation, by J. Merle D'aubigne 435, 437 Appendix

History of the Sabbath, J. N. Andrews should have published less than pefect first edition, then improved his book 97

J. N. Andrews spent too much time perfecting 97

Holiness, holier, holier still, is echo of God's voice in His law 202

reflection of God's glory in His people 203

Holy Spirit, constantly drawing attention to great official sacrifice 137

EGW declared that the, traced truths in Conflict Series books upon her heart and mind 122

enabled apostles to resist every species of idolatry and exalt Christ alone 137

our grand helper 137

our greatest need 189

outpouring of, at Pentecost brought unity to early church 20

pray earnestly for 189

when comes, many will turn against 375

works in a manner to commend itself to good judgment 371, 373

works with the mind to transform character 138

Home, is both a family church and a family school 214

Homes, less than ideal, the reason for EGW advocating lowering age for school entrance 216, 217

Hooks, Satan's, upon which to hang doubts 68, 69

Hope, for everyone, but only in fastening selves to Christ 155

Hopeless, not one should feel his case is 152

Horror, we need not marvel at any developments of, in last days 416

Horse, angry, four winds likened to, seeking to break loose and wreak destruction 409

How to Live 276, 277, 281

Human nature, Christ's, was created 129
    was identical with ours 129
    we are not to serve God as if we were not human, but in the, we have 140
    we now have, God demands everyone through faith to serve Him in the 140

Humanity, became Christ's purchased possession because He gave His life for life of human family 141

Humility, voluntary, equated with will-worship 251

Hypnotism, those who depart from faith using 412
    we are not to link up with those who use 412

I

Idol, anything that stands between the soul and supreme love to God 330

Idol Sabbath. See Sunday

Image of God, if we diligently obey God's precepts, we shall be conformed to 291

Image to the beast, made by deceiver that doeth great wonders 353
    Protestant world 385
    this persecuting power will compel worship of beast by insisting on Sunday observance 421

Immortality, finishing touch of, put on saints and they ascend to meet Lord 431

Imperfect, although, our service is accepted when we do our best, calling on God for help 195, 196

Imperfections, many in 1883 felt that, rendered them useless to God's cause 148, 149

Imprisonment, and chain gangs for Sunday-law violations in South 380, 381

Improvement, should be constant 25

Inaccuracies, in EGW's autobiographical writings, possible 57, 58

Incarnation 126
    and atonement, dwell more upon 187
    Christ as man could have yielded to temptation 129
    Christ as man did not even possess angelic powers 129
    Christ assumed human nature with its infirmities, liabilities, temptations 132

Christ became sin for man 194
Christ became subject to sorrow, weariness, hunger, thirst 141
Christ began work of redemption just where the ruin began, on appetite 128
Christ belonged to human family and Jewish race 127
Christ breathed the same air we breathe, traveled the same world we inhabit 130
Christ came as man, tempted as man, rendering obedience of man 139
Christ came to earth to stand as man before heaven and earth 127
Christ came to world as man 136
Christ came to refute Satan's lie that it was not possible for human beings to keep God's law 130
Christ condescended to connect our fallen humanity with His divinity 134
Christ consented to clothe His divinity with humanity to bring man moral power to overcome 154
Christ could have been born with a face bright with light, a form tall and beautiful, a personality that would have changed all, but this not God's plan 127
Christ could have come in such beauty as to have been unlike sons of men 127
Christ could have yielded to Satan's lying suggestions as did Adam 130
Christ could not be tempted as God, but could as man 129
Christ did not come to world to render obedience of lesser God to greater, but as man 140
Christ did not possess same sinful, corrupt, fallen disloyalty we possess or could not have been perfect offering 131
Christ endured Adam's test in our humanity 129
Christ had human body and mind 129
Christ, having taken our fallen nature, showed what it might become by our partaking of divine nature 134
Christ, helpless babe in manger, still divine Son of God 128
Christ passed through same test Adam and Eve passed through 129
Christ subject to trial and disappointment in own home 130
Christ tempted in human nature 130
Christ took on His divine soul the result of transgression 128
Christ took up relationship of true human being 135
Christ was God in humanity 128
Christ was not situated in surroundings calculated to preserve life of purity, yet was not contaminated 133, 134
Christ's features like those of other human beings 127
Christ's human nature created, identical with ours 129
Christ's innocence would have exempted Him from all anguish, but was His very innocence that made Him feel keenly Satan's assaults 129
Christ's obedience not something for which He was particularly adapted 139
Christ's power came directly from Father 128
divine and human were linked in Christ, both complete 135
EGW answers the question, Could Christ have fallen? 129, 130
God has given Himself to die for us 200
God sent a sinless Being to our world 132, 133
Godhead not made human; human not deified; the two natures blended 131
in coming to this world Christ did not become sinner 133
many say Jesus not like us, He overcame because He was divine 197
mystery to be studied throughout eternity 126
not God's will that Christ should exercise His divine power on own behalf 129
through, Christ brings moral power to man 198
when we give Christ's human nature power not possible for man to have, we destroy completeness of His humanity 139
will ever remain a mystery 126
Incident: of husband and wife getting ready for the Lord's coming in 1843 193
Independence, shown apart from God, a delusion of Satan 25
those acting, attract attention, but of little value 24
Infidel authors, danger of studying 232
prostitute their powers derived from God 232
Influence, center of, every individual striving to become 20
Christ's, to be felt through His believing children 15
deceptive, we must be prepared to withstand Satan's 39
EGW acknowledged that One mighty in counsel manipulated her writings 64
EGW resisted that of Brother E urging her, speak less about duty, more about Jesus' love; spoke as Spirit

impressed her 64
of those following worldly customs in
    dress, will come up in judgment
    247
on EGW. See White, Ellen
that would lead away from Christ, to be
    resisted 243
those who rejected EGW's Testimonies
    concluded she subject to 78, 79
Ings, Mrs. J. J. 457 Appendix
Insects, killing of, EGW condoned 329
Inspiration, drawing line between what is
    of and what is not 69
    Gaussen theory of verbal, never ac-
        cepted by EGW 454 Appendix
    of Bible, divine, more we study, more
        we shall find evidence of 359
    principles of 28
    thought versus dictational 28
    verbal, belief and position of pioneers
        454
        EGW always felt her duty to revise
            her talks or writing to make as
            effective as possible 441 Appendix
        EGW never claimed 437 Appendix
        neither Joseph Bates, J. N. An-
            drews, Uriah Smith, or J. H.
            Waggoner claimed, for EGW 437
            Appendix
        question of whether EGW had right
            to alter her own writings 441 Ap-
            pendix
        statement made at the 1883 General
            Conference session 454 Appendix
        W. W. Prescott's position on 454 Ap-
            pendix
Inspiration-revelation,   distinction be-
    tween common and religious sub-
    jects 58
    EGW's role clarified in hearts at Min-
        neapolis GC session 164
    General Conference action of Nov. 16,
        1883, stating its belief in thought
        inspiration 96 footnote
    making of none effect by defining what
        is inspired and what is not 68-70
    question of influence on EGW 62-67
    See also Messages of EGW, how they
        came, Revelation, inspiration
Inspired instruction, versus common
    topics, example of 59, 60
Instructor, EGW stated her messages
    consistent through the years be-
    cause had had same 73
Intellectual men of world, danger of SDA
    youths being misled by 232
Intemperance, Bible warns against 284
Irving, Agnes 263
Irwin, G. A., had a notebook in which
    wrote down perplexing questions
    for EGW 51
Isaiah 8:20 30
"I saw"; "I was shown"—why omitted
    from some EGW books 61, foot-
    note

J

Jackson, Dr. J. C. 276 footnote, 277
Jeremiah, article on, EGW preparing for
    Signs of the Times 107
Jesus, does not give us up because of our
    sins 149
    how He taught the people 188
    loves to have us come to Him just as we
        are 150
    waiting for sinner's return 151
Jewelry, abstain from display of, and or-
    naments of every kind 245
    and expensive dress, not give us influ-
        ence 249
    bracelets, gold, and ornaments should
        be sold, even at loss 248
    gold, silver, precious stones, a new
        convert taught SDA's did not wear
        246
    See also Rings; Adornment
Jewish race, Christ belongd to human
    family and the 127
John 15 35
Jones, A. T. 158, 159, 182, 386 footnote
    falsely stated to have influenced EGW
        at Minneapolis GC session 173
    prejudice against at Minneapolis GC
        session 173
    said some accepted Minneapolis mes-
        sage, others rejected, still others
        vacillated 158, 159
Jones, Dan, of Kansas 178
Judgment 380
    EGW had view of, soon after husband's
        death 148
    God not leading those who pronounce,
        upon church 18
    God will accuse in, those who now
        accuse Him of originating sin 179
    in day of supreme triumph will be seen
        righteous were strong ones 430
    influence of those following worldly
        customs in dress will come up in
        247
    no one who retains imperfection of hu-
        manity will be vindicated in 360
    of EGW developed under God's train-
        ing 60
    scales will be balanced accurately in 147
    those who follow own, will depart from
        faith 23
Judgments, human, EGW aware that
    some would view her communica-
    tions as 81, 82
Justification 144
    and sanctification, both accomplished
        through faith in Christ 191, 192
    by faith explained 193, 194
        faith that justifies first produces re-
            pentance, then good works 195
        moment the sinner exercises true
            faith in atoning sacrifice, that
            moment he is justified 195

sinner is filled with amazement at God's grace and love, which breaks down barriers 194

when sinner repents, is justified by God 193

when we repent, accept Christ by faith as Saviour, we stand before God as just persons 191

K

Kellogg, John Harvey, EGW refused to read certain of his letters lest he say, "I gave her that inspiration" 63

Kellogg, John P. 94, footnote

Kindergarten, for 5-year-olds at Haskell orphanage in Battle Creek praised by EGW 218

in Berrien Springs, Mich., W. C. White comments favorable on establishment of in 1903 223, 224

Kneeling, in prayer 236

Kuhn, Professor 464 Appendix

L

Lady, a true, shown by her simple, unpretending dress 245

Landmarks, will be a removing of, after truth has been proclaimed as witness to all nations 406

Lane, Sister 263

Language, strong, improper for Christians 146

Laodicean message, Christ presenting to His church 17

Last days, 109, 110, 112, 252, 253, 380

abundant light for, in EGW's writings 76

all appeals to highest authorities of land useless unless God works in us 385

all corrupt powers that have apostatized united in opposition to God in 392, 393

all great solemn events of Old Testament history repeating themselves in church in 339

anarchy in society 418

apostasies 381, 382

as we near, we either advance more rapidly in Christian growth or retrograde just as decidedly 407

Bible will be opened from house to house 390

carelessly spoken words will be produced against us by enemies 404

cause of selfishness, violence, and crime in, is excessive indulgence of appetites and passions 291, 292

closing scenes 114

cords of human sympathy will become fewer, fewer 418

corruption in public schools in 210, 211

crust of earth will be rent by outburst of elements 391

don't borrow trouble for future crisis 383, 384

EGW shown that many would listen to the warning in 114

EGW told that past history will be repeated in 113

every conceivable effort will be made to throw doubt on established SDA positions 408

every reason to fear that falsehood will gain mastery in land 385

evil angels in form of believers will work in our ranks 410

in human form will misinterpret and misconstrue statements of God's messengers 411

in human form will talk with those who know truth 411

fanaticism following 1844 will be repeated in 376

gift of prophecy placed in church to guide the church in 83

God promises that trial will not exceed strength given to bear 383

God's Spirit will first leave those who have failed to improve opportunities 154

in the future, special tokens of influence of God's Spirit 369

large accessions anticipated 381, 382

many children in mercy taken away before time of trouble 419

many of God's children in Protestant and Catholic church more faithful in living up to their light than SDA's 386

many who will come from other churches will show greater zeal than many SDA's 386, 387

martyrdoms 381, 382

misleading messages will be accepted by many in 403

misrepresentations, bearing of false witness, will grow into open rebellion 416

nations will be stirred to very center 385

need not marvel at any developments of horror 416

no need to dread being borne down by widespread apostasy, if have living experience 399, 400

not only earth's crust but religious world will be shaken 391

peace must not be disturbed by anticipated trials 383, 384

physical, mental, and moral degeneracy rapidly increasing in 289

power from beneath working in 1888 to change U.S. Constitution 166

purpose of health reform not only to

prepare people for heaven but to stand in day of God 283

ranks of God's people not diminish; those who have lived up to light they have had will fill vacancies left by apostates 422

Sabbath of fourth commandment will be great point at issue in 392, 393

Sabbath question, not style of dress, the great last question 254

Satan himself will work miracles 39

Satan's work will become more pronounced as we near 387

Satan will appear to succeed in 393

Satan will work with increasing power 83

scenes at destruction of Jerusalem repeated, but in a more fearful manner 417

SDA's should as far as possible cleanse camp of moral defilement 384, 385

some numbered among merchants and princes will take position to obey truth 421

some who refuse to harmonize with Christ will develop into warring element 37

support will be withdrawn from those who proclaim God's law 385

sword is coming 114

those who have not lived up to light they have will be swayed by Satan's temptations for advancement 421

those who live up to light they have will take place of those who do not 422

time will come when we shall see strange things 369

two distinct calls will be made to churches in 406

vermin and pests will multiply in 329

we are living amid perils of 311

we may have to forsake houses and lands, because of bitter opposition 401

we may struggle in vain as mighty man against Niagara, unless God pleads for us 385

we must soon wrestle with the powers of the land 385

we need not dread what will come in, but commit the keeping of our souls to God 339

we need to understand health reform in order to prepare for the 292

we shall be called to witness before kings, rulers, magistrates, and princes in vindication of truth 403, 404

we shall not receive grace by making time of trouble beforehand 383, 384

we shall not see the Sabbath in all its

importance and glory until voice of God, and gates of New Jerusalem are opened 261

when latter rain comes, we shall better understand importance of Sabbath 260, 261

will be army of steadfast believers in last test 390

will be demonstrations similar to those in Mackin case in the very 367

wonderful power accompanies proclamation of Word 375

See also Conflict, final

Last day delusions, of Satan will have great power 416

See also Satanic miracles

Latter rain, before giving us baptism of Spirit, God will try us, to see if we can live without dishonoring Him 426, 427

God will have a true, sanctified ministry, prepared for 385

importance of Sabbath will be better realized when, comes 260, 261, 388

many will turn against, when arrives 375

time of, when Satan is working with increasing power and gifts of the Spirit being poured out 83

when times of refreshing come, sins of penitent removed from heavenly record and placed on Satan 355, 356

Law, God's, Christ came to refute Satan's lie that it was not possible for human beings to keep 130

God wrote the whole, on tables of stone 318

immutable, hence the incarnation and atonement 179, 180

in Galatians, at Minneapolis a mere mote 175

   EGW declared that discussion of not vital 174, 175

   emphasis at the Minneapolis GC session 156

made void in face of convincing evidence of unchangeableness 390

of God, when made void God's people will be true and loyal to Him, but will show no defiant spirit 405

when made void, zeal of true and loyal will rise with emergency 405

of the nations to violate God's law, God will judge those who seek to establish 415

penitent sinner does not expect it to cleanse from sin, but looks to atoning sacrifice as only hope 194

royal law is the standard by which character is measured 169

when made void, and apostasy becomes national sin, God will work on behalf of His people 388

Laws, controlling conscience 392

Laws of Life 276, 282

Lawsuits, better to sustain loss and wrong than to institute a 299, 300

    EGW appealed that a brother withdraw lawsuit against the Review 304

    declares it a disgrace for Christians to lean upon arm of law 303

    declares those who institute, show have chosen world as their judge 302

    warned that, if a brother sued the Review, he would never recover from result 304, 305

    warns one who was planning to sue her, to desist 301, 302

    would rather share a brother's loss than see him sue and injure his soul 305

    God does not hear prayer of SDA's who institute, against their brethren 299

    God does not want His people to depend on worldly lawyers to settle differences 303

    will deal with unworthy member who defrauds his brother 300

    matters pertaining to the church should be kept within church 299, 300

    SDA's and 299-305

    SDA's who go to non-SDA lawyers dishonor God, injure themselves 299

    when Christians go to court, do the very thing God told them not to do 302

    when troubles arise in church, SDA's should not go to non-SDA lawyers 299

Lawyers, how Satan works through non-SDA, to the detriment of God's cause 300

    interests of the church not to be entrusted to non-SDA's 300

    when troubles arise in church, SDA's not to go to non-SDA 299

Lay, Dr. Robert 282

Leaders, danger of changing unconsciously 19

Learned men, no reason why opinions of, should be trusted when they measure divine things by own perverted concepts 308

Leighton, Brother 261

Lessons, of Christ, like the testimonies, often misunderstood 82

Letter, to Edson and Emma White, distinguishing instruction from the Lord from common, everyday topics 59

Letters, EGW endeavored to write, that would help others besides recipients 98

    EGW, more than just letters,

    prompted by God's Spirit 50

    how certain early EGW, came to be in White Estate 456 Appendix

Life of Christ, EGW felt inadequate to write on 115, 118

Life of Christ, EGW hoped to send her manuscript to Pacific Press in July, 1896 119

    EGW's manuscript on, not sent to Pacific Press until early 1897 119 footnote

    EGW's original work on 458, 459 Appendix

    manuscript on, written between 2 and 4 A.M. 118, 119

    (1876), running account of EGW writing 103-108

    things that did not concern EGW in writing 116

    See also *Desire of Ages*

Life of Our Lord, 459 Appendix

Life of St. Paul, Conybeare and Howson 459 Appendix

Life, spiritual, how to advance in 179

Light, EGW had none on who would constitute 144,000 51

    EGW received in night season, sometimes in the day before large congregations 89

    given EGW for individuals revived when she saw faces of those for whom given 66

    how came. Paul shown in advance general conditions that enabled him to judge in specific situations 55

    how came to EGW 40-47

    new, EGW declared that God had at Minneapolis GC session 174

Literary assistants, claim that, added material or changed meaning of EGW's messages declared untrue by her 89

    EGW directed to dismiss certain, because not spiritually qualified 455 Appendix

    God directed EGW in selection of 455 Appendix

    how helped EGW after death of James White 89

    of EGW 454-458 Appendix

    Mary Clough one of 103 footnotes

    Paul's and Jeremiah's 455 Appendix

Literary borrowing: EGW always felt her duty to use selection of matter for her books and discourses 441, 442, Appendix

    EGW's use of history 460 Appendix

    EGW's use of quotations 460 Appendix

    EGW used descriptions of other authors, added details seen in vision 459, 460 Appendix

    how EGW did 458-460 Appendix

Loaves and the fishes, miracle of, see 5,000, feeding of

Longing, after better life, evidence of

response to Christ's drawing
    power 198
Look and live, not one will perish who
    does this 152
Lord's supper 261, 263
Lord's supper. See also Communion;
    Footwashing
Loud cry, angel of Revelation 18 repre-
    sents giving of 412
  God is raising up class to give 410
  minds fully prepared to make decisions
    when third angel's message goes
    forth in 389, 390
  of third angel, will be heard in earth,
    and his glory will lighten world
    390
  Satan's attempts to divert minds with
    false interpretations one of great-
    est evidences that, soon to be
    heard 410
  Satan will stir up minds to give false
    interpretation of Scripture to di-
    vert minds from 410
Loughborough, John N. 104, 262, 454
    Appendix
  talked to congregation at Milton,
    Washington, camp meeting, June
    14, 1884 86

M

Mackin case 363-378
  EGW appealed for Mackins to halt
    their exhibitions 377
    considered souls of Mackins precious
      377
    declared strange exhibitions of Mrs.
      Mackin not from Holy Spirit 376
    shown Mackins misinterpreting
      Bible and Spirit of Prophecy 376
    stated that Mackins moved by wrong
      impulses 377
      told Mackins they were deceiving
        selves and others 376
      warned Mackins that Satan would
        insinuate himself through strange
        exhibitions 377
      warned Mackins that their exhibi-
        tions founded on false supposition
        377
      warned that Mackins were on wrong
        track 377
  Mackins claimed their experience tal-
    lied with God's Word 374
    led people to believe they were
      demon possessed 376
  R. Mackin offered to let EGW see his
    wife demonstrate powers 372
  strange work in, similar to fanaticism
    in Orrington, Maine, after 1844
    378
  W. C. White recommended praying
    and allowing matters to develop
    367

Mackin, Ralph, and wife 362, 363
  arrested while she singing by Spirit 367
  earnest students of Bible and Spirit of
    Prophecy 363
Man, may overcome temptation by same
    power by which Christ overcame
    in human nature 130
  none has all wisdom needed 24
  not made by God to be redeemed, but
    to bear His image 134
Man of sin, one fierce struggle before,
    disclosed for who he is 426
  Protestant world becoming tender and
    affectionate toward 426
Marian Davis. See Davis, Marian
Marion Party, Brother L who disregarded
    testimonies had been one of 86
Mark of beast, to be presented to every
    institution and individual 396
Martyrdoms 381, 382
Martyrs, if God would have us be, may be
    means of bringing many into
    truth 420
  in battle prior to last closing conflict,
    many imprisoned, many flee for
    lives, and many will be 397
  none after probation closes 399
  See also Persecution
Masons, EGW unwittingly giving secret
    sign of highest order of, a special
    evidence to N. D. Falkhead that
    God was working through her 85
  Free, N. D. Falkhead's connections
    with 85
Masturbation, bars way to eternal life 286
  EGW counsels parents that making
    eggs and meat a child's diet excites
    286
  harder to overcome than addiction to
    liquor or tobacco 286
  leads to deception and falsehood 286
  weakens the physical, mental, and
    moral powers 286
Matteson, J. G. 313, 315
McEnterfer, Sara, took letters by dictation
    and transcribed on typewriter in
    1886 111
Meat. See Butter
Meat eating, 277
  abstain from, for our spiritual and
    physical good 290, 291
  increases animal passions and lessens
    spiritual discernment 290
  injurious effect of, upon spirituality
    290
  permitted after Flood because vegeta-
    tion destroyed 289
  regular, causes higher faculties to be
    overcome by lower passions 290
  tends to corrupt taste and judgment
    289
  tends to make children peevish, irrita-
    ble, passionate, and impatient of
    restraint 290
Mediation of Christ began with Fall 194

Memoir, of Sylvester Bliss 463 Appendix

Memorials, expressing story of what God has done for us, urged 320
  Israel commanded to erect 320
  propriety of 320, 321
  set up by Israel to remind them of God's dealings 320, 321
  today God's cause needs, to remind us of His dealings 321

Memory, prophet's, of events may not be perfect 57, 58

Men, can never enter heaven with propensities of fallen nature 191
  "more humble," schismatics claim God has laid leaders of His work aside for 409, 410

Merits, creature, sink into insignificance in light of Christ's atonement 169
  of atonement, we must depend solely on 145
  of crucified and risen Saviour, childlike trusting in 193
  sinners urged to rely on 149
  of Jesus, each must depend solely on 145

Message, God will open ways for, to come to great men, authors, and lawmakers 389
  of Revelation 18 will triumph 390

Messages, inspired, confidence based on faith in Bible, conviction by Holy Spirit, fulfilling prophecy, fruitage in lives 28

Messages of EGW, blindness of mind result of rejecting 69
  faith in divine origin of, confirmed by many evidences of God's power 38, 39
  given by God for others, benefited her 75, 76
  how they came to her 175, 278
  how they were delivered, first wrote Dr. B in general terms, then specifically 52, 53
  minds must be first prepared spiritually to receive them 57
  once bore testimony, unexpected to her, to congregation at God's prompting 54
  many helped by, because they believed them 71
  those who acknowledged, as being from God were benefited 78
  those who have disregarded warning, have lost bearings 62
  written as God gave them to her 73
  See also White, Ellen; Inspiration-revelation

Messenger, why EGW described herself as God's 74

Millennium, temporal, in time of trouble wicked claim to be in 428

Miller, William 448, 449 Appendix

Mind, unenlightened by God's Spirit, will

ever be in darkness regarding His power 308

Minds, the greatest, become bewildered in attempt to investigate science and revelation if not guided by Bible 307

Minister, dress of: all black or dark, more becoming than two or three colors 250
  carelessness deplored 251
  in some cases, untidy, even slovenly 249
  negligence in, wounds those of good taste and refined sensibilities 251
  should recommend our holy religion 251

Ministry of Healing 458 Appendix
  prepublication title *Christian Temperance* 117

Minneapolis GC session 144, 156-163
  as soon as EGW did not agree with certain ideas, propositions, and resolutions at, some gave little weight to her words 164
  at a testimony meeting at, many declared it to be their happiest day 164
  began with presentations on dark, gloomy side 163
  blindness of many at 171, 172, 175
  busy and important 166
  debating spirit dominated some at 158
  differences of opinion made apparent at, to both believers and unbelievers 175
  discussions at, sometimes heated 159
  EGW battled prejudices and false accusations at 173
    believed that, would result in great good in spite of tug of war 177, 178
    burdened by spirit of many 171
    declared that question of law in Galatians not vital 174, 175
    encouraged open-minded study of law in Galatians at 174
    letter to her family regarding 177
    not the least discouraged in spite of opposition at 178
    tried to correct misguided views at 165
    urged delegates to look on bright side 163, 164
  E. J. Waggoner at, presented justification by faith and Christ's righteousness in relation to law 168
    his message at, old, not new, light 168
    presented series on law in Galatians near close of ministerial institute 158
  God was proving His people at 176
  held Oct. 17 to Nov. 4, 1888 156
  if all had come with Christ's spirit, He

would have instructed 171

law in Galatians, a point of difference at 167

many refreshed at, but not all 164

ministering brethren at, chose to pray by themselves 173

negative spirit controlling some at, seemed contagious 171, 172

preceded by seven-day ministerial institute 156

Satan's divisive strategy at 167

special need of God's grace at 166

spirit of, absent at 1889 session, EGW reported 160

spirit of discord almost leavened lump at 175, 176

subjects discussed at, included ten kingdoms, divinity of Christ, deadly wound, justification by faith 157

un-Christlike spirit prevailed at 174, 175

Minneapolis General Conference session of 1888. See Minneapolis GC session. See also Law in Galatians; Justification by faith; Righteousness by faith

Minneapolis message, EGW preached, at Colorado camp meeting 183

God raised up messengers to proclaim 189

hard-core opposition to 159

in S. Lancaster, Mass., favorable reaction to 180, 181

many in South Lancaster, Mass., blessed by 159, 180

no official rejection of, by church leaders 162

old, not new, light 168

one of first places EGW presented, was at S. Lancaster, Mass. 180 footnote

one of places EGW presented, was at Ottawa, Kans. 180 footnote

partial rejection of, tragic setback 162

received by church members 161

resisted by some, accepted by others 161

resistance on part of some leaders to 161

response to, in Ottawa, Kans. 159

uplifted the cross, which had been lost sight of 189

victory at Chicago and Denver 159

Minneapolis spirit, EGW acknowledged, was not dead by any means in 1890 161

Miracle(s), God's power seen in, when give selves wholly to Him 38

several of Jesus', EGW's writing on 106

those who look for, as sign of divine guidance, in grave danger of being deceived 408

See also Satanic miracles

Misrepresentation and falsehood, men and women who appear to believe truth demoralized through 417

Mistakes, we may make, but Christ does not reject us if we repent 149

but God does not leave us in our error 192

Model church. See Church, model

Moral faculties and physical powers of man, a transcript of God Himself 133

created by God 133

Morse [Washington?] 264

Moses, Satan triumphed that he had overcome 147

Mother, child's first teacher 210

influence of, on her children 220

Music, and music director 332-335

great power in 335

worldly, may be Satan's means of leading souls astray 332

See also Singing

Music director, exaggerated gestures of, detracted from singing 333-335

Mysteries, of future, SDA's anxious to penetrate 394

Mystery of godliness, how man is made righteous through Christ's merits 169, 170

N

"Narrative of the Life, Experience, and Last Illness of Henry N. White" 262 footnote

National apostasy in U.S., when apostasy becomes national sin and God's law is made void, He will work on behalf of His people 388

National councils, all who will not bow to decree of, and obey national Sunday laws, will be persecuted 385

National Sunday laws, those who refuse to obey decrees of national councils exalting, will be persecuted 385

See Sunday law, national

Nations, given a certain period of probation 396

Natural laws, idea prevails that God is restricted by His own laws 308, 309

skeptics fail to realize God can work above 309

some scientists, because they cannot explain, consider Bible record unreliable 307

some try to explain conversion by 309

Nature, a power, but God of, is unlimited in power 309

in one short hour God could dissolve whole frame of 312

many, who cannot measure Creator and His works by their imperfect knowledge of science, doubt

God's existence and attribute infinite power to 307

Nazareth, Christ in the synagogue at 164

Neatness, God desires, in His people 273, 274

Necklace, gold, EGW tells of new convert who proposed to sell her 246, 247

New Jerusalem 388
gates of, thrown back to admit saints 431

New light, many will arise claiming to have, which is but side issue, entering wedge 409
Satan's entering wedge; how it operates 409, 410
schismatics reject God's leaders because they fail to see importance of their 409, 410

New theories. See New light

Night seasons, light came to EGW in 89

O

Obedience, God presents right way, but compels no one to render 289, 290
of Christ not to be put aside as altogether different from, He requires of us 135
to God's requirements essential to happiness even in this life 151
willful, imperfect, not acceptable to God 199

Observances, outward, of no value; Christ's sacrifice is sufficient 190

Oct. 22, 1844, visions seen by EGW enabled her to speak very clearly and positively on what happened on 461, 462 Appendix

Olsen, Ole A., GC president 178

Olson, A. V. 162

One hundred and forty-four thousand, EGW had no light on who would constitute 51
who follow Lamb in heaven, will first have followed Him on earth 424
without guile 424

Only believe, Satan's greatest deception 153

Oppressors permitted to triumph for a time 414

Organization, God has, through whom He will work 17
greatest power to keep out spurious uprisings 26
religious, false notion advanced that near end every child of God will act independently 26
system of, built up by wise, careful labor 26
thorough, essential 26

Ornaments, abstain from display of jewelry and, of every kind 245
needless, ruffles, and trimmings should be left off 245

Orphan schools, J. H. Kellogg's, favorable comments by W. C. White on 223, 224

Overcome, we may, as Christ overcame—by prayer 195

Overcomers of Satan's power, some few in every generation have been representatives of 146

Overeating, physical and mental debility caused by 291
SDA's guilty of 291

P

Pantheism, EGW passed through intense agony for those who received 72
EGW positively denied right of anyone to use her writings to sustain 73

Paradise Valley San, EGW explains why she said it had 40 rooms 59

Pardon by Christ means not only forgiveness but renewal of mind 190

Parents, superscription of, impressed upon their children 229
responsibility of, for early education of children 214, 215
in education of children 210
should make lives of children as pleasant as possible 229, 230
should train children to do useful work 229
stand in place of God in relation to children 314
to represent Christ in dealings with their children 230
who allow their children to violate Sabbath, guilty of Sabbathbreaking 257

Passover, significance of 172, 173

Past, present, and future, representations of, given EGW as she wrote 110

Patriarchs and Prophets 102, 119, 121, 122, 462
amplified portions of Early Writings 443 Appendix

Patten, Adelia 262 footnote, 456

Pattern, Christ left us a plain 138

Paul, could not tell believers many things he had seen in vision because they would have misapplied them 57
listened to reports concerning church at Corinth, to counteract existing evil 65

Peace, true, among God's people when false, is disturbed 20

Peck, Sarah 218, 224, 225
experienced teacher 223
question of teachers' helping parents 225

Perfect, saved not because you are, but because you have trusted in Jesus 147

Perfection, before Christ comes, everything imperfect in us seen and put

away 427
God will carry on His work of, if we allow ourselves to be controlled by Him 201
is not reached in one bound 192
of character, we shall never attain or see God unless we strive for 148
when God's servants reach measure of stature of men and women in Christ, they will be sealed 427
Persecution, can do no more than cause death 421
counsels relating to, for Sabbathkeeping in South 394-400
God's commandments not to be ignored in order to have easy time 401
it is human nature to contemplate consequences of, and shrink from prospects of 398
if a fine will deliver from oppressor, pay it 400
not one word should be expressed to stir up dragonlike spirit 403
of God's people during time of trouble 427-430
redeemed come from mountains, rocks, dens, and caves of earth, dungeons, prisons, secret councils, torture chambers, hovels, garrets 430
scenes of Christ's betrayal, rejection, and crucifixion reenacted on immense scale 415, 416
some trying testimonies to be borne and bitter, finally endured 395
those who forsake God to save their lives will be forsaken by Him 401
those who refuse to obey national Sunday laws promulgated by national councils will suffer 385
we need not marvel at any developments of horror in last days 416
we shall be subject to heavy trials, bereavement, affliction, but they will be for our temporal and eternal good 407
when believer is incarcerated, Christ manifests Himself to him, ravishes his heart with love 420
when believer suffers death for Christ's sake, Christ assures him they may kill body but cannot harm soul 420
when many join commandment keepers prior to closing conflict, many will be imprisoned, many flee for lives, and many be martyrs 397
where opposition very pronounced, and lives endangered, privilege of God's people to go to another place 420
will be felt from not only popery but Protestant world 385
without controlling power of God's

Spirit, humanity a terrible power for evil 416
See also Martyrs
Persecutions, future, will more than rival past, of popery 387
when Protestants and Catholics unite, will more than rival past, of popery 387
Pests, killing of, EGW condoned 329
Peter's ladder, sanctification accomplished not instantaneously, but by climbing 153
Philosophy, all systems of, men have devised have led to confusion when God not recognized and honored 310
Photographs, idols if they tend to separate affections from God 331
some in EGW's day went to extreme of burning all 331
test of whether those who destroyed their, had right motives 331
Photography, and idolatry 330, 331
Picture making. See Photography
Pictures. See Photographs
Pillars, monumental, of what God has done for us ever to be kept before us 383
of SDA faith, some making efforts to sweep away foundation of, in EGW's day 38
Pioneers, attention should not be called to errors of those whose work has been accepted of God 342-347
danger of disparaging, of Advent message 342-347
disparaging 298
Plagiarism. See Literary borrowing
Plagues, present-day calamities are drops from 391
vial after vial to be poured out
Pleasure seeking, ball playing, and swimming on Sabbath a sinful neglect of God's sacred day 258
Posture in prayer. See Prayer, posture in
Power of God, mind unenlightened by God's Spirit will ever be in darkness regarding 308
miraculously manifested when give selves wholly to Him 38
reserve, none left to reach those who credit testimonies to human wisdom 70
Pratt, Brother 263
Prayer, attitude in 236
Christ's, for unity for all believers to end of world 18
cultivate habit of talking to Jesus when alone 267
for sick, EGW took no credit for healings 295, 296
how to pray 301
no time or place where inappropriate 266
posture in, D. E. Robinson stated

EGW repeatedly prayed in large assemblies with herself and audience standing 266 footnote

EGW asks GC delegates to stand for prayer at close of sermon 269, 270

EGW asks congregation to kneel after standing in consecration 267

EGW asks congregation to kneel for consecration prayer 268

EGW asks congregation to rise for consecration prayer 268, 269

EGW asks crowded congregation in Europe to remain seated 267

EGW asks SDA workers at institute to rise 269

EGW did not intend we must kneel on every occasion 270 footnote

EGW not known to kneel for benediction 270 footnote

growing lack of reverence 270 footnote

kneeling mainly for worship services in church, and family and private devotions at home 270 footnote

not always necessary to kneel 267

our privilege and duty to kneel both in public and private worship 269, 270 footnote

propriety of varying 266-270

we need not wait to kneel 266

public and private 269, 270 footnote

we may commune with God in our hearts any time 266, 267

we may speak to Jesus as we walk by the way 266

work in spirit of 336, 337

Preaching Christless discourses 184, 185

Prescott, Amos 457 Appendix

Prescott, W. W. 454 Appendix

Primacy of Word of God. See Word of God, primacy of

Probation, after, closes, death coming to God's people would not be testimony in favor of truth 399

Christ placed on 131

some feel they must be on 149, 150

Promises of God, let us gather, like flowers in a garden 192, 193

Propensities of sin, the original, are left in heart in full strength without divine transforming process 190, 191

Prophecy, Mr. Mackin claimed his wife had gift of 365, 366

Prophet, many who assume title of, are reproach to cause of Christ 74

Prophetess, why EGW laid no claim to be 74

Prophetic gift, can all have? 340, 341

claim that if we have right relation with God, all may have, is false 340

Prophets and Kings, 458 Appendix

Prophets, Old Testament, spoke not only of present truth but of what should occur in last days 419, 420

wrote more for our time than their own 338, 339

Protestant churches, many of God's children are in 386

Psychosomatic relationship between mind and body 284

Psychosomatic relationships and health, 280

Publication of EGW's books, controversy between EGW and her publishers 458 Appendix

Public schools, corruption in, in last days 210, 211

question of attendance of 210

wickedness in, reason for EGW advocating home education until age 10 216, 217

Punishment of sinners 380

Q

Questions on Doctrine, Seventh-day Adventists Answer, statements on the Incarnation 126

R

Rain, former and latter 203

Reasoning, sophistical, dangerous to SDA youth in worldly colleges 232

Redeemed, crowns of, some will be brighter than others, yet no one will envy 155

EGW deals with question of whether probation closes when certain number of, reached 315

those connected in family relationship here will know each other in first resurrection 316

when we are, Bible will be better understood 316

Refinement, constant work of, under Christ's discipline 243

Reform, do not try to, others until you reform 254

Reformation, events in the, presented before EGW 110

histories of, EGW read to help her locate events seen in vision 437 Appendix

Reformation history 464, 465 Appendix

how, was given EGW 447 Appendix

seen in vision refreshed in EGW's memory when she visited historic sites 465 Appendix

Reform dress, EGW cautions regarding resuming 252

EGW explains her testimony concerning length of 277-279

explanation regarding 253 footnote

not to be made test 253

some erroneously supposed EGW was given very pattern all were to

adopt 254
why burden for, removed 253
Reformers, Protestant, made mistakes,
but we are not to draw attention to
them 342, 343, 345, 346
the way, were treated passed in vision
before EGW point by point 121
Reliance on God without doubt makes all
difference in world with us spiritually 149
Religion, dwarfs in 189
goody-goody, encourages sinner to believe God will save him in his sins
155
makes light of sin 155
the principles of, first steps in acquisition of knowledge 311
true, means nothing short of full conformity to God's will 150
Religious amendment, in U.S. in 1889
386
Religious liberty, America to become
battlefield for 387
in coming crisis many will maintain
cause of 387
in U.S., attention of delegates to Minneapolis GC session diverted from
167
Satan's oppressive power will be expected against 392
Religious life, closely related to physical
habits 290
Religious subjects. See Revelation-inspiration. See also common subjects
Religious world, greater part of, will be
deceived by heresies, delusions,
false Christs 114
Remarrying, EGW had no idea of, after
James White's death 66
Remnant, those claiming to be, better not
be found hurling thunderbolts
against church 19
will be those among, unwilling to listen to advice or counsel 23
Renting SDA churches to other denominations 322, 323
Representations of past, present, and future given EGW when speaking or
writing 72
Research, scientific, a snare to men
overimpressed by opinions of
learned men 306, 307
Resurrection 380
first 430, 431
Christlikeness of those who come up
in, does not destroy, but transforms, their image 316
redeemed connected in family relationships here will know each
other in 316
we come forth in, to meet loved
ones, and recognize their faces 316
of righteous. See Resurrection, first
Revelation. See Inspiration-revelation
Revelation-inspiration. EGW got infor-

mation on number of rooms in
Paradise Valley San from those
supposed to know 59
GC delegates in 1867 believed light
given to prophets by enlighten-
ment of mind 49, 50 footnote
new EGW statements on 28
See also White, Ellen
Review, all EGW articles for, were what
God showed in vision 50
Reward in exact proportion to improvement of talents 147
Rich foods, health destroyed by 274
should not be prepared 274
See also Grease
Righteousness, weak if trust in own 150
Righteousness by faith 162
does not downgrade law 176
EGW did not speak on, at Minneapolis
GC session 179 footnote
preached at Colorado camp meeting
with good results 183, 184
fear of the message of 186
grace and salvation through Christ a
mystery to many church members
188
meaning of 186, 187
meetings on, extended a week at S.
Lancaster, Mass. 182
mere intellectual conviction not
enough; we must appropriate
merits of Christ to soul 191
message of, slighted, spoken against,
ridiculed, rejected 162
one of the first places EGW spoke on,
after the Minneapolis GC session
was at S. Lancaster, Mass. 180
footnote
places the law in correct light 176
presented by E. J. Waggoner at Minneapolis, merged with his presentation on Galatians 158
principles of, enunciated by EGW in
1883 148
set forth by EGW in her ministry
145-155
some erroneously believe they must do a
great work; Christ comes in to aid
only at very last, with finishing
touch 181
we need Christ formed within 186, 187
what it means 181, 182
work of righteousness cannot be carried
forward without implicit faith
201
See also Faith
Righteousness of Christ 160
the character we take to heaven has been
imparted to us through 191
Christ's perfection atones for our shortcomings 180
connected with law, presented by EGW
since 1844 168
connected with law, presented in testimonies 168

EGW sought ways to present, to icy hearts of Minneapolis GC session leaders 177
in the law reveals God's true character 170, 171
mystery of godliness 169
transaction by which sin is pardoned 172
unless sinner lays hold on, he is lost 173
we need 150
when we do our best, Christ becomes our righteousness 180
See also Righteousness by faith; Faith in Jesus; Faith of Jesus

Ring, EGW relates incident of SDA sister displaying gold, to new convert 247
wearing of gold, by SDA sister not in accordance with Christ's teaching 247

Robinson, Dores E., stated EGW repeatedly prayed in large assemblies with herself and audience standing 266 footnote

Ruin, moment's carelessness may cause irretrievable 154

Rules, unbending, versus love in teaching children 228

S

Sabbath, beginning of, marked by sunset 319
boisterous noise and loud-toned commands inappropriate on 257
children allowed to run, play, talk, and manifest evil tempers in church desecrate 257
children should not be permitted to violate 257
Christ performed miracles of healing on, but not common work 258
Creation, God's memorial of 318
demarcation line between loyal and true, disloyal and transgressor 423
great test question 423
guiding principles in, observance 256-265
hatred against those who keep will become more and more bitter 401
importance of, will be best realized when God makes covenant of peace 387
will be better realized when latter rain comes 388
is a test, not butter, meat, or eggs 287
made for round world 317
objection to teaching in Desire of Ages 119, 120
of fourth commandment, will be great point at issue in last days 392, 393
parents who allow their children to violate, are guilty of Sabbathbreaking 257

pleasure seeking, ball playing, and swimming on, sinful neglect of God's sacred day 258
question of, is great test, not dress 252-254
seal of living God 423
seventh-day, to be determining factor in final conflict 380
SDA's in danger of doing own pleasure on 258
sign of relationship between Creator and created beings 256
test question, how we treat places us either on God's or Satan's side 396
washing dishes on, should be avoided if possible 258
we shall not see, in all its importance and glory until voice of God and gates of New Jerusalem are opened 261
when latter rain comes we shall better understand importance of 250, 261

Sabbathkeeping, and EGW 258, 259, 260-265
EGW read to her children in afternoon 262, footnote
EGW rode cab to church on Sabbath 265
EGW spent a Sabbath afternoon on nature walk, conversing on religious subjects, writing, reading 263, 264
EGW traveled on Sabbath but baggage stored on board Friday 265
EGW wrote on sufferings of Christ 264
holding services in oak grove 264
in arctic regions 317
mothering the sick and elderly Sabbath afternoon 264
need of far-reaching example at headquarters 259, 260
one is keeping Sabbath as much while caring for sick as leading out in Sabbath school 259
sacred work of priests contrasted with secular labor 259
traveling by train on the Sabbath 265
visit by a non-SDA on Sabbath 264, 265
warming food in EGW's home 363 footnote

Sabbath meals in EGW's home 263 footnote

Sabbath observance, acceptable 236

Sabbath Readings 262 footnote

Sabbath service in Convis, Mich., 1859, lasted till two o'clock 262, 363

Sacrifice, atoning, not the law, is the sinner's only hope 194
official, Holy Spirit constantly drawing attention to the great 137

Saints, clothed in richer robes than earthly beings ever worn 430
come from mountains, rocks, dens and

caves of earth, dungeons, prisons, secret councils, torture chambers, hovels, garrets 430

those who would be in heaven, must first be saints on earth 191

urged "Look up! Look up!" in time of trouble 428

See also Redeemed

St. Helena Sanitarium, church school established in 1902 did not provide for children under 8 years of age 206

Salisbury, Sister W. 264

Salvation 298
by works, do all that we may, cannot pay ransom for our souls 198
cannot achieve by good works, but cannot be saved without good works 147
Christ does not save because you are perfect, but because have trusted in Him 147
matters essential to, more important than chronology 448 Appendix
our hope of, dependent on Christ's becoming one with us 128
plan of, plainly revealed 151
some look afar off and make intricate what is plain 151
we may have assurance of, now 356

Samaritans, Christ mingled with, though contrary to Jewish custom 238

Sanctification, Brother P had theory of truth but not special work of 201
daily, runs through all of God's design 201
definition of, given in Sermon on Mount 202
entire comformity to the will of God is alone 204
experience of continued growth 203
exultant feeling is no evidence of 204
false, taught by a non-SDA minister 152, 153
    wonder-working power to appear when men claiming sanctification 353
fruit that true produces 146
many who claim to be manifest a spirit that proves are not 203, 204
more than a flight of feeling 204
no saving faith that does not produce good fruit 195
not instantaneous but accomplished by climbing Peter's ladder 153
not reached at one bound, achieved by daily advancement in trusting Jesus 193
not outward work, takes hold of very life 146
of soul, accomplished through implantation of Christ's nature in humanity 198
progressive in nature 191
progressive work of a lifetime 202

Sanctuary, light on, given in clear, distinct rays to EGW in early days of message 32
Most Holy Place of, Jesus pleading in 149

Sanitariums, SDA, should have church schools connected with 215, 216

Satan, and his angels, will appear on earth as men and mingle with apostates 409
as angel of light, when wonderful miracle-working power shall be displayed 389
attacks on EGW when she began writing great controversy story 99, 100
bruising Christ's heel in all suffering he caused Him 129
Christ's personal enemy 407
could find no vantage ground in Christ in wilderness, so it may be with us 192
declared fallen man could not keep God's law, but Christ as man revealed it could be done 136
divisive strategy of, at Minneapolis GC session 167
endeavors distract from all-important subjects as end nears 23, 24
greatly disturbed because Enoch and Elijah stood untainted amid moral pollution 146, 147
has made masterly efforts to unsettle faith in testimonies 83
in heaven claimed to be sanctified 199
insinuates heresies by introducing things with some marks of truth 404
in wilderness claimed to be sanctified 199
makes fools and demons of some seen as excellent men when once controls the mind 164
miracles of, performed by apostates, even to bringing fire down from heaven 408
    pray for divine enlightenment to discern truth when, shall be displayed 389
miracle-working power of, EGW shown false Christs will appear 114
permitted to reveal his character as liar, accuser, murderer to the last 414
preparing to work through human agencies in secrecy 414
will appear to succeed in last days 393
will continue to bring in erroneous theories (pantheism) 73
will invent activities, if parents fail to furnish their children with them 229
will make effort to distract interest from all-important subjects as are near end 23

will seek to annoy, harass, falsify, accuse, misrepresent all whom he cannot compel to honor him 423

will steal heart from God, if fail to maintain godly jealousy over self 19

work of, will become more pronounced as we near end 387

Satanic miracles, angel of Revelation 18 proclaims his message while Satan working his lying wonders 408

God's Word to be our defense when Satan works with lying wonders 407

in time of trouble wicked claim miracles among them 428

right decisions will be made in spite of 390

when Satan works with lying wonders, those who have not stood firmly for truth are deceived, apostatize 407, 408

Satan's greatest deception, the idea that Christ did all and we can go on transgressing 153

Satan's hooks upon which to hang doubts 68, 69

Saviour, childlike trusting in, merits of crucified, risen 193

Scapegoat, when times of refreshing come, then sins of penitent removed from heavenly record and placed on Satan 355, 356

Scavengers, those who feed on suspicions, conjectures and suppositions regarding EGW's writings, like 351

Scenes, of great conflict opened to EGW through illumination of Spirit 110

of past, future, opened to EGW's mind in writing Great Controversy 111

of Second Advent, seemed like living reality to EGW 112

presented some before, forgotten, recalled vividly by EGW while speaking in public 43

See also Events; Visions; White, Ellen; Work

Schismatics, as soon as their new light accepted, is drawing away from leaders of God's work for "more humble" men 409, 410

how operate 409, 410

Scholar, EGW conceded she was no scholar when it came to writing 90

School, attendance by SDA children under 8 years of age 216, 217

Schools, in Switzerland, EGW favorable comments regarding 228

SDA, the Bible to be made essence of education in 227

School age, EGW advocated school for children as young as 7 if home situation less than ideal 216, 217

School-age attendance, interview with EGW in 1904 regarding school

for children under 8 years of age 207

School-age entrance, counsel regarding 214-226

8 or 10 221, 224

Science, aid to understanding God, when Bible is taken as one's counselor and guide 310

and Bible, correct understanding of, will always prove them to be in harmony 307, 308

and revelation 306-312

the greatest minds become bewildered in attempts to investigate, if not guided by Bible 307

skeptics, who read Bible to cavil, find contradictions between 308

deductions of, men treat the, and opinions of learned men, as incontrovertible truths 306, 307

latter-day discoveries of, permitted by God 307

must be viewed from religious standpoint to be fully appreciated 311

must be vitalized by God's Spirit to serve the noblest purposes 311

of the devil, great miracles will be performed in behalf of 408

some will exalt, and through them Satan will try to make void God's law 408

we shall soon hear of 408

will make God and Christ of no account 408

Scientific research. See Research, scientific

Scientists, when write upon discoveries of science merely from human standpoint, reach wrong conclusions 307

Scott, Sister 263

Scripture, some, not heeding testimonies, will claim as evidence 83

Sea, Jesus walking on, EGW writing about 105

Seal, of God 258

of living God, SDA's who use tobacco cannot be sealed with 273

Sealing, all-injurious, discouraging influences held in control until God's people sealed 409

God alone can hold four winds until angels seal God's servants 415

when God's servants reach measure of stature of men and women in Christ, sealed 427

Second Advent 380

just two classes at 391

vivid scene 112

Second angel's message 406

Second coming, when Christ comes we gifted with higher nature 427

Selected Messages, book 1 144

statements on the Incarnation 126

book 2 236

Self, let, be lost in Christ 357

look away from, to Jesus 145
    to Lamb of God 149
overcoming of 146
we not to make, the center and indulge
    in anxiety as to whether we saved
    357
Self-abuse. See Masturbation
Self-respect, he who wishes to preserve,
    will not needlessly wound others'
    240
Self-restraint, for efficient service 24
Separation, must be no, in this great test-
    ing time 21
Serpent, brazen, purpose of 149
Service, ours, accepted when we do our
    best, calling on God for help, al-
    though we are imperfect 195, 196
SDA's, had proclaimed commandments of
    God but not faith of Jesus as of
    equal importance 172
SDA Bible Commentary, vol. 1, statements
    on the Incarnation 126
    vol. 7a, statements on the Incarnation
    126
SDA Church, in 1892 EGW declared that
    had nothing to fear for future ex-
    cept as forget God's past leadings
    and teachings 162
    in 1907 EGW declared that was to
    increase in activity and enlarge
    162
SDA churches, renting to other denomi-
    nations 322, 323
Shaking, will weed out those not ap-
    pointed by God 385
Sharp, Smith, letter of W. C. White to
    157
Sifting, all the policy in world cannot save
    us from terrible 384, 385
    See also Shaking
Signs, will be, and wonders in heavens
    preceding sign of Christ's coming
    391
Sin, Adam's, and our guilt 179, 180
    blaming God for our 179, 180
    first, leads to second, third 154, 155
    freedom from, expecting before trust-
    ing God's power to save gives no
    strength 149
    if we, after forgiven, God forgives, we
    need not despair, we have an Ad-
    vocate 196, 197
    is, to talk discouragement and doubt
    instead of faith and courage 192
    leprosy of, healing from, cleanse soul-
    temple, then look to Christ 152
    soon as committed, flee to Christ 196
Sins, Jesus does not give us up because of
    149
    known only to those involved, EGW
    determined not to confess to
    others 75
Sinning, he who has not faith to believe
    Christ can keep him from, has not
    enough faith to enter God's king-

dom 360
Sinless, cannot say we are, until vile body
    changed to be like Christ's 355
    Moses, Daniel, Joseph, and Elijah
    never claimed to be 353
    only after conflict over will it be safe to
    claim to be 356
Sinlessness 298
    EGW never claimed 354
    only those far from Christ claim 354
    will meet those who claim, more and
    more 354
Sinless Being, God sent a, to our world
    132, 133
Sincerity, and uprightness, not atone for
    lack of kindness 238
Singing, drives away powers of darkness
    332
Skeptics, fail to realize God can work
    above natural laws 309
    who read Bible to cavil, find contradic-
    tions between science and Bible
    308
Skepticism, worldly wise men sow seeds
    of 232
Smith, Cyrenius 94, footnote
Smith, Harriet(?) 263
Smith, Uriah 94, footnote, 96 footnote,
    463 Appendix
    enthusiastic review of Spirit of Prophecy,
    vol. 2, in Review, Nov. 30, 1876
    108
    impressed with EGW's material on
    time of trouble in Spirit of Proph-
    ecy, vol. 4 111
Sophistry, spiritual, one to follow another
    74
South, counsels relating to persecution for
    Sabbathkeeping in the 394-400
Southern field, counsel regarding 56
Southern States. See South
Special Testimonies, Series A 457 Appendix
Special Testimonies to Ministers. See Special
    Testimonies, Series A
Speculation, EGW refused to engage in,
    regarding salvation of children of
    unbelieving parents 313-315
    regarding probation closing when cer-
    tain number redeemed 315, 316
Spirit, Holy, worked on EGW's mind,
    gave appropriate words to express
    truth 51
Spirit of discord, nearly leavened the lump
    at Minneapolis GC session 176
Spirit of God, being withdrawn from the
    world 154
    first to be left by, those who fail to
    improve opportunities 154
    minds were stirred by, at Minneapolis
    GC session 170
    prompted letters EGW wrote 50
Spirit of Prophecy, and Bible, have same
    author 30
    not to twist and turn, to suit what may
    want them to say 30

lesser light leading to the greater 30
See also Writings of EGW
Spirit of Prophecy 447, 452 Appendix
 vol. 1 102
 vol. 2, EGW believed would have
  completed in four weeks 108
  EGW felt God gave her light and
   truth as well as strength to write
   104
  enthusiastic review by Uriah Smith
   in *Review*, Nov. 30, 1876 108
  notice of publication of, in *Review*,
   Nov. 9, 1876 108
  on *Life of Christ* 103 footnote
  See also *Life of Christ* (1876); *Desire of
   Ages*
 vols. 2, 3 456 Appendix
 vol. 3 437, 438 Appendix
 vol. 4 114, 437, 438, 452, 453, 458,
  463
  development of 437, 438, 441, 442
   Appendix
  EGW felt there was nothing in to
   exclude from sale to general public
   111
  EGW regarded as expansion of *Spiritual Gifts*, vol. 1 442 Appendix
  EGW wanted first copy off press sent
   to her 112, 113
  published in late September, 1884
   111 footnote
  translation of, into other languages
   463, 464 Appendix
  writing of 109, 110, footnote
  written for U.S. Adventists 438 Appendix
  See also *Great Controversy*
Spiritual Gifts 447, 452, 455, 456 Appendix
 vol. 1 100, footnote, 442
  introduction by R. F. Cottrell 100
   footnote
  notice of publication in *Review*, Sept.
   9, 1858 100
 vol. 3, EGW began writing on Dec.
  21, 1863 100, 101
  states its source were visions 101
 vols. 3, 4 276, 281
 vol. 4, published in 1864 102
  writing of 101
 See also *Great Controversy*
Spraying fruit trees, EGW condoned 329
Spurious loud cry. See False loud cry
Spurious Sabbath. See Sunday
Standards, Christian, need to uphold 236
Starr, G. B. 455 Appendix
Stars, under law, influencing each other to
 do God's will 26
Stewardship, we handling Lord's money
 248
Story of Our Health Message 253 footnote
Strength, from concerted action 23
Struggle, fast-approaching. See Final
 conflict
Study, of Bible, the more we do, the more
 evidence we shall find of divine
 inspiration of 359
Sturgess, Emma 457
Subordination to God, only safety for soul
 20
Success, in God's work, dependent on
 laboring according to His rules
 and arrangement 25
Sunday, all who exalt worship idol Sabbath, cannot see it is entirely an
 institution of Catholic Church
 424
 help devil and his angels 423, 424
 anything we do that exalts, to take
  place of Sabbath, disloyal to God
  397
 enforced by oppressive law, after truth
  has been proclaimed as witness to
  all nations 406
 presented to be legislated into power
  387
Sunday labor, by SDA's, counsels relating
 to, in view of Sunday laws in
 South 394-400
Sunday law, agitation in U.S. waned 381
 appearing to harmonize with in South
  in 1889 would have lost all to
  SDA's 394, 395
 avoid provoking Sundaykeepers 384
 decision respecting, will be universal
  394, 395
 do not irritate Sundaykeeping neighbors by working on Sunday 394,
  396, 397, 399
 encourage no defiance to 395
 national, in U.S. 380
 when is legislated, will not be so great a
  danger of taking steps Heaven
  cannot sanction because Lord will
  give light 394
 while we cannot violate Sabbath, must
  speak no words to do harm 396,
  397
 See also Blair Amendment
Sunday laws, EGW advised caution 381
 in late 1880's 380
 in Southern States 380
 let there be no proud boast showing
  defiance of laws of land 396, 399
 make no resolutions that will lessen
  individual responsibility 396
 times may have changed, but issues and
  principles concerning remain 381
Supernatural powers, promised to those
 struggling with sin 137
Sweat, great drops of, stood on brows of
 Mackins 365
Sweden and other northern countries,
 work of child preaching in, presented before EGW 110, 111
Swimming, pleasure seeking, and ball
 playing on Sabbath, a sinful neglect of God's sacred day 257
Switzerland, schools in, EGW favorable
 comments regarding 228

T

Tables of stone, on which God wrote the
    law, now in ark to be brought
    forth when sentence pronounced
    122

Talents, lent to increase by use 228, 229
    reward will be in exact proportion to
    improvement of 147

Taylor, C. L. 224, 226
    raised question of church school be-
        coming curse when responsibility
        for education shed by parents 224
    raised question whether proper for
        qualified SDA parents to place re-
        sponsibility for educating young
        children on church school 219
    satisfied that work should be begun on
        the Crystal Springs church school
        226

Tea 272

Teachers, not to be facsimile copies of
    predecessors 228
    of schools in Switzerland, engaged in,
        guided student activities 228
    to teach according to own capabilities
        228

Temptation, man may overcome by the
    same power that Christ overcame
    in human nature 130
    many think it impossible not to fall to
        192
    resisted when man powerfully in-
        fluenced to do wrong but holds
        firmly by faith to divine power
        132
    unless possibility of yielding to, is no
        temptation 132

Temptations, man cannot overcome,
    without divine power 140

Testimony, EGW bore one, unexpected to
    her at God's prompting 54
    counsel sometimes based on cases of
        similar character 54
    interpreted in light of preconceived
        positions 79, 80
    of believers, must be one 20
    of reproof to parents who were not
        treating children right 53
    truthfulness of, publicly acknowledged
        79

Testimonies, bring plain lessons from
    Bible 31
    credited to human wisdom 70
    discrepancies and contradictions, so-
        called, in 349
    doubting shows measure of our faith 80
    EGW declared did not contain one he-
        retical sentence 52
    EGW found it discouraging to see
        SDA's pick out portions that
        pleased them, reject others 81, 82
    EGW omitted from published, some
        things some might use to hurt
        others 98
    EGW urged study of 358, 359
    EGW warns not to dissect into in-
        spired, mere human, wisdom 46
    given to leave Bible neglecters without
        excuse 31
    if speak not according to God's Word,
        reject 32, 46
    inspired and uninspired, discriminating
        between 68-70
    light in, not addition to Word of God
        31
    like lessons of Christ, often misunder-
        stood 82
    men have torn away barrier against un-
        belief when they weaken confi-
        dence in 83
    misinterpreted, results in confusion 79,
        80
    misuse of 359
    never contradict the Bible 32
    not new revelation, designed to set
        Bible lessons before disregarders
        of the Word 31
    our protection 360
    partial acceptance of because they con-
        demn an individual's sins 80, 81
    personal, published for the benefit of
        the church 95
    personal study of, would answer many
        questions 359
    perverting by quoting half a sentence
        82
    position that part human and part di-
        vine erroneous 68
    Satan has made masterly efforts to un-
        settle faith in 83
    SDA's who apostatize will first give up
        faith in 84
    some, not heeding, will claim Scripture
        as their evidence 83
    some profess to believe but accept only
        partially when personal sins
        pointed out 80, 81
    take no man's word for, but study them
        for self 359
    those who have carefully read need not
        be perplexed as to origin 50
    those who pay no heed to, will claim
        Scripture as evidence 83
    those who reject, reject not EGW but
        God's message to them 84
    those who specify what in is of God and
        what uninspired words of EGW,
        help devil in work of deception 70
    tide of errors will spring to life as, are
        unheeded 83
    timeliness of 84, 85
    to be a living letter in regard to EGW's
        faith 52
    written before EGW inquired regard-
        ing conditions 65
    written three years before acknowl-
        edged to be of God, heartily ac-
        cepted 86

See also Spirit of Prophecy

Testimonies for the Church, 281 footnote, 456, 459

early, acknowledged to be grammatically imperfect in General Conference action of Nov. 16, 1883 96 footnote

editing the published, in 1884 96, footnote, 97, 98

EGW approved of improving language, providing sense not destroyed 97

EGW read every article in, before published 98

EGW selected the most important matters for 98

No. 1, based on vision of Nov. 20, 1855 94, footnote

Nos. 1-10, of practical and general interest, omitted local and personal matters 95

published between 1855 and 1864 95, footnote

significant statements on how prepared 88, 94ff.

some SDA's in Battle Creek apparently objected to grammatically improving, which EGW approved of 96 footnote

vol. 5 380

See also Letters

Testimonies to Ministers 161, 453

Testimony meeting, many at Minneapolis GC session declared it to be their happiest 164

Testing time, must be no separating in this great 21

Testing truths, *Great Controversy* traces the unfolding of the great 112

Theories, erroneous, Satan will continue to bring in 73

Third angel, symbolizes those who proclaim three angels' messages 405

Third angel's message, believers in, Bible gives no advice or sanction for drawing apart 21

burden of, is the commandments of God and the faith of Jesus 172, 184, 287

minds fully prepared to make decisions when goes forth with loud cry 389, 390

See also Message

Thought inspiration, General Conference action of Nov. 16, 1883, stating its belief in 96 footnote

Thoughts From the Mount of Blessing 458 Appendix

Three angels' messages, all linked together 405

Satan constantly seeking to obscure 405

To exert their power on our religious experience while time lasts 405

Through Crisis to Victory 162, 179 footnote

Time of trouble, during, wicked claimed all world, except, SDA's, in harmony with Sunday law 428

EGW's vivid view of 427-430

God's people in great distress, weeping and pleading God's promises 427

God's people unable to buy, sell 428

many children in mercy taken away before 419

resources of saints cut off 428

saints urged to "Look up! Look up!" in 428

those who borrow trouble regarding future crisis will have a, beforehand 383, 384

Uriah Smith felt material on, in *Spirit of Prophecy,* vol. 4, should not be left out 111

wicked declared they had truth, miracles among them, angels walked and talked 428

wicked ridicule smallness of number of saints 427, 428

wicked trying to destroy saints 427

Tirades, against EGW and her work left her unmoved 74

Tobacco 272

SDA's must lay aside or give up 273

Tongues, false gift of 362

Mackins claimed spoke in, as Spirit gave utterance 365

Trall, Dr. R. T. 277

Translators, list of, of *Great Controversy* 463, 464 Appendix

Trees, EGW shown in vision how to plant fruit 328

Trial and perplexity, Christ's followers not to become discouraged when meet 131

Trumpet, trumpet after trumpet to be sounded 426

Truth, many are holding with only tips of fingers 415

never makes one coarse or discourteous 243

not merely to be presented but lived out 249

to be imparted to others 258

Two meals a day 294

Typewriter (calligraph), Sara McEnterfer took letters by dictation and transcribed on 111

U

Unbelief, the least cherished, involves soul in guilt 149

Union, of evil, Satanic forces and evil men will unite in desparate companionship 416, 417

of Satan's forces, there will be universal bond 392

See also Church unity

United States. See America

Unity, Christ's prayer for, for believers to
  end of world 18
  church members to answer Christ's
    prayer for 17, 18
  God's transforming grace leads to 20
  Holy Spirit will create 20, 21
  in the church 20-22
    to exist between members and with
      God 18
  in the early church, through outpour-
    ing of Holy Spirit 20
  need for 352
  of different minds, gifts, plans,
    methods needed where truth in-
    troduced 24
  See also Church; Church unity
Universalism, some who dwell on God's
  benevolent character try to forget
  there is also infinite justice 308
Universal Sunday law, God will judge
  those who seeking to establish law
  of nations to cause men to violate
  God's law 415
University, attendance of SDA's at non-
  SDA 207
University, of Michigan, at Ann Arbor,
  SDA youth that attend, to be
  converted 233
Unpromising ones, God has sometimes
  used to do great work for Him
  240
Unpublished EGW writings. See Writ-
  ings of EGW
Uprising, spurious, organization the
  greatest power to keep out 26

V

Van Ostrand, Brother 264
Verbal inspiration, General Conference
  action of Nov. 16, 1883, rejecting
  96 footnote
  See also Inspiration, verbal; White,
    Ellen
Vials. See Plagues
Vision, EGW at times conscious while in
  35
  EGW did not breathe while in, yet
    spoke 38, 39
  EGW had not control over her, despite
    accusations to the contrary 36
  EGW in, showed things in future and
    past 35
  EGW led by angel to room where
    young men playing cards, young
    girls watching 41, 42
  EGW preferred to die rather than have,
    could she choose 36, 37
  EGW taken into presence of Jesus and
    angels when had 35
  EGW's ability to speak in, while not
    breathing, substantiated faith in
    Spirit of Prophecy 39

EGW's experience of having, while
    writing an inspired message 36
  EGW's experience while conscious but
    in 35, 36
  EGW's first 34
    after coming out of it, unable to hear
      or see, for many hours 35
    disappointment on coming out of 35
    seemed participant in events viewed
      40
    those with her at first thought she
      was dead 34
  EGW's last, at camp meeting in Port-
    land, Oregon, in 1884 37 foot-
    note
  EGW's opinion about a matter nothing
    to do with what God showed her
    63
  eternal things crowded upon EGW in,
    day and night, as she wrote Spirit
    of Prophecy, vol. 4 109, 110
  evil angels escorting Dr. A from place
    to place 43
  great controversy, of March 14, 1858,
    given to EGW at funeral service
    99 footnote
  James White had no control over
    EGW's 37
  materials published in Testimonies given
    to EGW in 96, 97
    of adulterous worker 44
    of Dr. B who was not efficient as a
      physician 52, 53
    of earthquake while EGW in Loma
      Linda, Calif., April 16, 1906 40,
      41
    of establishment of bakery at Loma
      Linda Sanitarium 46, 47
    of general on horse with banner,
      "The commandments of God and
      the faith of Jesus" 42
    of jets of light shining from map 45
    of June 12, 1868 95
    of March 14, 1858, received at Lovett's
      Grove, Ohio, regarding great
      controversy 99
    of men rolling large stones up hill
      only to have them roll back down
      42
    of Nov. 20, 1855, basis for Testimonies,
      No. 1 94, footnote
    of One in authority giving counsel re-
      garding locating of a sanitarium
      45
    of One looking over shoulder of
      physician, warning him 42, 43
    of unreasonable sanitarium manager
      43, 44
    one so real it seemed to EGW that
      Battle Creek Sanitarium buildings
      had been constructed before were
      erected 55
    regarding members of family with
      whom EGW staying 41, 42

Satan pressing close to Dr. A
clothed in attractive garments 43
scenes EGW had witnessed, repeated
when wrote *Great Controversy* 112
symbolic, EGW enabled to comprehend 42
of fruit being given out 44, 45
that led EGW to separate Mary C.
Clough from her 456, 457 Appendix
why EGW rarely speaks of physical
phenomenon while in 35 footnote
Visions, at first EGW tempted to doubt
divine origin of her 37
at first EGW thought hers result of
mesmerism; resisted, struck dumb
37
at first not understood by EGW, made
plain by repeated presentations 56
basis of *Patriarchs and Prophets, Acts of
the Apostles,* and *Great Controversy*
462 Appendix
EGW given under variety of circumstances 37
EGW given a vivid picture of way
Reformers were treated 121
EGW makes only incidental reference
to her 28
EGW received more than one thousand
14
EGW shown, lives, character, history
of patriarchs and prophets in 121
of great controversy in different ages
40
EGW wanted to reproduce as vividly as
possible those God gave her 51
EGW's, concerning great controversy
first in outline later in greater detail 459 Appendix
confirmed conclusions derived from
Bible study in early days of message 31, 38
EGW's first, related to experience of
Advent believers, Second Coming,
and reward of faithful 34
false, dreams, and impressions, do not
open door for Satan to enter
through 404
given as object lesson of what might be
if certain plans carried out 47
given to guide and guard the remnant
14
how influenced writing of *Spirit of
Prophecy,* vol. 4 442 Appendix
later, of EGW, brought out more
clearly details seen in earlier visions 442, 443, 447 Appendix
importance of physical phenomena
connected with 454 Appendix
of past, present, future given while
EGW speaking in public or writing 36
previously seen presented to EGW
again and again as wrote *Spirit of*

Prophecy, vol. 4 442 Appendix
reasons why given in last days 29
some, as though the whole thing transpiring before EGW 42
came to EGW like flash of lightning
out of dark, stormy cloud 43
sometimes scenes EGW given located
events in point of time and place,
at other times not 459 Appendix
source for writing *Spiritual Gifts,* vol. 3
101
W. C. White had utmost confidence in
the divine origin of EGW's 461
Appendix
W. C. White stated had overwhelming
evidence and conviction that
EGW's writings descriptions of
what revealed to her in 449 Appendix
See also Light; Representations; Scenes;
White, Ellen
Voice, culture of, should accustom selves
to speak in pleasant tones 240
there is something peculiarly sacred in
human 335
Voice of God, covenant of peace made at
261
declares the day and hour of Jesus'
coming, but EGW could not recall after vision 112
delivers the everlasting covenant 112
importance of Sabbath will be best realized when, makes covenant of
peace 388
we shall not see Sabbath in all importance and glory until, and gates of
New Jerusalem opened 261
Voice of the Prophets 277
Volume 1. See *Patriarchs and Prophets,
Spirit of Prophecy,* vol. 1
"Volume 4," same as *Great Controversy*
(1888)
Vuilleumier, Jean 463 Appendix

W

Waggoner, E. J. 158, 159
exhibited Christlike spirit at Minneapolis GC session 174
message of, at Minneapolis GC session
old light, not new light 168
prejudice against, at Minneapolis GC
session 173
presentation of the law in Galatians 174
merged with his presentation on
righteousness by faith 158
presented justification by faith, and
Christ's righteousness in relation
to law, at Minneapolis GC session
168
Waggoner, J. H. 94, footnote, 96 footnote, 104, 263, 463
Waldenses, youth in worldly schools, how

they shared their faith 233

Water, beneficial use of 277

pure, soft, is God's great medicine 280

Water Cure Journal 282

Waymarks. See Memorials

Wheeler, Frederick(?) 264

White, Ella 111

White, Ellen, acknowledged that God impressed her to write *Great Controversy* 113

acknowledged that God worked her mind when writing 81

acknowledged that spirit of Minneapolis not dead by any means in 1890 161

acknowledged value of Marian Davis' works 91, 92

addressed delegates to 1883 GC session on righteousness by faith principles 148

addressed members of the St. Helena Sanitarium church, urging establishment of church school 206, 209-213

advocated educating children at home till age 10 when SDA's had no church schools 216, 217

all articles written for *Review* what God showed in vision 50

A. T. Jones, and E. J. Waggoner presented the Minneapolis message after GC session 159

always read back her manuscripts to see that everything as it should be 90

and her work, attacks on 298, 348-352

antagonistic attitude toward her messages, preceding Minneapolis GC session 159

approved of improving language in *Testimonies*, providing sense not destroyed 97

approved verbal corrections in her republished *Testimonies* 96 footnote

approved W. C. White's statement regarding revision of *Great Controversy* (1911) 123

as dependent on Spirit in relating or writing vision as in having 48, 49

assured that letter she had written given of God 79

astonished at what saw in health reform vision of June 6, 1863 280, 281

at 45 decided to improve her literary skills 90

battled prejudice and false accusations at Minneapolis GC session 173

believed in doing work, leaving consequences with God 75

believed that Minneapolis GC session would result in great good in spite of tug of war 177, 178

benefited by messages she presented under inspiration 75, 76

better judgment from being in Christ's

school 46

bidden to bear plain, pointed testimony and to make known to others what revealed to her 48

books of, witness to character of testimonies 50

written by help of Spirit 50

burden of, to prepare a people to stand in day of Lord 49

burdened by spirit of many at Minneapolis GC session 171

careful to choose words that could not be misunderstood 52

carefully examined and approved changes in wording in *Great Controversy* (1911 ed.) 124

case in which was able to give counsel because previously similar subjects presented to her 56

charges Sister F with making her a hypocrite and liar by saying EGW got her testimonies from those who told her, gave as message from God 64

claimed no special wisdom in herself 46

conceded she had imperfectly represented a subject 90

conceded she was poor writer 90

conscious of presence of God's angels while writing *Great Controversy* 112

considered all materials pertaining to agelong conflict between good and evil part of great controversy story 109 footnote

considered all parts of great controversy story parts of whole 88

could answer to "Who Told Sister White?" "God's angel" 62

could find nothing in her life of which to boast 148

counsels regarding postures in prayer 266-270

dared not speak when had no special light 60

decided not to write more until she became better scholar 90

declared God guided and sustained her in writing of *Great Controversy* 124

declared her confidence in church's standing in 1892 162

declared herself untrustworthy, if her mind prejudiced by individuals 63

declared her writings did not contain one heretical sentence 52

declared in 1907 that in spite of fierce contentions, SDA's had ever been on gaining ground 162

declared the Lord prompted her messages 69

declared Marian Davis as true as needle to pole as her literary assistant 93

declared that Minneapolis meeting will result in great good 159 declared that Minneapolis message had been indelibly imprinted on her mind by God's Spirit, was message for the time 172

declared she could never doubt unmistakable evidence of God's special blessing to her 72

declined to give any man or woman the right to control work God had given her 66

denied accusation that she gave as message from God things told her by others 64

denied accusation that Sister D had influenced her 63

denied that anyone influenced her messages 67

denied charges that in testimonies sent to Battle Creek she was giving own opinion 70

denied that hearsay affected testimony she had sent 64

denied her books the productions of Marian Davis 91

denied that inquiries into cases originated testimony 64, 65

denied that letter she wrote that Elder H. belittled was merely own opinion 69

denied reports that her copyists changed her language 90

denied she derived information of 1863 health reform vision from contemporaries 276, 277, 282

denied she taught we are sanctified by keeping law 153

described herself as the Lord's messenger 71, 74

described how she received and transmitted messages given her 278

determined not to be directed from writing on Life of Christ (1876) 103-107

determined not to confess to others sins known only to those involved 75

did not charge church leaders with official rejection of Minneapolis message 162

did not make certain J. H. Kellogg letters, lest he claim he gave her inspiration 63

did not relish giving reproof 54

did not remember all seen in vision until began to write 48

did not speak on righteousness by faith at Minneapolis GC session 158

disclaimed being originator of Conflict of the Ages books 50

discriminating between testimonies, defining what her judgment and what the Lord's Word, makes them of none effect 68, 69

divinely directed to most helpful books in preparation of her writings 462, 463 Appendix

do not look to, but to God, who gave instruction to her 30

doubters of inspiration of her messages have arguments of results of her work 62

drew distinction in writings between common subjects and religious subjects 58

duty of, not to make GC delegates believe her testimony, but to leave light with those who appreciate 33 footnote

enabled by God to define truth clearly in early days 31

enabled to comprehend symbolic visions given her 42

enabled to write, though weak, when put forth efforts at God's command 37

encouraged open-minded study at Minneapolis GC session 174

exalted Word of God 33

expected attacks to be made on her till Christ comes 350

expected her words would be distorted and misapplied 81

experience in choosing appropriate words, having the words come to mind as pen hesitated 51

explained why she made inquiries regarding family she had been shown in vision 64, 65

explained that listened to reports same as Paul listened to reports concerning church 65

expressed own mind, yet not hers but the word of the Lord 70

faith in divine origin of messages confirmed by many evidences of God's power 38, 39

faith of, testimonies to be living letter in regard to 52

faithfully wrote warnings God gave her 50

falsely accused of being influenced at Minneapolis GC session 173

fanatics will handle heresies in such a way that our enemies will charge fanaticism upon 404

feared that recipient of a message would misinterpret what she had written, because she had presented it imperfectly 90

fearful lest she belittle with cheap words plan of salvation revealed in Christ's life 115

felt God gave her light and truth as well as strength in writing Spirit of Prophecy, vol. 2 104

felt her part of the work done when she finished writing manuscript 107

felt herself severely alone in work God gave her to do 67

felt impelled continue to write earnest messages 50

felt impelled to write *Spirit of Prophecy,* vol. 4, soon as possible 109

felt inadequate to write on life of Christ 115, 118

felt intense interest in every soul that claimed to be child of God 71

felt it was her privilege to express wishes, and not speak by commandment, concerning Brother C. coming to Australia 58, 59

felt it was not necessary to issue perfect first edition of *Spirit of Prophecy,* vol. 2 108, footnote

felt she could never write *Spirit of Prophecy,* vol. 2, without divine help 105

felt she could respond to E. J. Waggoner's message at Minneapolis GC session with all her heart 172

felt she was constantly receiving evidence of miracle-working power of God upon her 72

felt she was imbued with God's Spirit and was indeed His child while writing *Spirit of Prophecy,* vol. 2 105

felt she was less than nothing and Jesus was her all while writing on His life 107

firm in her confidence in light given in Conflict Series books 122

first wrote Dr. B about his problem in general terms, then specifically 52, 53

forbidden to send testimony to N. D. Falkhead until right time 84, 85

found it discouraging to have SDA's pick out portions of testimonies that pleased them while rejecting others 81, 82

found last three chapters of *Spirit of Prophecy,* vol. 4, of thrilling interest 112

found sound of the voice in reading or singing almost unendurable 98

frequently did not foresee words God gave her to speak to congregation 81, 86

fully confident of divine source of her revelations 73

gave her messages in manner God gave them to her 67

given representations of past, present, future as wrote 110

given tongue of utterance that silenced opposition and convinced hearers her words from God 72, 73

God promised increased ability in writing, speaking 97

habitually did not read doctrinal articles in *Review,* lest her mind be molded by ideas of others 63

had many experiences since childhood

that strengthened her faith in divine origin of her work 37

had no idea of remarrying after James White's death 66

had no light on who would constitute 144,000 51

had vivid picture of way Reformers were treated from visions 121

held back testimony one year because was told would not be received 56

her understanding of duties and perils of God's people increased through study of Bible, and many visions 45, 46

how dealt with some cases that came to her attention, whose sins not especially shown her 53

how kept Sabbath 258, 259

influenced, those who rejected her testimonies concluded that 78, 79

inquired of Professor I. more to learn how he regarded conditions than to obtain information 69

instructed to speak words of Lord, leave consequences with Him 75

instructed to write out the great controversy vision she received March 14, 1858 99

in vision beheld fearful scenes of future 114

James White helped and encouraged but never tried to influence 66, 67

judgment developed under God's training 60

knew her writings would continue to witness after her death 76, 77

knew what to write as soon as took pen 49

letter of, called human work by Elder H. 69

letter reporting on Minneapolis GC session 159

letters more than letters, were prompted by Spirit 50

light given concerning individuals revived when she saw their faces 66

literary assistants of 88, 89-93

why made inquiries concerning cases after they opened to her in vision 64-66

made inquiries into cases after they opened to her to determine how to deal with 66

made no claim for inspiration of autobiographical writings 57, 58

made no effort to vindicate herself or her mission 74, 75

made use of good, clear historical statements, make plain what she trying to present 437 Appendix

maintained everything she had written to one who planned to sue her was true 301, 302

message consistent through the years 73

never claimed to be sinless 354, 355

never claimed to be authority on history 437 Appendix

never coveted her position, yet dared not resist Spirit or seek easier position 37

never wished SDA's treat her writings as authority regarding details of history or historical dates 446, 447 Appendix

no arguments would convince doubters of inspiration of her messages 62

not always certain whether what shown applied to past or future 54, 55

not always given special vision, but dealt with case based on cases of others she had seen 53

not least discouraged over the Minneapolis GC session, in spite of opposition 178, 179

not originator of her books 61 footnote

offered to lease land for establishment of church school in 1902 at Crystal Springs 212

omitted from published *Testimonies* some things that some might have used to hurt others 98

on one occasion bore testimony to congregation, unexpected to her, at God's prompting 54

only hope was in merits of Christ's blood 148

paralysis of, left arm when began writing *Spiritual Gifts*, vol. 1 99, 100 when she began writing great controversy story 99, 100

permitted to behold (in vision) the working in different ages of great controversy 110

perplexed by interruptions in her writing on life of Christ 116, 117

pleaded no excuse for doing work God gave her 72

preferred to die rather than have a vision could she choose 36, 37

prejudice against, at Minneapolis GC session 173

prepared statement soon after Minneapolis GC session 156

presented Bible principles first; if no reformation, appealed personally 30

promised to write much more when time was fully come 56

question "Who told Ellen White?" shows measure faith, confidence of rejectors of her message 62

read to her children on Sabbath afternoons 262, footnote

realized that anything of hers published liable to be criticized and distorted 97, 98

rebuked an editor for remaining silent when he should have defended her husband from slander 350

recounts evidences of her call and work 37-39

received increased light on Old and New Testament since 1845 90

received special divine help when speaking, writing 72

received wonderful representations of past, present, future as speaking or writing 72

recognized that partial rejection of Minneapolis message was tragic setback 162

refused to speak less about duty and more about Jesus' love, but spoke as God's Spirit impressed her 64

refused to varnish over case of adulterer who had been warned, reproved, and counseled 53

reported excellent meetings at 1889 GC session 160

reported in 1890 that message of righteousness by faith had been slighted, et cetera 162

requested Mary Kelsey to send her Bible histories to help with order of events 122

resolved not to write certain chapters on life of Christ suggested by Marian Davis unless Spirit led her 116

resolved to be more cautious lest what she wrote be misinterpreted 82, 83

reviewed success of Minneapolis message in 1889 160, 161

right hand preserved by God for more than half century so truth might be published 54

role clarified in hearts at the Minneapolis GC session 164

said need for reformation in SDA anti-kindergarten attitude 224

saw her life as it will appear in judgment 148

scenes of Second Advent witnessed in vision by, seemed like living reality to 112

separated from James White for 66 days while writing *Spirit of Prophecy*, vol. 2 103, footnote

set before brethren only that which presented to her 51

shown scenes of great controversy in different ages 40

shown that paralysis when began writing *Spiritual Gifts*, vol. 1, was Satan trying to take her life 100

sometimes aroused in middle of the night to write 49

sometimes astonished when she read things she had previously written 57

sometimes constrained not to reveal at one time all shown her 69

sometimes deferred giving counsel until minds spiritually prepared to receive 57 sometimes material previously written in her diary seemed new to her when read later 57

sometimes things revealed forgotten until with company to which applied, then would come to mind with force 48

sometimes unable to write unless Holy Spirit helped 49

Spirit of God opened to mind of, great truths of Bible and scenes of past and future 48

Spirit of God worked on mind, gave appropriate words to express truth 51

spoke nearly twenty times at Minneapolis GC session 177

spoke on righteousness by faith at the Denver, Colo., camp meeting 183

spoke twenty times at Minneapolis GC session 158
 but did not touch on righteousness by faith 179 footnote

stated that her messages were consistent through years because she had had same Instructor 73

stated that SDA's should be example in education of children 226

stated that she had been in communication with heavenly messengers for sixty years 71

stated that she professed to be only a humble instrument in God's hands 47

stated that Spirit moved her to write *Great Controversy* 113

strengthened by God to speak at Minneapolis GC session 176

supervision of her writings 460, 461 Appendix

teachings, harmony among 38

testimony of, all attempts to neutralize or gainsay, only compelled her to repeat more decidedly and stand on the light revealed to her 73

things that concerned, and did not concern, in writing on life of Christ 116

those who believe God has spoken through, will be safe from last-day delusions 83, 84

told Satan would try to hinder her writing great controversy story 99

took no credit for healings in answer to her prayers 295, 296

took no glory to self for messages she received 71

traveled reluctantly by ship, train, on Sabbath 265

tried to confine her work of correcting to smallest circle possible 65, 66

tried to correct misguided views at Minneapolis GC session 164, 165, 166

unable to proceed with work at own impulse 49

unable to recall revealed but forgotten things unless Lord brought to mind 48

unique position in SDA ranks 62, 63

unwavering in faith in third angel's message 38

unwittingly gave secret sign of the highest order of Masons to N. D. Falkhead 85

urged delegates at Minneapolis GC session to look on bright side 163, 164

urged withdrawing SDA children from public schools to suitable SDA schools 209

used own words in describing what revealed, unless quoting words spoken by angel 49

voice miraculously preserved after doctors said would lose in three months 39

vowed ever to do work faithfully 71, 72

vowed to bear decided testimony as long as God sustained her 72

wanted to reproduce as vividly as possible representations God had given her 51

was present and participated at the Ministerial institute and Minneapolis GC session 156

was shown in vision the lives, character, and history of patriarchs and prophets 121

"Who Told Sister White?" He who does not falsify, misjudge, or exaggerate 63
 really insult to Spirit 62
 really means, Who exposed my faults to her? 62

welcomed improvements in wording in *Spirit of Prophecy*, vol. 2, by J. H. Waggoner and J. N. Loughborough 104

what to write plain, clear as voice speaking soon as took pen 49

without divine instruction, refused to take responsibility for that which God not given her to bear 51

words, distorted, sounded new, strange when they came back to her 83

words sometimes wrested, misunderstood 82

work included more than that of prophet 74

work made doubly sure by word of mouth and printed form 54

work not unlike that of the Bible prophets 30

would check to see whether testimony she had been shown was substantiated by facts 64, 65

would not dare say God did not move

her to speak the things He gave 49

writing as fast as her hand could move over paper 49

writings of, light given in will condemn those who will not study and obey 358

wrote all the Lord gave her to write 49

wrote light had in answer to questions G. A. Irwin brought to her 51

wrote matters that Lord opened before her 49

wrote on *Spiritual Gifts*, vol. 4, from 7:00 a.m. to 7:00 p.m., then proofread 101

wrote out counsels rather than speak them, lest her words be misstated by some leaders 173

wrote what she had seen, knew to be true 49

White, Emma 122

White, Henry 262 footnote

White, James 99 footnote, 261-264, 272, 277, 280, 282, 322, 350, 438, 455-457, 463 Appendix

death, effect of upon EGW 148

EGW read D'Aubigne's *History of the Reformation* to, when W. C. White was a boy 437 Appendix

EGW's helper and counselor in sending out her message 89

had no control over EGW's visions 37

helped and encouraged EGW but never tried to influence her 65, 66

how helped EGW with editing of her material 89

illnesses prevented editing of *Testimonies* to be published 96

separation from EGW for 66 days while on itinerary 103 footnote

sought counsel of men of sound judgment in early days of work 25

White, James and Ellen, biography of, published by Pacific Press 108

White, James Edson 119, footnote, 122

White, Mary Kelsey 111, 122

White, W. C. 96 footnote, 111, 122, footnote, 178 footnote, 222, 363

acknowledged lack of peace and harmony at Minneapolis GC session but declared it profitable 157

children, EGW wanted them to attend the Crystal Springs church school 219

closely associated with production of EGW's books after James White's death 88

concerned about impact that school admitting children under 8 would have on world work 222, 223

did not assist EGW until death of James White 463 Appendix

falsely said to have influenced EGW at Minneapolis GC session 173

found the Minneapolis GC session most

laborious 177

had utmost confidence that EGW received revelations from God 461 Appendix

heavy burdens carried by, in 1889 92, footnote, 93

letter to L. E. Froom, concerning EGW's method of producing her writings 453-461 Appendix

concerning how EGW did her writing 451-453 Appendix

of December 13, 1934 461-465 Appendix

prejudice against, at Minneapolis GC session 173

reference to isolated EGW statements on education 221

reference to underlying principles in EGW's counsels 221

review of accomplishments of Minneapolis GC session 157

saw interview in 1904 with EGW regarding early school-age attendance as landmark 207

stated EGW had clear comprehensive understanding of conditions, and consequences, of publishing what she wrote 452 Appendix

statement made before General Conference council, October, 1911 433-440 Appendix

statement to W. W. Eastman 445-450 Appendix

statements from intimate knowledge of production of EGW's books 88, 433ff. (Appendixes A, B, C)

Whitney, Buel L. 464 Appendix

Whitney, Mrs. B. L. 457 Appendix

Wilcox, Milton C. 463 Appendix

Will, of God, conformity to, true religion means nothing short of full 150

Will-worship and bodily neglect condemned 251

Wisdom, of world, sought too much; of Christ, too little 151

Wolves in sheep's clothing. See Schismatics

Wonder-working power, to appear when men claiming sanctification 353

Word of God, additional light not given to take place of 29

given to bring light to confused minds 29

primacy of 29-33

recommended as rule of faith, practice 29

standard by which all teaching and experience to be tested 30

sufficient to enlighten beclouded mind 31

See also Bible

Words, EGW careful to use, that could not be misconstrued 52

of angel, EGW always enclosed in

quotation marks 278
Work, of first angel's message in Scandinavian countries presented before EGW 110, 111
everyone has a, to do for self 154
Works, do all that we may, we cannot pay a ransom for our souls 198
good, are the result of the working of Christ's sin-pardoning love 199, 200
cannot save, but cannot be saved without 147
merits of Christ make acceptable 199, 200
ordained to be rewarded through Christ's merits alone 200
when we have done all possible, have only done our duty, deserve no thanks, are to count ourselves unprofitable servants 200
of righteousness, our efforts in, will have decided influence on our recompense 147
Worker, no one has all wisdom needed 24
Worldliness, among SDA's, EGW saddened by 243, 244
Wretchedness, the sum of life's, largely made up of neglect of courtesies 240
Writing, while EGW, representations of past, present, and future given her 110
Writings, of EGW, corrections, EGW acknowledged Marian Davis had a point regarding Zedekiah having his eyes put out and the rock from which water flowed 121, 122
do not quote, until you obey the Bible 33
EGW divinely directed to most helpful books in preparation of her 462, 463 Appendix

how she prepared 458, 459 Appendix
in diaries to be brought before people 32
not to be used in public labor as authority to sustain position 29
relation to Bible 29-33
to continue to speak after her death 76, 77
See also Spirit of Prophecy
Wrongs, how EGW went about convicting of 63-67

Y

Yoke, of Christ, if men wear, will not pull apart 26
Youth, SDA, could safely enter colleges of land, if daily converted 231
EGW scarcely dared encourage, to attend worldly colleges because of danger of being led astray 234
in danger of being misled by Satan, if feel free to be off guard one day 231
who attend worldly colleges should do so to draw others to Christ 231-233
Youths, SDA, should not seek theological training in non-SDA schools 234
that attend University of Michigan, to be converted 233
who attend non-SDA colleges, not to stir up trouble, but be ready to share faith 233, 234
Youth's Instructor, statements on the Incarnation 126

Z

Zwingli, Ulrich 465 Appendix